MW01502543

# Introduction to Simulation with GPSS

The micro-GPSS system of this book is obtainable on diskette for the PC and Macintosh and on tape for VAX and some other mini-computers, from Professor Ingolf Ståhl, Stockholm School of Economics, Box 6501, S–113 83 Stockholm, Sweden. For ordering details and prices of the student version of micro-GPSS, the diskettes with 85 programs and commented solutions to the 80 exercises of this book as well as a dialogue program for easy program coding see the card enclosed with this book.

# Introduction to Simulation with GPSS

## on the PC, Macintosh and VAX

Ingolf Ståhl

*Professor, Stockholm School of Economics*

**Prentice Hall**

New York   London   Toronto   Sydney   Tokyo   Singapore

First published 1990 by
Prentice Hall International (UK) Ltd,
66 Wood Lane End, Hemel Hempstead,
Hertfordshire HP2 4RG
A division of
Simon & Schuster International Group

© Prentice Hall International (UK) Ltd, 1990

All rights reserved. No part of this publication may be
reproduced, stored in a retrieval system, or transmitted,
in any form, or by any means, electronic, mechanical,
photocopying, recording or otherwise, without the
prior permission, in writing, from the publisher.
For permission within the United States of America
contact Prentice Hall Inc., Englewood Cliffs, NJ 07632.

Printed and bound in Great Britain at the University Press, Cambridge

Typeset by Columns Design and Production Services Ltd, Reading

---

Library of Congress Cataloging-in-Publication Data

---

Ståhl, Ingolf, 1940–
    Introduction to simulation with GPSS on the PC, Macintosh, and VAX
/ Ingolf Ståhl.
        p.        cm.
    Includes bibliographical references and index.
    ISBN 0–13–483231–0
    1. Business—Computer simulation. 2. Business—Decision-making–
–Computer simulation. 3. Digital computer simulation. 4. GPSS
(Computer program language). 5. Microcomputers—Programming.
I. Title.
HF5548.2.S7724      1990
658.4'03'02855262—dc20                                              90–7622
                                                                        CIP

---

British Library Cataloguing in Publication Data

---

Ståhl, Ingolf, *1940–*
    Introduction to simulation with GPSS: on the PC, Macintosh and VAX
    1. Business firms. Applications of computer systems.
    Systems analysis
    I. Title
    658.05421

    ISBN 0–13–483231–0
    ISBN 0–13–483249–3 pbk

---

1 2 3 4 5 94 93 92 91 90

*To Thomas J. Schriber*

# Contents

## 20   Remaining micro-GPSS features

## 21   How to proceed in simulation

## *Appendices*

## References

## Index

# Preface

Simulation, already the most widely used management science method, is being used more and more for supporting business decisions. It implies that a computer model is used for systematically investigating the consequences of various decisions, completely risk free and at a low cost, before any resources are committed in reality. As managers get more accustomed to using the computer, e.g. a PC, for business analysis, the demand for more realistic modeling increases. Managers want to be able to consider both uncertainty, e.g. sales fluctuations, and the time factor, e.g. in form of project delays. Such stochastic and dynamic simulation is generally not possible using spreadsheets, but requires computer packages for discrete-event stochastic simulation.

The most widely used software for such dynamic stochastic simulation is GPSS (the General Purpose Simulation System). As discussed further in Chapter 1, this system has the advantage of being highly problem-oriented, representing reality in an intuitively natural way, using block diagrams. The programs are very compact, can be written in a short time and are easy to explain. All this helps to make GPSS models easy to implement. Although GPSS is an 'old' language (first version 1961), it has experienced a strong revival during the last few years, not least due to new versions on the PC.

The most recent 'up-to-date' version, micro-GPSS, is presented in this book. On the basis of over a decade of experience in teaching GPSS, micro-GPSS was designed as a 'streamlined subset' of the major commercial versions of GPSS to be as easy as possible to learn and use. To facilitate learning there are fewer concepts, which are less complicated, but more powerful, often well-known to students of other languages like BASIC. There are fewer technical details and many of the *ad hoc* features of mainframe GPSS have been removed. In micro-GPSS there is a greater stress on programming safety with an extensive error trapping system. These features have made learning micro-GPSS very easy. As demonstrated, to learn enough micro-GPSS to write a certain set of programs took less than half the time to learn enough mainframe GPSS to write the corresponding programs.

Although micro-GPSS is considerably smaller than full GPSS, almost all published programs in full GPSS can be written as compactly in micro-GPSS, since many features of full GPSS are redundant.

There are also several features (see Section 1.10) making micro-GPSS easier to use, such as completely free format, floating point numbers, built-in functions, facilities for very easy repetition of runs and for collection of queuing statistics, easily readable reports obtained directly at execution, etc. The coding of the program can be done very easily by using a special menu program, GPSSMENU.

Micro-GPSS is available on the PC, the Macintosh and the VAX, as well as some other mini-computers. It is the only GPSS on the Macintosh. The system functions identically on all the computers mentioned and this book is suitable for any of these systems.

The PC version for students uses only 256 kBytes and on PCs with more memory there is hence ample room for a memory resident editor and a graphic system interfacing with micro-GPSS. For the buyer of this book, the standard student PC version can be ordered at the price of $20. Special, very favorable quantity discounts apply for classes and PC labs. This book contains an order card for this, which can also be used for ordering other versions, e.g. for PCs using a floating point processor or for the Macintosh. You can also order diskettes with all the 85 programs and solutions to the 80 exercises in this book as well as with the GPSSMENU program or obtain information regarding mini-computer and professional versions and versions allowing for animation, block diagram generation and translation of micro-GPSS programs into GPSS/H.

Since simulation of this kind with a focus on uncertainty and the dynamic time aspect is of increasing importance as a decision-support tool in business, this book, written by a professor at a business school, is first of all aimed at business courses. It appears reasonable that every business student should acquire an understanding of the potential of simulation by actively working with a simulation package on a broad range of problems. The TIMS education committee has suggested a larger role for simulation in the first MS/OR course (Interface 5, 1988), where a concentration on three topics is suggested, one of which is simulation. Since micro-GPSS was created with the specific purpose that a student should be able to write programs for truly interesting problems after only 6–8 classroom hours and be able to cover almost all of micro-GPSS in around 15 hours, micro-GPSS would be very suitable to constitute, e.g., one-third of such a first, PC-oriented, MS/OR course, e.g. together with linear programming and decision analysis.

It must be stressed that this book on micro-GPSS does not require any specific background, either in computer programming or statistics. It should also be mentioned that working in micro-GPSS has proved to be very popular with students and resulted in good ratings of the courses where it has been included. For teachers there is a package with overhead masters and commented solutions to the exercises.

This book with the micro-GPSS system is suitable too for other courses and early versions have been used both in manufacturing, transport engineering and computer science courses. Also for those who want to continue in simulation with a full GPSS version, micro-GPSS provides a suitable starting point, since the main principles are the same for all GPSS versions. By starting with micro-GPSS, a student can rapidly progress to interesting applications.

The great number of programs and exercises as well as the general simplicity of the micro-GPSS system also make this book suitable for self-study. It has been used in two-day management education courses on dynamic simulation for business planning and has attracted professionals involved in manufacturing, telecommunications, transport, wholesale and retail trade, banking and construction. Among the functional problems covered in this book are inventory management, staffing planning, production planning, investment budgeting, traffic systems, etc.

Besides dealing with the easy-to-learn micro-GPSS version, this book distinguishes itself from other GPSS books by having many more examples, especially from a broad range of business areas. It also covers in a simple way a number of general simulation topics, including random numbers, statistical distributions like the exponential and Erlang distributions, a statistical method for analysing simulation data, and the design of simulation experiments. The aim is to cover so much that a basic understanding of the main ideas of simulation is obtained to allow for the application of these ideas to actual problems in business.

# Acknowledgments

I have been working on parts of this book since as long ago as 1976. In the process I have piled up a great amount of indebtedness for the help I have received, which I would like to acknowledge here.

By far my greatest debt is to Thomas J. Schriber, professor at the University of Michigan. First of all I would never have started in GPSS had it not been for reading his excellent introductory Chapter 12 on GPSS in McMillan and Gonzales (1973). After that I immediately ordered his now classic book *Simulation Using GPSS* and started to teach GPSS at the Stockholm School of Economics in 1976. For the first few years we used GPSS/360 on an IBM mainframe, but in 1979 we started using our own rudimentary GPSS, which eventually developed into the micro-GPSS of today. Throughout the development, Tom's book was our guide. One aim was that one should be able to write the programs in this book as compactly in micro-GPSS as in full GPSS.

Tom has generously allowed me to take a great many of the program examples as well as exercises in this book from his book. Furthermore he has done a very careful review of my book with many important suggestions for improvement. Finally, Tom has given me great encouragement in my work on this book. In recognition of my very great gratitude for all this inspiration and support, this book is dedicated to him.

As mentioned above, micro-GPSS started in a rudimentary form in 1979. The very first version with nine block types was programmed by Kerstin Claesson. Although the code of the micro-GPSS processor is now 15 times longer, I am still very thankful for this important first start.

In the further development of micro-GPSS I have received many good ideas from the many colleagues teaching GPSS to the students at the Stockholm School of Economics. From them I have also received helpful critical comments on the manuscript which has been used in a multitude of versions by students at this school. Among the many colleagues, I would in particular like to thank Ann-Sofie and Alf Westelius, Lars Söderfjäll, Frank Torstensson, Pär Mårtensson, Björn Thodenius and Fredrik Ewerlöf.

This book has been used in manuscript form in several other places in

Sweden, among others at the Chalmer Institute of Technology, Gothenburg, and Karlstad College. Important comments on the manuscript and the system have been given by Dr Kent Lumsden and Dr Tomas Martinsson, for which I am grateful.

During 1983–85 I was visiting professor at Hofstra University, NY, where the book started to take its present form. I am grateful to Professor Ivo Antoniazzi, my colleague at Hofstra, for valuable comments on the manuscript at different stages. I am also grateful for comments from Dr Peter Stratfold of Loughborough University, England. I also want to thank Professors Peter Jennergren, Brian Birtwistle, Geoffrey Gordon and Jerry Banks for providing interesting exercises.

The development of micro-GPSS has required a great amount of computer work. This has been greatly facilitated by the efforts of Lars Ledenholm, Kjell Franzén, Jörgen Östgren, Leif Robertsson and Azad Saleh of the Computing Service of the School of Economics, for which I am grateful. I am also indebted to Future Knowledge Systems Ltd, Windsor, UK, for the excellent technical- and copy-editing.

Since July 1985 my professorship at the Stockholm School of Economics has been based on a research grant by the Ericsson Corporation. I want to express my deep gratitude for this support.

Finally, I am truly indebted to some 1,500 students, at the Stockholm School of Economics and at Hofstra University, who by making errors and asking questions made me realize how GPSS had to change in order to be easy to learn.

# Trademarks

GPSS/PC is a trademark of Minuteman Software, Graph-in-the-Box of Ide-Data AB, Lotus 1–2–3 of Lotus Development Corp., Macintosh of Apple Computers, Inc., MS-DOS of Microsoft Corporation, Stella of High Performance Systems, Inc., UNIX of AT&T Bell Laboratories and VAX of Digital Equipment Corporation.

# Quoted material

Exercises 8.2, 8.3, 9.1, 9.2, 13.3, 13.4, 14.2, 16.3 and 20.1 are taken from Jerry Banks and John S. Carson, II, *Discrete-Event System Simulation*, © 1984, pp. 71–2, 107, 109, 111, 113, 115, 116, 201, 207. Adapted by permission of Prentice-Hall, Inc., Englewood Cliffs, N.J.

# How to use this book

This book is intended for both classroom use and self-study. In either case the reader is advised to work actively on the computer, using the micro-GPSS system which can be ordered at a discount price on the coupon provided. Each of the program examples in this book is also available on a diskette. It is highly recommended to run the programs of each chapter alongside the reading of that chapter. The programs available, called prog3.1, prog3.2 etc., correspond to the programs, Program 3.1, Program 3.2 etc., of the book. Instructions on how to run the programs are given in Chapter 3.

The student is also advised to work on the exercises at the end of most chapters. Suggested solutions to these exercises are also available on a special diskette. Writing new programs is most easily done using the dialogue program GPSSMENU, also available on a diskette (see Appendix C). The editing of the programs is system dependent, but instructions on editing are available together with the micro-GPSS interpreter in a document file to be started by the command GPSSDOC. This file will also contain instructions on how to produce graphic output from the micro-GPSS system.

The reader, especially when using the book for self-study, is advised to first read the book through at a reasonably rapid speed to obtain an overview, and then to go through the book again more slowly to study the details. There are parts of the book which deal with general simulation issues or comparisons with other GPSS versions and which are not necessary for the understanding of other parts of the book or for the use of micro-GPSS. These parts are all set in small print. When a whole section is of this character, the heading of this section is preceded by a black square.

# 1 The role of GPSS in simulation

## 1.1 Examples of GPSS use

1. A company loses customers because it does not have the capacity to answer all incoming calls. Would it be profitable to install a larger switchboard?

2. A company contemplates forming a secretarial pool to level off an uneven work load for secretaries who now work for specific managers. How will secretarial services change overall?

3. A store considers hiring an additional salesperson in order to decrease customer waiting times. Can the costs incurred be covered by sales to customers otherwise lost due to long waiting times? Should the salesperson be hired to work only during peak hours?

4. A bank with branch offices outside the city plans its daily cash holding. How much cash should be on hand in order to maintain a low risk of running out of cash?

5. A company contemplates buying a new computer system. What size should the primary and disk memories be in order to obtain the desired service in terms of response times for terminals?

6. A corporation plans its inventory policy. When should re-ordering take place to ensure that new products arrive before the inventory has been fully depleted?

7. A company is planning its financial policy for a period of foreseen market growth. It wants to take into account random variations in cash flow due to variations in sales and payment times. A production and inventory policy with a very low risk of financial crisis is required.

8. An engineering workshop makes its production plans using optimization methods which disregard variations in the machine time required for

various products. Production cannot reach planned levels and inventories of semifinished goods pile up because, in reality, machine times vary in a random fashion. New plans, taking these variations into account, are called for.

9. A construction company wants to estimate the total construction time for a building, taking into account the facts that some stages can start only after several others have been completed and that the time needed to finish a certain stage is not fixed but, rather, has been shown to vary considerably.

10. Traffic jams occur at an intersection during rush hours. Can this be solved by changing the timing of traffic lights?

In spite of outward differences, all the above situations have the following in common: they all concern systems where some service is carried out by 'servers', i.e. people or machines, for the benefit of 'transactions', i.e. 'customers' of the service in the widest sense of the word. Such a system is characterized by random variations in regard to when the 'customers' arrive and how long it takes to provide the services that they require.

Discrete-event stochastic simulation is a suitable method for investigating how such systems function for different server configurations, e.g. different numbers of salespeople, units of computer memory, etc. The most widely used computer language for such simulation is the General Purpose Simulation System, or GPSS. The use of GPSS in discrete-event stochastic simulation to support decision-making in situations similar to those described above is the topic of this book. Before going into any details about GPSS, we begin by discussing simulation more generally.

## 1.2 Computer decision-support systems and simulation

With the advent of cheap computer power, through mini- and micro-computers and modern time-sharing systems, managers increasingly use the computer as an aid and support in their decision-making. Decision-support systems include database systems, which provide access to different data in a fast and simple way, and scientific methods for decision-making. The latter field, often referred to as management science or operations research, is often divided into two main areas – optimization methods and simulation methods.

The aim of optimization methods is to find the particular decision which will, to the greatest possible extent, fulfill a certain objective, such as high profits or low costs. These methods have been around since the end of World

War II, but in general have not been quite as successful as was originally anticipated. The following two main problems are associated with optimization models:

1. Managers are often not really interested in optimizing, e.g. finding the solution which leads to the highest possible benefit. Rather, they appear to be more interested in determining whether at least one of a small number of contemplated solutions would lead to satisfactory results regarding a number of different objectives.

2. In order for computerized calculations to be simple, such that the best solution can be found with a reasonable amount of effort, optimization models are usually simplified drastically. Simple relationships are assumed between different variables. For example, one frequent assumption is that there is a linear relationship between total production and total costs. Another is that all data are given with certainty, i.e. the models do not allow for any random variations.

Many managers have reacted to this lack of realism by stressing their interest in models that take inherent uncertainty into account and allow for more complicated cost and demand relationships. Thus decision-makers have often been quite willing to relinquish the optimization aspect in order to be able to model a decision situation more accurately, in particular allowing for stochastic variations in the variables. This, in turn, has made management more interested in simulation, which can be defined as 'experimentation with a computer model of a real system'. The following three aspects of this definition should be emphasized:

1. We deal with a *model* of a real system. A model is a simplified picture of the real system in which only those characteristics of the system that are most relevant to the decision problem at hand are included.

2. In general, simulation necessitates computer use. If the model is to incorporate any kind of realism, and hence complexity, the repeated calculations required for experimentation with the model can be carried out most easily on a computer. The complexity of most simulation models is such that no analytical solutions could be obtained. Hence numerical methods for computer use are required.

3. Experiments imply that the model should be changed, preferably with regard to one aspect or variable at a time, in order to study the changes in results due to a specific change in the 'input' variable. By carrying out several experiments in this way, the effects of various changes in the system can be studied. We can answer such questions as 'how much will service level, sales and profits change in a store if we have different numbers of salespeople working at different times of the day'.

The possibility of experimenting with a model of a real system is one of the great advantages of simulation. Instead of experimenting with the real system, which might have negative consequences and hence be very costly, experiments can be performed using a computer model of the system. For example, rather than hiring an extra salesperson and paying for his or her salary for some months to see if sales will improve, the effects of this decision can be investigated on the computer at virtually no cost. Changes in the *real* system will be made only if these simulation experiments using the *model* of the system indicate that positive results are likely.

# 1.3 Main types of simulation

It should be noted that our definition of simulation does *not* include the word 'stochastic', i.e. a requirement that simulation involve some sort of randomness. In fact, simulation can be either *deterministic* or *stochastic*. In deterministic simulation, all data and relationships are given with certainty, while in stochastic simulation at least some of the variables studied change in a random fashion. For example, in a deterministic model it would be assumed that exactly 20 units are demanded each day; in a stochastic simulation daily demand could be allowed to vary between 10 and 30 units.

In some instances, managers have found deterministic simulation models sufficiently realistic and have been attracted by their simplicity and ease of use. This is especially true for so-called spreadsheet simulation, which has recently become popular through such systems as Lotus 1–2–3.

As managers have become more familiar with the general idea of simulation through the use of deterministic simulation models, an increased interest in stochastic simulation also seems to have evolved. Managers have found that in many situations the essential aspect of a problem which is deeply rooted in the uncertainty and random nature of certain variables cannot be handled by a deterministic model. This is true not only in queuing and inventory problems, but also in many other problem areas, not least finance. If all payments were known with absolute certainty, there would in fact be no need for a theory of finance.

Several of the situations outlined in Section 1.1 belong to areas which are sometimes dealt with using other methods such as queuing and inventory theory. However, rather than resorting to these more cumbersome and complex analytical methods, which have proved to be very difficult to learn, these problems can be handled much more conveniently, and often more accurately (see, e.g., Chapter 12), by stochastic simulation.

Another important distinction is between *static* and *dynamic* simulation. In static simulation there is no real explicit time, in the form of a simulation clock, which can take any value. An example of static simulation is spreadsheet simulation, where results can only be obtained for specific predetermined points in time such as the end of a quarter. In many cases, e.g. cash forecasting, the decision-maker is more interested in seeing the result after a specific event, such as the receipt or disbursement of a large cash amount, has taken place. An example is a corporation where cash at the end of each quarter appears sufficient but a financial crisis occurs in the middle of some quarter. Dynamic simulation, where *any* time value is possible, is required to establish this (see Chapters 17 and 19).

A third distinction to be made is that between *discrete* and *continuous* simulation. Discrete-event simulation deals with systems where there is a noticeable difference in time between the occurrence of significant events and where a noticeable change in the characteristics of the system components is caused by these events. This distinguishes discrete-event simulation from continuous simulation. Since, in continuous systems, it is impossible to distinguish between specific events taking place, under continuous simulation 'events' are allowed to happen at very short time intervals (in relation to total time) and each such 'event' causes a very insignificant change in the system attributes.

Discrete-event simulation usually concerns business-type systems involving clearly distinguishable events such as the arrival of a customer, the delivery of some goods, the breakdown of a machine, etc., while continuous simulation usually deals with physical systems such as the launching of missiles. When simulating the trajectory of a missile (i.e. the path it travels), travel time is divided into very small intervals. Then the path travelled and the amount of fuel consumed during this short time interval are computed.

This book deals with *discrete-event stochastic* simulation. Obviously this type of simulation is stochastic, not deterministic. Furthermore, the concept of discrete-event is twofold: it deals with discrete, not continuous, simulation and, since an event can take place at *any* desired *time*, it refers to *dynamic*, not static, simulation.

## 1.4 Computer systems for stochastic discrete-event simulation

There are three main ways, as follows, of performing stochastic, discrete-event simulation on a computer:

1. A program in a *general*-purpose, high-level language, such as FORTRAN, Pascal, BASIC, etc. – in principle, any kind of program can be written in these general languages.

2. A program in a *simulation* language, which is a language specially

designed for simulation, but is general as regards the type of simulation problems that can be investigated. There are several such languages, of which the best-known is GPSS, the General Purpose Simulation System, where General Purpose refers to the fact that it is intended to be general as regards the type of simulation problems. Among other well-known simulation languages we mention here only SIMSCRIPT, SIMULA, SIMPL/I and SIMPAS. (For a host of others, see Kreutzer, 1986.) It should be noted that these other simulation languages can be regarded as extensions to general high-level programming languages (with SIMSCRIPT similar to FORTRAN, SIMULA based on ALGOL 60, SIMPL/I based on PL/I and SIMPAS based on Pascal).

3. A simulation system geared to a *specific* type of simulation problem – this includes special languages such as SIMFACTORY and XCELL+ for simulating manufacturing systems, sometimes with animation, or languages such as SCERT and IPSS for simulating computer systems. Specific packages or code-generators for, say, queuing simulation, such as $SP^2$ (Greenwood, 1988), are even more limited as regards the area of application. These packages mainly allow the user to choose between different data for, say, customers per hour, service times, etc., but the basic structure of the model is given.

It should be recognized that this last category of systems for special areas of application is too limited in scope to be of real interest for a general introduction to simulation methodology. One of the most important aspects of simulation is to show that the same concepts, e.g. transaction, server, etc., can be applied successfully to a great diversity of problem areas.

It remains to be shown why I believe that GPSS is more suitable for this type of introduction to simulation than, on the one hand, other simulation languages such as SIMSCRIPT and SIMULA and, on the other hand, a general programming language such as FORTRAN or BASIC. This will be discussed in Sections 1.5–1.6.

# 1.5 Advantages of GPSS

Later, we will be in a better position to understand the main differences between GPSS and other languages for discrete-event stochastic simulation, but it may be appropriate here to outline the main advantages of GPSS over these other simulation languages, which are more similar to each other than they are to GPSS:

1. GPSS is by far the most *widely used* of these languages. It is used

extensively within industry, both in manufacturing, e.g. the automobile industry, and in retailing, transportation, banking and other services.

2. The wide use of GPSS implies the existence of many textbooks, many examples and also many users to consult. (I present some of the books on GPSS in the references.)

3. Although all the languages mentioned are specially designed for discrete-event simulation, GPSS is much more *problem-oriented* than these other languages. The general terms and concepts of GPSS are closely related to common English words used to describe simulation problems, whereas the other languages are more geared to how the computer will carry out a simulation. The GPSS 'world view' of temporary transactions, like customers moving to various permanent servers, is, in most real situations, close to the way that decision-makers actually look at these systems.

4. Closely related to the problem-oriented aspects of GPSS is the feature that GPSS programs can be described using a special type of *graphical representation*, called 'GPSS block diagrams'. These diagrams are much more problem-oriented and hence easier to explain to management users of simulation than the ordinary flow charts used in connection with other simulation languages. They can also serve as a basis for animation.

   Figure 1.1 gives an example of a block diagram which illustrates customer movements in a store. Customers are first served by a salesperson and they then pay a cashier. The numerical details in this block diagram will be discussed in Chapter 7. The only purpose here of the diagram is to stress the closeness between the actual problem and the block diagram.

5. One important advantage of GPSS, which is to some extent associated with the problem-orientation of the language, is that small but powerful programs can be written and made operational in a very *short time*. As demonstrated by many program examples in this book, some small programs can be quite powerful in the sense that they provide a great deal of insight into a real problem situation. Corresponding programs in, e.g., SIMSCRIPT or SIMULA might be three or four times longer in terms of program codes and would probably take correspondingly longer to write.

6. The subset of GPSS presented in this book is *easy to learn*, as proved by many years' experience in teaching GPSS. The process of learning, e.g., SIMULA to the extent that one can write the same type of programs as are given in this book would take much – perhaps five times – longer.

7. From a learning point of view, GPSS also has the advantage of being

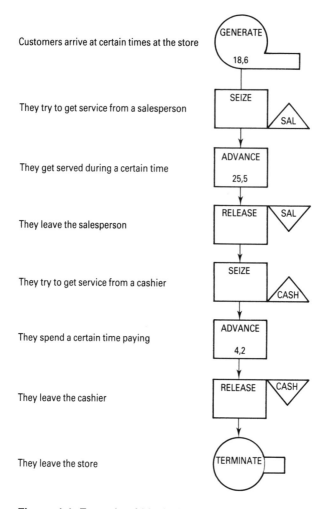

Customers arrive at certain times at the store

They try to get service from a salesperson

They get served during a certain time

They leave the salesperson

They try to get service from a cashier

They spend a certain time paying

They leave the cashier

They leave the store

**Figure 1.1** Example of block diagram

'fun'. The author's experience in teaching GPSS for many years has been very positive in this respect. The use of GPSS as, e.g., part of an OR course has greatly improved student ratings of such courses.

8. GPSS facilitates the task of the model-builder when *explaining* the model to the user of the results. This follows to some extent from points 3 and 4 above; i.e. the proximity of GPSS to actual problems and the availability of the block diagram method. It is also a function of the compactness of the programs and the ease with which at least the most fundamental GPSS concepts can be learned.

9. Lately, GPSS has gained the additional advantage of *availability on a wide range of computers* and is hence more widely available today than the other languages mentioned. GPSS was initially an IBM product; it was later implemented on other large mainframes. More recently, powerful subsets have become available on a wide range of minis and micros. The subset presented in this book – micro-GPSS – is implemented on the IBM PC and compatible machines, on the Macintosh, as well as on some mini-computers such as the VAX.

10. It should also be mentioned that GPSS has *influenced* many *other* languages and program packages for simulation. For example, there are packages similar to GPSS written in SIMULA, such as GPSSS and DEMOS (Birtwistle, 1979). There are also sets of FORTRAN subroutines with GPSS features, such as GPSS–FORTRAN (Schmidt, 1980). There is even a GPSS package in Prolog (O'Keefe, 1989).

11. In summary, it should be emphasized that GPSS is highly compatible with what we may call the *implementation approach* to simulation.

According to the implementation approach, the model-builder focuses on the usefulness of the simulation to the ultimate decision-maker. If the results of the simulation cannot be implemented, i.e. do not affect decision-making, then the simulation model is of no practical value, even if it is characterized by great elegance. Hence, in the development of the simulation model, the final implementation must always play a guiding role.

As much of the literature on implementation stresses – in line with the author's personal experience – successful implementation of a model requires that 'the user should not be left behind'; the user should feel confident about the model. This implies that the user should have a basic understanding of how the model functions. Managers are generally reluctant to make decisions on the basis of results whose derivations they do not understand, since they want to be able to determine which assumptions are explicitly or implicitly made in the model.

Models that have been implemented successfully have in general been developed step by step, starting with the development of a very simple model with a simple and easily understood structure. After this simple model has been presented and explained to management, a somewhat more detailed model can be developed on the basis of the feedback obtained, e.g. by making it more realistic along certain lines desired by management. After feedback on this second version, a third – even more detailed – model can emerge, and so on. The important element is the constant interaction with the final user of the simulation results during the model-building process.

GPSS seems to be eminently suitable for simulation according to this implementation approach. As mentioned above, it is problem-oriented. The speed with which small models can be written and the ease with which models can be explained facilitates the build-up of the model, step by step, in interaction with the user.

## 1.6 Limitations of GPSS

It should be acknowledged that GPSS is not superior to the other simulation languages in *every* respect. In my opinion, the major limitations of GPSS as compared to, say, SIMSCRIPT or SIMULA, are as follows:

1. Because it is problem-oriented and remote from ordinary General Programming Languages such as FORTRAN and ALGOL, etc., GPSS is less flexible and less general than SIMSCRIPT and SIMULA. The important advantages of GPSS, mentioned above, refer mainly to certain types of problems, which might be called GPSS problems. Some examples of these problems have already been listed at the beginning of this chapter and more will be given later in the book. Problems that are far removed from the main area of GPSS, however, might be easier to program in the other languages.

2. In the case of very large models, the use of GPSS might be more problematic than that of the other languages since they have a greater capacity for structured programming than does GPSS. It is difficult to generalize just how large the models have to be in order to be less suitable for programming in GPSS, but it seems safe to say that this limitation is not likely to be serious in models with, at most, a couple of hundred lines of GPSS code. In fact, the number of problems associated with long GPSS programs is heavily dependent on the situation to be modeled. Henriksen (1983) mentions that programs of several thousand lines of GPSS code have been written without major problems.

   However, even if another language might be more suitable for large models, it may still be advisable to *start* the modeling in GPSS. In this way a 'prototype model' could be running at a very early stage and feedback could be obtained from management at an early stage of the project. If management then turned down the simulation project, very few resources would have been wasted. In the case of management approval, better directions (as well as funding) might result from the early presentation. When – after a few rounds of model build-up and feedback – a certain complexity in the GPSS model has been reached (e.g. several hundred lines of code), it might in some cases be pertinent to switch to another simulation language. In such cases it might be appropriate to turn to a package which is similar to GPSS (e.g. DEMOS of SIMULA).

3. Another drawback of GPSS, often mentioned in the literature, is that it has proved to be fairly wasteful of computer time and hence is generally costly, although this critique refers mainly to 'standard' GPSS running on mainframes. In fact, simulation on a PC is generally less expensive. Also, some modern GPSS versions avoid the most time-consuming characteristics of standard GPSS: GPSS/H does so by compiling the programs; micro-GPSS does so by having a different internal structure (see Section 1.10).

## 1.7 Comparisons between simulation in GPSS and in a General Programming Language

We have already compared the use of GPSS to that of other simulation languages. Another alternative is to write the program in a General Programming Language (GPL) such as Pascal, BASIC, etc. Later, in Chapter 5, we compare one of our simplest GPSS programs with the corresponding program written in a GPL (BASIC). This comparison will highlight how much simpler it is to use the special simulation language GPSS, the main reason for which is that the GPSS processor automatically carries out numerous functions which the programmer has to write in the GPL. For the time being, let us list the most important tasks which the GPSS processor carries out automatically, but which have to be taken care of by the programmer in the case of most GPLs. (Many of the items may not become quite clear until later in the book.)

1. Production of random numbers: many common GPLs, such as FORTRAN and Pascal (standard), do not produce random numbers automatically, as GPSS does. Rather, the programmer has to supply a random number routine.

2. Production of numbers sampled (i.e. drawn at random) from various statistical distributions, e.g. the negative exponential distribution: when using a GPL, the programmer has to write the subroutine that transforms the random (fraction) number into a number sampled from the desired statistical distribution. In GPSS this is carried out in a simpler fashion. Generally, the desired statistical distribution is specified by one or several data lines. In some versions, e.g. micro-GPSS, some important statistical distributions are also supplied directly by the GPSS system.

3. In GPSS, such transactions as the arrival of customers at a store are generated by a single command.

4. In GPSS, the simulation clock is updated automatically.

5. One of the most important advantages of GPSS is automatic scheduling of future events, such as the arrival of the next customer, completion of

service for a customer, etc. This events scheduling requires considerable programming in a GPL.

6. Closely related to events scheduling, automatic 'looping' is performed by the GPSS processor. At a certain clock time, when all events that are to happen at this time have occurred, the GPSS processor will automatically 'go back in the loop' to look for the next future event.

7. The GPSS system will manage waiting lines and ensure that customers are served on a first-come, first-served basis. In this context, the system will also take into consideration whether certain customers have priority over other customers who have waited longer.

8. GPSS will automatically gather a large amount of statistical data, e.g. on how many minutes each customer spends in a waiting line or with a salesperson.

9. The GPSS processor will automatically carry out certain statistical calculations on the data gathered, grouping them into classes and calculating statistical measures such as means, standard deviations, etc.

10. One specific feature of GPSS is the automatic print-out of many relevant results such as statistics on the utilization of servers, waiting times in lines, the length of waiting lines, etc.

11. The GPSS processor will provide detailed and relevant error messages. Hence a programming error that could have led to a difficult-to-discover logical error in a GPL program will be found by the GPSS processor and will result in an error message.

12. The GPSS processor takes care of numerous programming details which might be quite burdensome when writing in a GPL. For example, in GPSS the programmer does not have to bother with the dimensioning of vectors.

There is obviously much more flexibility in writing a program in a GPL than in GPSS because, in principle, almost anything can be done in most GPLs. However, if something of a special nature is required and it cannot be done in GPSS, subroutines written in a GPL such as FORTRAN may be called by GPSS (see Chapter 17).

As programming spreads to those more general groups of users who are not computer specialists, there seems to be a trend in computer software away from the more general, but weak, languages and towards more powerful, easy to learn but less flexible 'fourth generation' languages which focus on a particular area of application. For the special purpose of discrete-event stochastic simulation, GPSS is the most powerful and easily learned language. While learning GPSS, many of the problems encountered by students with knowledge of a GPL are caused by this power of GPSS. Some students tend to forget that certain things are done automatically by the GPSS processor, while they would have to be explicitly programmed in the GPL.

# 1.8 Different versions of GPSS

The first version of GPSS was created as early as 1961 by G. Gordon for an IBM mainframe. This was followed in 1964 by a slightly revised version, GPSS II, and in 1965 by a more fundamentally revised version, GPSS III. The basic structure of GPSS has remained unaltered since this last release; GPSS/360 of 1967 contained several extensions (a total of 44 block types) and GPSS V, released in 1970, contained further extensions (a total of 48 block types). GPSS V is the latest IBM GPSS release; it is the GPSS version discussed in most textbooks and has also served as a kind of standard for most of the GPSS versions available today. Hence, the comparisons in this book are made mainly with reference to GPSS V. The comparisons will focus on cases where micro-GPSS is not a subset of GPSS V.

Several other mainframe versions of GPSS appeared in the late 1960s and early 1970s, e.g. on the Norden and UNIVAC computers.

A considerable upward extension of GPSS V in the form of GPSS/H was released in 1977 by Wolverine Software. With an earlier total of 58 and now over 60 block-types, GPSS/H is the most advanced GPSS version available today; it runs on IBM mainframes, VAXs, and work stations with Motorola 68000-type CPUs, as well as on the IBM PC (see below). In contrast to other GPSS systems it is compiling and not interpretative, and thus executes considerably faster. One of the main differences as compared to GPSS V is that it works with floating point numbers instead of integers. Since GPSS V is almost a pure subset of GPSS/H, all our comparisons with GPSS V also refer to GPSS/H, unless the opposite is indicated.

There are at least four versions on IBM compatible PCs, as follows:

1. GPSS/PC of Minuteman Software: this version is fairly close to GPSS V, but there are some differences, e.g. every GPSS block requires a line number. It allows for integers with no limit to magnitude. It lacks only a few GPSS V blocks, e.g. PRINT. It allows for animation based on block diagrams.

2. GPSSR/PC of Simulation Software: with over 40 block-types, this is a substantial subset of GPSS V. Similar systems such as GPSSR and GPSS/C (both with 48 block-types) run on several mini-computers and under UNIX; GPSSR/PC also allows for animation.

3. A PC version of GPSS/H was released in 1988: it is very similar to the mainframe version.

4. The author's micro-GPSS: the subject of the next section.

On the Macintosh there is at present only one GPSS version, i.e. micro-GPSS.

It should be stressed that GPSS has been subject to intense development during the 1980s and in several important respects the modern versions are superior to the versions available throughout the 1970s. Hence, much of the critique directed earlier at GPSS is not valid as regards the newest versions.

# 1.9 The ideas behind micro-GPSS

The basic idea behind micro-GPSS is that stochastic and dynamic simulation of the GPSS type is a very powerful and interesting tool for a great many decision situations and should therefore be included in the 'toolbox' of every manager who uses a PC. Thus it appears to be highly important that students in any university business program receive an introduction to the basic methodology of such stochastic and dynamic simulation.

In other words, the creation of micro-GPSS stems from a very specific educational need, namely to teach the basic aspects of discrete-event stochastic simulation, and specifically GPSS, in a very short time, e.g. a total of around 8–15 classroom hours, or one to two full days of teaching. This, for example, would allow GPSS to be part (say, one-third) of a one-semester college course in either OR (along with, e.g., linear programming and decision analysis), general simulation (along with, e.g., Dynamo or Stella and a term project) or micro-computer software (along with, e.g., Lotus 1–2–3).

The teaching of GPSS should focus on the most important and powerful concepts. When teaching GPSS in the 1970s, using GPSS/360, the author focused increasingly on a specific subset of GPSS, which mainly corresponds to the GPSS of this book, involving only a score of different block-types and a dozen control statements. In addition to the intention that this subset be very easy to learn, it should also be powerful enough for virtually all programs in popular GPSS textbooks to be re-written without a significant increase in code size. Thus blocks should be avoided if they were difficult to learn and use and if they could easily be replaced by another block.

The original decision to create a specific micro-GPSS system for teaching this subset, instead of merely using an existing system similar to GPSS V, was based on several considerations, as follows:

The use of full GPSS V for teaching a subset gave rise to several types of serious problem. Students wrote (due, e.g., to simple typing errors) statements that violate the subset GPSS syntax, but are allowed in the full GPSS. Serious and elusive logical errors resulted, instead of an immediate, clear error code. (An example is GATE NI FAC, meant to be GATE NU FAC.) Furthermore, students sometimes felt tempted to try to go outside the subset taught, which almost always resulted in logical errors since the students misunderstood these more complex GPSS concepts.

Finally, by creating a specific micro-GPSS for teaching GPSS, the educational community could be provided with an easy to learn GPSS, without serious restrictions on program size, at a low cost.

When I embarked upon the construction of this specific micro-GPSS system, I tried to follow GPSS V as closely as possible. However, the following considerations led me to introduce several improvements and extensions to what would be a pure subset of GPSS V. When trying to cut down on the number of different block-types, I realized that some GPSS V blocks carry out roughly the same functions. Some GPSS experts, such as Gordon and Henriksen, have also suggested that GPSS V contains too many block-types and that certain similar concepts could be merged into one concept (see Gordon, 1979 and Henriksen, 1985). These ideas were an additional inspiration to my efforts to cut down the number of different block-types by creating new more powerful blocks.

From my experience of teaching GPSS V, the greatest obstacles faced by students in the effective use of GPSS was that they all too frequently wrote programs in GPSS V that led to serious logical errors. An aim of micro-GPSS was to try to eliminate these sources of logical errors as far as possible. For example, one common source of logical errors in GPSS V is in the unintended use of a number and name for the same server. In micro-GPSS such mix-ups have been eliminated by restrictions on how servers can be named. The replacement of some of the blocks most commonly leading to logical errors in GPSS V with other, simpler and more straightforward, concepts has made programming in micro-GPSS safer. The highly increased programming safety in micro-GPSS has the advantage of eliminating the need to learn a complicated debugging system.

Furthermore, I wished to avoid some details in GPSS V that constantly led to student errors. One of the most important decisions in this regard was to introduce a completely free format.

Finally, some GPSS V elements had proved to run contrary to the thinking of those students who had some experience of other computer languages. Since my aim was to make it as easy as possible to learn GPSS, as an integrated part of the general learning of computer software for decision support, the following idea was important when creating new blocks: since almost all students have some elementary knowledge of BASIC, micro-GPSS should utilize this knowledge in order to make learning as smooth as possible. This refers not only to the use of such well-known terms as IF, but also to following more generally accepted ways of thought. For example, in order to direct a customer to label BYE if P1 is negative, micro-GPSS uses 'IF P1<0,BYE', while GPSS V requires 'TEST GE P1,BYE' which appears quite strange to the uninitiated.

Because of the introduction of these improvements and extensions, micro-GPSS, with only 22 block-types, has proved successful in several respects: over the last couple of years it has been possible to cover material and exercises in less than half the amount of time than was taken by the same type of students using GPSS V. Furthermore, all but one of the 27 case studies in Schriber's 'classical' textbook from 1974 could be re-written in micro-GPSS with roughly the same number of statements as in GPSS V.

It should, however, be stressed that virtually none of these changes is contrary to the 'spirit' of GPSS. Micro-GPSS is primarily true to the fundamental 'world view' of GPSS with temporary transactions and permanent servers and with blocks that are closely related to the actual system. The differences only apply to specific details where substantial improvements in learning efficiency can be obtained by minor changes. The objective is that the student who subsequently wishes to work in GPSS V should lose less than one hour by first learning these simpler micro-GPSS forms, rather than learning the complicated GPSS V forms directly. This is a very small disadvantage as compared to the very substantial savings in time from learning micro-GPSS instead of GPSS V.

Although the main target audience is made up of students who do not know GPSS V and are not likely to find any need to move from micro-GPSS to full GPSS, the micro-GPSS processor also allows some of the alternative, more complicated, GPSS V forms in order to facilitate a transition to GPSS V. They are presented in Appendix B. Furthermore, special software is presently being developed which will translate micro-GPSS programs so that they can run on the GPSS/H system.

## ■  1.10  Special features of micro-GPSS

The special micro-GPSS features will become clearer as the book is read chapter by chapter. However, to conclude this introduction, we give the following brief summary of the main differences between micro-GPSS and GPSS V. (You may prefer to read this later.)

1. *Free format and easy coding*: in contrast to GPSS V which specifies, e.g., that an operation has to start in a certain column, micro-GPSS has a *completely* free format. Hence any line could start in column 1. Both upper and lower case letters are allowed. Furthermore, coding in micro-GPSS can be performed even more conveniently thanks to the availability of an easy-to-use code-generating dialog program, GPSSMENU.

2. *Floating point numbers*: in contrast to GPSS V, which in almost all operands allows only for integer numbers and truncates almost all decimal values, micro-GPSS (like GPSS/H) also allows for floating point values, i.e. numbers with a decimal point. This eliminates many problems inherent in GPSS V, such as the requirement for careful choice of time units.

3. *Repeated runs*: in order to run a certain program, say 20 times with different set-ups of random numbers for each run, in GPSS V 39 and GPSS/H 4, extra control statements must be used. In micro-GPSS the number 20 is merely included in a control statement or written at run time.

4. *Built-in functions*: while in GPSS V all statistical functions must be defined

using a relatively large number of pairs of numbers, micro-GPSS and GPSS/H have several common statistical distributions as well as mathematical functions built in.

5. *General use of expressions*: whereas GPSS V only allows the use of expressions in special definition statements, micro-GPSS and GPSS/H allow for a much more general use of expressions.

6. *Greater program safety*: as mentioned above, micro-GPSS eliminates sources of logical errors as far as possible.

7. *Error codes*: another factor making logical errors less likely and increasing the likelihood of correct programming is that micro-GPSS has a more extensive error code and error trapping system than other GPSS systems.

8. *Simplified queue statistics gathering*: statistics on the waiting line in front of a server can be collected in micro-GPSS by just adding one letter to a block referring to this server, while GPSS V requires two additional blocks.

9. *No 'unnecessary details'*: in micro-GPSS such details as 'unnecessary' commas, for example, can be left out. Furthermore, one can use ordinary comparison characters like > and < instead of letter codes.

10. *More easily read output*: the output of micro-GPSS is in several respects more readable and understandable than the output generated by GPSS V. All output fits a normal 80 column screen.

11. *Easier key words*: since most students are familiar with the BASIC key words IF, GOTO and LET, learning of micro-GPSS is facilitated by allowing these words to replace more complicated words in GPSS V (ASSIGN, INITIAL, SAVEVALUE, TEST, TRANSFER). ARRIVE of micro-GPSS (as compared to QUEUE of GPSS V) is a more natural counterpart of DEPART.

12. *Conventional IF logic*: most students are used to IF blocks, where they go to an address if a condition is true and to the next block if the condition is false. Micro-GPSS keeps this logic construction, in contrast to GPSS V which uses inverted logic in so far as one goes to the next block if the test condition is true, and to the address if the condition is false.

13. *Statistical analysis and optimization*: in micro-GPSS it is easy to perform both statistical analysis (e.g. on the basis of Student's *t*-distribution estimate for a set of runs within which limits the true average will lie with 95 percent confidence) and optimization (e.g. in the form of automatically comparing the results from a great number of runs with different values of the decision variable).

14. *Better experimental facilities*: by providing for simple methods for obtaining antithetic random numbers for variance reduction, repeated runs of paired conditions, etc., experiments are greatly facilitated in micro-GPSS (as in GPSS/H) in comparison to GPSS V.

15. *More powerful interface with FORTRAN*: both in GPSS V and micro-GPSS a GPSS program can call a FORTRAN subroutine, but only in micro-GPSS can a FORTRAN program call a GPSS program, which in turn can call a FORTRAN subroutine, thus allowing for better structured programs. The call on FORTRAN subroutines can also be carried out from GPSS control statements, making interactive input easy.

16. *Different internal structure*: while GPSS V puts all waiting transactions on one

single waiting list, micro-GPSS uses one specific waiting list for every server as well as for every other kind of block where waiting can take place. In some cases this will lead to a dramatic improvement in time efficiency, which may well be important when running simulations on a PC. This also appears to make it easier for students to understand how the micro-GPSS processor works.

17. *Animation*: like GPSS/PC and GPSSR/PC, special versions of micro-GPSS allow for animation based on the block diagrams. Since animation works differently on different computers it is not covered in this book, but is covered in the documentation which accompanies the software.

# 2 Random numbers

## 2.1 Main characteristics of random numbers

Before presenting any specific details about GPSS, we examine one of the most important aspects of any stochastic simulation language, namely the generation of random numbers. We begin by dealing with random numbers that are integers, i.e. 0, 1, 2, 3, etc., and then (in Section 2.4) we discuss random fraction numbers between 0 and 1.

In everyday life we are quite familiar with the generation of random numbers, although we are perhaps not always aware of it. Coin flips or die throws are examples of processes which generate true random numbers. When throwing an ordinary unbiased (unloaded) die, we generate at random a number 1, 2, 3, 4, 5 or 6, where each of these six numbers is equally likely. There also exist, although they are less common, 10-sided dice, allowing generation of the digits 0, 1, . . . , 9, all equally likely. In the drawing of some state-lottery winnings the 'lucky number' is generated, digit by digit, by drawing one of 10 different balls.

All these processes are examples of true random numbers. This implies that no one, even with the help of very advanced calculating aids, can predict the next random number to be drawn. Furthermore, the number generated in, say, one throw of a die is completely independent of the number generated in the immediately preceding throw. As any student of statistics knows, the probability of throwing a six with an ordinary die is always 1/6, regardless of whether a six has just been thrown or not.

In the simulation of stochastic events, however, we do not use true random numbers, but, rather, a sequence of what are called *pseudo-random* numbers. These pseudo-random numbers have certain characteristics in common with true random numbers. An 'outsider' should perceive pseudo-random numbers as true random numbers. If someone who has not been involved in the generation of a sequence of pseudo-random numbers is confronted with a sequence of such numbers, he should not be able to determine whether the sequence of numbers is truly random (e.g. generated by repeated throws of a 10-sided die) or whether they are pseudo-random (generated by a special computer algorithm). This should hold, even if the 'outsider' is a statistician who performs various statistical tests; see Section 2.5. Hence, we wish the pseudo-random numbers to appear truly random to 'outsiders'.

However, pseudo-random numbers differ from true random numbers in several respects. All the differences stem from the fact that a sequence of pseudo-random numbers is generated by an algorithm, i.e. a computational procedure. This generally starts with a number, $r(0)$, called the seed. The next number in the random number sequence, $r(1)$, is then generated by carrying out some often fairly complicated transformation of $r(0)$; see Sections 2.2 and 2.3. The next number in turn, $r(2)$, is obtained by the same transformation of $r(1)$; $r(3)$ is obtained by the same transformation of $r(2)$, and so on.

Before giving examples of some of the transformation methods, it should be noted that when one number in a sequence is produced in such a way from the immediately preceding number in the sequence, the following are implied:

1. An 'insider' who knows the starting number $r(0)$ and the transformation algorithm can predict every random number in the sequence, provided he or she has a suitable computational tool. Hence, we can very well understand that a pseudo-random number generator cannot be used to pick the winner of a million dollar prize in a state lottery. It would then be too tempting to become an 'insider'.

2. The sequence of random numbers can easily be replicated. Once we use the same starting number $r(0)$ and the same transformation algorithm, the same random number sequence $r(1)$, $r(2)$, $r(3)$, etc., will be replicated. Such a replication of a sequence of numbers is obviously impossible with truly random numbers.

3. Eventually, the same random number that was generated earlier will be generated again after which the same sequence will start all over again. This is because when dealing with finite numbers, there is a maximum value to a pseudo-random number. For example, if we allow a maximum of three-digit numbers only, this would be 999. Allowing for non-negative integers only, but including 0, we would then have a maximum number of different random numbers, $m$, which is one higher. In the case of three digits we would thus have a maximum of 1000 different numbers.

   Obviously, if more than 1000 numbers were generated in this case, we are sure to have generated at least one number more than once. Once we repeat one number, we also repeat the whole sequence that follows on from this number. For instance, let us assume that at the $n$th number we obtain the same number as at the $j$th, i.e. $r(n) = r(j)$. Since we use the same transformation to obtain $r(n + 1)$ from $r(n)$ as we used to obtain $r(j + 1)$ from $r(j)$, we obviously have $r(n + 1) = r(j + 1)$ and likewise $r(n + 2) = r(j + 2)$, etc. The same sequence of numbers $r(j), \ldots, r(n - 1)$ will now be repeated again. The *length* of the sequence of random numbers, $r(j), \ldots, r(n - 1)$, which is repeated over and over again is called the *period* of the random number generator.

We are obviously interested in a long period, particularly if we have to use a great many random numbers, in order that we do not use the same random numbers over again unintentionally. The *maximum* period is obviously equal to $m$, as defined above. After $m$ numbers, at most, the same sequence is bound to start all over again. It should be stressed that in many cases the actual period is considerably shorter than this maximum period, as exemplified in Section 2.3. The *actual* period is equal to the maximum period only if $r(0) = r(m)$, i.e. the repetition does not occur until after $m$ numbers.

Before looking at some specific methods for generating random numbers, it should be mentioned that we wish the random number generator to operate quickly so that the generation of many random numbers does not slow down simulation significantly.

## ■ 2.2 The von Neumann method

In this and the next section, which can be skipped without affecting the understanding of later chapters, we present two methods for generating random numbers. We begin with the oldest method, that constructed by John von Neumann and sometimes referred to as the 'mid-square'-method, which has the advantage of great simplicity. We exemplify this method with a random number sequence involving three-digit numbers. Let us set the starting value, i.e. the seed, $r(0)$, at 239. We obtain $r(1)$ as the middle three digits in the product $239 \star 239 = 57\,121$, i.e. $r(1) = 712$. The generation of successive random numbers is shown below, where we have underlined the three digits in the middle:

$r(0) = 239 \qquad r(0) \star r(0) = 239 \star 239 = 57\,\underline{121}$
$r(1) = 712 \qquad r(1) \star r(1) = 712 \star 712 = 50\underline{6\,94}4$
$r(2) = 694 \qquad r(2) \star r(2) = 694 \star 694 = 48\underline{1\,63}6$
$r(3) = 163 \qquad r(3) \star r(3) = 163 \star 163 = 26\,\underline{569}$
$r(4) = 656 \qquad r(4) \star r(4) = 656 \star 656 = 43\underline{0\,33}6$, etc.

The von Neumann method has several drawbacks, however. The most serious is that the sequence might degenerate for certain seeds, in the sense that we are stuck with the same number, repeated over and over again. In other words, we get a period of 1. For example, the seed $r(0) = 252$ leads to the following sequence:

$r(0) = 252 \qquad r(0) \star r(0) = 252 \star 252 = 63\,\underline{504}$
$r(1) = 350 \qquad r(1) \star r(1) = 350 \star 350 = 12\underline{2\,50}0$

$r(2) = 250$    $r(2) \star r(2) = 250 \star 250 = 62\,500$
$r(3) = 250$    $r(3) \star r(3) = 250 \star 250 = 62\,500$

We see that all random numbers onwards will be 250.

## ■ 2.3 Lehmer's congruential method

Owing to the deficiencies of the von Neumann method, more complicated random number generators with better properties have been constructed. One of the methods used most widely today is the Lehmer congruential method, which is used by micro-GPSS in this book as well as by some other systems such as GPSS/H and GPSS/PC.

Before studying the computational algorithm of this method, we should look at the concept of *modulus*.

The result of $(a) \bmod (b)$, read as '*a* modulus *b*', is equal to the remainder in the division of $a$ by $b$. For example, $(10) \bmod (3) = 1$ and $(7) \bmod (5) = 2$. With INT ( ) as a function that truncates a number, i.e. takes away the decimals and keeps only the integer part of the (positive) number, we can write $(a) \bmod (b)$ as $a - \mathrm{INT}\,(a/b) \star b$, where $a/b$ reads $a$ divided by $b$. For example, $(10) \bmod (3) = 10 - \mathrm{INT}\,(10/3) \star 3 = 10 - 3 \star 3 = 1$ and $(17) \bmod (5) = 17 - \mathrm{INT}\,(17/5) \star 5 = 2$.

We are now better prepared to study Lehmer's method. We write the relationship between one random number $r(n + 1)$ and the preceding number $r(n)$ as $r(n + 1) = (a \star r(n) + c) \bmod (m)$. We begin by computing a linear transformation $y$ of $r(n)$ as $a \star r(n) + c$. Next, we compute $r(n + 1) = (y) \bmod (m)$. The following BASIC program summarizes the procedure for computing a stream of random numbers.

```
10  INPUT R
20  Y = A * R + C
30  Z = Y / M
40  R = Y - INT ( Z ) * M
50  PRINT R
60  GOTO 20
```

The table below shows how the program works, exemplified using $m = 25$, $a = 6$, $c = 1$ and with $r(0) = 1$.

| $i$ | $r(i - 1)$ | $y$ | $z$ | $r(i)$ |
|---|---|---|---|---|
| 1 | 1 | $6 \star 1 + 1 = 7$ | $7/25$ | 7 |
| 2 | 7 | $6 \star 7 + 1 = 43$ | $43/25 = 1 + 18/25$ | 18 |
| 3 | 18 | $6 \star 18 + 1 = 109$ | $109/25 = 4 + 9/25$ | 9 |
| 4 | 9 | $6 \star 9 + 1 = 55$ | $55/25 = 2 + 5/25$ | 5 |

When $m = 25$ we have a maximum period of 25. The actual period in this example is also 25, as can easily be checked.

A special case of the Lehmer congruential method, called the Lehmer multiplicative method, is obtained by setting $c = 0$. This special-case method is regarded by many statisticians as having numerous desirable properties. The maximum period in this case, however, is $m/4$.

The most suitable values of $a$, $m$, and $c$ depend on the computer system. (For efficiency reasons, $m$ is often a power of 2, e.g. 2 raised to 31.) Hence different micro-GPSS versions might not produce identical results and the result of the programs presented in this book might not be the same as those produced by a particular micro-GPSS version.

## 2.4 Uniform random fraction numbers

The random number generators discussed so far have produced an integer number from 0 to $m - 1$, where $m$ is the maximum value of these random numbers. For example, if $m = 1\,048\,576$, then we generate integer numbers from 0 to $1\,048\,575$. If $m = 32$ instead, we would only generate integer numbers from 0 to 31. Hence the numbers generated would be very different, depending on the choice of $m$. We are really interested in a more standardized random number, namely a number between 0 and 1. We call this the *uniform fraction* random number; *fraction* indicates that the numbers are between 0 and 1 and *uniform* that every number with a certain number of decimal digits, e.g. six, is equally likely.

To obtain this number we simply divide the integer random number, discussed above, by $m$. For example, in the case of $m = 32$, if we have an integer random number $r = 12$, we obtain a random fraction number $u = 12/32 = 0.375$ and if we have $m = 1\,048\,576$ and $r = 392\,901$, then $u = 0.3747$. It should be noted that since the largest integer number is $m - 1$ and this number is divided by $m$, $u$ will never quite become 1. With $m$ very large and with six-digit precision, $u \le 0.999\,999$. The fact that we cannot obtain exactly 1 does not play any practical role, since for most practical purposes 0.999 999 is close enough to 1.

As discussed further in Chapter 12, micro-GPSS has eight different generators producing different sequences of such uniform random fraction numbers.

### ■ 2.5 Testing of random number generators

We conclude this chapter with a brief discussion of the testing of random number generators. As mentioned, we want the random number sequence provided by a random number generator to appear truly random, even to a statistician making a careful statistical analysis of these random numbers. Here we mention only four of many possible statistical criteria for establishing whether pseudo-random numbers behave like true random numbers. It should be kept in mind that tests are not performed on the integer random numbers, but, rather, on the standardized uniform fraction numbers.

Let us assume that we have a sequence of, say, 1000 such random fraction numbers. The most obvious criterion for determining whether they appear to be truly random is that the average is very close to 1/2.

A second criterion would be that the variance of the numbers would be very close to 1/12, which is the expected value of the variance of fraction random numbers.

A third method would be to divide all random numbers into 10 groups with all numbers 0, . . . , 0.099 999 in one group, all from 0.1 to 0.199 999 in the second group, and so on. We would then expect roughly the same frequencies of observations for each of these groups.

A fourth method is to measure the percentage of random numbers that are higher than the immediately preceding random number. This percentage should be roughly 50. The sequence of 0.1, 0.2, 0.3, 0.4, 0.5, 0.6, 0.7, 0.8, 0.9 would fail on this criterion, although it would be successful on the other three.

# 3 Foundations of GPSS: transactions

## 3.1 Introduction

In this chapter we will present the most fundamental GPSS concepts, and in this connection will present our first simple programs. Since the material here is essential to understanding all the remaining chapters, readers are recommended to read this chapter very carefully.

We deal here with the concept of a transaction. As mentioned earlier, this can be seen as a customer in the wide sense of the word. Transactions are temporary entities which are generated, i.e. created, and terminated, i.e. destroyed, during the course of the simulation. They might thus remain in the system for only a small part of the total simulation time. In the next chapter we deal with servers, which are the permanent entities in the simulation. Some examples of transactions are as follows:

1. A patient in a hospital clinic who is served by a medical secretary, a nurse and a doctor.

2. A customer in a supermarket who is served at a meat counter and subsequently at a checkout counter.

3. A car which is served by various segments of a road.

More examples of transactions are given in Chapter 4.

The important aspect in GPSS when modeling transactions is that all transactions that are similar in some fundamental aspect are placed in one group. This similarity can, for example, refer to their arrival pattern or to the time they require from various servers. All transactions that can be regarded as similar can use the same program segment. Hence, if there is only one kind of customer in a model, the program requires only one customer segment. Our first program examples will be limited to the case of only one type of customer. Cases with several types of customer will appear in Chapter 7.

A transaction's movement through the system, a customer's walk through a store, say, consists of the four following main types of event:

1. Generation, e.g. a customer arrives at the store.

2. Planned delay, e.g. the customer obtains service over a certain time period.

3. Waiting, e.g. the customer waits for a server to become available.

4. Termination, e.g. the customer leaves the store.

This chapter will cover generation, termination and planned delay, presented in this order. Waiting is dealt with in the next chapter dealing with servers.

## 3.2 The InterArrival Time concept

We begin with the generation of transactions into the system, e.g. the arrival of customers at a store. The most important aspect of this generation is that we are dealing with stochastic systems. The systems discussed above are characterized by the fact that the transactions (e.g. customers arriving at a shop) do not enter the system (arrive at the shop) at a steady rate, but, rather, in a somewhat irregular pattern. Sometimes there will be a short time, sometimes a much longer time, between the arrival of two consecutive customers. Here we wish to model this random aspect of arrival.

In order to establish arrival times of transactions we first determine the time between one arrival and the next, i.e. the InterArrival Time (IAT). On the basis of this we determine the time of arrival (T).

For the first customer's arrival we start at time 0. We then sample the first InterArrival Time, IAT (1). For the sake of simplicity, we assume as a standard case that the first customer arrives at a time $T(1) = 0 + IAT(1) = IAT(1)$. If, for example, we sample $IAT(1) = 16$, the first customer arrives at time $0 + 16 = 16$. (Although the micro-GPSS system allows decimal values of time, in this section we use integer values of time for the sake of simplicity.)

For the second customer's arrival we first determine the second InterArrival Time, IAT(2), i.e. the sampled time between the arrival of the first and the second customers. We next calculate the time of the arrival of the second customer $T(2)$ as $T(1) + IAT(2)$, i.e. we add the just sampled time, IAT(2), to the time of the arrival of the first customer. If $IAT(2) = 23$ we obtain our example described in Figure 3.1 – $T(2) = 16 + 23 = 39$. Likewise, the arrival time of the third customer, $T(3)$, is obtained as $T(2) + IAT(3)$, (e.g. $39 + 13 = 52$), where IAT(3) is the sampled time between the arrival of the second and third customers.

The InterArrival Time of each customer is random in the sense that it is

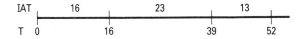

**Figure 3.1** Relationship between arrival times and IATs

drawn from a statistical distribution. This distribution can be regarded as a very large set of values from which we draw one value at a time at random, and can be described by certain characteristics of the numbers that can be drawn from this distribution.

Foremost among these characteristics is the average, i.e. in this case the average time between the arrival of two consecutive customers. If, for example, during a business day of 10 hours, i.e. 600 minutes, 100 customers arrive, the average InterArrival Time is 6 minutes. In this case, if we draw, say, 100 IAT values, then the sum of these values is expected to be close to 600 and the average value of these 100 sampled IATs should be close to 6.

Each specific sampled value might, however, differ markedly from 6 – sometimes higher, sometimes lower. Another natural characteristic of the InterArrival Time distribution is thus some measure of *dispersion* of these IAT values around the average value. When describing this dispersion, a balance must be struck between realism and simplicity. This chapter discusses the simplest possible kind of dispersion, while later chapters (Chapter 12 onwards) cover other distributions which are more realistic for many customer arrival processes.

## 3.3 The rectangular distribution

The simplest distribution of InterArrival Times, determining the average as well as the dispersion, is the rectangular distribution, defined by the following two assumptions:

1. There is an upper limit and a lower limit to the values.

2. All values between these two limits are equally likely, implying that the distribution is completely symmetric.

Figure 3.2 shows an example of the distribution. In this example, the average InterArrival Time (IAT) is 18 minutes, the lowest is 12 and the highest is 24; and all values between 12 and 24 minutes are equally likely. The distribution is completely symmetric around the average, i.e. the distance from the lower limit to the average (6 minutes) is the same as the distance from the average to the upper limit. Thus the distribution is completely defined by two factors,

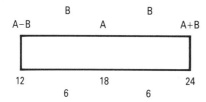

**Figure 3.2** A rectangular distribution

the average and the distance from the average to one of the limits, be it the lower or the upper limit. Since this distance is equal to half the total width (= the distance between the upper and lower limits), we call it the 'half-width' of the distribution. Thus this rectangular distribution is uniquely determined by the average 18 and the half-width 6.

Other rectangular distributions are obtained using different averages and different half-widths. For example, the average 200 and the half-width 50 defines a distribution with all IAT values between 150 and 250, i.e. $200 \pm 50$, as equally likely.

Following from the above, here I describe the connection in micro-GPSS between the sampled InterArrival Time and the uniform random fraction number $u$, discussed earlier in Chapter 2. Let us call the average $A$ and the half-width $B$. Thus $2B$ is the total width, i.e. the distance between the lower limit $LL$ and the upper limit $UL$. As $u$ goes from 0 to 1, IAT goes from $LL$ to $UL$. This is accomplished by defining IAT as $LL + u2B$. When $u = 0$, $IAT = LL$; when $u = 1$, $IAT = LL + 2B = LL + (UL - LL) = UL$. Since $LL = A - B$, $IAT = A - B + u2B$. When $u = 1/2$, $IAT = A - B + (1/2)2B = A - B + B = A$. Since $u$ never quite reaches 1 (see Section 2.4), $IAT$ can never be $A + B$, although it can get very close; $IAT$ can reach $A - B$ since $u$ can be 0.

## 3.4 The GENERATE block

We are now ready to study the first GPSS block, GENERATE. Blocks contain an operation, usually followed by one or several operands. The operation of the GENERATE block is the word GENERATE. In this case the block has two operands, referred to as the A and B operands, separated by a comma. The A operand is the average InterArrival Time, while the B operand is the mentioned half-width, i.e. the distance between the average and the lower limit. Hence the general expression GENERATE A,B implies that trans-actions are generated with InterArrival Times such that all IAT values from $A - B$ to $A + B$ are equally likely. GENERATE 18,6 thus generates InterArrival Times drawn from the distribution in Figure 3.2 above with all IATs from 12 to 24 being equally likely.

The GENERATE block is represented in block diagrams by the general symbol given in Figure 3.3, where the word GENERATE is written at the top and the operands are written below. It should be stressed that both the A and B operands, as used here for the rectangular distribution, are non-negative constants. In micro-GPSS both integers and decimal numbers are allowed. Integers can have a maximum of five digits and decimal numbers can have a maximum eight digits, including the period. (In GPSS V programmers are restricted to integers only, i.e. to 0, 1, 2, 3, etc.)

**Figure 3.3** Block symbol of GENERATE

Furthermore, it is required that A $\geq$ B. In the case of A $<$ B, the lower limit value A $-$ B would be negative. If we then sampled an IAT close to the lower limit, we would obtain an IAT $<$ 0, implying that the next customer would arrive before the present one, i.e. we would attempt to travel backwards in time. This is not allowed in GPSS and will result in an error message.

It should be mentioned here that the A and B operands of the GENERATE block have default values of 0. A default value is the value that is assigned automatically by the GPSS processor if no value is given to the operand by the programmer.

The use of the default value for the B operand is fairly common. GENERATE A implies the same value as GENERATE A,0, i.e. generating IATs that are all A. Hence GENERATE 10 implies that the first customer (transaction) arrives at time 10, the second at time 20, the third at time 30, etc.; i.e. we get a completely deterministic arrival pattern.

## 3.5 The TERMINATE block

We have described above how we insert the transactions in the simulation system, e.g. the customers enter a store. Next we discuss how we remove the transactions from the simulation system, e.g. the customers leave the store. This is accomplished by the block TERMINATE.

The block symbol of the TERMINATE block is illustrated in Figure 3.4, and is composed of a circle with the operation TERMINATE written inside and a small 'tail' on the right-hand side containing the A operand, which is a non-negative integer, 0, 1, 2, 3, etc.

**Figure 3.4** Block symbol of TERMINATE

If the TERMINATE block has no A operand, or if the A operand is 0, which is the default value of the A operand of the TERMINATE block, then the TERMINATE block merely effects the termination of the particular transaction, i.e. removes it from the simulation system.

To explain how the TERMINATE block works, let us look at a very simple example. Assume that customers arrive at a turnstile every $18 \pm 6$ minutes, i.e. at a rate such that the InterArrival Times vary between 12 and 24 minutes. Assume that the customers then leave the system immediately. Following the convention of this book, using lower-case letters for all (parts of) program listings, we write this segment of the simulation program as follows:

```
generate 18,6
terminate
```

This customer segment instructs the computer to first sample IAT(1), say 16, and then schedule the first customer to arrive at this time. As this first customer is brought into the system at time 16 (and is then immediately terminated), the computer samples IAT(2), say 23, and schedules the second customer to arrive at time $16 + IAT(2) = 16 + 23 = 39$. When one customer arrives, i.e. is brought into the system, micro-GPSS automatically schedules the arrival of the next customer. At time 39, when this second customer is brought into (and then immediately removed from) the system, the third customer's time of arrival is scheduled. In this way one customer after the other is brought into the system.

In principle, this process can go on forever. In order to stop the simulation, we must use the A operand of the TERMINATE block. In order to understand how the A operand is used in closing down the simulation, an understanding of the concept of the 'termination counter' is necessary. This is a counter that will stop the simulation when it is set to (or below) 0. As long as the termination counter has a value larger than 0 the simulation will continue.

In order for any simulation to occur at all, the termination counter must be given a value $> 0$ prior to commencement of the simulation. This is done by a special GPSS control statement, START A, where the A operand is a positive integer constant, i.e. 1, 2, 3, etc., given to the termination counter. START 50 will, for example, set the termination counter to 50 at the commencement of the simulation.

The difference between a GPSS block and a GPSS control statement is explained as follows. A block refers to an action taken by transactions and will be executed every time a transaction enters the block. In the block diagram all the blocks, but no control statements, will be represented. Control statements are commands which are either executed at the very start or the very end of the simulation or refer to general definitions possibly relevant to several blocks.

We can now demonstrate how the A operand of the TERMINATE block specifies the amount by which the termination counter will be decreased. TERMINATE 1 implies that when the transaction reaches the TERMINATE block and is taken out of the simulation system, the termination counter will also be decreased by 1. Every time the termination counter is decreased, a test is carried out to determine whether or not the termination counter has reached 0 (or turned negative). If this is the case the simulation is stopped. The ordinary TERMINATE without an A operand will thus not result in any decrease in the termination counter.

It should now be apparent that the following three lines result in stoppage of the simulation of the turnstile after the arrival of 50 customers:

```
generate 18,6
terminate 1
start 50
```

The control statement START 50, which, for reasons that will be explained later (Chapter 18), is placed after all blocks at the end of the program, will set the termination counter to 50. Hence the first customer will, when terminated (by the TERMINATE block), decrease the termination counter from 50 to 49; the second one will decrease it from 49 to 48; the third one from 48 to 47, etc., and finally the fiftieth one from 1 to 0. Since the termination counter then becomes 0, the simulation will stop.

## 3.6 Program 3.1

We are now ready to write our first, but very simple, program in complete form, simulating the arrival of 50 customers at a turnstile. Refer to the block diagram in Figure 3.5. Note that the two block symbols in the diagram are connected by an arrow which indicates the direction of transaction movement, i.e. in this case that the transaction goes from the GENERATE block to the TERMINATE block.

In addition to the two blocks illustrated in Figure 3.5, the program contains three control statements. The START statement has already been defined. The SIMULATE statement, usually without an operand, should head every program to be executed. (Without the SIMULATE statement the

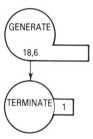

**Figure 3.5** Block diagram of Program 3.1

program will only be checked for syntax errors.) Finally, every program must end with an END statement, always without an operand. This statement is used merely to indicate the end of the program.

The whole program can now be written as shown in Program 3.1.

**Program 3.1** Micro-GPSS input format

```
simulate
generate    18,6
terminate   1
start       50
end
```

## 3.7 Program coding

When coding the program on the computer, the question of input format arises. Here micro-GPSS has the considerable advantage of a completely free format. For standard GPSS, originally run on cards, there are specific format requirements. The GPSS/360 format rules are generally also accepted by other versions, e.g. micro-GPSS and GPSS V, the latter having its own free format which, however, is more restrictive than the completely free format of micro-GPSS.

Micro-GPSS thus allows input in a free format, of which the GPSS/360 format can be seen as a special case used by micro-GPSS when listing the program since it improves the readability of the program listing. Only the free format of micro-GPSS and the GPSS/360 card format rules are discussed here.

In GPSS there are three types of field:

1. The *address* field (to be discussed later), where, for instance, statement addresses or labels are written.

2. The *operation* field, where we write the operation, e.g. GENERATE or START.

3. The *operand* field, where we write the operands, e.g. the A and B operands.

It is true for all systems that there must not be *any* blanks, i.e. blank spaces, in the operand field. The operands are only separated by commas. Hence 18,6 in Program 3.1 must *not* contain any blank. The GPSS processor regards the operand field as complete as soon as a blank is encountered.

In micro-GPSS the only other rule is that we must insert at least *one* blank *between* each of the three fields. This is very pertinent from the point of view of readability. In Program 3.1 we thus require at least one blank between GENERATE and 18,6. Otherwise, we are free to start each line in any column (provided all text is completed prior to column 72 to allow space for line numbers on the complete listing). If there is no address, as in Program 3.1, the operation field can start immediately in column 1.

The rules of GPSS/360 are more restrictive. Columns 2–6 form the address field, columns 8–17 the operation field and columns 19–71 the operand field. Hence each address starts in column 2, each operation in column 8 and each A operand in column 19.

In micro-GPSS the program is coded using whichever editor or word processor is most convenient on the computer system being used. The only restriction is that it should produce ASCII code. Furthermore, GPSS does not differentiate between upper- or lower-case letters. In this book we will consistently use lower-case letters in the programs, although this is not necessary. Finally, the program is saved in a file under a name with, at most, 25 characters.

To assist even further in the coding of a micro-GPSS program, a special code-generating dialog program, GPSSMENU, is available. This program, which is very easy to use, normally comes on a separate diskette and is described in Appendix C which also includes an example illustrating the coding of Program 3.1 using this facility.


## 3.8 Program output

The program illustrated above can now be run by first typing 'GPSS'. The micro-GPSS interpreter is then loaded into the primary memory and begins by asking for the GPSS program file name. The name of the program just saved is then typed. If the user does not wish to code Program 3.1, this is available, as are all other programs presented in this book, on the program diskette of the GPSS system, titled prog3.1.

This GPSS program is then executed and output is produced, provided that the program is correct. If there is a syntax error, e.g. due to misspelling of a key word, the micro-GPSS processor will print the incorrect line and allow the user to re-type the whole line. An alternative is to hit the return key and correct the program using the editor. (For hints on errors see Appendix D.)

The program output commences with a program listing, in GPSS/360 format, as shown in Table 3.1. As can be seen immediately, this program listing differs from the original Program 3.1 in the three following ways: (i) it follows the GPSS/360 format; (ii) we obtain a print-out of the block numbers as well as the line numbers; (iii) headings are printed out at commencement, indicating which field the output refers to.

**Table 3.1** Complete listing of Program 3.1

Extended program listing

| Block no. | *Adr. | Operation | A,B,C,D,E,F,G,H | Comments | Line no. |
|---|---|---|---|---|---|
| | | simulate | | | 1 |
| 1 | | generate | 18,6 | | 2 |
| 2 | | terminate | 1 | | 3 |
| | | start | 50 | | 4 |
| | | end | | | 5 |

The numbering of the blocks assists interpretation of the block statistics, which comprise the remaining part of the output received for Program 3.1 in micro-GPSS. This output is illustrated in Table 3.2 and is obtained after pressing the return (or enter) key.

At the head of the output is the time on the simulation clock when simulation stopped. There are two clocks, a relative clock and an absolute clock, both registering the value 892.24. At this stage there is no need to

**Table 3.2** Block statistics of Program 3.1

Relative clock     892.24 Absolute clock     892.24

Block counts

| Number | Adr. | Oper. | Current | Total |
|---|---|---|---|---|
| 1 | | GENER | 0 | 50 |
| 2 | | TERMI | 0 | 50 |

explain the difference between the two clocks; this is discussed in a later chapter (Chapter 18). As can be seen, however, it took 892.24 minutes for 50 customers to go through the turnstile in this simulation. This is as expected when the average InterArrival Time is 18, since $50 \times 18 = 900$.

The block count statistics are listed below the data on the simulation clock. These statistics refer to the situation at the end of the simulation, i.e. in this case at time 892.24. To the left is given the number of the block. In micro-GPSS the first five letters of the operation are printed after the block number, which makes it easier to determine the block being referred to. The block counts give two types of statistics for each block: the current count and the total count, as follows:

1. The *current* count refers to the number of transactions still inside a block at the end of the simulation. Since there is nothing in this simple program to stop a transaction in any of the blocks, these current counts are both 0.

2. The *total* count is the number of transactions that have entered the block during the simulation. Hence it can be seen that 50 customers have been generated and 50 customers have also left the simulation, which is what we wanted.

After printing out the program, the micro-GPSS processor asks if the user wishes to stop. The Y(es) answer exits the operator from the GPSS system. If the user types in the name of a new program this will be executed. A N(o) answer in turn leads to the question of whether or not the user wishes the same program to be repeated. By answering N(o) or directly giving another program name, another program can be run; by answering Y(es), the same program can be re-run. On some systems the operator is given the opportunity of editing the program before re-running it (see the documentation obtainable by GPSSDOC on the diskette with the micro-GPSS system). The answer 'END' to the request for a program name exits the operator from the GPSS system.

If a program is to be re-run the next question determines whether or not the seeds of the random number generators are to be reset. If the answer to this question is Y(es), the seeds are reset and the simulation is repeated with exactly the same random numbers as before (see Chapter 2). This leads to exactly the same InterArrival Times being sampled and thus to exactly the same output as before, i.e. the clock value 892.24.

If, instead, the answer to the question regarding resetting the seeds is N(o), the program is re-run, but rather than using the first 50 random numbers, it now uses the next 50 (i.e. 51–100). Since these next 50 numbers will be based on a different seed, namely the value of the fiftieth random number, the two sequences of random numbers will be different and hence the output of this repeated run will be different, giving a final clock of 894.37.

If the program is run a third time without resetting the random number seed, a third result is obtained, and so on.

This simple example of repeated runs demonstrates one of the most fundamental aspects of stochastic simulation, namely that different results are obtained in different runs. The result of each run can be seen as *one* sample from a large number of possible results. A simulation should *never* be run just *once* since in that case no estimate of the variation of results due to the random numbers could be derived.

The above aspect of simulation will be discussed at length in Chapter 18, together with details of different methods for producing different runs. Suffice it to say here that micro-GPSS also contains a simple way (not available in GPSS V) of running a program a *fixed* number of times with different random number streams: here SIMULATE is given an A operand. Thus SIMULATE 10 would run the program 10 times, probably with a different output each time. In this case, the program is listed at the first run only. For successive runs only the results are listed. Furthermore, with SIMULATE A, the output is printed in a stream without the need to press the return button for each separate item of output. SIMULATE 1 could thus be used if a single run with output produced in a stream were required.

## 3.9 Program 3.2

The simulation in Program 3.1 stopped once 50 customers had gone through the turnstile. The program exemplified how the simulation can be stopped after a certain number of transactions. However, in most situations it is more interesting to run the simulation for a given amount of time, e.g. one day. Program 3.1 can now be amended so that it will stop after 8 hours = 480 minutes.

If closure of the turnstile after 8 hours, or 480 minutes, is desired, a special transaction can be scheduled to close the turnstile and hence stop the simulation after 480 minutes. The stop transaction may be compared to a guard or janitor who arrives after 8 hours and shuts down the turnstile.

At time 480 this stop transaction is thus generated and, directly after entry, it moves into the TERMINATE block and decreases the termination counter by 1. If the termination counter had initially been set to 1, by START 1, the termination counter would then be decreased to 0 and the simulation would stop. In Program 3.2, as compared to Program 3.1, the customers terminate *without* affecting the termination counter. Termination is solely caused by the arrival of *one* stop transaction.

The model must therefore contain two separate segments, one for each type of transaction: i.e. one customer segment and one stop segment (see Figure 3.6 which illustrates the block diagram for Program 3.2). It should be

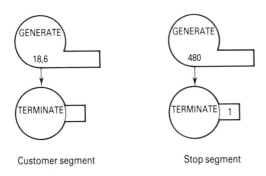

**Customer segment**

**Stop segment**

**Figure 3.6** Block diagram of Program 3.2

noted that the two segments are completely separate; there are *no* connecting lines. The GPSS block diagram is *not* a flow chart.

The following discussion centers upon the choice of time unit. Customers arrive with an InterArrival Time distribution of $18 \pm 6$ minutes and the simulation stops after 8 hours. Each GPSS program can only contain *one* type of time unit. Hence, if one segment uses minutes, the other segments must also use minutes. Using minutes is easier than using parts of hours. (Use of integers also renders the program compatible with GPSS V, which only allows integers.) It is usually convenient to use the time unit that allows for the lowest, but still integer, values.

Next, the same three control statements as are used in Program 3.1 are included to obtain a complete Program 3.2. In this case it is enough to have 1 as the A operand of START, since *one* transaction (the stop transaction) with TERMINATE 1 is sufficient to stop the simulation.

It should also be mentioned here that comments can be added to a program. Such comments will be included in the program listing, but are otherwise disregarded by the GPSS processor. Comments can most easily be inserted on special lines, which commence with an asterisk (*) in the first column of the line. Comments can also be written at the end of the line, where they should follow an exclamation mark (!); otherwise a comment could be mistaken for an operand (e.g. after TERMINATE).

Two comment lines are inserted commencing, as mentioned, with a * in column 1, and two end-of-line comments, after !. Program 3.2 in 'raw form' is shown below.

The output of this program comprises the complete program listing shown in Table 3.3 (the line numbers are omitted here).

It can be seen that all end-of-line comments in micro-GPSS are listed, commencing in the same column. In order that these end-of-line comments can be properly printed they should contain, at most, 38 characters. For large programs of a non-standard type, such end-of-line comments are highly

**Program 3.2** Micro-GPSS input format

```
simulate
generate 18,6! Arrivals 12..24 min. apart
terminate
generate 480! Close down after 8 hours
terminate 1
start 1
end
```

recommended. The reason that most of the programs in the following parts of the book refrain from end-of-line comments is that these simple GPSS programs are often extensions of earlier programs and are largely self-documenting. Also, the accompanying text will usually make the contents clear.

**Table 3.3** Complete listing of Program 3.2

```
Block
no.  *Adr.  Operation  A,B,C,D,E,F,G,H              Comments
              simulate
      * Customer segment
  1            generate   18,6         ! Arrivals 12..24 min. apart
  2            terminate
      * Stop segment
  3            generate   480          ! Close down after 8 hours
  4            terminate  1
              start      1
              end
```

**Table 3.4** Block statistics of Program 3.2

Relative clock     480.00 Absolute clock     480.00

Block counts

| Number | Adr. | Oper. | Current | Total |
|--------|------|-------|---------|-------|
| 1 | | GENER | 0 | 27 |
| 2 | | TERMI | 0 | 27 |
| 3 | | GENER | 0 | 1 |
| 4 | | TERMI | 0 | 1 |

The block statistics are as shown in Table 3.4. A total of 27 customers has been generated; the expected number was 480/18 = 26.67. If the program is re-run twice with other random numbers 25 and 26 customers, respectively, are generated.

# 3.10 Execution of the program and the scheduling of events

Before going on to more complicated programs, in order to increase the reader's understanding of how the GPSS processor works, there follows a brief account of how Program 3.2 is handled in the computer by the GPSS processor. (Below, for the sake of simplicity, this is exemplified using integer values of time, although micro-GPSS would generally use decimal numbers.)

1. The processor begins by reading the control statements, in this case SIMULATE and START. (END instructs the processor to stop reading.) SIMULATE simply instructs the processor that execution is to be carried out. As mentioned above, START 1 sets the termination counter to 1 and commences program execution.

2. The processor next schedules the very first arrival for each segment, i.e. for each GENERATE block. Hence, the computer first samples the first InterArrival Time IAT(1) for block 1: GENERATE 18,6, e.g. IAT(1) = 16. It then schedules, on a *list of future events*, the first customer arrival at time 16. The second segment, the stop segment, starts with GENERATE 480, implying that the (first) stop transaction is scheduled on the list of future events to occur at time 480. After this initial scheduling of events, the list of future events looks as follows:

   ```
   Time 16    Segment 1 (block 1)
   Time 480   Segment 2 (block 3)
   ```

3. Following initial scheduling of events, the real execution of the program begins. The computer searches the list of future events to find the most immediate event, i.e. the event with the lowest time. As seen above, this is the GENERATE of segment 1, which is to occur at time 16. Hence, the simulation clock is moved to time 16 and the GENERATE block is carried out, i.e. a transaction is brought into the simulation system. The GENERATE event is then removed from the list of future events. At the same time a new customer arrival is scheduled. Hence another IAT is sampled from the 18 ± 6 distribution. Assume that a value of 23 is obtained. Since the time of the arrival of the present customer is 16, the arrival of the next customer will occur at time 16 + 23 = 39. A new

arrival at time 39 is thus scheduled and the future events list looks as follows:

```
Time 39    Segment 1 (block 1)
Time 480   Segment 2 (block 3)
```

4.  After scheduling the next customer arrival, the first transaction is brought forward as far as possible, i.e. in this case to TERMINATE, when the transaction is removed from the system.

5.  After the transaction has been halted, the GPSS processor returns to the list of future events to search again for the most imminent event. Thus the GPSS processor continues to pick up one customer arrival after the other from the future events list, in a kind of automatic loop, while at the same time scheduling the arrival of the next customer on the same list.

6.  At some future point in time the future events list might look as follows:

```
Time 480   Segment 2 (block 3)
Time 493   Segment 1 (block 1)
```

At this point the most imminent event is the closing down of the turnstile. Thus at time 480 the stop transaction is brought into the simulation. When we remove it from the future events list, the processor will in fact schedule a second arrival of a stop event, namely at time $480 + 480 = 960$, i.e. at the present time 480 + the IAT of 480. This event will, however, never happen. Immediately after this scheduling has taken place the stop event will move directly into the TERMINATE 1 block and will thereby decrease the termination counter from 1 to 0, thus stopping the simulation.

This brief description of the internal mechanism of the micro-GPSS processor explains how the processor can keep track of which segment will be 'active' at various times during execution. It also explains why the order in the program between segments does not usually matter. We could just as well have put the stop segment prior to the customer segment; it would not have affected the future events list. The above discussion should also make it clear why the GPSS block diagram is quite different from an ordinary flow chart.

## 3.11 The ADVANCE block

In Program 3.2 presented above, the customers left the system – the turnstile – immediately after they had arrived, i.e. the transactions were terminated at the same time as they were generated. This led to all current block counts being 0 at time of simulation close-down.

As a further step towards more realistic simulation, the next program, Program 3.3, allows the transactions to remain in the system for some time, possibly for random periods. This is done using the ADVANCE block. The symbol for this block is a rectangle with the operation with the A and B operands below written inside, as shown in Figure 3.7. This chapter deals with the case when both the A and the B operands are constants, which implies sampling from a rectangular distribution. The time sampled from this distribution is the time spent in the ADVANCE block before the first attempt is made to move out of this block. (As will be seen in Chapter 4, it is in certain cases possible that a transaction will be unable to move out of one block into the next.)

**Figure 3.7** Block symbol of ADVANCE

Just as in the GENERATE block, the A operand denotes the average and the B operand denotes the half-width of the range of the distribution to be sampled. ADVANCE A,B thus samples times between $A - B$ and $A + B$, with all times in between being equally likely. The time sampled is thus the time that the transaction must spend in the ADVANCE block before it attempts to move into the next block. Hence, ADVANCE 25,5 implies that the time spent in the ADVANCE block, before any attempt to move out of the block is made, will be between 20 and 30, with all times between being equally likely.

As mentioned above, the time sampled in the ADVANCE block is the time that the transaction is scheduled to spend in the block before attempting to enter the next block. Hence the transaction is brought to a halt when it reaches the ADVANCE block. From a GPSS processor point of view the following happens: when the transaction is brought into the ADVANCE block, it schedules the time of the first attempted exit from the ADVANCE block on the list of future events. This scheduling process is discussed in Section 5.2.

Again as in the GENERATE block, the default values of the operands A and B are 0. Hence, ADVANCE 10 is the same as ADVANCE 10,0, implying that exactly 10 minutes are scheduled to be spent in the ADVANCE block before the first attempt to exit. (ADVANCE without any operands is the same as ADVANCE 0,0, implying that the transaction can, after being scheduled on the list of future events, but before the simulation clock changes, attempt to move into the next block. ADVANCE without any operands is thus a kind of 'dummy block' which has no real effect.)

Having introduced the ADVANCE block, the earlier model of Program

3.2 can be extended. Instead of assuming that people just walk in and then walk straight out of the door again – the turnstile case – they can now be allowed to stay in the system a while. It should be stressed that as yet there is no limitation on how many transactions can be in the ADVANCE block at any one time. 'Being in the ADVANCE block' only means that the exit from the ADVANCE block has been scheduled as a future event on the list of future events. There is obviously nothing to prevent that several transactions at the same time have their exit times from this ADVANCE block scheduled on the list of future events simultaneously. Furthermore, since there are no capacity limits, there are no waiting lines either. The system to be presented is similar to a large museum: visitors arrive in a random fashion and stay a random time. There is no real limit to the number of visitors at the same time.

For Program 3.3 assume the same arrival behavior as that in Program 3.2, but now assume that the visitors stay between 20 and 30 minutes in the system. The block diagram illustrated in Figure 3.8 is obtained.

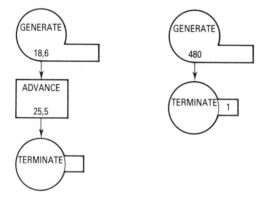

**Figure 3.8** Block diagram of Program 3.3

Next, turn to the program listing with the block numbers inserted by the GPSS processor:

**Program 3.3**

```
          simulate
1         generate    18,6
2         advance     25,5
3         terminate
4         generate    480
5         terminate   1
          start       1
          end
```

The computer produces the block counts shown in Table 3.5. It can be seen from this block count that 27 visitors have been generated, just as in Program 3.2. The current count of block 2, the ADVANCE block, shows that one visitor remains in the ADVANCE block at time 480. The reason for this is that at time 480 there is one 'exit from the ADVANCE block' event scheduled on the future events list to take place *after* time 480. This transaction might, for example, be scheduled to attempt exit from the ADVANCE block at time 487. Since the simulation is closed down at time 480, this transaction has, at time 480, not yet moved out of the ADVANCE block. It can be thought of as a visitor who is forced out of the museum at closing time before having spent the time he originally planned to spend.

**Table 3.5** Block statistics of Program 3.3

```
Relative clock      480.00 Absolute clock      480.00

Block counts
Number Adr.  Oper. Current  Total
   1           GENER    0      27
   2           ADVAN    1      27
   3           TERMI    0      26
   4           GENER    0       1
   5           TERMI    0       1
```

Before presenting the first exercises below, mention should be made of how to obtain the output in the form of a file rather than solely on the screen. If % is typed in the very first column on a separate *first* line, prior to SIMULATE, all output otherwise written on the screen (except for error messages and similar output) is written without any pause into a file with the same name as the program but with the extension .RES. A period (.) in the original program name is, however, not included. Thus prog3.1, if % were typed on the first line, would produce the result file PROG31.RES. This file can next be copied, edited and printed in a conventional manner.

For the coding of these exercises any editor or word processor that can produce an ASCII file can be used. A more convenient alternative might be to use the special interactive GPSSMENU code generator described in Appendix B.

---

## Exercise 3.1

Change Program 3.3 so that visitors stay between one and two hours in the museum, with all times in between being equally likely. Compare the current counts of the two programs (i.e. old Program 3.3 and your revised program), running each program three times.

## Exercise 3.2

Visitors arrive at a museum on average every 10 minutes, with InterArrival Times varying between 5 and 15 minutes. They stay there on average for half an hour, but some stay for only a quarter, while some might stay for up to three-quarters of an hour. Write a GPSS program and simulate a five-hour day in order to take account of those who at closing time had planned to stay longer. Run the program three times with different random numbers.

## Exercise 3.3

We study a turnstile where people arrive on average every 12 minutes but where InterArrival Times vary between 6 and 18 minutes. We wish to close down the turnstile after eight hours or 40 customers, whichever comes first. Run the program four times.

# 4 Simple servers: facilities

## 4.1 Different types of server

The three programs presented thus far are of strictly pedagogical interest. The print-outs do not yield any really interesting results. In this chapter I shall present the first 'interesting' program which produces non-trivial results. This is brought about by bringing a server into the model.

GPSS deals, as mentioned, with transactions and servers. Transactions are temporary entities, while servers are permanent in the sense that they are in the system throughout the whole simulation. The transactions are, as seen in the preceding chapter, generated and removed during the simulation. Table 4.1 gives some examples of transactions and servers in some different types of system.

In GPSS there are two types of server, facilities and storages. A facility can serve only *one* transaction at a time, while a storage can serve several transactions at a time. This chapter covers only facilities, which are the simplest kind of servers to understand and use. Storages will be studied in Chapter 7.

**Table 4.1** Systems with transactions and servers

| System | Transactions | Servers |
|---|---|---|
| Telephone system | Telephone calls | Switchboard |
| Secretarial pool | Tasks | Secretaries |
| Store | Customers | Salespeople |
| Bank | Customers | Cash |
| Transport company | Shipments | Trucks |
| Computer system | Programs | Disks, tapes |
| Inventory system | Goods | Inventory space |
| Engineering shop | Products | Machines |
| Harbor | Ships | Berths, cranes, tugs |
| Hospital clinic | Patients | Doctors, nurses |
| Traffic system | Cars | Roads, traffic lights |
| Water system | Water use, rain | Reservoir |

## 4.2 The SEIZE block

In order for a transaction to utilize a facility, it must come to a SEIZE block. The operation is SEIZE and it has an A operand. The block diagram symbol is a rectangle with the word SEIZE written inside and the A operand in a triangle to the right of the rectangle, as shown in Figure 4.1. The A operand is compulsory (no default allowed) and is the name of the facility to be used.

**Figure 4.1** Block symbol of SEIZE

In this context I will now present the GPSS rules for writing a symbolic name. The same rules used here for facilities apply, as discussed later, to other symbolic names, e.g. of queues, storages, addresses, etc.

In micro-GPSS a name must start with three letters to be followed by zero, one or two alphanumeric characters (i.e. letters A . . Z or digits). Hence a GPSS name consists of 3–5 alphanumeric characters of which the first three must be letters. Hence JOE, XPD1, SER12 and SALLY are valid names. Invalid names are AB (only two letters), AB3CD (not three letters in the beginning), JOE+1 (non-alphanumeric character included), INGOLF (six letters) and STÅHL (Å is not part of the English alphabet).

> The same rules apply to GPSS V, but GPSS/H allows names with up to eight characters. In GPSS V a constant, e.g. 1 or 2 can also be used as an A operand. This use of numbers instead of symbolic names is, however, strongly discouraged. Serious logical errors can occur, if symbolic names and numbers for, e.g., facilities are mixed in the same program. (See Chapter 16.) Furthermore, names have the advantage over numbers of making a program easier to use and understand. Hence micro-GPSS allows *only names*.

I shall now discuss the use of the SEIZE block. SEIZE A, e.g. SEIZE SAL, has the following meaning:

1. If A, e.g. the facility SAL, is *idle* when the transaction tries to move into the SEIZE block, the transaction is allowed to enter the SEIZE block and then go straight through it to try to enter the next block. At the time the transaction enters the SEIZE block the facility becomes busy. All this has its counterpart in reality. For example, if a single salesperson in a store is idle, a customer seeking service will (hopefully) get prompt attention. The salesperson then becomes busy and cannot give service to any other customer.

2. If the facility is *busy*, when a transaction tries to enter the SEIZE block, entry into the SEIZE block is refused. The transaction has to wait. In this way a *waiting line* is formed. This waiting line is represented in two different ways:

    (a) From the GPSS program and *block count* point of view the transaction is regarded as waiting in front of the SEIZE block, i.e. inside the block immediately prior to the SEIZE block.

    (b) From the micro-GPSS *processor* point of view, the transaction will wait on a special waiting list, completely internal to the processor. On this waiting list, a first-in, first-out (FIFO) discipline holds, i.e. the one who enters this waiting list first, will also be the first one to be allowed to leave the list and use the facility once it becomes *idle* again.

In a store with one salesperson, this implies that, when customers arrive and find the salesperson busy, they have to wait in a line until the salesperson becomes idle again and then they are served on a first-come, first-served basis.

## 4.3 The RELEASE block

We now need to explain how a salesperson becomes idle again. This is done by the RELEASE block. This block is the mirror image of the SEIZE block, as is depicted by the block symbol which has the triangle with the A operand inverted.

**Figure 4.2** Block symbol of RELEASE

The A operand of RELEASE is similar to that of the SEIZE block. In order to have this facility released, we must use the same name as the one used in the SEIZE block's A operand. It must also be stressed that, if there is a SEIZE block in a segment, then there should normally be a corresponding RELEASE block in the same segment. If the RELEASE block is missing, the facility will be busy for the rest of the simulation. Furthermore, a transaction should not enter a RELEASE A block, if it has not previously entered the corresponding SEIZE A block. If there is no preceding SEIZE block, a run time error occurs and the simulation is stopped. Thus, SEIZE and RELEASE blocks really come in pairs.

A transaction trying to enter a RELEASE block will always succeed. A RELEASE block cannot refuse entry. The transaction will then immediately attempt to enter the next block; there is no delay in attempting to leave the RELEASE block.

When a transaction enters a RELEASE A block, the facility A becomes idle again. Once the facility becomes idle, the GPSS processor looks through the internal waiting list mentioned earlier to see if there are transactions waiting. If that is the case, it will allow the transaction that has waited the longest time to be removed from this waiting list, leave the block prior to the SEIZE block and enter the SEIZE block.

## 4.4 Program 4.1

It is now possible to write our first non-trivial program, dealing with a system with one server and one waiting line, with both random arrival of customers and random service time.

Let us consider, for instance, a barber shop with one barber or a small shop with one salesperson. Assume, as before, that customers arrive on average every 18 minutes with InterArrival Times varying between 12 and 24 minutes, and with all InterArrival Times equally likely, just as in Program 3.3. Let us also assume the same service time of $25 \pm 5$ minutes. The major difference from Program 3.3 is that only one customer at a time can be served. To model this, we take Program 3.3 and introduce block SEIZE SAL before the ADVANCE block and block RELEASE SAL after the ADVANCE block. The block diagram shown in Figure 4.3 is then obtained.

The introduction of the SEIZE block has the effect that only one transaction at a time can be in the ADVANCE block. The time spent in this block will be the time that the transaction will spend with the facility SAL. Once a transaction is allowed to enter the SEIZE block it will go straight through this block and enter the ADVANCE block. Here it will be held in accordance with the time sampled from the rectangular distribution $25 \pm 5$. Once a transaction is allowed to leave the ADVANCE block it will go straight through the RELEASE block, since there is no reason for it to stop there.

> This is the way the program is written in micro-GPSS; in GPSS V it would have to contain one more block, a dummy ADVANCE block after GENERATE. (See Schriber 1974, p. 357.)

The program itself is presented as a computer listing, i.e. with the block numbers added by the computer.

Let us now consider the output, which begins with the block statistics, just as in any program (see Table 4.2). (The clock times are not repeated here, since they are the same as in Program 3.3.)

The current block counts are of particular interest. At the end of the

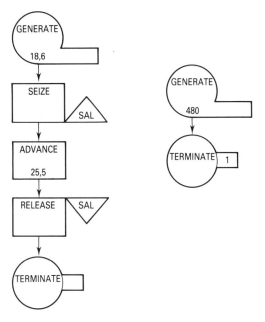

**Figure 4.3** Block diagram of Program 4.1

**Program 4.1**

```
            simulate
1           generate    18,6
2           seize       sal
3           advance     25,5
4           release     sal
5           terminate
6           generate    480
7           terminate   1
            start       1
            end
```

simulation there are eight people waiting in block 1, i.e. the block prior to the SEIZE block. From the total block counts it can be seen that a total of 27 customers have been generated (block 1) but only 19 have come into block 2, i.e. have received any service from SAL. Hence there is a waiting line of eight at the end of the simulation.

Note that this program produces a waiting line or queue, without having any specific block referring to queue statistics, as will be discussed in Chapter 6. A waiting line is therefore caused by the mere existence of a

**Table 4.2** Block statistics of Program 4.1

```
Block counts
Number Adr.  Oper. Current  Total
    1        GENER    8       27
    2        SEIZE    0       19
    3        ADVAN    1       19
    4        RELEA    0       18
    5        TERMI    0       18
    6        GENER    0        1
    7        TERMI    0        1
```

SEIZE block representing a facility. As mentioned above, when a transaction cannot obtain service from a facility, it waits in the block prior to the SEIZE block. The transaction is also put on a special internal waiting list, which allows for the handling of the waiting line on a first-come, first-served basis.

## 4.5 Facility statistics

Besides the block statistics, we also obtain after pressing the return key special facility statistics. These statistics are hence generated automatically in micro-GPSS once a SEIZE block is used. (The author, not the computer, has added a number above each item in Table 4.3 in order to make references easier.)

The three items can be explained as follows:

1. AVERAGE UTILIZATION is the fraction of total simulation time that the facility was busy. In this case, the facility was busy 467.5 minutes in total (not seen from the statistics directly, but calculated). Since total simulation time was 480 minutes, the average utilization fraction is $467.5/480 = 0.97$.

2. NUMBER OF ENTRIES is the total number of customers, which have started to obtain service from the facility SAL. This piece of information can also be obtained from the block statistics (total count for SEIZE block, block 2).

**Table 4.3** Facility statistics of Program 4.1

| Facility | (1)<br>Average<br>utilization | (2)<br>Number<br>entries | (3)<br>Average<br>time/trans |
|----------|-------------------------------|--------------------------|------------------------------|
| SAL      | 0.97                          | 19                       | 24.61                        |

3. AVERAGE TIME/TRANS is the average time per transaction. The total time that the facility has been busy is divided by the number of entries, giving $467.5/19 = 24.61$. There is a slight bias in the sense that we divide the time that the facility has been busy by the number of customers who have *started* to get service. At the time of close-down there is still one customer in the process of getting service. If instead this customer had just completed being served, this average service time would probably have been slightly higher. In any case, this average time should be fairly close to the average time in the ADVANCE block, i.e. the A operand 25.

In the output, we only receive information on the *final* length of the waiting line (in the current block counts). There is no information on how the waiting line behaved *during* the simulation. However, the final length of the waiting line does give us a general idea about whether the simulated system works or not. It is, however, necessary to run the simulation at least a couple of times with different random numbers before drawing any conclusions. For this program, the first re-run gives us a final waiting line of seven and the second re-run a final waiting line of eight. We might thus conclude that since the final waiting line is fairly long, it is probably advisable to increase the service capacity, e.g. hire another salesperson, at least part-time.

Since the average IAT, 18, is shorter than the average service time, 25, in Program 4.1, it is obvious that the waiting line will grow as simulation time increases. However, it is not necessarily the case that for a simulation of finite time, e.g. eight hours, the final or maximum waiting line will be unacceptably long, even if the average IAT is shorter than the average service time. This issue is dealt with further in Exercise 4.1. Furthermore, there might very well be a waiting line, even if the reverse is true; see Exercise 4.2.

## Exercise 4.1

Change the InterArrival Time of Program 4.1 so that customers arrive between 12 and 32 minutes apart, but keep the same service time. Run the program three times to find out whether the final waiting line is longer than four which is regarded as acceptable.

## Exercise 4.2

Change the InterArrival Time of Program 4.1 so that customers arrive between 22 and 34 minutes apart, but keep the same service time. Run the program three times to find out whether there will be any final waiting line.

## *Exercise 4.3*

Customers arrive at a store on average every 16 minutes, with 10 minutes as the shortest time and 22 minutes as the longest time between two arrivals (with all times between 10 and 22 being equally likely). The store is run by a single shopkeeper. It takes him between 10 and 20 minutes to serve a customer (all times between 10 and 20 being equally likely). Through an advertising campaign it should be possible to double the number of customers, i.e. to get one on average every 8 minutes, with 4 minutes being the shortest time between two arrivals and 12 the longest. The question is whether the shopkeeper would be able to handle all the new customers without the waiting line becoming too long. It is sufficient to estimate for the two situations the waiting line at the end of an eight-hour day. Write programs in GPSS to simulate the two situations.

# 5 The simulation process in the one-line, one-server case

## 5.1 Introduction

In this chapter the simple one-line one-server problem, which was presented in Program 4.1, will be studied more closely. In order to achieve a better understanding of the micro-GPSS system, I shall first give a brief description of how the micro-GPSS processor executes this program.

Then in Section 5.3 I will demonstrate how the problem dealt with in Program 4.1 would be written in a general-purpose high-level programming language like, for example, BASIC. This procedure has two objectives. Firstly, it might further illustrate certain aspects of the event scheduling process and hence complement the description of how the micro-GPSS processor works. Secondly, and most importantly, it will illustrate how much more difficult it is to do this type of discrete-event stochastic simulation in a General Programming Language. This will highlight some of the many things that the GPSS processor does automatically, but which the programmer has to specify in a General Programming Language. If your interest is in the practical use of GPSS and you already know the advantages of GPSS, you can omit Section 5.3 if you wish.

## 5.2 Scheduling of events

When describing how the micro-GPSS processor deals with Program 4.1, I shall build upon my earlier discussion of how the micro-GPSS processor worked on Program 3.2.

As mentioned, execution starts by the processor scheduling a transaction arrival on the list of future events for each of the segments, i.e. each of the GENERATE blocks. It then starts the actual execution by looking for the most imminent event on the future events list; in this case, the arrival of the first customer. When this customer is brought into the system, it will cause the scheduling of the arrival of the next customer. When a customer is taken away from the future events list and brought into the simulation, another customer arrival is always scheduled. Therefore there is always one transaction arrival from each GENERATE block on the future events list.

One difference in Program 4.1, as compared to Program 3.2, is that the future events list will also contain service completion events. In fact, the processor schedules each future (planned attempt to) exit from the ADVANCE block.

Let us illustrate this with the first customer. When he is brought into the system, he will be brought forward in his segment as far as possible. When he is allowed into the SEIZE block he will go straight through it and enter into the ADVANCE block. Here the transaction is brought to a halt.

The processor then schedules a service completion event: it samples the time to be spent in the ADVANCE block from the rectangular distribution specified in this block. The time of exit from the ADVANCE block is then obtained by adding this sampled time to the present clock value.

On the list of future events there will thus be both customer arrival and service completion events. These events scheduled on the list of future events are called *primary* events. All other events are called *secondary*. When the processor activates a primary event, e.g. brings a customer into the simulation or carries out a service completion, it might also cause secondary events, like putting another customer into service.

It should be stressed that putting a customer into service is *not* a primary event; it is not scheduled on the list of future events. It can either be initiated by the arrival of a customer, when the salesperson is idle, or by a service completion. In the latter case a waiting customer is brought into service from the waiting line.

I shall now summarize somewhat more formally how the micro-GPSS processor would handle a program like Program 4.1. It should be stressed, however, that this explanation of how a processor works is a simplification. It refers only to how the micro-GPSS processor works. (A much more detailed and precise description of the GPSS/360 processor is given in Schriber, 1974 and of the GPSS/H processor in Schriber, 1990.)

1. The processor schedules the first transaction for each segment, i.e. for each GENERATE block.

2. The processor searches the future events list for the most imminent event and brings this event into the system.

3. If this event is a transaction arrival, the processor schedules the next transaction arrival on the list of future events.

4. This transaction, just brought into the system, is moved through as many blocks as possible until it is stopped.

5. The transaction can be stopped (a) in front of a SEIZE block, because the facility is busy, (b) in the ADVANCE block or (c) in the TERMINATE block.

    (a) If it is stopped in front of the SEIZE block, because the facility is busy, it is put on a waiting list, until the facility becomes idle again. It can be regarded as waiting in the block prior to the SEIZE block.

    (b) If it is stopped in the ADVANCE block, an ADVANCE block exit (= service completion) is scheduled on the future events list.

    (c) If it is stopped in the TERMINATE block, it is brought out of the system.

6. When a primary event is activated, as well as moving the particular transaction through as many blocks as possible, the processor also activates one (or several) transactions on a waiting list. For example, if the primary event brings the transaction into a RELEASE block, the processor will check whether there is any transaction waiting (on the waiting list) that can now be moved, e.g. be brought into the SEIZE block.

7. The processor brings the transaction of this secondary event as far as possible through the blocks of its segment until it too is stopped, possibly causing the scheduling of new primary events, e.g. service completions, on its way.

8. When the transaction of this secondary event is brought to a halt, the processor goes back to point 2 above to search for the primary event which has now become the most imminent one on the list of future events.

## ■ 5.3 The program in a General Programming Language

Let us now write a program that simulates the same system as Program 4.1, the barber shop example, in a General Programming Language. Since all output commands have to be written explicitly, we shall, in order to make this program as short and simple as possible, only ask for the length of the waiting line at the end of the simulation. This might, as noted earlier, in some cases indicate whether or not satisfactory service is provided by the facility. (The following relies heavily on pp. 15–18 in Schriber, 1974.)

    This program must specifically handle the simulation clock. Updating the clock would take place in a main loop as described in Figure 5.1.

    This figure contains an infinite loop. A customer arrival event will, when brought into the system, schedule another customer arrival event. Hence there will always be new events and the simulation could go on forever. Therefore, we must have a stop event that shuts down the simulation and provides the desired output – in this case the final length of the waiting line.

    Furthermore, when a transaction obtains service, a service completion event will also be scheduled. Thus on the future events list there can in this case be three different primary events: a customer arrival event; a service completion

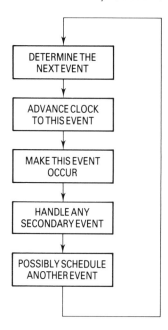

**Figure 5.1** Main loop

event; and a simulation stop event.

It should be noted, however, that while there is always a customer arrival event and a simulation stop event, there will be a service completion event only if the server is busy. The search for the most imminent event would therefore be different when a service completion event is scheduled (three time values are compared) as compared to the case of no service completion event being scheduled (only two time values are compared).

In order to have a simple algorithm, it seems best to *always* have a service completion time. Therefore, for the case when no service completion is scheduled the time of the service completion (TOSC) is set to STOPT + 1 (stop time + 1), i.e. to a time that comes *after* the simulation stop. When choosing the earliest of the three event times in the case of *no* service completion event being scheduled, we will thus in reality only choose between the time of (customer) arrival (TOA) and STOPT, since STOPT will then come earlier than TOSC = STOPT + 1.

The main loop of the program thus consists of determining the next event time, advancing the clock to this time, and choosing the earliest of three events: customer arrival, service completion and simulation stop. This loop is preceded by an initial segment for reading data and initializing variables as well as a final segment for printing output, as shown in the general flow chart of Figure 5.2.

In order to be able to transform this into computer code we need the more specific flow chart of Figure 5.3.

Five parameter values are input:

1.   IATA = The InterArrival Time A-parameter = average InterArrival Time =

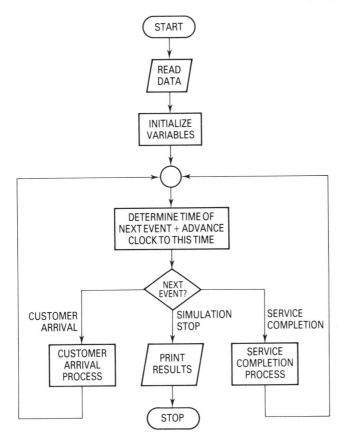

**Figure 5.2** General flow chart of barber shop problem

same as the A operand in the first GENERATE block in Program 4.1.

2. IATB = The InterArrival Time B-parameter = the half-width of the rectangular distribution of InterArrival Times = the difference between the average InterArrival Time and the lower limit of the InterArrival Time = the same as the B operand of the first GENERATE block in Program 4.1.

3. STA = Service Time A-parameter = average value of service time = the A operand in the ADVANCE block in Program 4.1.

4. STB = Service Time B-parameter = half-width of rectangular distribution of service time = difference between average service time and lower limit of service time = B operand of ADVANCE block in Program 4.1.

5. STOPT = time of stopping the simulation = the A operand of the STOP segment's GENERATE block in Program 4.1, e.g. 480.

Prior to the actual execution of the program three values are set to 0 initially:

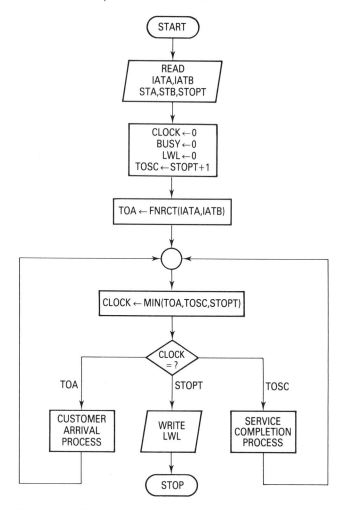

**Figure 5.3** Specific flow chart of barber shop problem

1.  CLOCK = time of the simulation clock.

2.  BUSY = an indicator of whether the facility is busy or not. BUSY = 0, if the facility is idle and = 1, if the facility is busy. This can also be seen as the number of customers being served at present by the facility.

3.  LWL = the length of the waiting line.

Furthermore, TOSC, the time of service completion is set to STOPT + 1 in line with the reasoning above.
The final task of the initial part of the program is to determine the first

TOA, i.e. the first time of arrival. This is a value sampled from the rectangular distribution function FNRCT, using the parameters IATA and IATB.

In order to determine this FNRCT function value, the program must contain a definition of the function FNRCT with the parameters A and B, such that $FNRCT(A,B) = A - B + 2 \star B \star RND$, where RND in turn is a random number fraction $u$, such that $0 \leq u < 1$ (see Section 3.3). In BASIC, RND needs no further definition. When using another programming language, a special subroutine program for RND may have to be written.

Inside the loop the simulation CLOCK is set to the time of the most imminent event, i.e. to the lowest value of TOA, TOSC and STOPT. MIN is a function which calculates the lowest of three values. MIN might have to be defined in a specially written subroutine. Next there is a test of whether CLOCK = TOA, = TOSC or = STOPT.

If CLOCK = TOA, the customer arrival process is carried out (see below). After this the processor goes back to update CLOCK again.

If CLOCK = TOSC, the service completion process is carried out. After this the processor goes back to update CLOCK again.

Finally, if CLOCK = STOPT, the program prints the desired output, i.e. the length of the waiting line, LWL, and stops the simulation.

In the customer arrival process, the program first of all determines the time of arrival of the next customer, by adding to the present clock time an InterArrival Time sampled from the rectangular distribution FNRCT with IATA and IATB as parameters. Next there is a test of whether the server is busy or not.

If the server is *busy*, the length of the waiting line is increased by one.

If the server is *not busy*, the program brings the newly arrived customer into service and makes the server busy. It also determines the time of service completion for this customer by sampling the service time, from the rectangular distribution with STA and STB as parameters, and adding it to the clock.

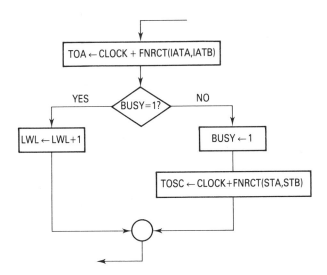

**Figure 5.4** Customer arrival process

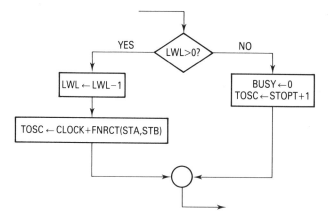

**Figure 5.5** Service completion process

In the service completion process the program first asks if there is anybody waiting, i.e. whether or not the length of the waiting line > 0.

If this is true, i.e. there is *someone waiting*, one waiting customer is put into service. This implies that the length of the waiting line is decreased by one. Furthermore, the next service completion time is determined by adding to the present clock a value sampled from the rectangular distribution with the service time parameters STA and STB.

If, on the other hand, there is *no one waiting*, the server is made idle (BUSY is set to 0) and a dummy service completion event is scheduled at time STOPT + 1.

On the basis of this, we can write a computer program. One possible solution, written in a simple form of BASIC (Microsoft BASIC for the PC), including comments, is given in Table 5.1. From this program we can see that the program in a General Programming Language is considerably more complicated than the corresponding program in GPSS, Program 4.1. Programs in FORTRAN, PL/I, PASCAL etc. would be roughly equal in complexity to the BASIC program.

**Table 5.1** BASIC program

```
10   REM DEFINITION OF RECTANGULAR FUNCTION
20   DEF FNRCT(M,R)=M-R+2*R*RND
30   REM INPUT OF DATA
40   INPUT "GIVE AVERAGE INTERARRIVAL TIME     ",IATA
50   INPUT "GIVE HALF-WIDTH OF INTERARRIVAL TIME    ",IATB
60   INPUT "GIVE AVERAGE SERVICE TIME    ",STA
70   INPUT "GIVE HALF-WIDTH OF SERVICE TIME    ",STB
80   INPUT "GIVE TOTAL SIMULATION TIME    ",STOPT
90   REM INITIALIZATION OF VARIABLES
100  CLOCK=0
```

```
110   BUSY=0
120   LWL=0
130   TOSC=STOPT+1
140   TOA=FNRCT(IATA,IATB)
150 REM LOOP STARTS HERE
160   IF TOA<TOSC THEN MIN=TOA ELSE MIN=TOSC
170   IF STOPT<MIN THEN MIN=STOPT
180 REM CLOCK=MIN(TOA,TOSC,STOPT)
190   CLOCK=MIN
200 REM DETERMINE NEXT EVENT
210   IF CLOCK=TOSC THEN 330
220   IF CLOCK=STOPT THEN 430
230 REM CUSTOMER ARRIVAL
240   TOA=CLOCK+FNRCT(IATA,IATB)
250   IF BUSY=1 THEN 300
260   REM SERVER IDLE
270     BUSY=1
280     TOSC=CLOCK+FNRCT(STA,STB)
290     GOTO 150
300   REM SERVER BUSY
310     LWL=LWL+1
320     GOTO 150
330 REM SERVICE COMPLETION
340   IF LWL>0 THEN 390
350   REM NO ONE WAITING
360     BUSY=0
370     TOSC=STOPT+1
380     GOTO 150
390   REM SOMEONE WAITING
400     LWL=LWL-1
410     TOSC=CLOCK+FNRCT(STA,STB)
420     GOTO 150
430 REM STOPSEGMENT
440   PRINT "FINAL WAITING LINE = ";LWL
450   END
```

# 6 Gathering time statistics

## 6.1 Gathering of queue statistics by use of Q as B operand

In Program 4.1 there were queues or waiting lines in the system. Customers were waiting in a queue: from the block count point of view in the block prior to the SEIZE block and from the processor point of view on a special waiting list. The block statistics also contained data on the length of this queue at the end of the simulation, but there were no statistics on the average length of the waiting line or average waiting time.

In micro-GPSS, but *not* GPSS V, such statistics can be obtained in a very simple fashion, namely by just adding a Q as a B operand to the SEIZE block. It should be stressed that the queue is *not* created by this Q as B operand. This Q only causes statistics to be gathered and printed.

This can be illustrated with Program 6.1. (The block numbers of the extended listing are left out, since no block statistics will be referred to here.) In this context it should be mentioned that in block diagrams the SEIZE block with Q as B operand can have the Q written in the lower right-hand corner of the rectangle as shown in Figure 6.1. Except for this one difference in the SEIZE symbol, the block diagram of Program 6.1 is exactly the same as that of Program 4.1 in Figure 4.3.

Running Program 6.1, we obtain block statistics and facility statistics which are exactly the same as for Program 4.1. In addition the queue statistics shown in Table 6.1 are obtained. (The author, not the computer, has added a number above each item in order to make references easier.)

In the output, the first item, SAL, is the symbolic name of the queue, which in this case is equivalent to the name of the facility in front of which the customers wait. (The words AD set will be explained in Section 6.2.)

The eight items of data require further explanation:

1. MAXIMUM CONTENTS, 8, is the highest number of transactions in the queue obtained at any time during the simulation.

**Program 6.1**

```
simulate
generate    18,6
seize       sal,q
advance     25,5
release     sal
terminate
generate    480
terminate   1
start       1
end
```

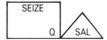

**Figure 6.1** Block symbol of SEIZE with Q

2. AVERAGE CONTENTS are calculated as follows: the computer keeps track of how much time each transaction spent in the queue. These times are added together, giving in this case a total of 1816 minutes. (This figure cannot be read directly in the output, but can be calculated.) This time spent in the queue is divided by the total simulation time of 480 minutes, resulting in an average contents figure of 3.78.

3. TOTAL ENTRIES, 27, is the same figure as given in the total block count of block 2 (see Table 4.2).

**Table 6.1** Queue statistics of Program 6.1

| Queue (AD set) | (1) Maximum contents | (2) Average contents | (3) Total entries | (4) Zero entries | (5) Percent zeros |
|---|---|---|---|---|---|
| SAL | 8 | 3.78 | 27 | 1 | 3.70 |

| Queue (AD set) | (6) Average time/trans | (7) $Average time/trans | (8) Current contents |
|---|---|---|---|
| SAL | 67.25 | 69.83 | 8 |

$Average time/trans=average time/trans excluding zero entries

4. ZERO ENTRIES, 1, refers to the number of transactions that spent 0 time in the queue, because the facility was idle. Obviously only the very first customer did not have to wait.

5. PERCENT ZEROS is the ratio (4):(3) expressed as a percentage, i.e. 1 in 27.

6. AVERAGE TIME/TRANS, i.e. average time per transaction, is the total time spent by all transactions in the queue, which, as mentioned, was 1816 minutes, divided by total entries into the queue, 27, giving us 67.25 minutes.

7. $AVERAGE TIME/TRANS is the average time per transaction excluding the zero entries. The total queuing time of 1816 minutes is divided by 26 (= 27 − 1), the number of non-zero entries, leading to 69.83 minutes. This is the average waiting time of those who really had to wait, because the facility was busy.

8. CURRENT CONTENTS is the final number of transactions in the queue. This number can also be obtained from the current count of block 1 in the block statistics of Table 4.2.

It should be noted that the values (6) and (7) might be downward biased. Total waiting time is divided by the total number of entries into the queue. Only 19 customers have left the waiting line, while eight are still waiting. If we had wanted to know how long customers would really have to wait on average before being served, we would have to close down the simulation in a slightly different manner, so that everybody who ever started waiting was served before closing time. This will be done in Chapter 10.

Program 6.1 would be different in GPSS V where two extra blocks would be required (see Section 6.2).

## 6.2 The ARRIVE and DEPART blocks

Program 6.1 gathered statistics on the actual waiting line formed in front of a facility. Our next example is similar, but instead of statistics on how long customers waited in the line to obtain service, we require statistics on the total time they spent in the store. We can now no longer just add Q to the SEIZE SAL block, but must instead use two new micro-GPSS blocks, ARRIVE and DEPART.

Just as the SEIZE and RELEASE blocks come in pairs, being mirror images of each other, the ARRIVE and DEPART blocks also come in pairs and are likewise mirror images of each other, as can be seen by the block symbols in Figure 6.2. The basic symbol is a rectangle with a circle on the

**Figure 6.2** Block symbols of ARRIVE and DEPART

right-hand side. The circle has a small 'slash' to its right: at the top of the circle for the ARRIVE block and at the bottom of the circle for the DEPART block.

In micro-GPSS these blocks have only A operands. These operands have no default values and must contain a name. The DEPART block should have the same A operand as the ARRIVE block. This name should preferably differ from the name used in the SEIZE block. The rules regarding the names of the A operands of ARRIVE–DEPART blocks, or what we can call names of *AD sets*, are the same as for facility names.

Neither the ARRIVE block nor the DEPART block can refuse a transaction entry. The transaction will go straight through the block and try to enter the next block. However, if this next block, e.g. a SEIZE block, refuses entry, the transaction will have to wait in this block.

The ARRIVE and DEPART blocks keep track of the number of transactions and the time spent by each transaction between *entering* the ARRIVE block and *entering* the DEPART block. This is achieved as follows: when a transaction enters an ARRIVE block, e.g. ARRIVE TIM, the time of its arrival is noted by the processor. The transaction becomes a member of the AD set TIM. When the same transaction enters the DEPART block, it will give up its membership of the AD set TIM and the time is recorded again. The processor computes the total time spent by the transaction in the AD set TIM. It also keeps track of the number of transactions that at any time are members of the AD set TIM.

To measure the time spent in the store, it is necessary for the customers to enter an ARRIVE block just after being generated and to enter a DEPART block just before being terminated. The block diagram of Figure 6.3 is then obtained. (Since the stop segment is identical to that of Program 4.1, the block diagram of this segment is left out.)

When the program is run, part of the output obtained is the block statistics shown in Table 6.2.

In addition the statistics of Table 6.3 are obtained, referring to time spent between the ADVANCE and DEPART blocks, i.e. in what we call the AD set. These statistics are of the same type as the queue statistics in Table 6.1, since the queue and AD set statistics have the same format.

Comparing Table 6.3 with Table 6.1, we see that the statistics in Table 6.3 refer not only to the time spent in the block prior to the SEIZE block, i.e. the ARRIVE block, but also to the time spent in the ADVANCE block. In the block statistics, the current contents of the ARRIVE block is 8, but the

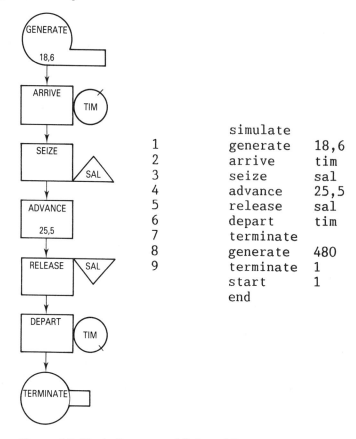

| | |  | |
|---|---|---|---|
| | | simulate | |
| 1 | | generate | 18,6 |
| 2 | | arrive | tim |
| 3 | | seize | sal |
| 4 | | advance | 25,5 |
| 5 | | release | sal |
| 6 | | depart | tim |
| 7 | | terminate | |
| 8 | | generate | 480 |
| 9 | | terminate | 1 |
| | | start | 1 |
| | | end | |

**Figure 6.3** Block diagram and listing of Program 6.2

**Table 6.2** Block statistics of Program 6.2

```
Block counts
Number Adr.   Oper. Current   Total
       1      GENER    0        27
       2      ARRIV    8        27
       3      SEIZE    0        19
       4      ADVAN    1        19
       5      RELEA    0        18
       6      DEPAR    0        18
       7      TERMI    0        18
       8      GENER    0         1
       9      TERMI    0         1
```

**Table 6.3** AD set statistics of Program 6.2

| Queue (AD set) | Maximum contents | Average contents | Total entries | Zero entries | Percent zeros |
|---|---|---|---|---|---|
| TIM | 9 | 4.76 | 27 | 0 | 0.00 |

| Queue (AD set) | Average time/trans | $Average time/trans | Current contents |
|---|---|---|---|
| TIM | 84.56 | 84.56 | 9 |

$Average time/trans=average time/trans excluding zero entries

current contents of TIM is 9, i.e. there are nine transactions that have entered the ARRIVE block, but not yet entered the DEPART block. These nine transactions consist of eight in the ARRIVE block waiting to be served, and one in the ADVANCE block in the process of being served.

The average time per transaction is also different from the corresponding time in Table 6.1. One might expect that the average time in the store would be roughly 25 minutes longer, since it also includes the time spent in service, which on average is 25 minutes. However, since nine of the customers have not yet finished being served at closing time, the average added time (84.56–67.25 = 17.31) is considerably shorter.

Program 6.2 dealt with total time spent in the store, *not* time spent queuing. In micro-GPSS, use of the word ARRIVE will avoid misleading the reader into thinking that the time refers only to time spent queuing, whereas GPSS V uses the word QUEUE instead of ARRIVE. It has been found that the use of the word QUEUE for the general measurement of time has misled users into believing that queuing times were involved when in fact completely different times were being measured.

In order to avoid such misunderstandings and thus improve the implementation of GPSS programs, micro-GPSS uses the term ARRIVE as the standard one. However, in order to increase compatibility with GPSS V, as an alternative to ARRIVE you can use the word QUEUE, which works exactly like ARRIVE. (See Appendix B.) In fact, both words will be translated to the same internal code by the micro-GPSS processor. QUEUE uses the same block symbol as ARRIVE, but with QUEUE as text.

## 6.3 More detailed statistics with QTABLE

The statistics automatically printed, by using Q as B operand of SEIZE or by having an ARRIVE–DEPART pair, might be insufficient for many purposes. One limitation is that there are only statistics on *average* times. We are often interested in more specific values, e.g. knowing how many waited more than

10 minutes, more than 20 minutes, etc. This is particularly important if we are interested in avoiding very long waiting times. It is therefore often desirable to obtain a table with waiting times distributed into different classes, e.g. showing how many waited 0–10 minutes, 10–20 minutes, etc.

A QTABLE statement will lead to such statistics. This is a control statement, not a block. It is placed after SIMULATE, but before the first GENERATE block. If only one table is required from a program, there is then no need to give the table a name (for tables with table names see Chapter 15), and the format of this control statement is as follows:

    QTABLE A,B,C,D

In the operation field we write the operation code: QTABLE.
    The QTABLE statement has four operands:

A. The A operand contains the name of the queue or the AD set to be described in the table. This name must be the same one used as A operand of a SEIZE block with Q as B operand, or identical to the one used as A operand of an ARRIVE block and its corresponding DEPART block.

B. The B operand specifies the upper limit of the lowest class presented in the table. This will be explained in more detail later. However, the B operand is normally set to 0.

C. The C operand is the class width of each class, except the highest and the lowest class. The class width is the number of time units in each of these classes.

D. The D operand specifies the total number of classes.

This can be illustrated by the following QTABLE statement:

    QTABLE SAL,0,10,5

This is incorporated into Program 6.1, resulting in Program 6.3.
    The QTABLE statement produces a table that contains the statistics for waiting times in front of the facility SAL. The times are divided into five classes (in accordance with the D operand) as follows:

1.      –0
2.  0.01–10
3. 10.01–20
4. 20.01–30
5. 30.01–

## Program 6.3

```
simulate
qtable      sal,0,10,5
generate    18,6
seize       sal,q
advance     25,5
release     sal
terminate
generate    480
terminate   1
start       1
end
```

The first class contains in principle all waiting times from minus infinity to 0. Since waiting times cannot be negative, the first class will only contain those transactions that spend 0 time in the queue. The second class contains those transactions that spend 0.01–10 minutes, etc. The fifth and highest class contains, in principle, all transactions that spend more than 30 minutes waiting. If there is data in the highest class, there will be a special print-out of OVERFLOW. This might be seen as a recommendation to re-run the program with a higher number of classes.

Running Program 6.3, we obtain Table 6.4, in addition to all earlier obtained print-outs of Program 6.1.

Prior to the actual table there is a line of extra statistics. This includes first of all the number of entries in the table. This number, 19, is different from the number of entries in the queue statistics, 27 (see Table 6.1). While the earlier queue statistics include all transactions that have started waiting, the QTABLE statistics include only those transactions that have also *finished* waiting and have gone into service. Hence the difference of 8 (27 − 19) refers to the transactions that are still waiting at closing time. For the same reason there is a different mean waiting time (68.85), referring to the 19 customers who went into service before closing time.

The first line of the QTABLE statistics also includes the standard deviation of the waiting times. The standard deviation, a well known statistical measure of dispersion, is here defined as

$$\sqrt{\frac{1}{n-1}\sum_{1}^{n}(x_j - \bar{x})^2}$$

where $n$ is the number of entries into the table, $x_j$ is an individual value and $\bar{x}$ the average value. The standard deviation, often denoted as $s$, will together with the average give a rough idea of the limits within which the bulk of the

**Table 6.4** QTABLE statistics of Program 6.3

```
Table
Entries in table Mean argument Standard deviation Sum of argument:
```

| Entries in table | Mean argument | Standard deviation | Sum of argument: |
|---|---|---|---|
| 19 | 68.85 | 39.97 | 1308.15 |

| Range | | Observed frequency | Per cent of total | Cumulative percentage | Cumulative remainder |
|---|---|---|---|---|---|
| – | 0 | 1 | 5.26 | 5.26 | 94.74 |
| 0.01 – | 10 | 1 | 5.26 | 10.53 | 89.47 |
| 10.01 – | 20 | 1 | 5.26 | 15.79 | 84.21 |
| 20.01 – | 30 | 1 | 5.26 | 21.05 | 78.95 |
| Overflow | | 15 | 78.95 | 100.00 | 0.00 |
| Average value of overflow | | 83.63 | | | |

values will lie. If the distribution of values approximately follows the normal distribution, one can then expect roughly two-thirds of all values to lie between $\bar{x} - s$ and $\bar{x} + s$.

There is also a value called SUM OF ARGUMENTS. This is the total time spent by all the 19 transactions in the table.

The actual table has five columns. The first column, RANGE, indicates that the first class concerns 0 minutes (see above), the second 0.01–10 minutes, the third 10.01–20 minutes, etc. The fifth class, here called OVERFLOW, includes all values from 30.01 and upwards.

The second column, OBSERVED FREQUENCY, gives the number of transactions that belong to each class.

Column 3, PER CENT OF TOTAL, gives what percentage the numbers in column 2 constitute of the total 19 transactions.

In column 4 the percentages in column 3 have been added cumulatively to make it easier to answer questions such as: how many wait *at most* 20 minutes? The answer is given on line 3 (upper limit 20): around 16 percent waited at most 20 minutes.

The final column, column 5, is the value in column 4 subtracted from 100. This helps us to answer a question like: how many waited more than 30 minutes? The answer, seen on line 4 in column 5, is 79 percent.

Finally there is a print-out of the average value of the overflow. This is the average waiting time of those 15 customers who waited more than 30 minutes. This value gives some indication of how many more classes are needed in order to avoid overflow. Probably a dozen more classes are needed. In order to be safe we change the D operand of Program 6.3 to 20 (obtaining Program 6.3b). This produces the revised QTABLE statistics of Table 6.5. (Program 6.3b is not presented here.)

**Table 6.5** QTABLE statistics of Program 6.3b

| Range | | Observed frequency | Per cent of total | Cumulative percentage | Cumulative remainder |
|---|---|---|---|---|---|
| – | 0 | 1 | 5.26 | 5.26 | 94.74 |
| 0.01 – | 10 | 1 | 5.26 | 10.53 | 89.47 |
| 10.01 – | 20 | 1 | 5.26 | 15.79 | 84.21 |
| 20.01 – | 30 | 1 | 5.26 | 21.05 | 78.95 |
| 30.01 – | 40 | 2 | 10.53 | 31.58 | 68.42 |
| 40.01 – | 50 | 0 | 0.00 | 31.58 | 68.42 |
| 50.01 – | 60 | 2 | 10.53 | 42.11 | 57.89 |
| 60.01 – | 70 | 1 | 5.26 | 47.37 | 52.63 |
| 70.01 – | 80 | 1 | 5.26 | 52.63 | 47.37 |
| 80.01 – | 90 | 3 | 15.79 | 68.42 | 31.58 |
| 90.01 – | 100 | 1 | 5.26 | 73.68 | 26.32 |
| 100.01 – | 110 | 1 | 5.26 | 78.95 | 21.05 |
| 110.01 – | 120 | 2 | 10.53 | 89.47 | 10.53 |
| 120.01 – | 130 | 2 | 10.53 | 100.00 | 0.00 |

Remaining frequencies are all zero

This time there is no overflow, but although the D operand specified 20 classes, there are only 14. The highest one goes from 120.01 to 130. The message 'REMAINING FREQUENCIES ARE ALL ZERO' explains that the remaining classes contain no observations and the GPSS processor will not print any empty classes at the bottom of the table.

It should finally be mentioned that a QTABLE statement can be added just as effectively to Program 6.2, resulting in Program 6.4.

**Program 6.4**

```
simulate
qtable      tim,0,10,20
generate    18,6
arrive      tim
seize       sal
advance     25,5
release     sal
depart      tim
terminate
generate    480
terminate   1
start       1
end
```

Here the A operand of the QTABLE statement is the name of the AD set, i.e. the same name used as A operand of the ARRIVE and DEPART blocks. This program will produce a table of statistics for the times between transactions entering the ARRIVE block and entering the DEPART block, i.e. in this case for the time spent in the store by those 18 customers who at closing time had already entered the DEPART block and then left the store.

---

## Exercise 6.1

Combine Programs 6.1 and 6.2 so that from the same program you can get statistics on both waiting time and time spent in the store.

---

## Exercise 6.2

Change Program 6.3b, in the first instance so that customers come on average every 28 (instead of 18) minutes apart. Next change also the half-width of the ADVANCE block from 5 minutes to 25 minutes, implying that service time varies between 0 and 50 minutes. Compare the tables of the two runs and study the effect on the longest waiting times.

---

## Exercise 6.3   (Case study 2A in Schriber, 1974)

The InterArrival Time of the customers at a one-chair barber shop is uniformly distributed over the range 18 ± 6 minutes. Service time for haircuts is 16 ± 4 minutes, uniformly distributed. Customers coming to the shop have their hair cut, on a first-come, first-served basis, then leave. Model the shop in GPSS, making provisions to collect data on the waiting line. Then run the model through eight hours of simulated time. Interpret the output produced by the model in the context of the barber shop.

---

## Exercise 6.4

Rewrite the program in Exercise 6.3 so that the program also produces statistics on how many waited more than 10 minutes, 15 minutes and 20 minutes and how long the customers who got service spent on average in the barber shop.

# 7 Systems with different customers and several servers

## 7.1 Different types of customer

The preceding chapters were limited to very simple systems with only one type of customer, i.e. only one kind of transaction besides the stop transaction, and only one server. In this chapter systems with different types of customer as well as several servers will be considered.

We will first deal with a system with two different types of customer, but still only one server. Let us consider a small '7–11' store with just one salesperson, but where two types of customer arrive: newspaper buyers, who need very little time (between 15 and 75 seconds) for service, and food buyers, who need considerably longer time (between 90 and 390 seconds). The newspaper buyers also arrive more frequently, with InterArrival Times of between 90 and 150 seconds, while the food buyers have IATs between 240 and 480 seconds.

The two types of customer hence differ in two respects: the frequency of arrival and the required service times. Since the difference between the averages of the two groups is greater than in-group differences, i.e. differences between the members in each group, it is reasonable to model these customers differently by using two different segments, i.e. one separate segment for each group of customers. We would like to measure the waiting times for each of the two groups of customers, i.e. having one statistical queue for the newspaper buyers and one for the food buyers.

My store is open 14 hours (not 16), i.e. 840 minutes or 50 400 seconds, each day and we wish to simulate one day. All this is represented by the block diagram of Figure 7.1.

Each customer group has its own segment, starting with a GENERATE block and ending with a TERMINATE block. It should be stressed that these segments are drawn completely separately in the diagram. No lines go from one segment to the other. In particular, note that *no* lines lead *into* the GENERATE blocks.

It should also be stressed that the three segments can be put in any

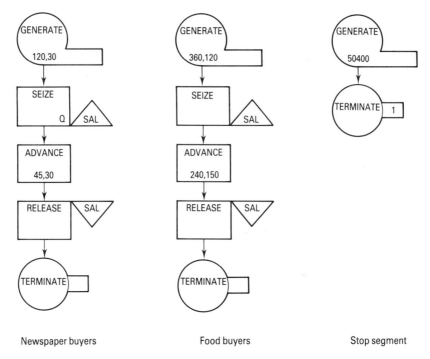

**Figure 7.1** Block diagram of Program 7.1

order in the program. It is equally possible to begin with the food buyer as with the newspaper buyer segment. It should again be stressed that the block diagram is not like an ordinary flow chart. Program execution does not follow a block diagram as if it were a flow chart. The events are instead executed according to which event is at any one moment the most imminent event on the list of future events. The processor will initially schedule the first newspaper buyer, the first food buyer and the stop event. After this each arrival event will then schedule the arrival of the next customer of this type. Since the block diagram covers all the essential aspects of the program, no program listing is necessary.

In the block diagram there is one SEIZE block in each of the two customer segments. They both refer to the same facility, SAL. When a transaction tries to enter a SEIZE block and is admitted because the facility is idle, the facility status indicator is changed to busy. Assume a newspaper buyer makes the salesperson busy. If a food buyer soon afterwards tries to obtain service, he will find the salesperson's status indicator in the busy state. No entry into the SEIZE block is then possible.

When a customer is refused entry into the SEIZE block he is, as mentioned earlier, forced to wait. This can be seen from two view-points: the block view-point, according to which he is waiting in the preceding block, and the waiting list view-point, according to which he is put on a list of waiting transactions, which the customers (transactions) leave on a first-in, first-out basis.

The programs presented earlier with only one SEIZE block are not markedly different from this program with two SEIZE blocks: from a block perspective, the food customers wait in one block (GENERATE 120,30) and the newspaper buyers in another (GENERATE 360,120). One might therefore be tempted to assume that the food customers wait in a different waiting line from the newspaper buyers. This is, however, *not* the case. When food buyers are said to wait in the GENERATE block prior to the SEIZE block in the food segment, this is only how the waiting is represented with regard to the block statistics. In reality during program execution all transactions waiting to enter the facility SAL are placed on the *same* internal waiting list. On this list the GPSS processor will also keep track of the particular block in which the transaction is waiting, so that when the transaction is allowed to move into service it will go to the SEIZE block of the appropriate segment.

Thus the processor correctly models the real-life situation where the food buyers and newspaper buyers join the same waiting line and the customers are served on a first-come, first-served basis, regardless of what type of buyer they are.

In order to gather statistics on the average time spent waiting by *all* customers, a Q is used as B operand of the first SEIZE block. It should be noted that it is enough for a facility to have *one* SEIZE block with a Q as B operand in order to have its queue statistics gathered. It is permitted also to add a Q to the other SEIZE block but this is unnecessary. The kind of queue statistics shown in Table 7.1 are now produced.

Although there is a stop time of 50 400 time units (= seconds), the real time required for running the program is not very long. The simulation clock will in this case make a significant jump every time it is updated. The

**Table 7.1** Queue statistics of Program 7.1

| Queue (AD set) | Maximum contents | Average contents | Total entries | Zero entries | Percent zeros |
|---|---|---|---|---|---|
| SAL | 14 | 5.90 | 560 | 6 | 1.07 |

| Queue (AD set) | Average time/trans | $Average time/trans | Current contents |
|---|---|---|---|
| SAL | 531.39 | 537.15 | 6 |

$Average time/trans=average time/trans excluding zero entries

processing time is dependent on the number of events, not on the final value of the simulation clock.

## 7.2 Several types of queue statistics

Program 7.1 produced statistics on only *one* queue, namely the joint waiting line in front of the facility SAL. We might, however, also be interested in seeing how long the two different groups of customers have to wait, since the newspaper buyers are probably less willing to wait than the food customers.

In order to obtain such statistics we must use pairs of ARRIVE and DEPART blocks, since the B operand of a SEIZE block can *only* be used to gather the statistics for *all* customers of a facility as one group. ARRIVE and DEPART pairs of blocks can, on the other hand, be used to measure time

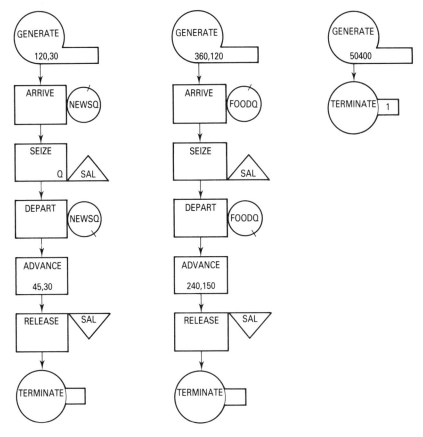

**Figure 7.2** Block diagram of Program 7.2

between *any* two points in the block diagram. This is where the block diagram of Figure 7.2 is used.

For newspaper buyers time is measured from the moment when they arrive at the end of the waiting line, called NEWSQ, and the moment they depart from this line. Since they start waiting when they have been refused entry into the SEIZE block, a block ARRIVE NEWSQ is put in front of the SEIZE block. The newspaper buyers who are refused entry to the SEIZE block are then regarded as waiting in the ARRIVE NEWSQ block.

A newspaper buyer will depart from the waiting line NEWSQ at the same time as he is allowed through the SEIZE block and enters the ADVANCE block. Consequently, the DEPART NEWSQ block is placed immediately *after* the SEIZE block in the newspaper buyer segment. In the same way we put an ARRIVE FOODQ block before the SEIZE block in the food buyer segment, and a DEPART FOODQ block after it.

For the same reason as for Program 7.1, the program listing is omitted. The program produces the kind of queue statistics shown in Table 7.2 with three separate lines of statistics, one for each of the three groups. The total entries into the joint queue SAL is the sum of entries into NEWSQ and FOODQ. The average time in the joint queue SAL is a weighted average of the NEWSQ and FOODQ averages.

It should now be clear that the Q as B operand of the SEIZE SAL block could be replaced with, e.g., a block ARRIVE TOTQ prior to *each* SEIZE block and a block DEPART TOTQ after *each* SEIZE block. This is of course more complicated, but this is the way it has to be done in GPSS V, with the word QUEUE replacing ARRIVE. (See furthermore Appendix B.)

**Table 7.2** Queue statistics of Program 7.2

| Queue (AD set) | Maximum contents | Average contents | Total entries | Zero entries | Percent zeros |
|---|---|---|---|---|---|
| NEWSQ | 11 | 4.62 | 421 | 3 | 0.71 |
| SAL | 14 | 5.90 | 560 | 6 | 1.07 |
| FOODQ | 3 | 1.28 | 139 | 3 | 2.16 |

| Queue (AD set) | Average time/trans | $Average time/trans | Current contents |
|---|---|---|---|
| NEWSQ | 553.09 | 557.06 | 5 |
| SAL | 531.39 | 537.15 | 6 |
| FOODQ | 465.67 | 475.94 | 1 |

$Average time/trans=average time/trans excluding zero entries

# 7.3 Several facilities working in series

The systems in the last two programs had two types of customer and one facility. We shall now study a case which also has several facilities, taking the simplest case with two facilities being utilized one after the other. The programs used in Chapters 4–6 regarding a store with one server will now be extended. Assume that the store also has one cashier. The customers first select the goods, e.g. articles of clothing, with the aid of the salesperson, and next proceed to the cashier to pay for the goods. The service time of the salesperson is the same as in the earlier programs, but that of the cashier varies between two and six minutes. The block diagram of Figure 7.3 is obtained.

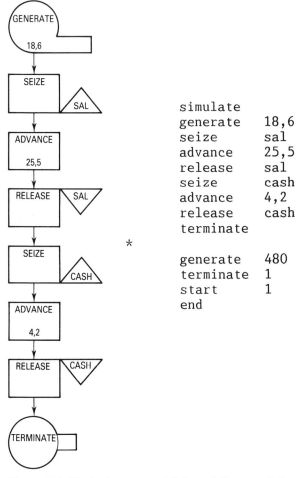

```
simulate
generate    18,6
seize       sal
advance     25,5
release     sal
seize       cash
advance     4,2
release     cash
terminate
      *
generate    480
terminate   1
start       1
end
```

**Figure 7.3** Block diagram and listing of Program 7.3

The program is quite straightforward. It illustrates that we can allow a transaction to get service from one facility after another. A waiting line can be formed in front of each facility. The two facilities must be given different names, e.g. SAL and CASH. If the name SAL had been used erroneously (instead of CASH) in the last pair of SEIZE–RELEASE blocks as well, the program would have meant that a customer, after having been served by SAL the first time, would immediately try to get service from SAL a second time. If SAL had been busy, he would have gone back to the end of the internal waiting line in front of SAL.

# 7.4 A GPSS program to test an optimal production plan

I shall now discuss a very simple version of a common type of situation in industry. An engineering workshop has two machines, one lathe and one grinder, and produces two products, A and B. The products first go through the lathe, then the grinder. The production process can be explained by Figure 7.4, which shows for each machine how the amount of time each product requires can vary.

Hence, for example, in the lathe one unit of product A needs on average 20 minutes, but times can vary between 15 and 25 minutes because of various random factors.

The gross profit, or contribution, per unit (sales price − unit cost of materials) for product A is $2.00 and for product B $3.00. At these prices all the products that can be produced can also be sold. We want to establish which daily production schedule maximizes total gross profits when there are 500 minutes available during a day and there are no machine set-up times.

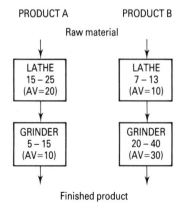

**Figure 7.4** Production flow of Program 7.4

If the random variations in the time requirement were completely disregarded and only the average values were used, the production problem could be solved by a conventional optimization method, called linear programming (LP). The problem is then formulated in the following way.

With $Q(A)$ being the quantity of product A and $Q(B)$ the quantity of product B, we seek to maximize total gross profits $Q(A) \star 2 + Q(B) \star 3$ under the following pair of restrictions:

1.   $Q(A) \star 20 + Q(B) \star 10 \leq 500$
2.   $Q(A) \star 10 + Q(B) \star 30 \leq 500$

Restriction (1) means that the total time spent in the lathe must not exceed 500 minutes and (2) that the total time needed in the grinder must not exceed 500 minutes.

It can be shown that the largest profit ($70) is obtained when 20 units of A and 10 units of B are produced. In this case both the lathe and the grinder are used to capacity. The question is whether this production schedule is suitable since it disregards the considerable time dispersions around the averages. In order to answer this question, GPSS is used to simulate this production situation, taking these time variations into account.

Producing 20 units of A and 10 units of B during 500 minutes can be seen as equivalent to starting the production of one A every 25 minutes and one B every 50 minutes. This would be in line with a 'just-in-time' production policy. (A different policy will be tested in Exercise 8.5.)

In order to start the production of one unit of A every 25 minutes, i.e. to have an InterArrival Time (between the start of the production of each A) of 25 minutes, the block GENERATE 25 could be used. This is, however, not very realistic. GENERATE 25 implies that the first transaction is generated first at time 25 $(= 0 + \text{IAT}(1) = 0 + 25$; see Chapter 3). No production would thus take place during the first 25 minutes of the day.

In order to remedy this, the C operand of the GENERATE block is used. We have until now only used the A and B operands of the GENERATE block. There is also a C operand, which is a constant that specifies the time of arrival of the first transaction. If the C operand is not stated, as in all the previous programs, the first arrival is established as the first InterArrival Time. This is the default value of the C operand of the GENERATE block. If the C operand is explicitly stated, the first transaction will be generated at time C (and hence the second at $C + \text{IAT}(1)$). Writing GENERATE 25,0,1 will generate transactions with an InterArrival Time of exactly 25 (B operand is 0), but with the first transaction generated at time 1. (The reason why 1 instead of 0 is used in this example is that we do not want production of new units to start just at closing time 500.)

If we want an operand to take its default value and a later operand has a *no*-default value (i.e. a value different from the default value), we can, however, just write an extra comma to denote that the operand has a default value. Instead of writing GENERATE 25,0,1, where the 0 is the default value for the B operand, we can simply write GENERATE 25,,1. (Note that there is no blank between the two commas.)

Summing up, if we require the production of one unit of A to take place every 25 minutes, with the first commencing at time 1, we write GENERATE 25,,1. Likewise GENERATE 50,,1 will generate one product start every 50 minutes with the first at time 1.

Let us next look at the block diagram of the whole program in Figure 7.5. In the block diagram it can be seen that each type of product first seizes the lathe and then, after a sampled time in the ADVANCE block (i.e. in the lathe), releases the lathe before it can seize the grinder.

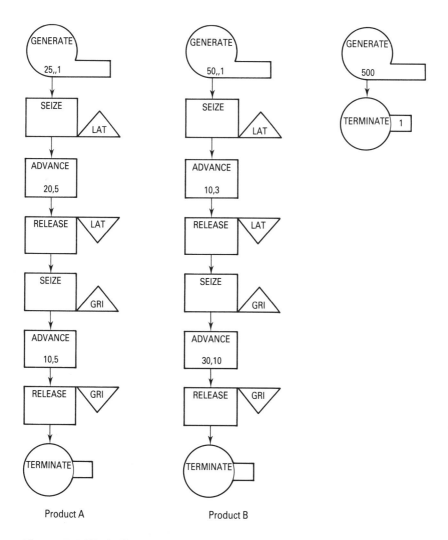

**Figure 7.5** Block diagram of Program 7.4

The listing of the program follows the block diagram closely.

**Program 7.4**

```
                simulate
        *  Product A
1               generate    25,,1
2               seize       lat
3               advance     20,5
4               release     lat
5               seize       gri
6               advance     10,5
7               release     gri
8               terminate
        *  Product B
9               generate    50,,1
10              seize       lat
11              advance     10,3
12              release     lat
13              seize       gri
14              advance     30,10
15              release     gri
16              terminate
        *  Stop segment
17              generate    500
18              terminate   1
                start       1
                end
```

The block statistics obtained are shown in Table 7.3.

From these statistics it can be seen that it is impossible to follow the production plan based on linear programming which ignored time variations. Instead of the 20 As to be produced according to that plan, only 17 As were finished. Two units of A and one unit of B are waiting in front of the grinder, resulting in temporary inventories of semifinished goods.

The facility statistics presented in Table 7.4 reveal a further discrepancy with the LP model. Utilization is not at full capacity.

There are two main lessons to be learnt from this simple example:

1. From a purely GPSS point of view, facilities can be used in series with different types of transaction using the same facilities.

2. From an application point of view, this is an example of a business situation where random variations and time considerations are important

**Table 7.3** Block statistics of Program 7.4

Relative clock     500.00 Absolute clock     500.00

```
        Block counts
        Number Adr.  Oper. Current  Total
            1        GENER    0       20
            2        SEIZE    0       20
            3        ADVAN    0       20
            4        RELEA    2       20
            5        SEIZE    0       18
            6        ADVAN    1       18
            7        RELEA    0       17
            8        TERMI    0       17
            9        GENER    0       10
           10        SEIZE    0       10
           11        ADVAN    0       10
           12        RELEA    1       10
           13        SEIZE    0        9
           14        ADVAN    0        9
           15        RELEA    0        9
           16        TERMI    0        9
           17        GENER    0        1
           18        TERMI    0        1
```

**Table 7.4** Facility statistics of Program 7.4

| Facility | Average utilization | Number entries | Average time/tran |
|---|---|---|---|
| LAT | 0.96 | 30 | 16.07 |
| GRI | 0.96 | 27 | 17.73 |

and where it might be suitable to use discrete-event stochastic simulation of the GPSS type to complement static deterministic planning methods that disregard these factors. On the basis of such simulations, new production plans could be made that take these dynamic random factors into account.

# 7.5 Several parallel servers with a common waiting line

In the program examples studied so far, customers either use only one facility or, in the case of several facilities, use them one after the other in series (as in the preceding section). Let us now consider the case of a system in which there are several servers, but if one server is busy, a customer does not necessarily have to wait, but can get service from other similar servers. We may speak of servers that work in parallel.

A distinction can be drawn between two specific types of parallel server:

1. There is only a single waiting line, which is in front of all the servers and the servers have similar characteristics, in particular with regard to service time (group A).

2. Each server has its own waiting line and/or the servers are significantly different, in particular with regard to service time (group B).

Figure 7.6 illustrates the difference between group A and group B as regards queue formation.

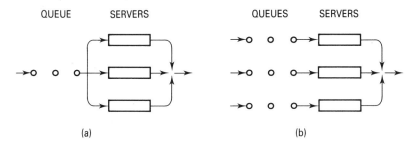

(a)                                    (b)

**Figure 7.6**  Two types of parallel server

Examples of situation A are:

1. A store with several salespeople giving service to whichever person in the store has waited the longest.

2. A bank or post office with several tellers but only one waiting line.

3. A multi-barber barber shop.

4. A parking garage.

5. Tables in a restaurant.

Some obvious examples of situation B would be a supermarket with several checkout counters, a railway station with several ticket booths or a bank, where each teller has his own waiting line.

This chapter only deals with the first case, i.e. where there are several similar servers with *one* waiting line. Case B will be dealt with in Chapters 9 and 16.

As mentioned in Chapter 3, GPSS distinguishes between two types of server:

1. Facilities, which can serve only one transaction at a time.

2. Storages, which can serve several transactions at a time.

The rest of this chapter covers the GPSS storage concept.

## 7.6 Syntax rules for storages

The concept of a storage will be used for servers that work in parallel, have a single waiting line and where differences between the individual servers, e.g. as regards service time, is so small that it is not worth the extra trouble of modeling each server separately.

The use of the word 'storage' in GPSS for this type of server is probably connected with the fact that physical storage provides good examples of such a kind of server. Each part of a storage, be it a shelf in a warehouse or a byte of computer memory, is very similar to other parts, i.e. there are a number of identical servers working in parallel.

In order to use the storage concept in a GPSS model, three different types of statement need to be used:

1. A storage definition statement.

2. An ENTER block, and

3. A LEAVE block.

### 1. The storage definition statement

This is a control statement to be placed after SIMULATE, but before the first GENERATE statement.

The storage definition statement is used to define how many servers are working in parallel. For facilities with only one server no such statement was necessary or possible, but for a storage this statement for defining the maximum number of servers must be used.

In the address field the name of the storage, e.g. STOR, is written using the micro-GPSS rules for names in the address field. The rules are the same as for facilities, i.e. three letters followed by 0–2 alphanumeric characters (see Section 4.2). Furthermore, the name of a storage must *not* be the same as that of a facility used in the same program.

The operation field contains the word STORAGE.

The only operand, the A operand, is a constant, which denotes the maximum number of transactions to be held in the storage at any time, which is equal to the maximum number of servers that work simultaneously. This is called the *capacity* of the storage. The A operand has a very high default value (2 billion in micro-GPSS). In micro-GPSS all storages have to be defined, with or without an A operand, to avoid logical errors.

It should be noted that a storage can have a capacity of one, i.e. a storage can act like a facility. It makes sense to give a storage the capacity of one, if you want, for example, to determine the effect of having one, two or three salespeople in a store using several runs of the same program, by changing only the value of the A operand. Otherwise there is no reason to use a storage instead of a facility. The facility concept is simpler (no definition statement is required), runs faster on the computer and allows for interruption of service (see Chapter 11).

## 2. The ENTER block

The ENTER block is used in order to allow a transaction to obtain service from a storage. This chapter covers the simplest case, namely when ENTER has only one 'true' operand, the A operand.

The symbol of the ENTER block is shown in Figure 7.7. Next to the rectangle with the operation ENTER (and a possible B operand) there is a half-circle with the round side upwards and the A operand inside.

**Figure 7.7** Block symbol of ENTER

The A operand is the name of the storage, e.g. STOR. No default value is allowed.

The B operand will be discussed in detail in Chapter 12. This chapter only deals with the case when the B operand is Q, an alternative only allowed in micro-GPSS.

When a transaction reaches the block ENTER A, the transaction will attempt to enter this block. What happens then depends on whether or not the storage is full. The storage is full if there is no free capacity, where the free capacity is equal to the defined capacity (the A operand in the STORAGE statement) *minus* the current contents of the storage.

If the storage is *full*, the transaction attempting to enter will be refused entry and it will have to wait, just as for a SEIZE block: in the block sense it will wait in the block preceding the ENTER block; in the processor sense on a special waiting list, on a first-in, first-out basis, together with all other transactions waiting to move into the storage.

If the storage is *not full*, i.e. there is at least one unit of capacity free, then the following will happen, when ENTER has only an A operand or the B operand is Q:

1. The transaction will enter the ENTER block and proceed to try to enter the next block.

2. The total block count is increased by 1.

3. The current contents of the storage of the A operand is increased by 1.

4. The free capacity of this storage is decreased by 1.

## 3. The LEAVE block

Just as ENTER is the storage counterpart of SEIZE, LEAVE is the storage counterpart of RELEASE. LEAVE can hence be seen as the mirror image of ENTER, with the block symbol of Figure 7.8, where the half-circle has the rounded part downwards.

**Figure 7.8** Block symbol of LEAVE

The LEAVE block, just like the RELEASE block, will not refuse entry. When there is no B operand, LEAVE STOR implies that:

1. The current contents of the storage STOR will decrease by 1.

2. The free capacity of this storage will increase by 1.

3. If the free capacity of STOR consequently goes from 0 to 1, another transaction will be able to come into the ENTER STOR block. The GPSS processor will at this point check if there is any transaction on the waiting list of the storage STOR. If this is the case, the transaction at the front of the waiting list will enter the appropriate ENTER STOR block.

## 7.7 A store with several servers

The use of the storage concept can be illustrated with a simple program. It deals with the same store as presented in Programs 4.1–6.4, but there are now two salespeople instead of one. The block diagram and listing of this program, Program 7.5, is in Figure 7.9.

Although the storage definition statement STOR STORAGE is not represented in the block diagram, since it is a control statement, it must be part of the program. If this statement were omitted, micro-GPSS would produce an error message.

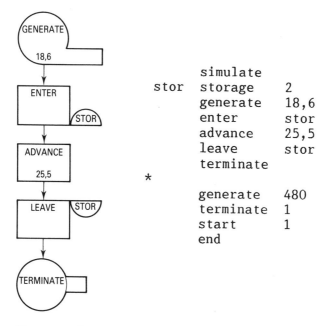

```
             simulate
        stor storage    2
             generate   18,6
             enter      stor
             advance    25,5
             leave      stor
             terminate
*
             generate   480
             terminate  1
             start      1
             end
```

**Figure 7.9** Block diagram and listing of Program 7.5

In addition to the block counts and the queue statistics, which do not contain any new concepts, Program 7.5 produces the storage statistics shown in Table 7.5. (The author, not the computer, has added the numbers above the data items in order to make references easier.) These statistics are similar to the facility statistics, although more extended. The ideas behind some of the storage statistics are also in some regards similar to those of the queue statistics.

Besides the name of the STORAGE, there are seven items of information:

**Table 7.5** Storage statistics of Program 7.5

| | (1)<br>Capacity | (2)<br>Average<br>contents | (3)<br>Average<br>utilization | (4)<br>Entries | (5)<br>Average<br>time/trans |
|---|---|---|---|---|---|
| Storage | | | | | |
| STOR | 2 | 1.39 | 0.70 | 27 | 24.73 |

| | (6)<br>Current<br>contents | (7)<br>Maximum<br>contents |
|---|---|---|
| Storage | | |
| STOR | 1 | 2 |

1. CAPACITY is the A operand of the storage definition statement, i.e. the maximum number of transactions that can be served simultaneously by the storage.

2. AVERAGE CONTENTS (in this program where ENTER lacks a B operand) is calculated by dividing the total time spent in the storage by all transactions, e.g. customers (667.6 minutes; not printed, but calculated), by the total simulation time (480 minutes), giving 1.39. (Micro-GPSS computes total simulation time as follows: for each transaction it notes the times of entry into the ENTER block and of entry into the LEAVE block and on the basis of these it calculates the time spent by each transaction in the storage. These times are then added together.)

3. AVERAGE UTILIZATION is the average contents divided by the capacity of the storage, i.e. in this case $1.39/2 = 0.70$. (Micro-GPSS rounds off to two decimal places.) This indicates that on average the salespeople are busy 70 percent of the time.

4. ENTRIES is the total number of transactions which have entered into the storage. This number is equivalent to the number of transaction entries also found in the total count of the ENTER block.

5. AVERAGE TIME/TRANS is the average time per transaction. This is the total time spent in the storage by all transactions (667.6 minutes) divided by the total block count of the ENTER block (27), i.e. $667.6/27 = 24.73$ minutes. Since the total time is divided by the total number of entries into the storage, not by the transactions that have also left the storage after service, this time is slightly underestimated, in a way similar to that discussed for queues (see Section 6.1).

6. CURRENT CONTENTS, 1, is the number of transactions that are inside the storage at simulation stop time. This is equivalent to the sum

of the current block counts for each of the blocks between (and including) the ENTER block and the LEAVE block; and in this case is the same as the current block count of the ADVANCE block.

7. MAXIMUM CONTENTS, 2, is the maximum number of units inside the storage at any one time, which in this problem equals the maximum number of salespeople who have been busy simultaneously. With a capacity of two salespeople, both busy at the end, this last piece of data does not provide any new information. It can, however, be quite significant if the program is re-run with, e.g., three, four or five salespeople to see how service improves with a further increase in the number of salespeople. If, for example, a re-run with four salespeople (i.e. with a storage definition statement STOR STORAGE 4) yields a maximum contents of 3, we would know that one salesperson would always be idle in this case and that three salespeople would be sufficient.

Program 7.5 will not yield any queue statistics. To obtain these in micro-GPSS it is possible to use the simple alternative of inserting a Q as B operand of the ENTER block. As in the case of facilities, a Q as B operand of one of the ENTER blocks connected to a storage will make the micro-GPSS processor collect queue statistics for this storage. (The B operand of ENTER and LEAVE can also contain other attributes, having a value $> 1$, as discussed in Chapter 12.) Thus Program 7.6 will collect the queue statistics for the store with two salespeople.

**Program 7.6**

```
        simulate
stor    storage      2
        generate     18,6
        enter        stor,q
        advance      25,5
        leave        stor
        terminate
*
        generate     480
        terminate    1
        start        1
        end
```

In GPSS V the program would need a QUEUE–DEPART pair surrounding the ENTER block to gather queue statistics.

Finally the queue statistics for this store can be compared with the equivalent statistics for the same store with only one salesperson (Program 6.1).

**Table 7.6** Comparison of queues of Programs 6.1 and 7.6

|  | Average contents | Number of customers who did not wait | Average time spent in queue |
|---|---|---|---|
| 1 salesperson | 3.78 | 1 | 67.25 |
| 2 salespeople | 0.00 | 26 | 0.02 |

## Exercise 7.1

Using two GPSS programs (with attached GPSS block diagrams) compare the functioning of small stores in the USA and the USSR. In both systems, customers are allowed to arrive at a rate of every 4 to 10 minutes ($7 \pm 3$ minutes). (Assume a rectangular distribution for all time data.) For both systems also assume that the store is closed after eight hours and that all service is then stopped and all customers have to leave.

1.  In the US store there are two salespeople who both sell the goods and receive payments for the goods. Total service time is between 7 and 17 minutes ($12 \pm 5$ minutes).

2.  In the Soviet store there are also two people working, one salesperson and one cashier. Customers first go to the salesperson and choose the goods and find out how much they have to pay. This takes between 3 and 7 minutes ($5 \pm 2$ minutes). Next they go to the cashier to pay for the goods and obtain a receipt. This also takes between 3 and 7 minutes. Finally, they return to the salesperson to pick up their goods after presenting the receipt, which is then stamped. This takes between 1 and 3 minutes ($2 \pm 1$). There is one waiting line in front of the salesperson and one in front of the cashier. Customers returning to the salesperson to pick up their goods have to start at the end of this line again.

The two programs should be written so that times spent by customers in the two types of store can be easily compared. How many customers will spend more than 15, 20, 25 minutes, etc. in the store in the two types of system? (Hints: Look at Programs 7.3 and 7.6! If you work in DOS on a PC, do not give a program file the name USA!)

## Exercise 7.2 (Case study 2B in Schriber, 1974)

Two types of customer arrive at a one-chair barber shop. Customers of the first type want only a haircut. Their InterArrival-Time distribution is 35 ± 10 minutes. Customers of the second type want a shave as well as a haircut. Their InterArrival-Time distribution is 60 ± 20 minutes. The barber provides service to his customers on a first-come, first-served basis. It takes the barber 18 ± 6 minutes to give a haircut. When he gives a shave, 10 ± 2 minutes are required.

   Model the barber shop in GPSS, making provisions to collect data on the waiting line that forms ahead of the barber. Then run the model through eight hours of simulated time.

## Exercise 7.3

An engineering shop processes two products: clutches and spindles. Clutches arrive at the shop according to a uniform distribution with a mean of 30 minutes and a half-width of 20 minutes. Spindles have an InterArrival Time of 35 ± 15 minutes.

   When clutches arrive they are placed in a grinder, of which there is only one available; there they are processed by the only worker. The processing takes 14 ± 6 minutes. As soon as the processing is over, the grinder can be used by another waiting job. Spindles are also processed by the worker with the processing taking 10 ± 4 minutes. No grinder is required to process spindles. Simulate the operation for an eight-hour day.

## Exercise 7.4 (Based on Example 2 in Birtwistle, 1979)

A port has two jetties each of which can be used for unloading by one boat at a time. Boats arrive at the port periodically and must wait if no jetty is currently free. When a jetty is available, a boat may dock and start to unload. When this activity has been completed, the boat leaves the jetty and sails away. The port authority has a pool of three tugs. One tug is required for docking and when a boat leaves its jetty. On average boats arrive 10 hours apart, but this can vary between 7 and 13 hours. It takes 14 ± 6 hours to unload. Docking and leaving, using tugs, take 2 hours each. Simulate for 28 full days of 24 hours.

## Exercise 7.5

One doctor and two nurses work in a clinic. Patients arrive every 15 ± 10 minutes.

Patients first go to one of the nurses (whichever one is free) for tests, etc., which takes 25 ± 10 minutes. They then proceed to the doctor for examination, which takes 15 ± 10 minutes. Since some patients have complained about very long waiting times, the doctor is considering a different arrangement. He realizes that if the nurse who has just made the tests on the patient also stayed with the patient during the examination, the time for examination would decrease to 10 ± 9 minutes. Write GPSS programs for both the present and the proposed alternative and simulate for a seven-hour day to see if there will be fewer patients who have very long waiting times.

# 8 The GOTO block

## 8.1 Introduction

So far the transactions have gone from block to block within each segment without any possibilities for jumping over some blocks. In many General Programming Languages, like BASIC, FORTRAN, etc. such jumps, carried out with the aid of GOTO statements, play an important role. In a similar way, GOTO statements play an important role in micro-GPSS. In this chapter two types of GOTO statement will be considered: the unconditional GOTO and the statistical GOTO. While the unconditional GOTO is very similar to the GOTO statements of many high-level programming languages, the statistical GOTO is a construction unique to micro-GPSS.

## 8.2 The unconditional GOTO

As already mentioned, the unconditional GOTO is very similar to the GOTO construction in many languages like BASIC, FORTRAN, etc.

In micro-GPSS this statement contains GOTO, written as *one* word, as the operation and an A operand, which is the address. Such a statement implies that the execution does not proceed to the next block, but instead jumps to the block that has this A operand in the address field. Just as GOTO 100 in BASIC means that the next statement to be executed will be that one which has 100 as its statement number, GOTO with the A operand BEGIN means that the next block to be executed is the one that has the address BEGIN. A transaction entering this GOTO block will thus next go to the block with the address BEGIN.

It should be stressed that there must be a block with the address BEGIN preceding the operation, i.e. in the address field. If there is no block with such an address an error message is given. Note that it is not incorrect to have an address that is not referred to by another block. This type of redundant address may help make a program easier to understand.

The block symbol of the unconditional GOTO block is shown in Figure 8.1. The GOTO operation is symbolized by a diamond, and the address to which the transaction goes next (the A operand) is written within parentheses on the line leading to the block with the same address as this A operand.

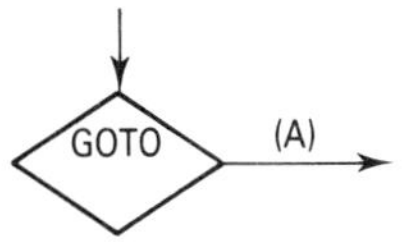

**Figure 8.1** Block symbol of unconditional GOTO

While micro-GPSS uses the word GOTO, familiar to all BASIC users, GPSS V uses the word TRANSFER. The address in GPSS V must be in the B operand. The A operand is given its default value and is hence in GPSS V written as a comma (see Section 7.4). Thus in GPSS V the only way of writing the unconditional transfer to the address BEGIN is TRANSFER ,BEGIN. In order to be more compatible with GPSS V, micro-GPSS also allows for the more complex GPSS V construction TRANSFER ,B. (See Appendix B.)

## 8.3 GENERATE with a D operand

We shall next, in Program 8.1, study how the unconditional GOTO is used. However, this program requires the introduction of the D operand of GENERATE.

Earlier (in Sections 3.4 and 7.4) we studied the A, B and C operands of the GENERATE block. The D operand, which is an integer constant, defines the maximum number of transactions that the GENERATE block can generate during the simulation (i.e. until the termination counter becomes 0). If the A, B and C operands all take their default values, this could be indicated by three commas. Hence, GENERATE ,,,D implies GENERATE 0,0,,D and (since IAT(1) = 0) GENERATE 0,0,0,D, i.e. D transactions are generated at the very start of the simulation and no more transactions will be generated by this block.

The default value of the D operand of GENERATE is a very high value (in micro-GPSS 32 000). If the default of the D operand is used, as in earlier programs, the number of transactions generated will have limits set by other factors, such as time.

## 8.4 Program 8.1

Our next example is a modified version of an example in Schriber, 1974 (case study 2D). Consider a pottery where a certain number of workers produce large pots. It takes between 25 and 35 minutes to throw one pot. When this is done, the pot has to be put into an oven (or a kiln) and stay there for between 6 and 10 minutes. The worker has to watch the pot all the time it is in the oven to check that it does not crack. Once the pot has been taken out of the oven the worker can start throwing a new pot. Work continues along similar lines all day. With only one oven available, the question arises as to how many workers should be employed: four, five or six. The program is to be run with three different values of the number of workers. This will be represented by the D operand of the GENERATE block, which will therefore change between the runs. The block diagram of Figure 8.2 applies to the case of four workers.

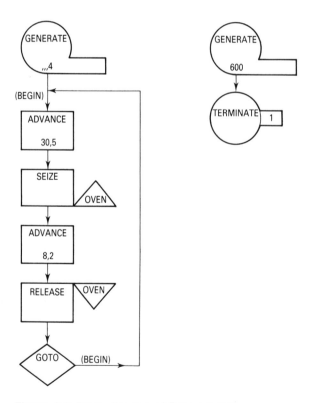

**Figure 8.2** Block diagram of Program 8.1

Firstly, four transactions are generated. This is equivalent to four workers arriving in the morning. The first ADVANCE block indicates that a worker throws a pot in 30 ± 5 minutes. The first worker who has finished his pot will seize the oven and use it for 8 ± 2 minutes, before he releases it. The other workers may have to wait until the oven becomes idle again.

Here is how the unconditional GOTO works: once a worker has finished using the oven, he will go back to the first ADVANCE block, which, as mentioned earlier, indicates the throwing of a pot. This ADVANCE block has the label BEGIN, written within parentheses on the upper left-hand side on top of the rectangle. Thus GOTO with the address BEGIN will bring the transaction, i.e. the worker, back to throw another pot.

The simulation is run for 10 hours, i.e. 600 minutes. The program is listed below.

**Program 8.1**

```
        simulate
        generate   ,,,4
begin   advance    30,5
        seize      oven
        advance    8,2
        release    oven
        goto       begin
        generate   600
        terminate  1
        start      1
        end
```

The output which is of interest to us is the total number of pots completed each day, i.e. the total block count of the RELEASE block. This corresponds to the total number of times that a worker has taken a finished pot out of the oven.

If the program is run with 4, 5 and 6 as the D operand, i.e. with four, five or six workers, we find that 58, 68 and 70 pots, respectively, are produced. If a fifth worker is taken on, production increases substantially, by 10 pots, while adding a sixth worker will increase production by only two pots. The reason for this smaller improvement is that the more workers there are, the greater the time that will be spent waiting in front of the oven. This can be seen from the figures for facility utilization. With four workers there is 80 percent utilization, with five workers 91 percent and with six workers 96 percent.

# 8.5 Statistical GOTO

The statistical GOTO is, as already noted, a concept unique to GPSS. Micro-GPSS uses the operation GOTO, with two non-default operands A and B.

As in the unconditional GOTO the A operand is an address. The new B operand is a probability larger than 0 and less than 1. In micro-GPSS it can have a maximum of four significant *digits*. Hence the lowest value is .0001 and the highest .9999. In most cases one or two digits will, however, be sufficient. In micro-GPSS the decimal point of this probability can be optionally preceded by 0.

A transaction leaving a statistical GOTO block will have a probability B of going to the block with the address of the A operand and the remaining probability, 1 − B, of going to the *next* block.

The block symbol of the statistical GOTO statement is depicted in Figure 8.3. Again it is symbolized by a diamond. Below the word GOTO there is the B operand = the probability of going to the block with the address of the A operand. This address is written to the right within parentheses.

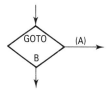

**Figure 8.3** Block symbol of statistical GOTO

The block GOTO PLAY,.25 is read as 'GOTO PLAY with 25 percent probability'. When executing this block the micro-GPSS processor will sample a uniform random fraction number between 0 and 1. If this random number is smaller than the B operand, the transaction is brought to the address in A. If the number is greater than (or equal to) the B operand, the transaction proceeds to the next block. If in the example GOTO PLAY,.25, 0.1713 is sampled, the transaction would go to PLAY; if 0.473 is sampled, it would go to the next block.

> GPSS V uses the word TRANSFER instead of GOTO. The use of the operands is also different. The A operand is the probability and the address connected with this probability is the C operand. GOTO PLAY,.25 must be written as TRANSFER .25,,PLAY in GPSS V (with *two* commas and with *no* 0 before the decimal point). In order to increase compatibility with GPSS V, micro-GPSS also allows for this more complicated form (see Appendix B).

# 8.6 Program 8.2

The following program is also a modified version of a program from Schriber, 1974 (case study 2F). The problem concerns a quality control unit of a TV set factory. Sets arrive at the inspection unit with InterArrival Times of 35 to 75 minutes. The sets are first tested by one of two inspectors. It takes one man 60–120 minutes to make an inspection. Fifteen percent of the sets are defective and have to be repaired by an adjustor, who works alone. It takes 200 to 400 minutes to adjust the set. The set then goes back for re-inspection.

It needs to be determined how long sets are delayed waiting for inspection and for readjustment. A total of 4800 minutes are simulated. On the basis of the block diagram in Figure 8.4, the program can be written as follows:

**Program 8.2**

```
        simulate
test    storage     2
        generate    55,20
begin   enter       test,q
        advance     90,30
        leave       test
        goto        fix,0.15
        terminate
fix     seize       fixer,q
        advance     300,100
        release     fixer
        goto        begin
        generate    4800
        terminate   1
        start       1
        end
```

The program involves both a statistical and an unconditional GOTO. GOTO FIX,0.15 implies that 15 percent of all transactions (on average) go to the block FIX SEIZE FIXER,Q, while 85 percent go straight to the TERMINATE block. By using Q as B operands of both the ENTER and the SEIZE blocks it is possible to gather the desired statistics on waiting times.

In Section 14.1, this program will be modified by allowing the probability of error to change: instead of the constant 0.15 increasing from 0.1 to 0.2 over time in order to reflect increasing weariness as the day progresses.

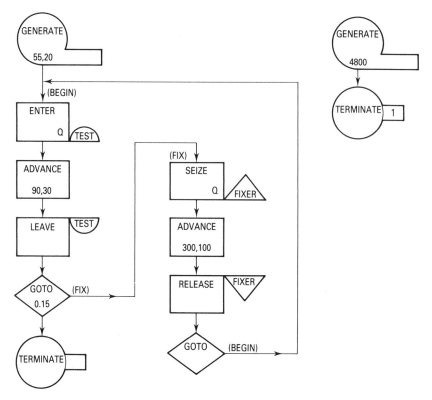

**Figure 8.4** Block diagram of Program 8.2

---

## Exercise 8.1

Draw a GPSS block diagram and write a GPSS program for the following problem.

    Customers arrive at a food store with InterArrival Times between 3 and 9 minutes (with all times between 3 and 9 minutes being equally likely). Twenty-five percent of the customers go to the fish counter, run by one person, who needs between 17 and 23 minutes to serve a customer (with 20 minutes as the average). Customers wait on a first-come, first-served basis at this counter. The remaining 75 percent of the customers go to the meat counter, where two butchers of equal ability serve them, which takes between 8 and 24 minutes. There is a single waiting line in front of the meat counter. No customer goes to both the fish and the meat counter.

    Simulate a day of eight hours to find out the maximum waiting line in front of the fish counter and how many customers waited more than 10 minutes, 20 minutes, etc., at the meat counter. Assume that all service stops after exactly eight hours and all customers then have to leave.

**Exercise 8.2**  (Based on Exercise 3.10 in Banks and Carson, 1984)

Ambulances are dispatched at a rate of one every 10 ± 7 minutes in a large metropolitan area. Fifteen percent of the calls are false alarms which require 12 ± 2 minutes to complete. All other calls can be one of two kinds. The first kind are classified as serious. They constitute 25 percent of the non-false alarm calls and take 25 ± 5 minutes to complete. The remaining calls take 20 ± 10 minutes to complete. Assume that there are three available ambulances, and that they are on call at any time. Simulate the system for 500 calls to be completed. Give statistics on how long serious alarm cases have to wait before an ambulance is on its way.

**Exercise 8.3**  (Based on Exercise 3.25 in Banks and Carson, 1984)

People arrive at a self-service cafeteria at the rate of one every 30 ± 20 seconds. Forty percent go to the sandwich counter where one worker makes a sandwich in 60 ± 30 seconds. The rest go to the main counter where one server spoons the prepared meal on to a plate in 45 ± 30 seconds. All customers must pay a single cashier, which takes 25 ± 10 seconds. For all customers, eating takes 20 ± 10 minutes. After eating, 40 percent of the people return to buy a coffee and pay the cashier for this. Drinking coffee takes 10 ± 2 minutes. Simulate a day of five hours. The output should include data on average time spent in the cafeteria, maximum number of people at any time and average waiting time in front of the cashier.

**Exercise 8.4**  (Based on case study 2E in Schriber, 1974)

In a garment factory there are 50 sewing machines operated eight hours a day, five days a week. There is a problem in that machines break down on average every 157 hours (with times between break-downs varying between 132 and 182 hours). If there are fewer than 50 machines available, production is lost, leading to a loss of $20 an hour for each machine break-down. The broken machines are brought to a repair shop, where between 4 and 10 working hours are needed to repair a machine. In order to make up for the time lost owing to the broken machines being repaired, reserve machines can be brought in. How many repairers are needed in the repair shop and how many reserve machines ought there to be?

Each alternative would be simulated for three years of 52 weeks of 40 hours. Although it is desirable to test various numbers of repairers and reserve machines, only write the specific GPSS program for the case of three repairers and three reserve machines, hence allowing for a total of 53 machines. (Remember that only 50 of the 53 machines can be used at the same time.)

Draw the GPSS block diagram and write a GPSS program for this simulation,

which will provide output from which it is possible to calculate the total cost of
production lost through having too few machines.

---

## *Exercise 8.5*

Modify Program 7.4 so that instead of starting production of a unit of A every 25
minutes and one of B every 50 minutes, production of a unit of A or B commences as
soon as the lathe has free capacity. Compare the results of this new program with
those of Program 7.4.

# 9  The IF block

## 9.1 The Standard Numerical Attribute

In the preceding chapter we studied the GOTO block, which in its simplest form is very similar to the GOTO concept of many ordinary programming languages like BASIC, FORTRAN, etc. In these languages another concept is even more important, namely the IF concept, which allows program execution to follow different paths dependent on certain conditions which vary according to different data. The IF statement has its corresponding IF block in micro-GPSS.

Before turning to the details of the IF block, we must examine a very fundamental GPSS concept, the Standard Numerical Attribute, abbreviated SNA. An SNA is a variable, which takes the value of some specific system attribute. When an SNA is referred to by a transaction entering a block, the SNA has the present (i.e. current) value of that system attribute.

In the examples in this chapter only one SNA will be used – the length of a queue or an AD set, i.e. either the number of people waiting in front of a facility or the number of transactions that have entered an ARRIVE block, but have not yet entered the corresponding DEPART block. The queue (AD set) statistics contain the length of this queue (or AD set) at the time of the simulation stop (see e.g. item 8 in Table 6.1). By using an SNA we can determine the value of this queue length at *any* time during the simulation.

The SNAs have different symbolic names. The length of a queue or AD set has the name Q, followed by a $-sign, in turn followed by the name of the queue or the AD set. Thus, if there is a block SEIZE SAL,Q, as in Program 6.1, Q$SAL refers to the length of the queue SAL, i.e. the number of transactions that are waiting in front of the facility SAL. Likewise, if there is a block ARRIVE TIM and a block DEPART TIM, as in Program 6.2, Q$TIM refers to the number of transactions that have entered block ARRIVE TIM, but have not yet entered the block DEPART TIM.

In later chapters several other SNAs will be used, but in Section 9.5 I will briefly refer to the SNA which gives the current contents of a *storage*. This SNA is called S$ followed by the storage name.

## 9.2 Syntax of the IF block

The IF block consists of a test condition and an address to which the transaction goes if the condition is fulfilled.

The test takes place between the A and B operands and these two operands are separated not by a comma but by one of the following six sets of characters:

1. >   : greater than

2. >= : greater than or equal to

3. =   : equal to

4. <> : not equal to

5. <   : less than

6. <= : less than or equal to

The C operand, which is *compulsory* in micro-GPSS, is the address to which the transaction in the IF block goes if the test condition is true. If the condition is *not* true, the transaction proceeds to the next block.

We put the relationship symbol, e.g. <>, *between* the A and B operands, as in the block symbol of the IF block, which is shown in Figure 9.1. Once again a diamond is used, but this time with a horizontal line across the middle. The IF is written below this line and above it is written the relationship, here denoted by X, which stands for >, >=, =, <>, < or <=. The A operand is written to the left and the B operand to the right, so that the whole relationship to be tested can be read above the line.

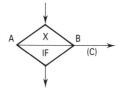

**Figure 9.1** Block symbol of IF

The C operand is written in parentheses to the right, *below* the line which leads to the block with the address of the C operand.

As regards the A and B operands it is necessary to distinguish between two types of IF blocks. The first, called the SNA type, is very similar to that of BASIC and involves Standard Numerical Attributes and constants. This form is discussed and exemplified in Sections 9.2–4. The second, called the server type, involves server names and is presented and exemplified in Sections 9.5 and 9.6.

Having studied the SNA concept in general and Q$ in particular in Section 9.1, the use of the IF block involving SNAs will now be studied.

IF Q$LIN=4,BYE implies a test of whether or not Q$LIN = 4, i.e. whether or not there are four transactions in the queue LIN. If this condition is *true*, the transaction goes to the address BYE. If the condition is *false*, the transaction goes to the next block.

Thus the micro-GPSS IF block works like a BASIC statement: IF LIN = 4 THEN 100, i.e. if LIN is 4 then the transaction goes to the address with the label 100. The difference from BASIC is that micro-GPSS uses names instead of numbers as addresses and a comma instead of THEN.

GPSS V does not have this simple IF statement with SNAs but uses instead the TEST block. Besides a different key-word, there are several important differences:

1.  There are no characters between the A and B operands. GPSS V requires instead special auxiliaries (G, GE, E, NE, L, LE) placed in a special format after the operation code, but before the operands.

2.  The TEST block works in a completely opposite way to the IF block of General Programming Languages. If the TEST condition is true, the transaction proceeds to the next block, but if it is false, it goes to the address in the C operand. This difference in terms of other programming languages has been known to cause many errors by students.

3.  The C operand is optional. The use of the C operand of the TEST block is, however, in most situations highly recommended even in GPSS V. For some programs omitting the C operand will slow down execution dramatically.

The TEST block of GPSS V generally leads to the code being much more complicated. GPSS V requires, e.g., TEST NE Q$LIN,4,BYE or TEST LE Q$LIN1,Q$LIN2,BACK, which are more difficult to read and understand than the corresponding IF Q$LIN=4,BYE or IF Q$LIN1 > Q$LIN2,BACK of micro-GPSS.

In order to be more compatible with GPSS V, the micro-GPSS processor *also* allows use of these more complicated TEST blocks. The micro-GPSS processor will, however, *require* a C operand. (See Appendix B.)

In this context it should be mentioned that micro-GPSS also has an IF block with a value assignment, which will be presented in Section 15.3. This powerful concept does not exist in GPSS V.

## 9.3 Program 9.1

In the one-person barber shop of Program 6.1, the waiting line became quite long (a maximum of eight was obtained, see Table 6.1) and consequently waiting times were also quite long (67 minutes on average). It is probable that customers do not wish to wait that long for service. When they arrive at the shop, they will probably look at the length of the waiting line and leave if it contains more than a certain number of people. Let us, for example, assume that the barber shop has only four chairs for waiting and that a customer will therefore leave, if there are four people already waiting. To model this, it is sufficient to add the block IF Q$SAL=4,BYE and an additional TERMINATE block with the address BYE to Program 6.1. The block diagram of this new program is in Figure 9.2.

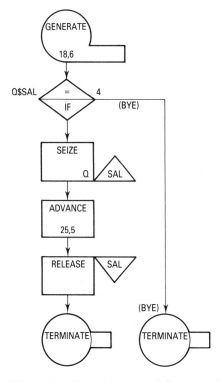

**Figure 9.2** Block diagram of Program 9.1

The IF block comes directly after the GENERATE block, i.e. the customers will *not* join the waiting line if there are four people already waiting. Hence, if there are, e.g., three people waiting, a customer will join the waiting line, which will then contain four people. If four people are already waiting, he will not do so, but will instead go to the TERMINATE block, with the address BYE (written on top on the left-hand side). The reason for having separate TERMINATE blocks is that in the block statistics it can be clearly seen how many customers were lost because of too long a waiting line.

The program can be written straight from the block diagram. Note the address BYE in the address field of the second TERMINATE block (block 7).

**Program 9.1**

```
              simulate
1             generate    18,6
2             if          q$sal=4,bye
3             seize       sal,q
4             advance     25,5
5             release     sal
6             terminate
7    bye      terminate
8             generate    480
9             terminate   1
              start       1
              end
```

The program works as follows: when the first customer arrives, there is obviously no waiting line, i.e. Q$SAL = 0. (The SNA Q$ is always automatically set to 0 at the start of the simulation.) The first customer will thus enter and go directly into service (in the ADVANCE block). The value of Q$SAL is then still 0. If the second customer arrives, while the first customer is still in service, the second customer will have to wait in front of the SEIZE block, i.e. as a member of the queue SAL, making Q$SAL = 1. In this way Q$SAL can increase in value as the simulation proceeds.

As long as Q$SAL < 4, each customer joins the waiting line. Once Q$SAL becomes 4 the next customer will not join, but will go directly to BYE TERMINATE. Hence the maximum length of the waiting line in this example is 4.

From the total count of block 7 in the block statistics in Table 9.1 it can be seen that four customers were lost.

From the queue statistics in the computer output a few figures can be taken to compare with the corresponding case where there is no IF block (i.e. Program 6.1) (see Table 9.2). The maximum length of the waiting line has decreased from 8 to 4, and the total number of customers joining the line has

**Table 9.1** Block statistics of Program 9.1

```
Block counts
Number Adr.  Oper. Current  Total
    1        GENER    0       27
    2        IF       4       27
    3        SEIZE    0       19
    4        ADVAN    1       19
    5        RELEA    0       18
    6        TERMI    0       18
    7   BYE  TERMI    0        4
    8        GENER    0        1
    9        TERMI    0        1
```

**Table 9.2** Comparison of queue statistics of Programs 6.1 and 9.1

|            | Entries | Maximum contents | Average time/ transaction |
|------------|---------|------------------|---------------------------|
| Without IF | 27      | 8                | 67                        |
| With IF    | 23      | 4                | 60                        |

decreased from 27 to 23, owing to the four customers lost because the line was too long. Finally, the average waiting time has decreased somewhat. This average time now applies to fewer people.

# 9.4 Program 9.2

I shall now turn to another example of how the IF block is used, this time with SNA values for both the A and the B operand. This example concerns the other form of parallel servers (i.e. not the storage type), namely when each server has its own waiting line, as in a supermarket, where there is a separate waiting line in front of each checkout counter. The storage concept cannot be used in this case, since this would presuppose that there is a joint waiting line for all checkouts. Rather than using a somewhat inaccurate model, we shall instead use several facilities, working in parallel, even though these facilities might be similar as regards service times.

In this chapter we shall discuss a very simple supermarket with only two checkout counters. (Chapter 16 covers supermarkets with many checkout counters.) It is assumed that the two counters are identical as regards service time.

When there are two identical facilities, the crucial question is which checkout counter a customer chooses. If one checkout counter is free, while the other one is busy, the customer will naturally proceed to the one which is free. If both checkout counters are busy, then the customer goes to the one with the shortest waiting line.

Thus there are two things to consider: is one of the checkout counters idle, and (if this is not the case), which checkout counter has the shortest waiting line? It might be thought that two separate tests are required. However, this can be achieved with only one IF block, which makes a test involving an AD set that measures the number of transactions that have chosen one specific checkout counter, but have not yet finished obtaining service there. Figure 9.3 shows the particular set of blocks that defines this AD set.

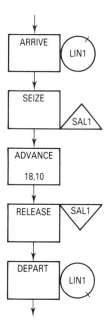

**Figure 9.3** Block diagram of the ARRIVE–DEPART pair of Program 9.2

From this part of the total block diagram note the following: since Q$LIN1 refers to *all* transactions that have entered the block ARRIVE and have not yet reached DEPART, Q$LIN1 involves *both* the customers who are in the actual waiting line before the block SEIZE SAL1 *and* the customer who is now being served at the checkout counter, i.e. is in the ADVANCE block. If the checkout counter is idle then Q$LIN1 = 0. If one person is being served but there is no waiting line then Q$LIN1 = 1. Otherwise, i.e. if there is a waiting line, Q$LIN1 is equal to the number of customers in this waiting line plus 1, i.e. *plus* the one person being served.

If there are several such checkout counters, each with its own AD set of this type, then if the customers go to the counter with the shortest AD set, they will go first to the one which is idle and, if all are busy, to the one with the shortest waiting line.

This example is, as mentioned, limited to the case of only two checkout counters. Let us assume that customers arrive with InterArrival Times varying between 3 and 13 minutes and that the service time at a checkout counter varies between 8 and 28 minutes. This is represented in the block diagram in Figure 9.4.

A customer arriving at the store decides whether Q$LIN1 > Q$LIN2. If this is the case, i.e. the number of customers (waiting or being served) at checkout counter 1 is greater than the corresponding number at checkout

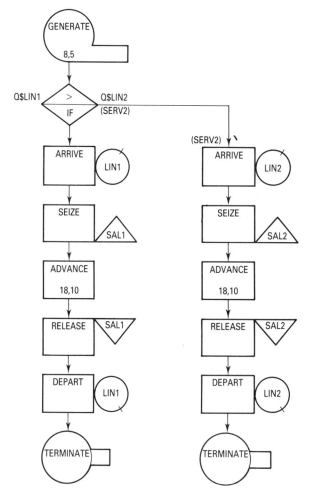

**Figure 9.4** Block diagram of Program 9.2

counter 2, the newly arrived customer goes to the second checkout counter (at the address SERV2) in the right-hand part of the customer segment. If this is not true, the customer goes to the next block, i.e. to checkout counter 1.

Note that if both checkout counters are idle, or the two checkout counters have equally long waiting lines, the customer goes to the first checkout counter, perhaps because it is the one closest to the entrance.

The program is closely related to the block diagram.

**Program 9.2**

```
        simulate
        generate    8,5
        if          q$lin1>q$lin2,serv2
        arrive      lin1
        seize       sal1
        advance     18,10
        release     sal1
        depart      lin1
        terminate
serv2   arrive      lin2
        seize       sal2
        advance     18,10
        release     sal2
        depart      lin2
        terminate
        generate    480
        terminate   1
        start       1
        end
```

It yields the AD set statistics shown in Table 9.3. From these statistics the following can be seen: at simulation stop, after eight hours, the AD set of people at counter 1, Q$LIN1, is 7, i.e. the checkout counter is busy and there are six people waiting in line. Likewise, the contents of Q$LIN2 (= 6) imply that the second counter is also busy and that five people are waiting in line there.

## 9.5 The server type of IF block

It should be mentioned that SNAs can deal with servers, e.g. the contents of a storage (S$ followed by storage name) and that it is thus possible to carry out

**Table 9.3** AD set statistics of Program 9.2

| Queue<br>(AD set) | Maximum<br>contents | Average<br>contents | Total<br>entries | Zero<br>entries | Percent<br>zeros |
|---|---|---|---|---|---|
| LIN1 | 7 | 4.10 | 34 | 0 | 0.00 |
| LIN2 | 7 | 3.74 | 28 | 0 | 0.00 |

| Queue<br>(AD set) | Average<br>time/trans | $Average<br>time/trans | Current<br>contents |
|---|---|---|---|
| LIN1 | 57.88 | 57.88 | 7 |
| LIN2 | 64.08 | 64.08 | 6 |

$Average time/trans=average time/trans excluding zero entries

tests on these SNAs. However, in order to carry out certain common tests on servers in a very simple and efficient manner, micro-GPSS also allows for a *server form* of IF block.

The A operand then consists of a server name, i.e. the name of a facility or storage, and the B operand consists of a code representing one of the following six conditions:

1. U   : (The facility is) in **Use**

2. NU : (The facility is) **Not** in **Use**

3. E   : (The storage is) **Empty**

4. NE : (The storage is) **Not Empty**

5. F   : (The storage is) **Full**

6. NF : (The storage is) **Not Full**.

The A and B operands are here separated by =.

Note that, if the capacity of STOR is defined to be 3 units (by the statement STOR STORAGE 3), then

```
STOR = E,   if STOR contains 0;
STOR = NE,  if STOR contains 1, 2 or 3;
STOR = F,   if STOR contains 3; and
STOR = NF,  if STOR contains 0, 1, or 2 units.
```

The C operand is, as before, the address where the transaction goes if the condition is fulfilled. Thus IF SAL=U,BYE reads 'If SAL is in Use, go to BYE' and IF STOR=E,BEGIN reads 'If STOR is Empty, go to BEGIN'.

In GPSS V this type of IF block must be represented either by a TEST block with SNAs or by a GATE block. Using TEST, GPSS V would have TEST G S$STOR,0,BEGIN instead of IF STOR=E,BEGIN. The GPSS V GATE block is presented briefly in the next chapter and in Appendix B.

## 9.6 Program 9.3

Taking Program 9.1 as a starting point, assume furthermore that if the facility (= salesperson) is busy, *no* customer wants to wait, but all customers decide to leave. The easiest way to model this is to use an IF block with a server name in the A operand and a condition in the B operand, like IF SAL = U,BYE. Except for the corresponding change in the IF block, the block diagram would be the same as in Figure 9.2. The program looks as follows:

**Program 9.3**

```
         simulate
         generate    18,6
         if          sal=u,bye
         seize       sal,q
         advance     25,5
         release     sal
         terminate
bye      terminate
         generate    480
         terminate   1
         start       1
         end
```

When a customer arrives, he will go directly to BYE if the facility SAL is busy. In this case no waiting line would be built up, as would be seen from the empty queue statistics. The SEIZE and RELEASE blocks are still needed in order to inform the IF block whether the facility is in use or not. Running this program once, the block statistics show that almost half of all customers are lost in spite of facility utilization being less than 70 percent.

---

### Exercise 9.1 (Exercise 3.30 in Banks and Carson, 1984)

The University of Lower Altoona has one computer terminal. Students arrive at the terminal every 15 ± 10 minutes to use the terminal for 12 ± 6 minutes. If the terminal is busy, 60 percent will come back in 10 minutes to use the terminal. If the terminal is still busy, 50 percent (of the 60 percent) will return in 15 minutes. Given that 500 students complete their work on the terminal, calculate how many students fail to use the terminal over the same period. The terminal is used and in demand 24 hours a day.

---

### Exercise 9.2 (Exercise 3.34 in Banks and Carson, 1984)

Jiffy Car Wash is a five-stage operation that takes 2 ± 1 minutes for each stage. There is waiting room for six cars. The car wash facility holds five cars which move through the system in order, one car not being able to move on until the car ahead of it moves. Cars arrive every 2.5 ± 2 minutes for a wash. Estimate the balking rate per hour. That is, how many cars drive off per hour? Simulate for one 12-hour day.

---

### Exercise 9.3

Modify Program 7.2 to take into account the fact that newspaper buyers will not wait in the '7–11' store if there are already four people in the waiting line. Instead they will buy their paper from the boy selling papers on the nearby street corner. The boy also has his 'own' customers arriving with an InterArrival Time of 60 ± 20 seconds. It takes him 45 ± 30 seconds to sell a paper. How many papers will the boy sell? How are waiting times in the store affected?

---

### Exercise 9.4

Modify Program 9.2 regarding the store with two checkout counters to take into consideration the fact that customers will not wait if there are already three people waiting in the *shortest* waiting line.

# 10 The WAITIF block

## 10.1 Syntax of the WAITIF block

Besides the IF block, micro-GPSS has a special kind of IF block called the WAITIF block. This block refers to specific conditions concerning facilities and storages and works in what is called a WAIT-mode. The conditions to be tested are described by A and B operands in exactly the same way as for IF blocks in the server-mode in Section 9.5. The A operand is the name of the facility or the name of the storage. The B operand is the letter code of one of six different conditions: U (in **U**se), NU (**N**ot in **U**se), E (**E**mpty), NE (**N**ot **E**mpty), F (**F**ull), NF (**N**ot **F**ull). The A and B operands are separated by =.

The WAITIF block does *not* have any C operand, in contrast to the IF block, which always has a C operand.

The block diagram symbol of the WAITIF block differs very little from the symbol of the IF block: it contains the word WAITIF, it only involves '=' and there is no line to the right, since WAITIF *never* has a C operand.

A      =      B

WAITIF

**Figure 10.1** Block symbol of WAITIF

The WAITIF block implies the following: *if, and as long as*, the waiting conditions of the A and B operands are fulfilled, the transaction has to wait. Thus WAITIF STOR=E implies that the transaction waits if and as long as the storage STOR is empty. As soon as the condition is *not* fulfilled, the transaction proceeds to the next block.

The checking of the wait condition is done the first time when the transaction comes to the WAITIF block. If the condition is *not* true, the transaction will immediately proceed to the next block, just as with the ordinary IF block. Otherwise it will have to wait as long as the condition is true.

The transactions that have to wait are, from the block point of view, waiting in the block preceding the WAITIF block. From the processor point of view they are waiting on a special list for this WAITIF block.

*Each* time a transaction engages or disengages a server, e.g. through an ENTER, LEAVE, RELEASE or SEIZE block, the micro-GPSS processor will check if there are any waiting transactions on any WAITIF list referring to this server, for which the waiting condition is now no longer true. The following then happens: the processor picks up one transaction at a time from the waiting transactions, starting with the transaction that has waited the longest. It lets this transaction go through the WAITIF block, and the transaction is then brought as far forward in the segment as possible. When this transaction is halted, the processor checks to see if the waiting condition is still no longer true, in which case it allows another transaction to go through the WAITIF block and so on.

It should be stressed that there is no sense in using a WAITIF block immediately before a SEIZE or ENTER block referring to the same server, since the transaction will in any case wait before the SEIZE or ENTER block. Thus it is meaningless to have, e.g., WAITIF SAL = U immediately followed by SEIZE SAL.

GPSS V uses a similar but more complicated block – GATE. In GPSS V the B operand of the micro-GPSS WAITIF block is placed as what is called an auxiliary operator after the operation GATE. There is also an additional initial S in the case of storages, e.g. SE instead of E for Empty. The B operand of the GATE block is an optional address for a *false* result of the test condition, unlike micro-GPSS. As with the IF block, the testing is done in the reverse way, so that the transactions wait if the test condition is *false*. In order to increase compatibility, the micro-GPSS processor also allows for the GPSS V GATE block. (See Appendix B.)

## 10.2 Proper close-down of a store

In all our simulations we have until now assumed a very abrupt stop. If this were taken literally it would imply the following in the barber shop case of Program 6.1: at closing time, after 480 minutes, the barber would stop cutting the hair of the customer sitting in the barber's chair and throw him out of the shop! He would also throw out all the customers who are waiting! This is obviously a simplification made in the hope that the desired statistics, e.g. on the length of the waiting line, would not be very different from those of a program in which a more realistic close-down was simulated.

A realistic close-down in a store would probably include the following assumptions: at closing time, no new customers are let into the store, but all customers inside the store at closing time obtain service. Thus not only the customers just being served at closing time, but also those in the waiting line, are served. The simulation can be closed down only when all those waiting have been served.

This proper close-down hence requires two specific things:

1. At closing time the door is locked so that no new customers can enter.

2. The simulation continues until all those still waiting after closing time have gone out, i.e. the simulation is stopped when the store is empty. In order to keep track of whether the store is empty or not, a storage is defined to represent the total capacity of the store in which people can wait. By having all customers ENTER and LEAVE the store we can keep track of the number of people inside the store.

When studying the block diagram of this program in Figure 10.2 below, let us look first at the *stop segment*. When the stop transaction arrives at time 480 it will seize the facility LOCK, which implies that the door is then closed. (The facility LOCK comes into Use.) After this, the stop transaction is kept in front of a WAITIF block as long as the store is **Not Empty**, i.e. STOR = NE. Only when the store is finally empty, is the stop transaction allowed into the TERMINATE block to close the store. The store will thus be closed as soon as the store is empty of customers after time 480.

It should be noted that it is *not* necessary to have a block RELEASE LOCK. The effect of a SEIZE block not followed by a corresponding RELEASE block, is that the facility becomes busy for the remainder of the simulation. This is permissible in this case, since the store is not to be re-opened after closing time.

We shall now consider the *customer segment*. Immediately after the GENERATE block the customers will come to a WAITIF block, representing the door to the store. At this point the customers check whether or not the door is locked, i.e. whether or not the facility LOCK is in Use. If the LOCK is in Use, i.e. the door is locked, the customer cannot enter the store. If the door is still open, the customers enter the store, i.e. go to the ENTER STOR block. Provided STOR has been given a substantial capacity (see below), all customers will be able to enter. STOR is used as a kind of counter to indicate when the store is empty.

The customers next come to the blocks SEIZE SAL, ADVANCE 25,5 and RELEASE SAL, which are all the same as in Program 6.1.

After the RELEASE block the customers come to the LEAVE STOR block and will hence leave the storage STOR. The moment that the last customer to enter the store comes to this LEAVE block, the store becomes empty. Then the stop transaction waiting in front of the block WAITIF STOR=NE

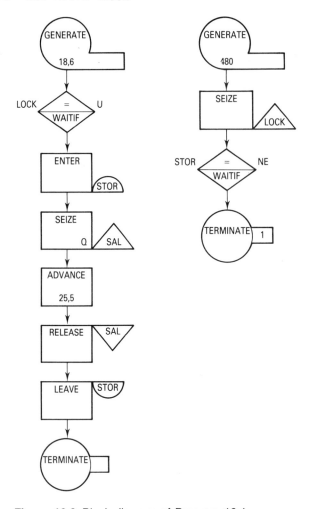

**Figure 10.2** Block diagram of Program 10.1

will be able to go through this block to terminate the simulation. The block diagram of this program is shown in Figure 10.2.

The program also uses a STORAGE definition statement. Since there is no reason to put a limit on the number of people waiting in the store, the A operand of the STORAGE statement is omitted. This gives the store STOR a very large capacity.

The whole program, Program 10.1, is presented below.

The program produces the block statistics shown in Table 10.1. It can be seen that the simulation (i.e. the store) is finally closed down over 200 minutes after closing time. At this time (684.13) there are 11 customers in

**Program 10.1**

```
               simulate
               qtable      sal,0,10,20
         stor  storage
 1             generate    18,6
 2             waitif      lock=u
 3             enter       stor
 4             seize       sal,q
 5             advance     25,5
 6             release     sal
 7             leave       stor
 8             terminate
 9             generate    480
10             seize       lock
11             waitif      stor=ne
12             terminate   1
               start       1
               end
```

the current count of block 1, i.e. 11 customers were locked out after the closing time of 480. This means that if the door had been open for new customers until time 684.13, 11 more customers would have arrived. The current count in all other blocks is 0, i.e. there are no customers left inside the store.

**Table 10.1** Block statistics of Program 10.1

Relative clock      684.13 Absolute clock      684.13

Block counts

| Number | Adr. | Oper. | Current | Total |
|--------|------|-------|---------|-------|
| 1      |      | GENER | 11      | 38    |
| 2      |      | WAITIF | 0      | 27    |
| 3      |      | ENTER | 0       | 27    |
| 4      |      | SEIZE | 0       | 27    |
| 5      |      | ADVAN | 0       | 27    |
| 6      |      | RELEA | 0       | 27    |
| 7      |      | LEAVE | 0       | 27    |
| 8      |      | TERMI | 0       | 27    |
| 9      |      | GENER | 0       | 1     |
| 10     |      | SEIZE | 0       | 1     |
| 11     |      | WAITIF | 0      | 1     |
| 12     |      | TERMI | 0       | 1     |

The QTABLE statistics would reveal that waiting times really become extreme. Some customers will wait over three hours!

## 10.3 WAITIF blocks in a traffic system

The next example of WAITIF blocks deals with a very simple version of a problem often solved by GPSS simulations, namely traffic systems, in particular the timing of traffic lights.

Let us consider a simple street crossing (e.g. in New York City) with two one-way streets. No right turns are allowed on red and all traffic has to wait for a green light. When a car has to stop for a red light it loses time in two ways. Firstly, it has to wait until the light turns green; secondly, having stopped for a red light, it will take a certain length of time before the car can accelerate up to the speed it would have had if it had not stopped for the red light. In our system we shall thus consider the part of the intersection in which the cars' speed is affected because of stopping at the lights. Once the lines 'back to normal speed' are reached, the effect of the traffic lights is over. These lines thus define the boundaries of the system studied.

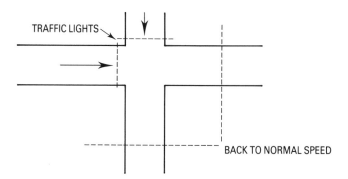

**Figure 10.3** Picture of street crossing in Program 10.2

Program 10.2 contains four segments: one segment generating the traffic lights; two segments for cars, with one for each street, and finally a stop segment. Only the block diagrams for the traffic light segment and for one of the two street segments will be studied here. The other street segment is virtually identical. The traffic light segment is shown in Figure 10.4. This is a loop, similar to that of the workers putting pots in the oven (Program 8.1). The start of the traffic light system is at time 0. First it turns on the red light for street 1 and it stays red for this street for 50 seconds; after this it

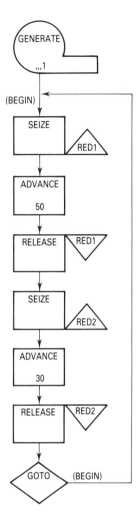

**Figure 10.4** Traffic light segment of Program 10.2

turns off the red light for street 1 and turns on the red light for street 2, which is the busier street. Here it is only red for 30 seconds. After this it goes back to turn on the red light for street 1 again. There is hence an infinite loop, turning on the red light for street 1 for 50 seconds and then for street 2 for 30 seconds in a continuous cycle.

Let us now examine the segment for one of the streets, namely the less busy street, street 1. Cars arrive here on average every 20 seconds, but with IATs varying between 13 and 27 seconds. On the busier street, street 2, they arrive with IATs ranging from 8 to 16 seconds, which is the only difference between the two segments, except that DIR1, RED1, WAIT1 and JOIN1

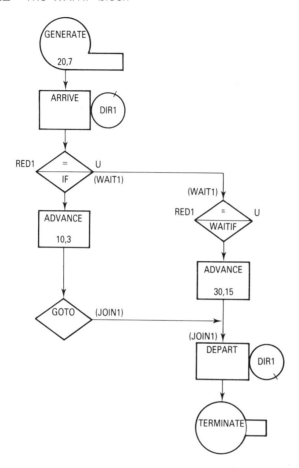

**Figure 10.5** Street segment 1 of Program 10.2

become DIR2, RED2, WAIT2 and JOIN2.

A car first enters the AD set DIR1, used for measuring the total time spent by the cars on street 1 at this crossing. Note that the ARRIVE DIR1 block comes immediately after GENERATE and the DEPART DIR1 block immediately prior to TERMINATE.

Next the car comes to the block IF RED1=U,WAIT1, implying that if the red lights on street 1 are in Use, i.e. are *on*, it goes to WAIT1; otherwise it proceeds to the next block, i.e. to ADVANCE 10,3, implying that the car drives at normal speed, taking $10 \pm 3$ seconds, to leave the area being modeled (see Figure 10.3 above). It then leaves the system by way of the DEPART block.

If the facility RED1 is on, i.e. there is a red light on street 1, the car proceeds, as mentioned, to the right-hand part of the segment, i.e. to the

**Program 10.2**

```
        simulate
* Light segment
        generate    ,,,1
 begin seize        red1
        advance     50
        release     red1
        seize       red2
        advance     30
        release     red2
        goto        begin
* Street 1 segment
        generate    20,7
        arrive      dir1
        if          red1=u,wait1
        advance     10,3
        goto        join1
 wait1 waitif       red1=u
        advance     30,15
 join1 depart       dir1
        terminate
* Street 2 segment
        generate    12,4
        arrive      dir2
        if          red2=u,wait2
        advance     10,3
        goto        join2
 wait2 waitif       red2=u
        advance     30,15
 join2 depart       dir2
        terminate
* Stop segment
        generate    14400
        terminate   1
        start       1
        end
```

address WAIT1. In this way the cars that have to wait are separated from those that do not have to wait. The address WAIT1 is for the block WAITIF RED1=U. The car is kept waiting here as long as the red light RED1 is on. After this the car goes into ADVANCE 30,15, implying that it requires between 15 and 45 seconds to leave the intersection, i.e. to reach normal speed again. It then goes through the DEPART and TERMINATE blocks.

The reason for using both a WAITIF block and an IF block is that it is necessary to keep certain cars waiting, dependent on RED1, and to have these cars go through a different ADVANCE block from the other cars. If there was only the WAITIF block, it would not be possible to have the waiting cars go through their own ADVANCE block which includes time for acceleration. If, on the other hand, there was only an IF block, it would not be possible to keep the cars waiting, while the red light was on. Hence both types of block are necessary.

Since there is no true closing down of the street intersection, an ordinary stop segment is used, arbitrarily closing down the simulation after a certain number of hours, e.g. four hours, i.e. 14 400 seconds.

It is interesting to vary the time values of the A operands of the ADVANCE blocks in the traffic light segment, in order to see if the time spent by cars in the intersection can decrease. Actual case studies have shown considerable improvements in traffic flow by changing traffic light times from those of present policies. A large-scale use of this kind of simulation of traffic light systems could significantly cut down the time spent motoring in metropolitan areas without significant costs.

---

### Exercise 10.1 (Example 5–10 in Gordon, 1975)

A doctor opens an office at 2 p.m. Patients arrive at the rate of one every $8 \pm 2$ minutes beginning at 2 p.m. The office can hold up to 10 patients, including the patient being examined. If the office is full patients are turned away. The patients are examined, one at a time, for $10 \pm 5$ minutes. The office is closed at 5 p.m. but the doctor will see patients who are still waiting at that time. What time will the doctor finish work, and how many patients will have been examined?

---

### Exercise 10.2 (Based on an example of Section 12–4 in Gordon, 1975)

A port is to be simulated. Ships come to this port from two sources.

Ships from one source are ready to sail every $15 \pm 10$ hours. They will not sail, however, unless there is a high tide. The tide changes every 12 hours. It will be high tide 6 hours after the start of the simulation.

When a ship sets out it travels for $6 \pm 2$ hours before selecting a route. It prefers to go to the particular port to be simulated, port 1, and will do so if it knows there is a free berth at that time. If not, it goes to another port, port 2. After a ship has selected port 1 it takes $40 \pm 10$ hours to reach this port and to get a berth. It might have to wait here for a free berth, since it cannot reserve a berth in advance. Port 1 has five berths.

Ships from the other source arrive at port 1 every 30 ± 15 hours irrespective of the tide and of whether there is a free berth or not. Unloading and loading will take 65 ± 30 hours for ships from either source.

Run the simulation for 1000 ships that leave port 1 to estimate the average utilization of the berth capacity of port 1.

## Exercise 10.3

Close down the US and Soviet stores in Exercise 7.1 in a proper way, i.e. so that no new customers are allowed into the stores after closing time, but all other customers are served before the stores are closed down. Do not change the old programs of Exercise 7.1 more than necessary.

## Exercise 10.4

In traffic systems like that of Program 10.2 it is possible that when the light is green for a short time (i.e. there is a red light on the other street), all the cars waiting might not be able to cross the street before the traffic light turns red again. Take this problem into account by modifying Program 10.2 according to the following assumptions: before crossing the street each car will be in the position of first car in the waiting line. It will be in this position for 1–3 seconds and from there can cross the street only if there is a green (i.e. not red) light.

# 11 Priority and service interruption

## 11.1 Introduction

We have until now assumed a strict FIFO (first-in, first-out) discipline for all waiting lists, implying that the customer who has waited the longest time will be the first one to leave the waiting line. Furthermore, no transaction has been allowed to interrupt the service given to other transactions.

In this chapter different kinds of queuing disciplines will be allowed. Some customers will be permitted to go ahead of other customers in the waiting lines by being given a higher priority. A customer (or more generally a transaction) can obtain this higher priority, either at the moment of generation (as described in Section 11.2) or some time afterwards during the simulation (as described in Section 11.3). Finally, in Sections 11.4–6 we shall study how certain transactions can be allowed to interrupt the service of other facilities.

## 11.2 Priority established by the E operand of the GENERATE block

In the earlier example of a '7–11' store used in Programs 7.1 and 7.2 there were two types of customer: newspaper buyers and food buyers. Both categories had to wait in line for fairly substantial times. For food buyers this might not be unreasonable, but for newspaper buyers, who require short service times, it might be annoying. It might hence be advisable to allow the newspaper buyers to go to the front of the waiting line, since they require such short service times. This can be achieved by giving the newspaper buyers a higher priority than the food buyers.

The priority level can be determined by the E operand of the GENERATE block. Until now we have only used the A, B, C and D operands of this block without perhaps even realizing that there was an E operand. We have hence used the default value of the E operand, which is 0. The E operand defines the priority level of the transaction generated in the GENERATE block. Hence with the E operand set to 0 above, all transactions have been on the *same* 0 level of priority. This E operand is in micro-GPSS a constant with a value from 0 to 99 999.

A transaction that has a higher priority level than another transaction will always go ahead of the other transaction in a waiting line, regardless of how long this other transaction has waited. The waiting line discipline is thus as follows: exit from the waiting line occurs first of all in accordance with the priority level. Only for transactions with the *same* priority level will a FIFO discipline hold, implying that the customer who has waited the longest among those with the same priority leaves the waiting line first. In other words, priority overrules waiting time. Thus if the newspaper buyers in Program 7.2 are to go ahead of the food buyers in the waiting line, the GENERATE block of the newspaper buyer segment should be as follows:

    GENERATE 120,30,,,1

Note that there are three commas between the B operand and the E operand, indicating the default values of the C and D operands in the general expression GENERATE A,B,C,D,E. The letters, not the commas, are deleted.

In this case the newspaper buyers are generated with a priority level 1, while the food buyers are generated with the E operand having the default value as in the earlier program, and have priority level 0. This implies that the newspaper buyers will go ahead of the food buyers in every waiting line.

This can be illustrated with Program 11.1, which is identical to Program

**Table 11.1** Queue statistics of Program 11.1

| Queue (AD set) | Maximum contents | Average contents | Total entries | Zero entries | Percent zeros |
|---|---|---|---|---|---|
| NEWSQ | 4 | 1.04 | 420 | 15 | 3.57 |
| SAL | 7 | 2.52 | 558 | 28 | 5.02 |
| FOODQ | 4 | 1.48 | 138 | 13 | 9.42 |

| Queue (AD set) | Average time/trans | $Average time/trans | Current contents |
|---|---|---|---|
| NEWSQ | 124.96 | 129.59 | 1 |
| SAL | 227.68 | 239.71 | 3 |
| FOODQ | 540.31 | 596.50 | 2 |

**$Average time/trans=average time/trans excluding zero entries**

7.2, except that the GENERATE block for the newspaper buyers now has 1 in the E operand. It might produce the queue statistics shown in Table 11.1, to be compared with the earlier queue statistics in Table 7.2.

Note that there is a drastic reduction in the waiting times for the newspaper buyers. The average waiting time for the food buyers has increased somewhat, but the average waiting time for *all* customers has decreased, because of the large decrease in waiting times for the newspaper buyers who constitute the majority of the customers.

Let us study another example of the use of GENERATE with an E operand. The problem is based on the barber shop in Program 6.1. Assume that the barber SAL now takes a lunch break of 30 minutes as soon as possible after 1 p.m. (The shop opens at 9 a.m.) This implies that SAL takes his lunch break as soon as he has finished with the person being served at 1 p.m. The waiting customers are assumed to remain waiting during the lunch break. We are only interested in how this will affect queuing times, not utilization.

The simplest way to model this in micro-GPSS is to have a special lunch transaction. This can be thought of as a friend coming to take SAL to lunch. One such transaction is generated so that it arrives exactly 240 minutes after simulation start. Since SAL gives priority to lunch even if customers are waiting, the lunch transaction is generated with priority. Thus both the D and the E operands are set to 1.

The lunch transaction now renders SAL busy for 30 minutes during which SAL cannot serve customers. This is accomplished by SEIZE SAL, ADVANCE 30 and RELEASE SAL. The block diagram of the segment dealing with the lunch transaction is shown in Figure 11.1 together with the whole program.

From the queue statistics it can be seen that the average waiting time has increased by approximately 10 minutes. The facility utilization statistics are, however, misleading since they include lunch time. To obtain correct facility statistics a somewhat more complicated program is needed (see Exercise 17.7).

Finally, it should be mentioned that giving a transaction a higher priority level does more than allow the transaction to go ahead in the waiting lines. It also allows an event to have a certain priority when scheduled on the future events list. This is covered in Section 11.3, which deals with changes of priority during the course of the simulation. It should be noted that what is said in Section 11.3 regarding the effect of priority in the list of future events also refers to the initial priority setting using the GENERATE block. However, the higher priority level does *not* include the right to interrupt service. This requires other blocks dealt with in Section 11.4.

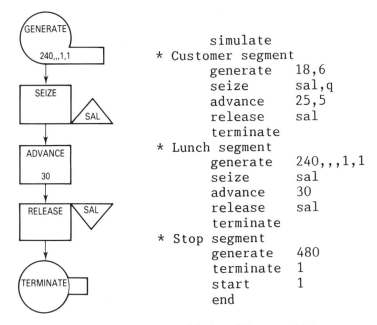

```
             simulate
* Customer segment
             generate   18,6
             seize      sal,q
             advance    25,5
             release    sal
             terminate
* Lunch  segment
             generate   240,,,1,1
             seize      sal
             advance    30
             release    sal
             terminate
* Stop  segment
             generate   480
             terminate  1
             start      1
             end
```

**Figure 11.1** Lunch segment and listing of Program 11.2

## 11.3 Changing priority during the course of the simulation

In the preceding section a transaction had the same priority during its whole life in the simulation and this was determined only by the GENERATE block. In this section we shall also study how to change the priority level for a transaction after it has left the GENERATE block. This change in priority level is accomplished by a specific block, PRIORITY, with an A operand. The symbol is shown in Figure 11.2. The main rectangle has the operation PRIORITY written inside and a smaller rectangle on top contains the A operand.

The A operand is a non-negative constant and is the new priority level given to the transaction. The A operand has to be positive (or 0) and in micro-GPSS it is at most a five-digit number, i.e. the priority level can take a value

**Figure 11.2** Block symbol of PRIORITY

0,1,...99 999. We can also use an SNA as A operand (see e.g. Program 20.8), provided the SNA value < 100,000. No default value is allowed for the A operand.

When a transaction enters a PRIORITY block, it is given the priority level of the A operand. This will have two effects:

1. Most importantly, the transaction will go ahead of all transactions with a lower priority in any waiting line it joins, be it in front of a server or a WAITIF block.

2. If a future event involving this transaction is scheduled to occur at *exactly* the same time as another event, the event with the higher priority will be executed first.

Program 11.3 will exemplify effect (1) and Program 11.4 effect (2).

## 1. Example of priority in a waiting line – Program 11.3

At an attraction at an amusement park, 50 percent of the children who have taken a ride want to repeat the ride. Those who already have taken the ride have to wait in line after those who have not yet taken the ride. Hence a child will have a higher priority when he is a new arrival than when he has already taken the ride. The block diagram and the program listing are in Figure 11.3. Note the GENERATE block with three consecutive commas (indicating default values on the C and D operands) and the priority in the E operand set to 1.

After completing the ride, i.e. after releasing the attraction, a child's priority is decreased to 0, so that he will wait after the newly arrived children. Before the TERMINATE block there is a statistical GOTO. Fifty percent of those who have taken the ride will be content and go to TERMINATE, while the other 50 percent will go to the address BEGIN, i.e. to the ENTER RIDE block, for yet another ride. Thus those who have taken a ride repeat the ride with 50 percent probability, implying that (in the long run) half the children make one ride, 25 percent two rides, 12.5 percent three rides, etc.

The program produces the block statistics shown in Table 11.2. At time 300 there is a waiting line of 4 in block 6, representing four children who have taken at least one ride and want to take another. There are no newly arrived children waiting in block 2.

If the block PRIORITY 0 is deleted and this modified program (= Program 11.3b) is then run, the block statistics change. Three newly arrived children would be waiting in block 1 and only one child would be waiting for a repeated ride. Thus the priority block does have an important effect.

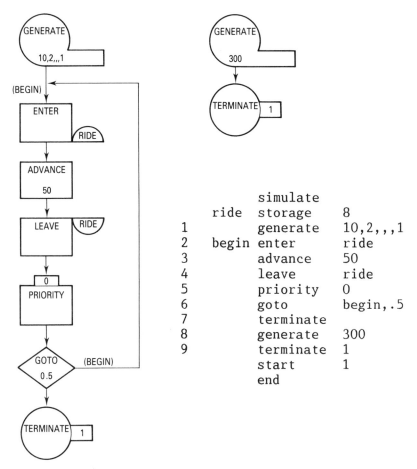

```
                          simulate
                ride    storage     8
         1              generate    10,2,,,1
         2      begin   enter       ride
         3              advance     50
         4              leave       ride
         5              priority    0
         6              goto        begin,.5
         7              terminate
         8              generate    300
         9              terminate   1
                        start       1
                        end
```

**Figure 11.3** Block diagram and listing of Program 11.3

## 2. Correct order of simultaneous events – Program 11.4

As already mentioned, at each stage of execution the GPSS processor picks up the most imminent event, i.e. the event with the lowest event time. We still need to consider what will happen when two events are scheduled to occur at *exactly* the *same* time. In this situation an event involving the transaction with a higher priority will occur before the event involving the transaction with a lower priority. If the two events have the same priority, the programmer *cannot* generally control which event is picked up first. Priority must therefore be assigned, if it is important to execute one event before another when they are simultaneous. However, on the list of future events,

**Table 11.2** Block statistics of Program 11.3

Relative clock     300.00 Absolute clock     300.00

Block counts

| Number | Adr. | Oper. | Current | Total |
|--------|------|-------|---------|-------|
| 1 | | GENER | 0 | 30 |
| 2 | BEGIN | ENTER | 0 | 45 |
| 3 | | ADVAN | 8 | 45 |
| 4 | | LEAVE | 0 | 37 |
| 5 | | PRIOR | 0 | 37 |
| 6 | | GOTO | 4 | 37 |
| 7 | | TERMI | 0 | 18 |
| 8 | | GENER | 0 | 1 |
| 9 | | TERMI | 0 | 1 |

priority will only have an effect on events scheduled to occur at the same time.

Table 11.3 summarizes the effects of priority as compared to waiting/scheduling time.

As an example of the effect on simultaneous events we shall study a program, dealing with the store of Program 9.3, where no customers wish to wait, but rather leave the store. If in this program a customer arrival and a service completion are scheduled to occur simultaneously at a time when the server is busy, the order of execution of these two events will be of great importance. If the customer arrival is executed first, the arriving customer will find the server busy and hence leave the store. If on the other hand the service completion is executed first, the customer will find the server idle and stay.

It appears most realistic to assume the second type of order. If a customer arrives at the moment when the server is in the process of finishing service, the server will probably inform the arriving customer that he or she is almost ready to serve. The customer will then enter. Therefore it is desirable to schedule service completion first. This is done by increasing the priority level prior to the ADVANCE block, where service completion scheduling takes place. Program 11.4 is obtained. The block diagram for the customer segment and the program listing are shown in Figure 11.4.

**Table 11.3** Effect of priority and time

| | For ordering in | |
|---|---|---|
| | Waiting lines | Future events lists |
| 1st criterion | Priority | Scheduling time |
| 2nd criterion | Waiting time | Priority |

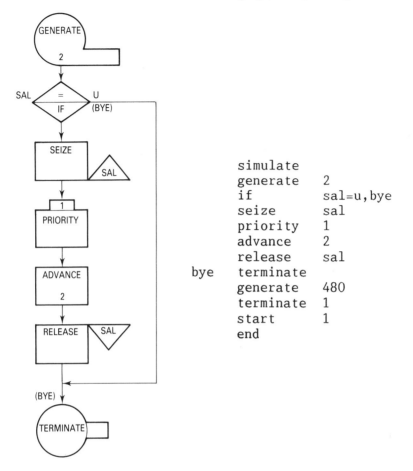

```
          simulate
          generate    2
          if          sal=u,bye
          seize       sal
          priority    1
          advance     2
          release     sal
bye       terminate
          generate    480
          terminate   1
          start       1
          end
```

**Figure 11.4** Block diagram of customer segment and listing of Program 11.4

In principle the PRIORITY block could be placed in front of the SEIZE block, but it is generally easier to understand the program if the PRIORITY block is in front of the ADVANCE block. In order to ensure that a customer arrival will come at exactly the same time as a service completion, the operands of the GENERATE and ADVANCE blocks are such that all IATs and service times = 2.

A run of this program shows that all 240 customers generated obtain service. The importance of the PRIORITY block becomes clear when the program is re-run *without* this block (= Program 11.4b). Then only half the customers will be served, while the rest will proceed directly to TERMINATE, because their arrival will now be scheduled prior to the service completion.

It should finally be mentioned that this usage of PRIORITY to distinguish between simultaneous primary events is much more important in GPSS V, where clock values only take integer values, than in micro-GPSS, where the clock can take any real value. When only integer values are involved there are far fewer possible values and hence much greater probability of two events being scheduled at the same time.

# 11.4 Service interruption

Sections 11.2 and 11.3 discussed how the priority level of a transaction could be established and changed respectively. This referred to the transaction's priority in waiting lines and also to the order in which simultaneous events involving this transaction were executed. It should again be stressed that the priority level does *not* refer to any kind of interruption of service. Thus the newspaper buyers in Program 11.1 were allowed to go to the front of the waiting line, but they were *not* allowed to interrupt the service given to a food customer. The newspaper buyers could only be served when the food buyer had finished his or her purchase.

It is, however, possible in GPSS to have some transactions interrupt service, e.g. to let a newspaper buyer interrupt the service given to a food buyer. Service interruption then implies that the food buyer halts his or her shopping temporarily, while the newspaper buyer pays for his paper.

The modeling of this service interruption requires a special pair of blocks – PREEMPT and RETURN.

It should first be stressed that service interruption applies *only* to *facilities*, not to storages. Here is one important difference between a facility and a storage which has its capacity defined as 1. Because only facilities allow for interruption, PREEMPT is similar to SEIZE, while RETURN is similar to RELEASE.

## The PREEMPT block

Chapter 11 only deals with the case where the PREEMPT block has an A operand only, while PREEMPT's B operand is covered in Chapter 20.

The block symbol is shown in Figure 11.5. It is almost identical to that of the SEIZE block. The only difference, except for the operation, is that the A operand triangle is now drawn with double lines. As with the SEIZE block, the A operand is the name of the facility. The A operand is compulsory.

The PREEMPT block of the type studied here (without a B operand) is used only in programs where some transactions use a facility by entering a SEIZE block, while others – the preempting transactions – use it by entering a PREEMPT block. Hence, the A operand of the PREEMPT block must be the

**Figure 11.5** Block symbol of PREEMPT

same symbolic name as that used as the A operand of a SEIZE block somewhere else in the program, probably in another segment.

Now, if a transaction tries to enter a PREEMPT block, there are three possibilities:

1. The facility is idle. The PREEMPT block then works exactly as the SEIZE block would. The transaction is admitted into the PREEMPT block and the facility is made busy.

2. The facility is busy and the transaction that has made it busy did so by entering a PREEMPT block. The PREEMPT block, used without a B operand, does not allow a preempting transaction to interrupt another preempting transaction. Thus a transaction entering the PREEMPT block cannot interrupt another transaction that has also come to the facility through a PREEMPT block. Therefore, the PREEMPT block will in this case have to wait: in the block sense in the block prior to the PREEMPT block; in the processor sense on a special waiting list, until the facility becomes idle again.

3. The facility is busy and the transaction that has made it busy did so by entering a SEIZE block. This is a true service interruption, which requires a more detailed explanation.

Let us here first distinguish between two transactions:

1. The SEIZE transaction, called ST below, which is a transaction that has made the facility of the A operand of the PREEMPT block busy by previously entering a SEIZE block. It should at this point be noted that micro-GPSS requires that this SEIZE block is followed in the same segment by an ADVANCE block without any GOTO, IF or WAITIF (or GPSS V equivalent) block, or without an ENTER or another SEIZE block, coming between the SEIZE block and the ADVANCE block. Otherwise errors might occur.

2. The PREEMPT transaction, called PT below, which is the transaction now going into the PREEMPT block.

When the PT attempts to enter the PREEMPT block referring to a facility that is giving service to an ST, the following happens:

(a) The ST's service is interrupted. The processor records the remaining service time of the ST, i.e. the time remaining until its scheduled exit from the ADVANCE block, if it had not been interrupted.

(b) The ST is then placed on a special waiting list, to return later back into service, before any transactions waiting in front of the SEIZE block are allowed to go into service.

(c) The PT goes into service, i.e. it goes through the PREEMPT block and on to an ADVANCE block, which schedules the service completion time of the PT, i.e. the time when the PT will try to leave the ADVANCE block.

## The RETURN block

Just as RELEASE is the mirror image of SEIZE, RETURN is the mirror image of PREEMPT. Hence the PT leaves the facility through a RETURN block. The symbol is shown in Figure 11.6. The only difference in the symbol as compared to RELEASE, besides the operation, are the double lines in the triangle for the A operand.

**Figure 11.6** Block symbol of RETURN

The A operand is the symbolic name of the facility to be disengaged. The A operand is compulsory. It should be the same name as that used in the PREEMPT block in the *same* segment. Note that there should be a complete pair in the same segment, not merely a PREEMPT block or merely a RETURN block. The transaction must have gone through the PREEMPT block before reaching the RETURN block.

RETURN implies different things, depending on whether or not the transaction, now coming to the RETURN block, previously caused the PREEMPT block to act like a SEIZE block or to cause a true service interruption.

I shall first deal with the case when PREEMPT works like SEIZE. This happens, as mentioned, when the facility is idle at the time of the PT entering the PREEMPT block or is busy with another PT. In this case, the RETURN block acts like a RELEASE block. Since there is no service interruption, the only thing that happens is that the transaction goes through the block and the facility becomes idle. The processor then checks whether there is any transaction waiting, which can now be served by the facility.

In the other case, when there is a true service interruption, the following happens.

Firstly, the PT goes through the RETURN block and moves on as far as possible.

If there is no other PT waiting in front of the PREEMPT block, but only STs waiting (in the block sense prior to the SEIZE block), then the facility becomes busy again with the interrupted ST. As mentioned above, the processor would have recorded how much service time remained for this ST when it was interrupted. This ST will now be moved back from the special waiting list and is re-scheduled on the list of future events to attempt to exit from the ADVANCE block at the present clock time *plus* this remaining service time. It will thus be scheduled to stay in the ADVANCE block for the service time which remained when it was interrupted.

If there is another PT waiting in front of the PREEMPT block, this new PT will go into the facility first, before the ST can obtain service again. This PT can be seen as interrupting the service of the ST again. It should be noted that the same ST can be preempted several times, e.g. after getting into service again for a short time.

It should be stressed that the PREEMPT–RELEASE pair in no way affects the priority levels of the transactions. Therefore, one must often complement the PREEMPT block with a specific determination of priority, e.g. in the E operand of the GENERATE block.

It should finally be mentioned that Q as the B operand for a SEIZE block will *not* work for a facility that can also be preempted. Thus, in a program where we use both SEIZE and PREEMPT blocks for a certain facility, we need pairs of ARRIVE and DEPART blocks to gather statistics on the time spent waiting in front of this facility.

As we have seen, the use of the PREEMPT–RETURN block pair is fairly complicated. I hope the presentation of two examples below will make it somewhat easier to understand these blocks.


## 11.5 The '7–11' store revisited

Let us return to the '7–11' store with food and newspaper buyers which was discussed earlier. We shall now allow the newspaper buyers to preempt the food buyers. Program 11.1 is now changed to obtain Program 11.5 and the block diagram for the two customer segments is shown in Figure 11.7. The program listing is also given.

In contrast to Program 11.1, in *both* segments there is an extra AD pair regarding TOTQ. This is in order to measure the total waiting line, since Q as the B operand of SEIZE SAL is no longer allowed owing to the existence of PREEMPT SAL. Apart from this addition the food buyer segment is as

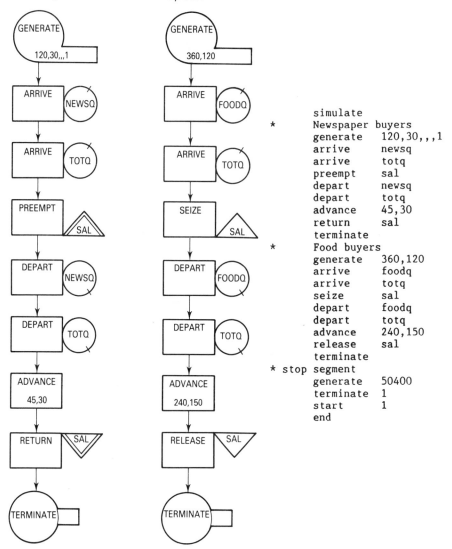

```
           simulate
    *      Newspaper buyers
           generate    120,30,,,1
           arrive      newsq
           arrive      totq
           preempt     sal
           depart      newsq
           depart      totq
           advance     45,30
           return      sal
           terminate
    *      Food buyers
           generate    360,120
           arrive      foodq
           arrive      totq
           seize       sal
           depart      foodq
           depart      totq
           advance     240,150
           release     sal
           terminate
    * stop segment
           generate    50400
           terminate   1
           start       1
           end
```

**Figure 11.7** Block diagram and listing of Program 11.5

before, but the newspaper customer segment needs to be studied more closely.

In this segment the 1 in the E operand of the GENERATE block remains, since we still wish the newspaper buyers to go first in the waiting line. Without this priority the following could occur: a newspaper buyer comes to the PREEMPT block, but SAL is already busy with another newspaper buyer. The newly arrived newspaper buyer then has to go into the waiting line, and without priority might have to go behind a food buyer. By

**Table 11.4** Queue statistics of Program 11.5

| Queue (AD set) | Maximum contents | Average contents | Total entries | Zero entries | Percent zeros |
|---|---|---|---|---|---|
| NEWSQ | 1 | 0.00 | 421 | 421 | 100.00 |
| TOTQ | 17 | 7.86 | 564 | 426 | 75.53 |
| FOODQ | 16 | 7.86 | 143 | 5 | 3.50 |

| Queue (AD set) | Average time/trans | $Average time/trans | Current contents |
|---|---|---|---|
| NEWSQ | 0.00 | 0.00 | 0 |
| TOTQ | 702.68 | 2871.84 | 16 |
| FOODQ | 2771.43 | 2871.84 | 16 |

$Average time/trans=average time/trans excluding zero entries

keeping the E operand of the GENERATE block, we ensure that newspaper buyers will not get behind food buyers in the waiting line.

The PREEMPT–RETURN pair allows a newspaper buyer to interrupt a food buyer. When the newspaper buyer goes through the RETURN block, the food buyer will come back into service for the part of the scheduled service time which remained at the time of the interruption, provided there is no other newspaper buyer waiting to interrupt again.

Finally let us consider the queue statistics that might be generated (see Table 11.4). The newspaper buyers now do not have to wait at all, but waiting times for the food buyers increase drastically compared to Table 11.1. In order to be able to say anything more certain about total waiting time, one would have to run the model many times and use a carefully planned experimental design. This will be discussed in Chapter 18.

# 11.6 A secretarial pool

The second example of PREEMPT deals with the administration of secretarial work in a company. At present, the president has a secretary, who works only for him and has no other tasks. The secretarial tasks of the other employees are handled by three secretaries, who work in a secretarial pool. Thus all these general tasks go into this pool and are handled by the first secretary available in the pool.

The present situation has led to some problems. While there is often a long waiting line for the general tasks at the secretarial pool, the utilization of the president's secretary (called PSEC) is not very high (less than 50 percent). A consultant has therefore suggested an arrangement whereby PSEC can to some extent be involved in the pool to do general tasks, when idle. Furthermore, the president should be able to use the pool if PSEC is busy.

The president is, however, afraid of obtaining a poorer service than before. The consultant therefore outlines the following specific proposal: the president's tasks would first of all go to PSEC. If she was busy (with whatever job), the task would go to the pool. If this was also fully occupied, the task would go back to PSEC. She would in this case interrupt her present work, if this was a general task, and instead carry out the president's task. She would resume work on the interrupted general task only when the president's task was finished. General tasks would first of all go to the pool. If the pool was completely occupied, the task would go to PSEC. If she was busy, the work would return to the pool to go into a waiting line there.

The question arises of how service would change if this proposal was implemented. Therefore the consultant wishes to do a simulation study, comparing the present system with the proposed system.

For this study the following is assumed: the InterArrival Times for the president's tasks vary between 20 and 50 minutes, while the IATs for the general tasks vary between 6 and 18 minutes. The president's tasks take between 15 and 25 minutes, when carried out by PSEC, and between 16 and 30 minutes when performed by someone in the pool, since the secretaries in the pool are less experienced. The general tasks take between 20 and 40 minutes when done in the pool and between 17 and 33 minutes when done by PSEC.

## Present system – Program 11.6

It is in many cases desirable to simulate the present system in addition to the proposed system. This is because differences due to stochastic variations can be eliminated more easily when comparing the systems (see Chapter 18). The modeling of the present system is quite straightforward. The president's tasks will seize the facility PSEC and release it after going through ADVANCE 20,5. The general tasks will simply enter and, after ADVANCE 30,10, leave the storage POOL, defined with capacity 3 in the STORAGE statement. Pairs of ARRIVE–DEPART blocks are used to measure the total time it takes for a job of either type to be finished.

The program is as follows:

**Program 11.6**

```
        simulate
 pool   storage      3
* The president's  tasks
        generate     35,15
        arrive       pre
        seize        psec
        advance      20,5
        release      psec
        depart       pre
        terminate
* General tasks
        generate     12,6
        arrive       gen
        enter        pool
        advance      30,10
        leave        pool
        depart       gen
        terminate
        generate     400
        terminate    1
        start        1
        end
```

## Proposed system – Program 11.7

The modeling of the proposed system is more complicated so it is necessary to look at the block diagrams in this case.

Let us first examine the block diagram of the president's tasks in Figure 11.8.

An ARRIVE block comes after the GENERATE block and a DEPART block comes immediately before the TERMINATE block (as in Program 11.6). This AD set PRE hence measures the total time required to complete the president's tasks.

Next, the task goes into the block IF PSEC=U,POL1. This will allow the tasks that should normally go to PSEC to go to the pool if PSEC is busy. At the pool part we have a new IF block which leads the task back to PSEC if the pool is fully occupied. PSEC will in that case be interrupted, if she is busy with a general task. For this return to PSEC a connector symbol (a circle with 1 inside) is used in the block diagram in order to avoid a very long connecting line.

It should be noted that the block pairs PREEMPT and RETURN are

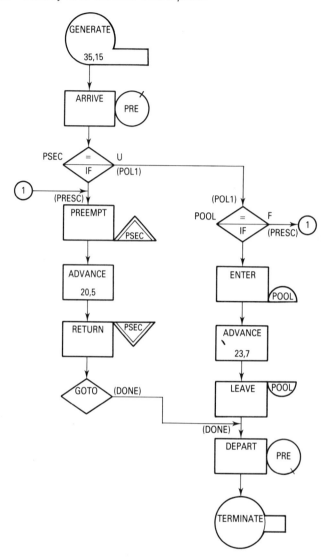

**Figure 11.8** Block diagram of president's tasks

*also* used when PSEC is idle. If PSEC is idle, PREEMPT works just as SEIZE, and RETURN just as RELEASE. In this way the program is shorter and the risk of having one presidential task interrupt another is avoided.

Figure 11.9 contains the block diagram of general tasks.

This is a similar kind of diagram. First there is an IF block, which leads to another IF block at PSECG if the pool is fully utilized. This IF block, in turn, tests the facility PSEC, and leads the general tasks back to the pool if PSEC is busy.

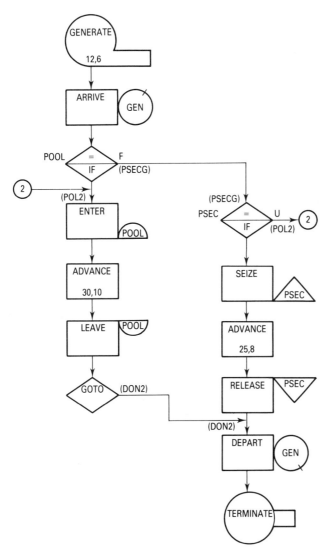

**Figure 11.9** Block diagram of general tasks

The full program, listed below, simulates a day of 400 minutes.

Running the program and comparing the outputs with that of the old system (modeled in Program 11.6), it can be seen from the facility and storage statistics that the utilization of PSEC has increased, while the utilization of the pool has decreased. This has had the beneficial effect of reducing the average time needed for the presidential tasks without increasing the time for the general tasks very much. If similar results were

**Program 11.7**

```
        simulate
pool  storage      3
* The president's tasks
        generate     35,15
        arrive       pre
        if           psec=u,poll
presc preempt        psec
        advance      20,5
        return       psec
        goto         done
poll  if             pool=f,presc
        enter        pool
        advance      23,7
        leave        pool
done  depart         pre
        terminate
* General tasks
        generate     12,6
        arrive       gen
        if           pool=f,psecg
pol2  enter          pool
        advance      30,10
        leave        pool
        goto         don2
psecg if             psec=u,pol2
        seize        psec
        advance      25,8
        release      psec
don2  depart         gen
        terminate
* Stop segment
        generate     400
        terminate    1
*
        start        1
        end
```

obtained when running the program a number of times, a switch to the new system would probably be recommended.

## Exercise 11.1

Modify Program 7.6 so that one of the two salespeople only works part-time – for three hours a day, starting at noon and stopping at 3.00 p.m. The store opens at 9.00 a.m. and closes at 5.00 p.m. Only statistics on waiting time are required.

## Exercise 11.2 (Case study 2C in Schriber, 1974)

In a factory a tool crib is manned by a single clerk. The clerk checks out tools to mechanics, who use them to repair failed machines. The time (in seconds) to process a tool request depends on the type of tool.

| Category of tool | Mechanic IAT | Service time |
|---|---|---|
| 1 | $420 \pm 360$ | $300 \pm 90$ |
| 2 | $360 \pm 240$ | $100 \pm 30$ |

The clerk has been serving the mechanics first-come, first-served, irrespective of their requests.

Owing to lost production it costs $9 per hour when a mechanic waits for service at the tool crib, regardless of the tool to be checked out. Management believes the average number of waiting mechanics can be reduced if Category 2 requests are serviced at the tool crib before those in Category 1.

Model the tool crib for each of the two queue disciplines indicated, simulating each case for an eight-hour work day. Does 'first-come, first-served, within Priority Class' reduce the average number of mechanics waiting in line? Calculate manually what daily savings in terms of cost of lost production can be realized when priority distinctions are made.

## Exercise 11.3 (Exercise 6–6 in Gordon, 1975)

An office has two copying machines. Secretaries from the general office arrive to use a machine at the rate of one every $5 \pm 2$ minutes. They choose a machine at random, whether it is busy or not, and they stay with their choice. A secretary from the president's office arrives at intervals of $15 \pm 5$ minutes. If a machine is free it is used. If not, the secretary goes to the head of the line for machine number 1. Assuming that all jobs take $6 \pm 3$ minutes, simulate the completion of 100 jobs of all types.

## Exercise 11.4  (Exercise 6–4 in Gordon, 1975)

Messages are created at the rate of one every 30 ± 10 seconds. They are sent over a communication channel, one at a time. Twenty percent of them require a reply, which returns over the same channel after a delay of 60 ± 30 seconds. Assume the transmission time for the original message to be 25 ± 15 seconds and for the reply 15 ± 5 seconds. Assume also that both messages and replies can be stored for transmission, if necessary. Compare the time it takes to complete 100 replies: (1) when the replies have priority and (2) when the messages have priority.

## Exercise 11.5  (Based on an example in Davies and O'Keefe, 1989)

At a hospital, patients arrive every 45 ± 15 hours for a short hospital stay of 30 ± 10 hours. Other patients arrive for an operation every 16 ± 4 hours. These patients must first have a pre-operative stay of 10 ± 5 hours, then an operation taking 1 hour followed by a post-operative stay of 7.5 ± 2.5 hours. The number of beds is limited to 20. When beds are not available, patients requiring only a stay in hospital are given preference over the patients requiring an operation. The operating theater is open only 8 hours and is then closed for 40 hours. Simulate for 14 full days of 24 hours.

# 12 General random functions

## 12.1 Introduction

Until now all GENERATE and ADVANCE blocks have used the rectangular distribution, where all values between the lower limit and the upper limit are equally likely. This is often a restrictive and unrealistic assumption, as might have been realized in connection with several of the programs in the preceding chapters.

The rectangular distribution is first of all a distribution which is completely *symmetric*. Many realistic distributions for InterArrival Times and service times are skewed. For example, in many situations, the majority of customers come with very short InterArrival Times, but a few customers come with very long InterArrival Times.

Secondly, the rectangular distribution is a distribution with sharply defined lower and upper limits. Many distributions are in reality instead characterized by 'tails', allowing for some very extreme values, which have very low probabilities.

Hence, it is desirable to be able to generate distributions other than the rectangular one. In principle, one would like to be able to generate any kind of distribution. GPSS provides for a very general methodology, which allows for the generation of any type of distribution. This chapter deals with defining functions of a random variable. At the end of the chapter these distributions will also be used in blocks other than GENERATE and ADVANCE blocks.

## 12.2 Discrete functions

In order to understand the main idea of a function definition in GPSS, let us start by considering a very simple distribution, based on empirical data. The idea is to generate each value of the function by a 'table look-up', whereby the probability of picking each value is proportional to the relative frequency of this value in the empirical distribution.

Let us assume that the service time of a certain facility has been measured and the empirical distribution shown in Table 12.1 was found.

**Table 12.1** Example of empirical distribution

| Service time | Frequency |
| --- | --- |
| 2 minutes | 15 percent |
| 5 minutes | 20 percent |
| 8 minutes | 40 percent |
| 12 minutes | 25 percent |

Next it is necessary to sample values from this distribution by generating uniform random fraction numbers between 0 and 1. The first step towards defining a function that relates such random numbers to the empirical values is to calculate the *cumulative* frequency. The cumulative frequency of a value is the sum of the relative frequencies of all values less than or equal to this value. This cumulative frequency will take values up to 1, since the cumulative frequency of the highest value will always be 1 (100 percent of all values are less than or equal to the highest value). Figure 12.1 shows the relationship between the original frequency distribution and the derived cumulative distribution.

The cumulative frequencies can be directly connected to the random number, since both take values between 0 and 1. This relationship between

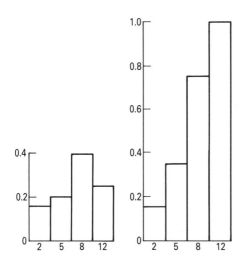

**Figure 12.1** Frequency and cumulative distribution

**Table 12.2** Table of cumulative frequency

| Service time | Frequency | Cumulative frequency | Corresponding random number |
|---|---|---|---|
| 2 | 0.15 | 0.15 | 0.00000–0.15 |
| 5 | 0.20 | 0.35 | 0.15001–0.35 |
| 8 | 0.40 | 0.75 | 0.35001–0.75 |
| 12 | 0.25 | 1 | 0.75001–1 |

the service time and the random number is shown in Table 12.2. A random number between 0 and 0.15 gives the service time 2; a random number between 0.15 and 0.35 gives the time 5, etc. This relationship between the random number and the service time is expressed in GPSS by function statements such as the following:

```
TIME  FUNCTION  RN2,D4
.15,2/.35,5/.75,8/1,12
```

There are two statements here; the first one is called the function header statement; the second the function data statement.

Let us look first at the function header statement. The address field contains the *name* of the function, in this example TIME. As discussed in more detail later, the value of the function will be called FN$TIME, since FN$ is the SNA of the function value. The operation field contains the operation, FUNCTION.

The compulsory A operand is the *independent* variable of the function. In the function presented above, the independent variable is the random number called RN2. This value is a uniform random fraction number sampled by random number generator 2. As mentioned earlier, micro-GPSS has eight different random number generators, producing different sequences of random numbers. (They are discussed in more detail in Chapter 18.) Thus RN4, for example, would be a random number produced by random number generator 4 and would be different from RN2. The actual value of RN2 will vary from call to call, since the generator will sample a different value each time it is used. The purpose of the function above is thus to relate a random number, RN2, produced by the second random number generator, to a specific service time, FN$TIME, which is the dependent variable.

The compulsory B operand is a code which also consists of two parts: first a letter, and then a number. The letter is C or D, where C stands for continuous and D for discrete. We shall in this section look at the discrete case (case D), and cover the continuous function (case C) in the next section. The number of the B operand is the number of pairs in the function data statement(s). In this example with four such pairs we therefore write D4.

The function data statement(s) contain the pairs defining the function. The first value in each pair is the independent variable, the random number, in this case RN2; and the second value represents the dependent variable, in this case FN$TIME. We can represent each such pair as a point on a diagram. The first value of each pair, the random number, is the value on the horizontal $x$-axis; hence it is the $x$-value; the second value, the service time value, is the value on the $y$-axis, i.e. the $y$-value.

We can thus also consider the values in the function data statement above as

$$x_1 = .15, y_1 = 2/x_2 = .35, y_2 = 5/x_3 = .75, y_3 = 8/x_4 = 1, y_4 = 12$$

Each pair can be plotted as a point as in Figure 12.2a below (left-hand side). This method of plotting the points is the same for both the discrete and the continuous cases. It shows what values $y$ takes for some specific values of $x$. The remaining problem lies in what value $y$ takes for values of $x$ other than those plotted. What is for example the value of $y$ when $x$ lies between $x_1$ and $x_2$?

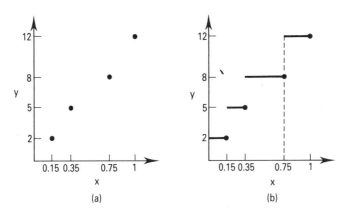

**Figure 12.2** Discrete function

In the discrete case this question can be answered by drawing from each point a horizontal line towards the left, until it reaches the $x$-value for the next point on the left, as shown in Figure 12.2b above (right-hand side).

We see that the left-most line is drawn until it reaches the $y$-axis, implying that $x = 0$. Hence the examples above yield the following results:

for $0 \le x \le .15$: $y = 2$

for $.15 < x \le .35$: $y = 5$

for $.35 < x \le .75$: $y = 8$

for $.75 < x \le 1$: $y = 12$

(It should, however, be noted that when $x$ is a random number, the highest value never quite reaches 1, only 0.999999; see Section 2.4.)

The above procedure can be compared with Table 12.2 and the discussion at the beginning of this section.

More generally, for the case of $n$ pairs, note that

for $0 \leq x \leq x_1$: $y = y_1$

for $x_{j-1} < x \leq x_j$ (where $2 \leq j \leq n$): $y = y_j$

Since the line is drawn towards the left, 1 must be the highest $x$-value. If the highest value was lower than 1, say 0.9, we would not know what $y$-value to assign if we sampled, e.g., RN2 = 0.95.

I shall now explain in detail how the pairs are written in the micro-GPSS data statement. As already mentioned, each value consists of a pair (independent variable, dependent variable), i.e. in the case studied here (random number, FN$-value). The random number value ranges from 0 to 1.

The above presentation demonstrates that the $x$-values have to be successively higher and higher, i.e. we require that

$x_1 < x_2 < x_3 < \ldots < x_n$, where $n$ is the number of pairs.

There is always a comma between the $x$-value and the $y$-value. All pairs are *separated* by a slash (/). It should be noted that there must *not* be a slash after the *last* pair of each statement.

We can write as many pairs as we like in one function data statement, provided no columns to the right of column 71 are used. Furthermore, there must not be any blank spaces inside or between the data pairs. As soon as a blank space is encountered, everything to the right of it will be disregarded by the GPSS processor.

The probabilities can be written with or without a 0 before the decimal point (e.g. both .7 and 0.7 are allowed). Furthermore, in line with the free format, the function data statement can start in any column, not necessarily column 1.

We do not have to put all pairs in one function data statement, but can have several such statements. However, we *cannot* split a single pair between two statements. The number of pairs in each statement is optional. The only important rule is that all function data statements follow in a direct sequence after the function header statement. Since the number of pairs is defined in this first statement, the GPSS processor will know how many pairs to look for. If not enough pairs are found, an error message will be printed.

The function statements are control statements to be placed at the beginning of the program, i.e. *before* the first GENERATE block, but after SIMULATE.

The rules for the function data statements are thus fairly complicated. Input of these data pairs can, however, be done much more easily using the GPSSMENU program (see Appendix C).

I shall now discuss how the discrete function is used. As mentioned, the function value is accessed using the SNA FN$, i.e. in this example FN$TIME. Hence, every time a block accesses or 'calls on' FN$TIME, a random number RN2 is sampled, i.e. produced by the second random number generator. Using the rules presented above, a value FN$TIME corresponding to this RN2 value is picked from the 'table', defined in the function data statement.

Let us next examine in detail how FN$TIME is used for sampling the service time in the block ADVANCE FN$TIME. The A operand of this ADVANCE block is FN$TIME and there is no B operand. Use of the ADVANCE block with *only* an A operand implies, as mentioned before, that the advance time is exactly the A operand.

When in the earlier examples, there was only an A operand (i.e. with the default-value $B = 0$), the A operand was a constant. The advance time then also became a constant. If, however, the A operand is FN$TIME, which has changing values from call to call, the advance time will also vary, even without a B operand. Hence a B operand is not needed in this case to cause the advance time to vary. When an FN$-value is used as A operand, a varying advance time will thus be obtained, provided the function is stochastic, i.e. that it depends on a random number, e.g. RN2.

Let us now turn to another discrete function. This will generate four IATs, 2, 3, 4 and 5 minutes, with equal probabilities. This cannot be done with GENERATE 3.5,1.5, i.e. with the A and B operands as constants. In micro-GPSS all *real* numbers between 2 and 5 would then be equally likely. To generate IATs of 2, 3, 4 and 5 minutes, each with 25 percent probability, depending on a random number, e.g. RN1, the following type of function definition can be used:

```
IAT FUNCTION RN1,D4
.25,2/.5,3/.75,4/1,5
```

The block GENERATE FN$IAT will then generate 2, 3, 4 and 5 minutes as equally likely InterArrival Times. (Program 16.1 will exemplify another method for generating integer random numbers.)

The following simple program illustrates the use of the discrete functions TIME and IAT defined above. If at most three people are allowed to queue, is it sufficient to have two salespeople in a store for arrivals following the function IAT and service times dependent on the function TIME? One way to answer this is to write Program 12.1. Running this we find that two salespeople are not enough, since there is a waiting line of eight at the end of the day.

**Program 12.1**

```
        simulate
*
 stor   storage     2
 iat    function    rn1,d4
.25,2/.5,3/.75,4/1,5
 time   function    rn2,d4
.15,2/.35,5/.75,8/1,12
*
        generate    fn$iat
        enter       stor
        advance     fn$time
        leave       stor
        terminate
        generate    480
        terminate   1
        start       1
        end
```

## 12.3 Continuous functions

While the preceding section dealt only with discrete functions, this section covers continuous functions. The main difference is with regard to the function header statement, where, as mentioned, the B operand starts with C instead of D.

As regards the function data statements, the syntax rules are the same as for the discrete case. In micro-GPSS there is only one difference as regards the values. The first value of the independent variable, i.e. the x-value in the first data pair, must be the lowest conceivable value of this independent variable. In the case studied here, i.e. functions of a random number, this implies that the first pair must start with the probability 0. The reason for this will be clear after the determination of the y-values for continuous functions has been explained. It is here that the difference between the continuous and the discrete functions can be seen clearly.

Let us look at the following function statements:

```
RTIM FUNCTION RN3,C6
0,15/.17,30/.32,50/.55,70/.75,80/1,90
```

This is a function where the value FN$RTIM depends on the random number RN3. The function is defined by six pairs and is continuous. Let us first plot the six pairs in Figure 12.3a, with the first value in the pair, the probability, plotted along the x-axis, and the second value, the FN$-value, along the *y*-axis. The question arises as to how the value of *y* is determined for any value *x* lying between two plotted *x*-values. It is in the determination of these 'inbetween-values' that the continuous function differs from the discrete one. Instead of drawing a horizontal line towards the left from a point, we obtain the *y*-values by *connecting* the points by straight lines, as shown in Figure 12.3b. A *y*-value is determined for an *x*-value as follows: draw a vertical straight line from the *x*-value until it reaches the curve composed of the straight lines connecting the points. From this intersection draw a horizontal line to the *y*-axis to obtain the desired *y*-value.

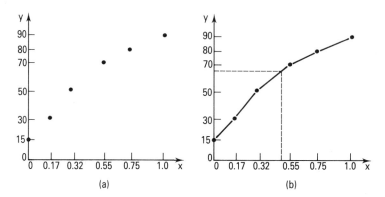

**Figure 12.3** Continuous function

For those with some mathematical background, the following is a more exact description: let us assume a value *x*, lying between $x_i$ and $x_j$. The slope of the line connecting the two points $(x_i, y_i)$ and $(x_j, y_j)$ is $(y_j - y_i)/(x_j - x_i)$.

The *y*-value thus becomes $y_i + (x - x_i)(y_j - y_i)/(x_j - x_i)$.

More generally, for *x* such that $x_j < x < x_{j+1}$,

$$y = y_j + (y_{j+1} - y_j)(x - x_j)/(x_{j+1} - x_j).$$

The *y*-value to be determined is hence the first of the two defined *y*-values *plus* the distance between the two defined *y*-values multiplied by the fraction that the distance between *x* and the lower defined *x*-value constitutes of the total distance between the two defined *x*-values.

As an example, if RN3 = 0.5, we obtain for function RTIM, defined above, $y = 50 + (70 - 50)(.5 - .32)/(.55 - .32) = 50 + 20 \star .78 = 65.6$.

This explains the micro-GPSS requirement that the first *x*-value must be the lowest possible *x*-value, in this case 0, and the last *x*-value must be the highest possible *x*-value, in this case 1. If $x_1 = 0.05$, *y* would be undefined for RN*j* < 0.05.

These are the only differences between continuous and discrete functions. Calling a continuous function is done in exactly the same way as in the discrete case, i.e. with FN$ followed by the function's name. Hence IATs can be generated according to the continuous function RTIM above by GENERATE FN$RTIM. Using a continuous function we can approximate virtually any function, since almost any function can be approximated by a succession of straight lines.

Finally, I shall deal with how rectangular distributions can be generated with continuous functions. It should first be noted that the GENERATE and ADVANCE blocks with the A and B operands as constants (as in all preceding programs) use RN*1*, i.e. random numbers produced by the *first* random number generator. As will be discussed in Chapter 18, there are in many cases good reasons for using a random number other than RN1 in GENERATE or ADVANCE blocks. In that case a function definition for the 'ordinary' rectangular distribution would also be required.

As seen in Section 12.2, a discrete function can produce a rectangular distribution, but it requires one data pair for every integer value. This would of course be very cumbersome for cases involving a great many values, e.g. when generating IATs between 200 and 400, i.e. corresponding to GENERATE 300,100. This would require 200 pairs when using a discrete function. A continuous function needs only two pairs in this case.

The function data statement which, together with the function header statement RECT FUNCTION RN2,C2, makes GENERATE FN$RECT correspond to GENERATE 300,100 is quite straightforward in micro-GPSS, namely 0,200/1,400. If RN2 = 0, FN$RECT = 200; if RN2 is almost 1, FN$RECT is almost 400 and, if RN2 is 0.5, FN$RECT = 300, i.e. the average. This is illustrated in Figure 12.4.

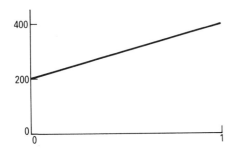

**Figure 12.4** A rectangular distribution (cumulative form)

In GPSS V the function data statement is written as 0,200/1,401. The reason for this is that GPSS V truncates real values into integer values and hence the highest value, obtained when RN2 = 0.999999, is INT(400.999) = 400.

As a simple example of the use of the continuous function let us rewrite Program 7.6 by using RN2 instead of RN1 for sampling the service times, ranging from 20 to 30 minutes. As will be discussed further in Chapter 18, it is highly appropriate to use one random number generator for the arrival of the customers and another one for the service times. In this way RN1 will only be used for arrivals and we will hence have the same arrival pattern regardless of whether we have one, two or three salespeople in the store. The output is very similar, but *not* identical, to that of Program 7.6. The differences are due to the use of RN2 instead of RN1 for the service time and the fact that the random number generators produce different sequences of 'random numbers. If RN1 is used instead (= Program 12.2b) *exactly* the same result is obtained as when Program 7.6 is used.

**Program 12.2**

```
        simulate
*
 stor   storage     2
 serv   function    rn2,c2
0,20/1,30
*
        generate    18,6
        enter       stor,q
        advance     fn$serv
        leave       stor
        terminate
        generate    480
        terminate   1
        start       1
        end
```

# 12.4 ENTER and LEAVE blocks with B operands

So far in this chapter functions have only been used in GENERATE and ADVANCE blocks. We shall also study how functions can be used in other ways. Before doing so, we must learn to use ENTER and LEAVE blocks with real B operands, i.e. B operands that are *not* Q.

Chapter 7 dealt with ENTER and LEAVE blocks with only an A operand. In this case each transaction only brings *one* unit into the storage, i.e. each transaction only requires one unit of free capacity in the storage in order to be able to enter the storage. In these two blocks a real (non-Q)

B operand is also allowed. This B operand is usually a constant, but does *not* have to be. It can also be, e.g., a function value, as will be exemplified in Programs 12.4 and 12.5. The value of the B operand, however, must be a positive integer.

The B operand defines how many units each transaction brings into the storage at the ENTER block or out of the storage at the LEAVE block. Defaulting on the B operand or setting it to Q, we have until now assumed that each transaction brings *one* unit into or out of storage. Thus it can be seen that the default value of the B operand is 1, and that Q as B operand is also equivalent to the number 1. Now allowing the B operand also to take any larger *integer* value (i.e. 2, 3 ... and upwards), we must clearly distinguish between the transaction and the number of units brought in or out of the storage by a specific transaction.

What I wrote earlier in Section 7.6 about ENTER and LEAVE must now be expanded. The block ENTER A,B implies that the transaction will only be able to enter the storage if the remaining free capacity of the storage $\geq$ B, i.e. there must be at least B units of remaining capacity. If this is true, the transaction will bring B units into the storage.

While the total block count increases by only one unit (block counts refer to transactions), the current contents of the storage is increased, and the remaining capacity decreased, by B units. If remaining capacity $<$ B, the transaction will not enter at all and hence no units will be brought into the storage. Thus, entry concerns either 0 or B units.

Let us consider a couple entering a restaurant. The transaction is the couple and their attempt to enter the restaurant can be modeled by the block ENTER RESTA,2. This implies that there must be space for both of them in the restaurant if they are to enter. If they do enter, there will be two more guests in the restaurant and two fewer seats free. If only one seat is free, they will both wait until two seats become free.

The capacity, defined in the STORAGE statement, refers to the maximum number of *units* that can be brought into the storage, and not to the number of transactions.

In addition some of the storage statistics presented in Section 7.7 will be affected. In particular, note the following (with the numbers referring to Table 7.5 in that section):

2. AVERAGE CONTENTS will refer to the number of units. In the above example the total time spent by all units will increase by two hours if the couple spends an hour in the restaurant.

4. ENTRIES also refers to the number of units. If the couple goes into the restaurant, the number of entries will increase by two. In this case with B $>$ 1, the ENTRIES statistics will differ from the total block count statistics.

5. AVERAGE TIME/TRANS is, however, *not* affected, since this refers strictly to transactions.

6. CURRENT CONTENTS refers to the units that have entered. This number will go up by two, if the couple enters. In this case with $B > 1$, this number will differ from the current count in the block statistics.

It should at this point be noted that if we have ENTER with a real B operand (e.g. 2) and want this block to initiate the gathering of queue statistics, we can place the Q as a C operand, e.g. as in ENTER STOR,2,Q.

The usage of the B operand of ENTER and LEAVE will be illustrated with Program 12.3 dealing with a coffee shop with 20 seats. Customers either come singly or as couples. Couples do not enter unless there are two seats free. (To simplify matters, assume that customers are willing to move around so that if there are two seats free they are always next to each other.) Thus two segments are required: one with single people and one with couples. In the couples' segment we have ENTER and LEAVE with a B operand of 2.

In order to facilitate the study of the effect of the B operand, let us assume that there will on average be just as many couples as single people arriving. When a couple leaves, two seats become available and two single transactions might enter, but two single transactions might have to leave, before a couple can enter. Using LIN1 to measure the waiting time for singles and LIN2 to measure waiting time for couples, the queue statistics in Table 12.3 show that this causes waiting times to be longer for couples than for single people.

**Table 12.3** Part of queue statistics of Program 12.3

| Queue (AD set) | Average time/trans | $Average time/trans | Current contents |
|---|---|---|---|
| LIN1 | 40.60 | 46.05 | 17 |
| CAFE | 49.45 | 54.53 | 41 |
| LIN2 | 56.86 | 61.28 | 24 |

$Average time/trans=average time/trans excluding zero entries

## 12.5 Value of lost customers

I shall end this chapter with two examples of the use of a *function* value in the B operand of the ENTER and LEAVE blocks. Before the problems are discussed, it should be stressed that ENTER and LEAVE are *not* necessarily

**Program 12.3**

```
        simulate
  cafe  storage     20
  iat   function    rn1,c5
0,0/.5,3/.7,6/.9,12/1,25
* Singles' segment
        generate    fn$iat
        arrive      lin1
        enter       cafe,q
        depart      lin1
        advance     30,5
        leave       cafe
        terminate
* Couples' segment
        generate    fn$iat
        arrive      lin2
        enter       cafe,2
        depart      lin2
        advance     50,20
        leave       cafe,2
        terminate
*
        generate    540
        terminate   1
        start       1
        end
```

required to be in the *same* segment. It is possible to have an ENTER block in one segment without a LEAVE block, and a LEAVE block in another segment without an ENTER block. There can also be programs with only ENTER blocks, but no LEAVE blocks.

The first example concerns the store dealt with earlier. In the previous examples (e.g. in Program 7.6) an attempt was made to determine a suitable number of salespeople. There was also the case of customers leaving if there was a waiting line of a certain length (Program 9.1). In that program the benefit of having another salesperson could only be measured by looking at the number of lost customers, but it was not possible to find out, for example, how much sales income would be lost. Now that the function concept and the B operand of ENTER have been introduced, a more realistic and interesting program can be written.

Firstly, a customer's decision on whether or not to leave the store, depending on the length of the waiting line, can now be modeled in a more realistic way. It seems reasonable to assume that customers have different degrees of patience. Some will not wait at all, while some may join even a fairly long waiting line. Let us assume that 10 percent leave if there is a waiting line of one or more; 20 percent leave if there are two (or more); 25 percent leave if there are three; 20 percent leave if there are four; 15 percent leave if there are five, and 10 percent leave if there are six people in the waiting line. This can be represented by defining a discrete function LIMIT as follows:

```
LIMIT FUNCTION  RN3,D6
.1,1/.3,2/.55,3/.75,4/.9,5/1,6
```

This function is used in the following block:

```
IF Q$SAL >= FN$LIMIT,BYE
```

Let us also assume that the amount sold is a random variable with nobody spending more than $500, 75 percent spending less than $100, 50 percent spending less than $40 and 25 percent spending less than $10. This can be represented by the following function SALES, which is continuous, since it is reasonable to assume that sales can take many different values:

```
SALES FUNCTION  RN4,C5
0,0/.25,10/.5,40/.75,100/1,500
```

As in Program 12.2 a function SERV is used based on RN2 in the ADVANCE block in order to ensure that the customer arrivals are identical, whether there are one or two salespeople (see Sections 12.3 and 18.4). Finally, assume that the payment for the goods takes place at the end of the service time. The whole program appears opposite.

This program illustrates another important difference compared to earlier programs, e.g. Program 7.6. Besides the block ENTER SAL, there is another ENTER block, ENTER REVNU,FN$SALES. While the first block ENTER SAL implies, as before, that one transaction tries to get service, ENTER REVNU,FN$SALES implies that the transaction brings FN$SALES units into the storage REVNU. Since the B operand of ENTER is an integer, the truncated value of FN$SALES is used.

Since there is no A operand in the STORAGE definition statement for REVNU, its capacity is defined to be very large. This is permissible, since the storage is only required to accumulate the sales income. Every time a transaction enters REVNU with a certain number of units, these units are added to the current contents of the storage. At the end of the simulation, i.e. at the end of the day, the current contents of the storage REVNU will correspond to total sales during the day.

The program is run in pairs of runs, first with STORAGE SAL 1 and then with STORAGE SAL 2 (= program 12.4b) to see how much more is sold if there are two salespeople instead of one. This can be done by comparing the statistics for the two runs. For the first pair of runs the facility and storage

**Program 12.4**

```
        simulate
sal     storage     1
revnu   storage
limit   function    rn3,d6
.1,1/.3,2/.55,3/.75,4/.9,5/1,6
  sales function    rn4,c5
0,0/.25,10/.5,40/.75,100/1,500
  serv  function    rn2,c2
0,20/1,30
        generate    18,6
        if          q$sal>=fn$limit,bye
        enter       sal,q
        advance     fn$serv
        enter       revnu,fn$sales
        leave       sal
bye     terminate
        generate    480
        terminate   1
        start       1
        end
```

statistics shown in Table 12.4 could be obtained. Sales amount to $1994 with one salesperson and $3363 with two salespeople. Hence according to this first pair of runs, additional sales due to one more salesperson amount to more than $1000. (In this connection note that in micro-GPSS facility statistics are printed instead of storage statistics, when the storage is given a capacity of 1.)

## 12.6 A bank branch office simulation

The last situation to be simulated in this chapter is that of a small branch office of a bank. Since the branch office is a fair distance from the central office, there will be great problems (e.g. two hours delay in cash delivery), if the branch office runs out of cash during the day. Hence, the bank management wants to balance the cost (in the form of lost interest) of having excess cash at the branch office against the losses made owing to bad service (thereby possibly losing customers) by running out of cash during the day. A decision has to be made concerning how much cash the branch office shall start with each morning. An armored truck comes in the evening to pick up

**Table 12.4** Some statistics of Program 12.4

| Facility | Average utilization | Number entries | Average time/trans |
|---|---|---|---|
| SAL | 0.97 | 19 | 24.61 |

| Storage | Capacity | Average contents | Average utilization | Entries | Average time/trans |
|---|---|---|---|---|---|
| REVNU | 2000 mill. | 1172.00 | 0.00 | 1994 | 282.13 |

| Storage | Current contents | Maximum contents |
|---|---|---|
| REVNU | 1994 | 1994 |

| Storage | Capacity | Average contents | Average utilization | Entries | Average time/trans |
|---|---|---|---|---|---|
| SAL | 2 | 1.38 | 0.69 | 27 | 24.56 |
| REVNU | 2000 mill. | 1667.90 | 0.00 | 3363 | 238.06 |

| Storage | Current contents | Maximum contents |
|---|---|---|
| SAL | 2 | 2 |
| REVNU | 3363 | 3363 |

excess cash or to deliver more cash so that the branch office has the same amount of cash each morning.

The risk of running out of cash will depend on both the initial amount in the morning, and the cash fluctuations during the day, which are in turn dependent on how much money is deposited and how much is withdrawn. The program must hence represent the stochastic fluctuations in deposits and withdrawals. The program also checks if *one* bank cashier is sufficient.

The block diagram is shown in Figure 12.5. Two types of customer are modeled, those making deposits and those withdrawing money. Random functions are used to sample the deposits and withdrawals. The continuous function INN gives the distribution for the deposits, implying, e.g., that no one deposits $50 or less; 10 percent deposit between $50 and $100; 20 percent deposit between $100 and $300, etc. The continuous function OUT gives the distribution for the withdrawals, implying, e.g., that 7 percent withdraw between $5000 and $10 000; 2 percent between $10 000 and $20 000 and finally 1 percent between $20 000 and $40 000. It is these small probabilities of substantial withdrawals which might particularly cause the problem of running out of cash.

It is not necessary to define the size of the storage, i.e. to give an A operand to the STORAGE statement, since there is no upper limit to the amount of cash that can be held during the day. The capacity of CASH is

**Program 12.5**

```
        simulate   10
cash    storage
inn     function   rn3,c7
0,50/.1,100/.3,300/.6,500/.8,1000/.9,4000/1,10000
out     function   rn4,c8
0,100/.2,300/.5,600/.8,1000/.9,5000/.97,10000/.99,20000/1,40000
        generate   8,3
        seize      sal
        advance    5,4
        release    sal
        goto       outbl,.7
        enter      cash,fn$inn
        terminate
outbl   leave      cash,fn$out
        terminate
        generate   ,,,1
        enter      cash,80000
        terminate
        generate   400
        terminate  1
        start      1
        end
```

hence set to the very high default value.

Assume that the customers arrive with IATs varying between 5 and 11 minutes. No distinction is made between the customers making deposits and those making withdrawals in the first part of the customer segment. This first part of the customer segment deals with ordinary service and waiting line computations. It is assumed that deposits and withdrawals require an equal amount of time, between 1 and 9 minutes. For the sake of simplicity changes in CASH are assigned to the moment when the customer's service is finished, i.e. after the RELEASE block.

There is a statistical GOTO whereby 30 percent of the customers become depositors and go directly to the block ENTER CASH,FN$INN. Here they bring FN$INN dollars into the storage CASH and then leave. Seventy percent of the customers go to the address OUTBL where the customer withdraws FN$OUT dollars from CASH and then leaves (through TERMINATE).

It is important to note that it is possible for the amount to be withdrawn, FN$OUT, to be larger than the current contents of the storage CASH. Since no storage is allowed to have negative contents, this will lead to the simulation being stopped and we then obtain a print-out prior to the time 400. Run time errors are usually followed by a complete standard print-out in

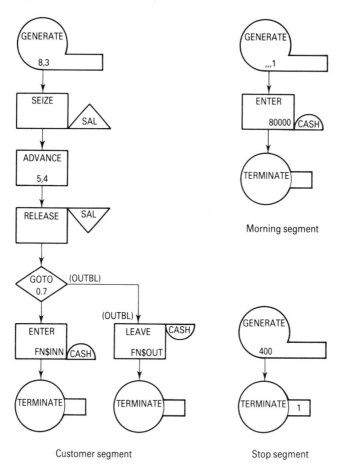

**Figure 12.5** Block diagram of Program 12.5

micro-GPSS in order to facilitate debugging.

Let us now consider the morning segment, where one transaction is created at the very start of the simulation. We default on the A, B and C operands and then set the D operand (= the total number of transactions to be generated by this block) to 1. This transaction will bring a certain number of dollars into the storage CASH at the start of the simulation. This is the decision variable, a number which can be changed between different simulations.

Let us assume that the criterion which determines whether this amount of cash is sufficient is that the simulation can run for a certain number of days without the bank running out of cash. In the above program the simulation is run for 10 days (due to SIMULATE 10, see Section 3.8). If the program runs without errors for all 10 days there is enough cash. This is true, for example, for the above case of $80 000.

However, if the program is run with only $50 000 in initial cash (Program 12.5b), the cash could be used up on the first day at time 326.39, i.e. five hours after opening. An error message is then obtained in micro-GPSS, indicating that the server in the block LEAVE CASH has a negative contents. This error message is followed by the usual statistics, but now all referring to time 326.39.

## Exercise 12.1 (Case study 3A in Schriber, 1974)

In Program 8.1, the times required to throw a pot (production time), and use the oven, are uniformly distributed over the interval 30 ± 5 and 8 ± 2 minutes, respectively. Suppose now that, instead of being uniformly distributed, 'production time' and 'oven-use time', both measured in minutes, follow the distributions shown below.

| Production time | 25 | 26 | 27 | 28 | 29 | 30 | 31 | 32 | 33 | 34 | 35 |
|---|---|---|---|---|---|---|---|---|---|---|---|
| Frequency | .01 | .03 | .05 | .10 | .18 | .26 | .18 | .10 | .05 | .03 | .01 |

| Oven-use time | 6 | 7 | 8 | 9 | 10 |
|---|---|---|---|---|---|
| Frequency | .05 | .25 | .40 | .25 | .05 |

These distributions are *symmetric*, and are centered about 30 and 8, respectively, i.e. the *average* production and oven-use times are identical to those in Program 8.1. Compare the number of pots made in this exercise with that of Program 8.1 for four, five and six workers.

## Exercise 12.2

The quality of a pot (in Exercise 12.1 above) and hence the price that can be charged varies in a random fashion. Thirty percent of the pots are of low quality and can fetch a price of $100; 60 percent are of medium quality, fetching a price of $150, while 10 percent are of high quality, fetching a price of $200. Have the simulation also calculate the revenues that the production during the day can lead to.

## Exercise 12.3

In Exercise 10.3 the comparison between a US and a Soviet store was simulated more accurately by closing down the stores in a proper way. Now improve the comparison even more by making sure that the customer arrivals will be *exactly* the same in the two stores.

---

## Exercise 12.4

In a factory a certain product requires processing in a special machine. The product comes in single format and double format size. Thirty percent of all product orders refer to the double format. The machine can either process two single format size products or one double format size product at the same time. There is a machine set-up time of 3 minutes per product, whether double or single size. The processing time for a single size product varies in a random fashion. For 30 percent of the products it varies between 10 and 15 minutes and for the remaining 70 percent it varies between 15 and 20 minutes. With regard to processing time the double size product can be regarded as consisting of two independent single size products. How long does it take to finish processing 100 product orders?

# 13 Built-in standard statistical functions

## 13.1 Introduction

The preceding chapter dealt with ways of defining any kind of function. I also discussed some severe drawbacks of using rectangular distributions for customer InterArrival Times and service times. Several of the objections raised against the rectangular distribution are taken care of by some common statistical distributions that are built into micro-GPSS.

In particular, for customer arrivals the so-called exponential distribution, implying a skewed distribution with a 'tail' of high values with low probability, provides several suitable features. This distribution will be discussed in Section 13.2 and its use in GPSS in Section 13.3.

For service times, a normal distribution, implying a symmetric distribution with 'tails' on both ends, is often considered as suitable. This distribution is presented in Section 13.4. In connection with the use of the normal distribution, the micro-GPSS concepts *expression and variable* are dealt with in Section 13.5. In Section 13.6, the exponential and normal distributions are applied to an inventory problem. Finally two distributions which allow for functions with varying degrees of skewness are studied, namely the Erlang distribution in Section 13.7 and the triangular distribution in Section 13.8.

■ **13.2 The exponential distribution**

The exponential distribution (often also called the negative exponential distribution) is very commonly used in the analysis of queuing systems. It is in particular used for describing customer arrival patterns. It is connected with several fundamental statistical distributions. Since this distribution is much used in GPSS, it is helpful to obtain a better understanding of the basic assumptions behind this function. (Readers interested only in micro-GPSS can go directly to Section 13.3.) With this purpose in mind, I shall provide the three main steps for deriving the exponential distribution from certain fairly basic assumptions.

**Step 1**

Let us assume that during a period of time, say 5 minutes, a certain number of customers, say 100, pass by a store. As each customer goes by the store, he throws a 10-sided die (or picks a random digit from 0 to 9) to determine whether to enter the store or not. If, for example, a 1 comes up, he will enter; otherwise he will not. Hence, a customer enters with a probability of 1/10.

The probability of one customer entering the store, i.e. throwing a 1, is completely independent of the probability of another customer entering the store. This assumption of independence of entry is important, since this excludes psychological phenomena such as people entering a store because they see other people enter.

If 100 customers come by the store, 'on average' 10 customers can be expected to enter the store, i.e. over many runs of 100 persons, the average would be 10 entries. The question arises as to what the probability is of a specific number of people out of 100 entering, e.g. of exactly two people entering the store.

Let us first determine the probability of having these two as the *first* two customers. This is equivalent to the probability that the first two enter and the next 98 do *not* enter. The probability of the first two entering is $(1/10)^2 = 1/100$ and the probability of the next 98 not entering is $(9/10)^{98}$ and hence the probability of *only* the first two entering is $(1/10)^2 (9/10)^{98}$. This can also be written as $(1/10)^2 (1 - 1/10)^{100-2}$.

We are, however, interested in how any two entries can occur. The first two customers do not need to be numbers 1 and 2; they can be 1 and 3, 1 and 4, etc.; or 2 and 3, 2 and 4, etc.; or 3 and 4, etc. The probability of any such combination of the $i$th and the $j$th person entering is the same as the probability of the 1st and 2nd entering. We hence want to determine how many possible ways 2 out of 100 customers can arrive. With the first being number 1, the second 2,3,... or 100 we have 99 possibilities; with the first being 2 and the second 3,4,... or 100 there are 98 possibilities, and with the first being 99 and the second 100, there is 1 possibility. Hence the total number of ways we can choose 2 out of 100 is $1 + 2 \ldots + 98 + 99$. Summing this we get 99 times the average value of $(99 + 1)/2 = 100/2$, i.e. we get $99 \star 100/2$. It should be mentioned that $(100 \star 99)/2$ can be written as $(100!)/(98!2!)$, where $n! = n(n - 1)(n - 2) \star \ldots \star 2 \star 1$.

Hence, the probability of getting exactly two entries from 100 persons, when each enters with a probability of 1/10, is

$$\frac{100!}{(100 - 2)!2!} \left(\frac{1}{10}\right)^2 \left(1 - \frac{1}{10}\right)^{100-2}$$

This can be written more generally for the case of $n$ persons going by and with the probability of one entry $= p$. Replacing 100 with $n$, 1/10 with $p$ and 2 with $r$, the probability of exactly $r$ customers entering the store is the well-known formula of the *binomial distribution*:

$$\frac{n!}{(n - r)!\, r!} p^r (1 - p)^{(n-r)} \text{ or } \binom{n}{r} p^r (1 - p)^{n-r}$$

**Step 2**

In the above example we assumed that 100 customers passed by every

5 minutes. Seen over many 5-minute periods, an average of $100 \star 0.1 = 10$ customers arrive per 5-minute period. More generally, $n$ customers pass by and $np$ customers enter on average during $t$ minutes.

The average arrival rate per minute is $10/5 = 2$ in the example. Generally when $np$ customers enter during $t$ minutes, the average arrival rate is $np/t$ per minute. The probability above (defined by the binomial distribution) can hence in the example be defined as the probability of getting exactly 2 arrivals during a 5-minute period when the average is 2 arrivals per minute or of getting $np$ arrivals during a $t$ minute period, when the average is $np/t$ arrivals per minute.

Making a mathematical simplification which keeps the average number of entries per minute, $np/t$, constant, and calling it $\lambda$, assume that $n$ becomes larger and $p$ correspondingly smaller, so that the product $np$ is constant, then as $n$ tends towards infinity and $p$ tends towards 0, the binomial distribution turns into the so-called *Poisson distribution*. This specifies the probability $P(r, t)$ of getting $r$ arrivals during $t$ minutes, if on average there are $\lambda$ arrivals per minute as

$$\frac{(\lambda t)^{r}}{r!} \, e^{-\lambda t},$$

e is here the base in the natural logarithmic system.

If, for example, the average is 1 arrival per minute ($\lambda = 1$), then the probability of having exactly $r$ arrivals during 1 minute ($t = 1$) is $e^{-1}/r!$. Hence, the probability of having 0 arrivals is $e^{-1} = 0.368$ (since $0! = 1$). The probability of 1 arrival is likewise 0.368. The probability of 2 arrivals is $0.368/2 = 0.184$; of 3 is $0.368/6 = 0.061$, of 4 is $0.368/24 = 0.015$ and of 5 is $0.368/120 = 0.003$. Plotting these values in Figure 13.1, we obtain a skewed distribution with low probabilities of high values of $r$.

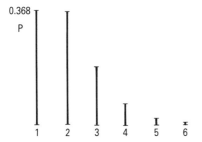

**Figure 13.1** A Poisson distribution with $\lambda = 1$

### Step 3

Furthermore, since $(\lambda t)^{0} = 1$ and $0! = 1$, the probability of exactly 0 arrivals during $t$ minutes is $e^{-\lambda t}$. This is the (negative) *exponential distribution*, in its basic frequency or probability form. The distribution is shown for $\lambda = 1$ in Figure 13.2.

We next want to establish the *cumulative* distribution, i.e. the probability that the time between two arrivals is less than or equal to a certain time. If there are *no* arrivals during $t$ specific minutes, the time between two arrivals is

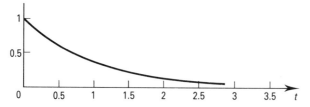

**Figure 13.2** The exponential distribution

larger than $t$ minutes. Hence we can write $P(IAT > t)$, i.e. the probability that the time between two arrivals $> t$, as $e^{-\lambda t}$. This implies in turn that $P(IAT \le t)$, is $1 - e^{-\lambda t}$, when the average is $\lambda$ arrivals per minute. This gives us the desired cumulative distribution, based on the frequency distribution in Figure 13.2. We plot this new cumulative distribution (for the case when $\lambda = 1$) in Figure 13.3. The probability gradually approaches 1 as $t$ becomes large. In almost two-thirds of the cases, $IAT$ is less than 1 minute and in almost 40 percent of the cases $IAT$ is less than half a minute. The distribution is quite skewed.

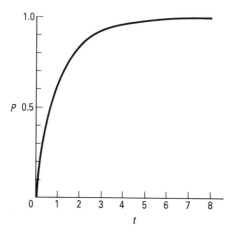

**Figure 13.3** The cumulative exponential distribution

The function in Figure 13.3 gives us the probability $P$ as the dependent variable (on the $y$-axis) and the InterArrival Time, $IAT$, as the independent variable (on the $x$-axis). In GPSS it is required the other way around, i.e. with $IAT$ as the dependent variable and $RNj$, a random number generated by the $j$th random number generator, as the independent $x$-variable. This will give us the GPSS XPDIS function illustrated in Figure 13.4.

This transformation can be done in two ways. We can do it graphically, by rotating the function above, so that the $x$-axis becomes the $y$-axis and vice versa. We then obtain Figure 13.4, which represents the case of $\lambda = 1$.

The other way is to regard the function formula above as an equation, where we want $t$ alone on the left side of the equals sign. From $P = 1 - e^{-\lambda t}$ we have $e^{-\lambda t} = 1 - P$, i.e. $-\lambda t = \ln(1 - P)$, i.e. $t = (1/\lambda)(-\ln(1 - P))$.

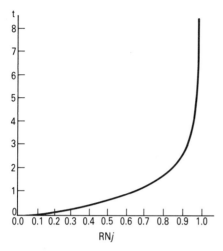

**Figure 13.4** The function XPDIS

For the case of $\lambda = 1$, $t = -\ln(1 - P)$, which is the formula of the function XPDIS in Figure 13.4.

Once this function XPDIS is defined for the case of $\lambda = 1$, we only need to multiply it by $1/\lambda$ to obtain the corresponding sampled IAT from the exponential distribution with an average IAT of $1/\lambda$. This can be explained as follows: $\lambda$ is the average number of arrivals per minute. If $\lambda = 1$, there is 1 arrival on average per minute. This means in turn that the average time between each arrival is 1 minute. If $\lambda = 2$, i.e. there are 2 arrivals per minute, the average time between two arrivals is 1/2 minutes. More generally, IAT (average) $= 1/\lambda$.

Hence, the sampled general IAT is this average InterArrival Time *times* the value sampled from the function in Figure 13.4, i.e. the sampled IAT when the average IAT = 1. To get this IAT we draw an $RNj$ value and use this $RNj$ as $P$ in the function above. It should in this context be mentioned that the standard deviation of this XPDIS function is 1 and that the standard deviation of IATs from a general exponential distribution is thus equal to the average IAT.

## 13.3 Use of the exponential function

The negative exponential function XPDIS, presented in Figure 13.4 and defined by the equation FN$XPDIS $= -\ln(1 - RNj)$, is built into micro-GPSS. There are two ways of using this built-in exponential function in GPSS:

1. The simplest way can be used if it is satisfactory for the exponential function to depend on the *second* random number generator. In this case the function FN$XPDIS can be used without any additions.

2. A slightly more complicated way is needed if it is necessary to use a different random number generator from the second one, e.g. if we wish to use the third instead of the second for an exponential function. We then add the *number* of the random number generator within parentheses to FN$XPDIS, e.g. obtaining FN$XPDIS(3). Note that in micro-GPSS the random functions can, as a parameter within parentheses, have only an integer 1 . . . 8, denoting the number of the random number generator used. We can of course write FN$XPDIS(2) instead of FN$XPDIS when using the second number generator, but the expression without parentheses is not only more convenient, but also more in line with GPSS V, where there are *no* parentheses after FN$ names.

In GPSS V (but not GPSS/H) we *have to* use the much more cumbersome general method of a function definition with a great many data pairs. (This method can of course also be used in micro-GPSS, but is obviously *not recommended.*) The statements normally used are presented in Table 13.1 (taken from Schriber, 1974).

**Table 13.1** Function statements for XPDIS in GPSS V

```
XPDIS FUNCTION    RN2,C24
0,0/.1,.104/.2,.222/.3,.355/.4,.509/.5,.69/.6,.915/.7,1.2/.75,1.3
.8,1.6/.84,1.83/.88,2.12/.9,2.3/.92,2.52/.94,2.81/.95,2.99/.96,3.
.97,3.5/.98,3.9/.99,4.6/.995,5.3/.998,6.2/.999,7/1,8
```

I shall now deal with how these functions are used in programs. If customers arrive with an average InterArrival Time of one hour, i.e. average IAT = 1, in micro-GPSS it is possible to just write GENERATE FN$XPDIS and then obtain InterArrival Times sampled from the distribution in Figure 13.4.

Varying IAT (average) from 1 is quite straightforward in micro-GPSS. If customers arrive one hour apart, but we want to have minutes as time units, we need to generate IATs that are $60 * \text{FN\$XPDIS}$. If FN$XPDIS = 2 is sampled, IAT is two hours or 120 minutes. In micro-GPSS this is written as GENERATE 60*FN$XPDIS (or GENERATE FN$XPDIS*60). The A operand in micro-GPSS takes the value of the whole expression $60 * \text{FN\$XPDIS}$. Micro-GPSS allows a general expression as the A operand of GENERATE and ADVANCE blocks. (The rules for these expressions in micro-GPSS are presented in Section 13.5 below.)

Such cases are much more complicated in GPSS V, where it is not possible to have an expression as an operand (except in VARIABLE or FVARIABLE statements, presented below in Section 13.5). In GPSS V, in order to generate customers with an IAT of $60 * \text{FN\$XPDIS}$, GENERATE 60,FN$XPDIS must be written, where 60 is the A operand and FN$XPDIS is the B operand. GPSS V relies on a very strange and special rule here. With FN in the B operand, the B operand will, in GPSS V, *not* have the same significance as in the earlier cases, when the B operand was a constant. In GPSS V the B operand is the half-width of the rectangular distribution *only* when the B operand is *not* an FN$ value. If the B operand starts with FN$, the value sampled in a GENERATE (or ADVANCE) block is A $\star$ B (and hence *not* A $\pm$ B as is the case when the B operand is a constant).

This rule of GPSS V is quite arbitrary. The use of a comma to signify a $\star$ also makes it more difficult to explain the program to outsiders. Because of these very substantial drawbacks, micro-GPSS does *not* follow GPSS V in this particular case. This is really the most important instance when the same correctly written program will in general give substantially different outputs in micro-GPSS and GPSS V. (Two less important cases are mentioned in Sections 4.4 and 14.1.) In micro-GPSS the A and B operands of GENERATE and ADVANCE blocks will *always* produce a distribution of A $\pm$ B.

Even when average IAT = 1 there will be severe problems in GPSS V (but not GPSS/H), because of truncation to integers. In almost two-thirds of all cases GPSS V gives an IAT of 0, although the true value of XPDIS is always larger than zero. Such truncation problems, of consequence for all values of average IAT < 50, forces the GPSS V user to choose a shorter time unit, e.g. seconds instead of minutes. The micro-GPSS user is spared this problem.

I shall illustrate the use of FN$XPDIS with Program 13.1. Let us consider the same store as in Program 6.1, but let us now suppose that customers arrive according to the exponential distribution with an average InterArrival Time of 18 minutes. Assume in this case that service time also follows the exponential distribution with an average service time of 25 minutes. The same averages as in Program 6.1 are therefore used. For the service time, the assumption of an exponential distribution is not as natural as for the IATs, but it might approximate the service time distribution in a case where a few customers require very long service times. The standard RN2 is used for IATs and RN3 for service times in order to ensure that the customer arrivals have their own random number generator.

**Program 13.1**

```
simulate
generate    18*fn$xpdis
seize       sal,q
advance     25*fn$xpdis(3)
release     sal
terminate
generate    480
terminate   1
start       1
end
```

If the results of running Program 13.1 a few times are compared with those obtained when running Program 6.1, two main differences are found: the results will vary much more from run to run, and waiting lines and times are often much longer in the case of Program 13.1. This difference is due to the much higher standard deviation of the exponential distribution (= 18 and 25 compared to 3.46 and 2.89 in the rectangular case of Program 6.1).

It should in this context be mentioned that Program 13.1 has a characteristic making it of interest as an illustration of *queuing theory*, namely that both InterArrival Times and service times follow the (negative) exponential distribution. One-line, one-server systems with exponential interarrival and service times are in the literature called M/M/1 systems.

For these systems it is easy to deduce theoretically the length of the waiting line, for instance, under so-called 'steady state' conditions, obtained when the simulation is run for a very long time. Such steady state solutions only exist when the InterArrival Times are *longer* than the service times. Otherwise, the waiting line will grow indefinitely.

Program 13.1 can be altered to become a true M/M/1 system by replacing 18 with, e.g., 37.5 in the A operand of GENERATE. An average waiting line of 4/3 customers and an average waiting time of 40 minutes would then be expected (see, e.g., Banks and Carson, 1984, p. 201). A simulation time of 480 is, however, far too short to obtain any stable results (over several runs) close to these theoretical values. A simulation time that is at least a hundred times longer is required to obtain stable results close to these values. It thus appears that the results of queuing theory are of little interest for simulation systems that are closed down within a fairly short time.

## 13.4 The normal distribution

The second distribution I shall discuss is the normal distribution. This is a distribution which is symmetrical in the sense that the average value has the highest probability and that the probability decreases at the same rate whether going to the left or the right of this average, as seen in Figure 13.5. The normal distribution also has what can be called tails on both sides, implying that there is a small probability of values far away from the average value. It is this gradual decrease in probability as values move away from the average that makes the normal distribution more attractive from the point of view of realism than the rectangular distribution.

Earlier I dealt with a service time having an average of 25 minutes, but with values varying between 20 and 30 minutes. For a rectangular distribution, this implies that a value of 20 is just as likely as the average value 25, but that a value of 19.99 is not possible. This sudden drop from a

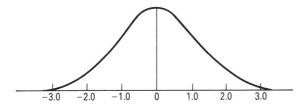

**Figure 13.5** Normal probability distribution ($\mu = 0$ and $\sigma = 1$)

high probability to a 0 probability, when going from one value to the most immediate value, appears quite unrealistic. When the service time is described as varying between 20 and 30 minutes it is generally meant that the bulk of values lie within this range, but there is some smaller probability of values outside this range. This makes the use of the normal distribution attractive.

It is possible, for example, to assume that 95 percent of all values lie between 20 and 30 minutes. The normal distribution can then be adjusted to our estimates as follows: a general normal distribution is defined by two parameters: the average $\mu$ and the standard deviation $\sigma$. The normal distribution is such that around 99.5 percent of all values lie within the area of $\mu \pm 3\sigma$; around 95 percent within $\mu \pm 2\sigma$, and around 68 percent within $\mu \pm 1\sigma$. If the service time is thought to be symmetrically distributed in roughly a bell-shaped fashion (as in Figure 13.5) and 95 percent of all times lie between 20 and 30 minutes, then $\mu = 25$ and $\mu - 2\sigma = 20$, i.e. $2\sigma = 5$ and $\sigma = 2.5$.

The use of this general normal distribution involves two steps:

1. The sampling of a value $s$ from a standardized normal distribution, which has an average $\mu = 0$ and a standard deviation $\sigma = 1$.

2. The calculation of a general value allowing for the desired values of $\mu$ and $\sigma$, on the basis of $s$, which was sampled from the standardized normal distribution.

## The standardized normal distribution

Let us first consider the standardized normal distribution. The function in Figure 13.5 gives the probability of an exact service time $t$, e.g. of $t = 2$. It is necessary to establish the cumulative distribution, i.e. to establish the probability that a value $\leq t$, e.g. $\leq 2$. Once this cumulative probability is obtained, with the probability as the dependent variable on the $y$-axis and time as the independent variable on the $x$-axis, we need to rotate (or invert) this cumulative function to have time $t$ as the dependent $y$-variable and the random number ($RN_j$) as the independent $x$-variable. Without going through

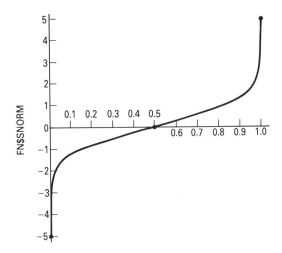

**Figure 13.6** Cumulative standardized normal distribution

complex mathematical derivation, I shall simply state that if these two steps are carried out, the function in Figure 13.5 can be transformed into the function in Figure 13.6.

In micro-GPSS there is a built-in function for this standardized normal distribution, FN$SNORM. I shall first deal with how micro-GPSS calculates FN$SNORM as a value sampled from this standardized normal distribution with an average of 0 and a standard deviation of 1. It samples 12 uniform random fraction numbers (0 to 1), adds them together and deducts 6, as in the following BASIC program:

```
10 S = 0
20 FOR K = 1 to 12
30 S = S + RND
40 NEXT K
50 S = S - 6
60 IF S > 5 THEN S = 5
70 IF S < -5 THEN S = -5
```

As can be shown by the so-called central limit theorem, the values will approximately follow the normal distribution. Since the expected average fraction number is 0.5, the expected average sum of 12 such numbers is 6, and by deducting 6 we obtain an expected value of 0. The values first obtained can thus vary between −6 and +6. The probability of obtaining a value < −5 or > 5 is, however, exceedingly small, much less than 0.0001. In order to be compatible with the way this function is usually calculated in GPSS V and to avoid certain problems (see below), micro-GPSS finally rules out any values < −5 or > 5.

Since the variance of these uniform random fraction numbers is 1/12, the expected variance, $\sigma^2$, of the sum of 12 random fractions is $12(1/12) = 1$ and the expected value of $\sigma = \sqrt{1} = 1$.

As for the exponential distribution, there are two ways of using the built-in standardized normal distribution in micro-GPSS:

1. Use of FN$SNORM without any additions, based on the *third* random number generator. Note that FN$XPDIS and FN$SNORM use different random number generators; FN$XPDIS uses the second and FN$SNORM uses the third.

2. A slightly more complicated method is needed if we want to use a random number generator other than the third one for FN$SNORM. The number of the random number generator is then added, within parentheses, to FN$SNORM, obtaining, for example, FN$SNORM(5). Thus, FN$SNORM and FN$SNORM(3) are equivalent.

In GPSS V, but not GPSS/H, the much more cumbersome method of function data statements must be used, a total of 25 data statements usually being required (see Schriber, 1974, p. 263).

## 13.5 Expressions and the variable concept

I have just discussed the function SNORM that gives values, such that they have an average of 0 and a standard deviation of 1. If we want to produce service times such that the average service time is 25 and the standard deviation is 2.5, we have to multiply FN$SNORM by 2.5 and then add 25.

This is very straightforward in micro-GPSS, since it allows an expression in the A operand of an ADVANCE or a GENERATE block (as well as some other blocks; see Appendix A). We simply write ADVANCE 2.5*FN$SNORM+25 (or ADVANCE 25+FN$SNORM*2.5 etc.).

If we want to do this calculation in several places in the same program without repeating a long expression, or if we want our program to be compatible with GPSS V, which (in contrast to micro-GPSS and GPSS/H) does not allow an expression in a block operand, we need a new GPSS concept – the *variable*. A variable is defined by a VARIABLE statement. This is a control statement to be placed before the first GENERATE (but after SIMULATE). In the address field we write the name of the variable. The operation field contains the word VARIABLE.

It should be mentioned that in order to be compatible with GPSS V, this can alternatively be written as FVARIABLE, i.e. starting with an F. In contrast to GPSS V, which ultimately uses integer mathematics, micro-GPSS (like GPSS/H) uses floating point numbers consistently.

VARIABLE has only *one* operand, the A operand. This contains a mathematical expression. Since such expressions can generally have between 4 and 59 characters in micro-GPSS, this A operand can thus be quite long. Such an expression allows for addition (+), subtraction (−), multiplication (⋆) and division (/). It also allows for parentheses. Terms are SNAs or constants. The constants can be either integers or decimal numbers. (In GPSS V, but not GPSS/H, only integers are allowed.)

The calculation of the value of this mathematical expression follows the normal rules of priority: first of all the processor calculates the values of expressions within parentheses. Within an expression without parentheses it gives priority to multiplication and division. The lowest priority is given to addition and subtraction. Within each priority group it carries out the evaluation from left to right. Thus in A + B ⋆ C the product B ⋆ C will first be calculated and finally A will be added to this product.

We can define a general normal distribution with $\mu = 25$ and $\sigma = 2.5$, using the function SNORM defined as above, with the following statement: GNORM VARIABLE 2.5⋆FN$SNORM+25. It is equally possible to write GNORM VARIABLE 25+FN$SNORM⋆2.5.

The value of the defined VARIABLE statement is called by the SNA V$. Hence the value of GNORM is called by V$GNORM.

Let us next examine the use of the V$-value as the A operand in an ADVANCE block. Since in this case all necessary definitions have been already made in the VARIABLE statement, the call on the V$-value will sample the needed stochastic value. For example, in the case where there is a variable GNORM defined as above, the block ADVANCE V$GNORM will sample values from a general normal distribution with a standard deviation of 2.5 and an average of 25. Thus the control statement GNORM VARIABLE FN$SNORM⋆2.5+25, when used with the block ADVANCE V$GNORM, does exactly the same sampling as the expression ADVANCE FN$SNORM⋆2.5+25. (In fact, the micro-GPSS processor will internally transform the expression into a hidden variable statement.)

At this point it should be noted that care is needed over the choice of the average value and the standard deviation, lest a negative value is obtained. In this case the simulation would be stopped, since the GPSS processor does not allow time to go backwards. We thus require that V$GNORM is not given a negative value, i.e. that $\mu + \sigma \star \text{FN\$SNORM} \geq 0$, i.e. $\mu/\sigma \geq -\text{FN\$SNORM}$.

Since it is possible to obtain $\text{FN\$SNORM} = -5$, we require that $\mu/\sigma \geq -(-5) = 5$, i.e. that $\mu \geq 5\sigma$. If $\mu$ is less than $5\sigma$, we run the risk of the simulation being stopped. (This problem can be avoided using an IF assignment statement; see Chapter 15.)

Finally let us study a program example involving the normal distribution, Program 13.2. This is based on Program 13.1, when there was a service time with an average of 25 minutes, following the exponential distribution. Let us alter the problem slightly by assuming a normal distribution for the service time, but assume the same average time as before.

For the normal distribution, the establishment of the standard deviation is required. Let us assume, as above, that the values lie between 20 and 30 in approximately 95 percent of all cases. This would imply that the half-width 5 would be approximately equivalent to two standard deviations, i.e. $\sigma$ is set to 2.5. Thus $\mu/\sigma = 25/2.5 = 10$, which is permissible according to the above discussion.

There are two versions of this program: the simpler 13.2a, using an expression in the ADVANCE block, and the slightly more complicated 13.2b, using a VARIABLE definition.

### Programs 13.2a and 13.2b

```
simulate                                    simulate
generate    18*fn$xpdis           gnorm variable   fn$snorm*2.5+25
seize       sal,q                       generate    18*fn$xpdis
advance     fn$snorm*2.5+25             seize       sal,q
release     sal                         advance     v$gnorm
terminate                               release     sal
generate    480                         terminate
terminate   1                           generate    480
start       1                           terminate   1
end                                     start       1
                                        end
         a                                         b
```

## 13.6 An inventory problem

To summarize what has been studied thus far, let us consider the inventory and re-ordering policy for a particular book in a student book store. One of these books is requested on average every day. The time between the arrivals of students asking for the book follows a negative exponential distribution. If the book is not in stock, the students can sign a list and have it sent to their home address when the new book arrives. Forty percent of the students make use of this service. The remaining 60 percent will instead go to another book store.

At the start of the year there is an initial inventory of 30 books. Every fifth workday an inventory manager checks whether the inventory has fallen to 10 books or less. If this is the case, he sends an order to the publisher for five books, provided there are *no* orders outstanding, i.e. he does not send an order if he has already ordered some books, but they have not yet reached the book store. Books take on average 10 workdays to arrive. For 95 percent of all deliveries, the time between ordering the books and their arrival lies between six and 14 workdays.

We want to simulate this system for one year (250 workdays). The program should answer the following questions:

1. How many books are sold during the year?

2. How many sales are lost because students go to another book store?

3. How many students sign up to have the book delivered at home?

4. How many books are delivered from the publisher during the year?

5. How large is the final inventory at the end of the year?

We shall disregard weekend effects and treat each of the 250 workdays in the same manner (i.e. disregard holidays, etc.).

Program 13.3 has been written to answer these questions. This program is divided into four segments: one customer segment; one re-ordering segment; one entering inventory segment and one stop segment.

The block diagram of the *customer segment* is shown in Figure 13.7. The customers (= students) arrive by means of the block GENERATE FN$XPDIS, which implies one potential customer on average per day. Next there is an IF block referring to a storage. If the storage is not empty, one book is sold directly and the student takes one book out of storage in the block LEAVE STOR and leaves the system through a TERMINATE block. If the storage is empty, the student goes to the stochastic GOTO block with the address NODIR. Here 60 percent of the students go to the TERMINATE block with the address NOSEL. The remaining 40 percent of the students wait for new books to arrive, in the block ARRIVE TIM in front of the block WAITIF STOR=E. Here the student will wait as long as the storage STOR is empty, i.e. until new books arrive in the re-ordering segment. Then the student will pass through the block DEPART TIM, which measures (together with the ARRIVE block) his or her total waiting time, and in the LEAVE STOR block, he or she will take out one book and proceed to TERMINATE.

The block diagram of the *re-ordering segment* is in Figure 13.8. One inventory transaction is generated, i.e. an inventory manager arrives, every fifth workday. In the block IF S$STOR>10,NOBUY, he or she checks if there are more than 10 books in stock. If so, he or she goes to NOBUY TERMINATE.

Otherwise, i.e. if there is a maximum of 10 books in stock, the manager will check whether ordered books are on their way, i.e. whether or not the facility ORDER is in use. If this order indicator is in use and there are new books on their way, the manager goes to NOBUY TERMINATE. Otherwise, i.e. if there are no new books already on order, he or she will proceed to place an order, i.e. causing the facility ORDER to then be in use.

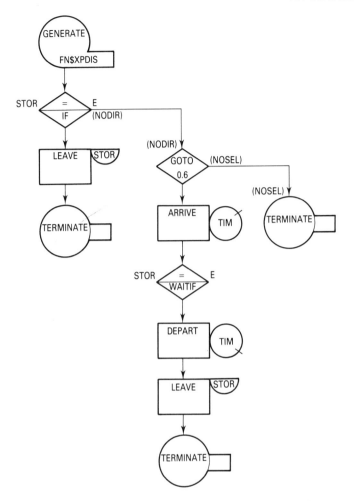

**Figure 13.7** Customer segment of Program 13.3

Next the inventory manager has to wait for the arrival of the new books. The average time is 10 days and since 95 percent of ordered books arrive within $10 \pm 4$ days, $2\sigma = 4$, i.e. $\sigma = 2$. We hence write ADVANCE FN$SNORM*2+10. After this time the ordered books arrive and the facility ORDER is released and five books are brought into storage.

The entering inventory segment and the stop segment can be studied in the program listing.

From the program listing we first see that the storage STOR is allowed a very high capacity by defaulting on the A operand of the STORAGE statement. The capacity is in fact the space available for books, which are brought in by an explicit ENTER block.

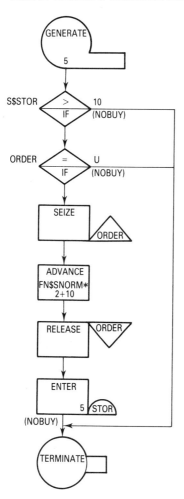

**Figure 13.8**   Re-ordering segment of Program 13.3

The customer and re-ordering segments are straightforward translations of the block diagrams already presented. Let us now examine the three statements of the entering inventory segment. Only one transaction is generated at time 0. Default values apply for the A, B and C operands and the D operand is set to 1 (see Program 8.1). This transaction brings 30 units into storage at time 0 by means of the block ENTER STOR,30 and then the transaction terminates.

We shall now study the output in Table 13.2, to answer the five questions listed at the beginning of this section.

**Program 13.3**

```
        simulate
 stor   storage
 *   Customer segment
        generate    fn$xpdis
        if          stor=e,nodir
        leave       stor
        terminate
 nodir goto         nosel,.6
        arrive      tim
        waitif      stor=e
        depart      tim
        leave       stor
        terminate
 nosel terminate
 *   Re-ordering segment
        generate    5
        if          s$stor>10,nobuy
        if          order=u,nobuy
        seize       order
        advance     fn$snorm*2+10
        release     order
        enter       stor,5
 nobuy terminate
 *   Entering inventory segment
        generate    ,,,1
        enter       stor,30
        terminate
 *   Stop segment
        generate    250
        terminate   1
 *
        start       1
        end
```

1. The total number of books sold during one year can be determined from the total block counts, and is the sum of the total block counts of the two LEAVE blocks in the customer segment, namely blocks 3 and 9, giving a total of 51 + 74 = 125 books. The number 125 can also be determined from the storage statistics as the difference between the number of ENTRIES (= 125) and the CURRENT CONTENTS (= 0).

2. Looking at the total block counts we find that 112 customers have come to block 11 NOSEL TERMINATE and hence 112 sales have been lost.

**Table 13.2** Results of Program 13.3

```
Relative clock      250.00 Absolute clock      250.00

Block counts
1           GENER    0      242    12           GENER    0      50
2           IF       0      242    13           IF       0      50
3           LEAVE    0       51    14           IF       0      47
4           TERMI    0       51    15           SEIZE    0      20
5   NODIR   GOTO     0      191    16           ADVAN    1      20
6           ARRIV    5       79    17           RELEA    0      19
7           WAITI    0       74    18           ENTER    0      19
8           DEPAR    0       74    19   NOBUY   TERMI    0      49
9           LEAVE    0       74    20           GENER    0       1
10          TERMI    0       74    21           ENTER    0       1
11  NOSEL   TERMI    0      112    22           TERMI    0       1
                                   23           GENER    0       1
                                   24           TERMI    0       1
```

| Facility | Average utilization | Number entries | Average time/trans |
|---|---|---|---|
| ORDER | 0.75 | 20 | 9.40 |

| Storage | Capacity | Average contents | Average utilization | Entries | Average time/trans |
|---|---|---|---|---|---|
| STOR | 2000 mill. | 2.08 | 0.00 | 125 | 4.16 |

| Storage | Current contents | Maximum contents |
|---|---|---|
| STOR | 0 | 30 |

| Queue (AD set) | Maximum contents | Average contents | Total entries | Zero entries | Percent zeros |
|---|---|---|---|---|---|
| TIM | 15 | 4.63 | 79 | 0 | 0.00 |

| Queue (AD set) | Average time/trans | $Average time/trans | Current contents |
|---|---|---|---|
| TIM | 14.65 | 14.65 | 5 |

3. The number of students signing up to have the book delivered at home, 79, can either be determined from the total block count of block 6 ARRIVE or from the queue statistics as TOTAL ENTRIES.

4. The number of books delivered from the publisher during the year can be determined from the storage statistics as the ENTRIES, 125, *minus* the entering inventory of $30 = 95$.

5. The closing inventory at the end of the year, 0, is also determined as CURRENT CONTENTS in the storage statistics.

## 13.7 The Erlang distribution

Another standard statistical distribution that is built into micro-GPSS is the Erlang distribution. This distribution is closely related to the (negative) exponential distribution. In fact, the Erlang distribution is obtained by drawing a certain number of independent samples from this exponential distribution and taking the average of these sampled values. The Erlang distribution thus has a parameter $n$ which is the number of samples drawn from the exponential distribution. Thus, the exponential distribution can be seen as a special case of the Erlang distribution with $n = 1$. Since the average of the exponential distribution is 1, the mean value of the Erlang distribution is obviously also 1, since it is the average of the $n$ values drawn from the exponential distribution.

In order to appreciate the usefulness of the Erlang distribution for simulation it is important to study how the distribution looks graphically for different values of $n$. Figure 13.9 shows that the Erlang distribution for values of $n > 1$ has the characteristic that the modal (peak) value is not 0, but is a value that moves towards the average of 1 as $n$ increases. The modal value is around 0.5 for $n = 2$ and around 0.7 for $n = 3$. It can also be seen that the Erlang distribution is quite skewed for low values of $n$. For $n = 10$ it is already very close to the normal distribution. Hence its main usefulness is for values of $n$ from 2 to 9.

Since standard GPSS only works with functions with *one* parameter, for statistical functions the number $j$ of RN$j$, it is sensible to let the last character of the *name* of an Erlang function be the value of $n$. Hence, micro-GPSS has eight built-in Erlang functions, RLNG2, ..., RLNG9, where RLNG$n$ consists of the average of $n$ samples from the exponential function.

Just as the statistical functions presented earlier, the Erlang distribution RLNG$n$ can be used in two different ways:

1. *Without* any additions, RLNG$n$ will use the *fourth* random number generator, regardless of the value of $n$.

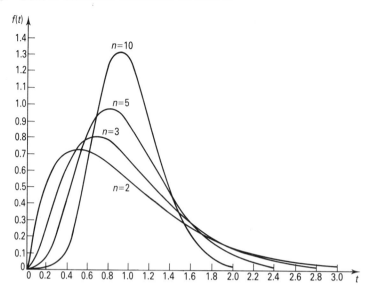

**Figure 13.9** The Erlang probability distribution

2. *With* the number of the random number generator within parentheses, any random number generator can be used. RLNG*n*(4) is thus equivalent to RLNG*n*.

In Chapter 15 (Program 15.5) the Erlang distribution will be used to simulate payment behavior. In this case a company gives 30 days of credit. Most people pay within 30 days ± a week. Some pay earlier, but very few pay right away. There are also quite a few who pay after considerably later than a month. Perhaps at least 5 percent do not pay until after three months or more. Since these long delays in payment strongly outweigh the days saved by early payments, the average payment time will be considerably longer than the modal value of 30 days. The average might be around 45 days. An Erlang distribution with *n* = 3 and an average time of 45 days might be a suitable approximation of such payment behavior. Thus this payment behavior can be simulated with an Erlang distribution with *n* = 3 using the block ADVANCE 45★FN$RLNG3.

## 13.8 The triangular distribution

The exponential and the Erlang distributions are skewed, but always with the mode, i.e. the most frequent value, to the left of the average and hence

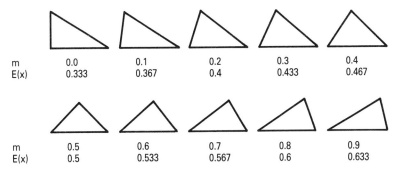

| m | 0.0 | 0.1 | 0.2 | 0.3 | 0.4 |
|---|-----|-----|-----|-----|-----|
| E(x) | 0.333 | 0.367 | 0.4 | 0.433 | 0.467 |

| m | 0.5 | 0.6 | 0.7 | 0.8 | 0.9 |
|---|-----|-----|-----|-----|-----|
| E(x) | 0.5 | 0.533 | 0.567 | 0.6 | 0.633 |

**Figure 13.10** The triangular probability distribution

with the 'tail' to the right. In some situations it might be desirable to use a distribution that can be skewed in either way, i.e. with the mode either to the left or the right of the expected average value. The simplest distribution with these characteristics is the triangular distribution. It is similar to the rectangular distribution in the sense that there are distinct lower and upper limits.

As with the other statistical distributions, we shall use it in a standardized form, such that the width, i.e. the distance between the upper and lower value, is 1. The triangular distribution takes various shapes dependent on how far the mode, $m$, is from the lower limit. This is shown in Figure 13.10 where there are different triangular distributions for the mode $m$ going from 0.0 to 0.9. The expected value $E(x) = (1 + m)/3$ is also indicated. Since the triangular distribution can only be a very rough approximation of reality, it would be misleading to use the distribution with a finer calibration than that above, i.e. with more than one decimal place of the mode. Hence, micro-GPSS uses the triangular distribution in very much the same way as the Erlang distribution, i.e. with a special parameter, in this case representing the mode $m$, as the last character of the function name. We shall thus use the names TRIA0, TRIA1, ..., TRIA9 for the 10 different types of triangular distribution presented in Figure 13.10, i.e. with the decimal *digit* of the mode $m$ as the last character of the name.

I have not covered the case when the mode $m = 1$, but this can easily be handled in another way. (See Section 14.2.)

Like the statistical functions discussed earlier, the triangular distribution TRIA$m$ can be used in two different ways:

1. *Without* any additions, FN\$TRIA$m$ will use the *fifth* random number generator, regardless of the value of $m$.

2. *With* the number of the random number generator within parentheses,

any ,random number generator can be used. FN$TRIA*m*(5) is thus equivalent to FN$TRIA*m*.

Now that all the statistical functions built into micro-GPSS have been discussed, note that the rectangular distribution uses the first, the exponential the second, the normal the third, the Erlang the fourth and the triangular the fifth random number generator, unless indicated otherwise.

Let us finally illustrate the triangular distribution with a situation from a quality control department, which assumes that the number of rejected chips can be approximated by a triangular distribution (Banks and Carson, 1984, p. 159). The maximum number of chips rejected during one hour is 10, the minimum is 0 and the mean is 4. Standardizing by dividing by the width ($= 10$), we obtain an average $E(x) = 0.4$. From Figure 13.10 it can be seen that the distribution with $m = 0.2$ will be used. Thus FN$TRIA2 $\star$ 10 can be used to sample the number of rejected chips during one hour.

---

## Exercise 13.1 (Case study 3B in Schriber, 1974)

At a one-car wash facility, it must be decided how many spaces to provide for cars waiting to use the facility. Cars arrive in a Poisson stream (= according to an exponential distribution) with an average InterArrival Time of 5 minutes. Car-washing time is exponentially distributed with a mean of 4 minutes. Potential customers who find no waiting space available go elsewhere to have their car washed. Build a GPSS model for this simple system, then use the model to observe system behavior for the alternatives of one, two and three waiting spaces. For each configuration, simulate for one eight-hour day of operation. Basing your answer on model output, estimate the fraction of potential customers who actually remain at the car wash to be served.

---

## Exercise 13.2

Modify Program 12.4 as follows: customer arrivals follow an Erlang distribution with $n = 3$ and service times follow the normal distribution. Average times are not changed, but service times are, such that 95 percent of all times lie between 15 and 35 minutes. Run the program for one and two salespeople.

**Exercise 13.3**  (Example 3.5 in Banks and Carson, 1984, which contains solutions to this problem solved in FORTRAN, GASP, SIMSCRIPT II.5, GPSS V and SLAM)

The system, a grocery check-out counter, is modeled as a single server queue. The simulation will run until 1000 customers have been served. In addition, assume that the InterArrival Times of customers are exponentially distributed with a mean of 4.5 minutes, and that the service times are (approximately) normally distributed with a mean of 3.2 minutes and a standard deviation of 0.6 minutes. When the cashier is busy, a queue forms with no customers turned away. The output should contain data on how many waited for at least 4 minutes.

**Exercise 13.4**  (Based on Examples 5.12 and 5.18 in Banks and Carson, 1984)

In a barber shop with only one barber there is waiting room for only two customers. Additional customers are turned away. Time between arrivals averages 1/2 hours, exponentially distributed, and the service time averages 20 minutes, also exponentially distributed. Run the simulation for 500 minutes as well as 5000 and 50 000 minutes. According to queuing theory, in the steady state, the average length of the queue would be 0.43 customers and the utilization of the barber 0.585 (see p. 208 in Banks and Carson, 1984).

**Exercise 13.5**

Customers come to a store with two salespeople on average every 10 minutes, following an exponential distribution. The average service time is 15 minutes. It is estimated that hardly any customer takes less than 5 minutes or more than half an hour. It appears that the triangular distribution could be a convenient but rough approximation of service times. Simulate for a day of nine hours.

**Exercise 13.6**  (Program CLAYWORKS in Jennergren, 1984)

Customers (trucks) pass through the following servers: weighbridge (on the way in), unloading bay, washer, loading bay, weighbridge (on the way out). Queues q1 to q5 form in front of these servers. q1 and q5 both form in front of the weighbridge, and q5 (customers about to leave) has priority over q1. InterArrival Time between successive customers is exponential with 17 minutes as the average IAT. The first customer arrives at time 5. No customers are accepted after time 360, but customers already in the system finish being served. Service times are all uniform between the limits: weighbridge 3–7; washer 5–7; unloading bay 8–16; loading bay 15–20. Investigate the reduction in average customer waiting time obtained by acquiring a second loading bay.

# 14 Other types of function

## 14.1 Functions with any SNA as independent variable

In the preceding two chapters we studied functions with a random number RN$j$ as the independent variable. Before we proceed further, it should be stressed that RN$j$ (with j = 1 . . . 8) is also an SNA. RN$j$ can hence be used, for example, in IF blocks to replace stochastic GOTO blocks which always use RN1. If, for a statistical GOTO, we do not want to use the first random number generator, but the third one instead, in micro-GPSS it is possible to write IF RN3 < .25,PLAY instead of GOTO PLAY,.25. In 25 percent of the cases the transaction then goes to PLAY.

> It should be stressed that in GPSS V, RN$j$ when used in blocks takes a completely different type of value, namely a three-digit integer. Because of this strange internal inconsistency in GPSS V, micro-GPSS is *not* compatible with GPSS V as regards RN$j$ usage in blocks. (This use is, however, infrequent.)

Since RN$j$ is an SNA, it is reasonable to ask whether other SNAs can also be used as the independent variable in a function. The answer is that any SNA can be used as the independent $x$-variable in a function. As an example, the time spent in an ADVANCE block can depend on the length of a queue or an AD set. Let Q$ROAD measure the number of cars that have come to a certain part of a road and have not yet left it. Then the following function makes time spent driving on that part of the road depend on the number of cars on the road, reflecting lower speeds, when there is more traffic:

```
QTIM  FUNCTION  Q$ROAD,C2
0,100/50,200
```

This is a simple linear function. If there are no cars, i.e. Q$ROAD = 0, it takes 100 seconds to drive this part of the road. If there is the maximum number of cars, 50, the time required increases to 200 seconds.

In a function it is possible to use as independent variable the following SNAs that we have already studied:

Q$, the length of a queue or an AD set

S$, the current contents of a storage

At this point we shall also study five other SNAs that can be used in this way.

Firstly there is another SNA for storages, R$, which is the remaining (free) capacity of a storage.

The second new SNA is PR, the priority of the *current* transaction. It lacks $ and a name, since transactions lack names.

The third new SNA is N$, denoting the *total* number of entries into a block. The name following N$ is the address given in the address field of the block. Thus, if there is a block INN ENTER STOR, N$INN will refer to the total number of transactions that have entered this block, e.g. the total number of customers that have entered STOR during the day.

This N$INN value can, for example, be used in a function to represent daily cleaning costs, which are composed of a fixed cost of $120 (e.g. for wages) plus a variable component (e.g. for paper, etc.) of $1.00 per 100 customers. With a maximum of 7000 customers per day, leading to a total cost of $120 + $70 = $190, the following function can represent the daily cleaning costs:

```
CLNCS  FUNCTION  N$INN,C2
0,120/7000,190
```

The next SNA, W$, also refers to the block statistics. While N$ refers to the total block count, W$ refers to the *current* block count. Thus, with reference to the block example above, W$INN would be the current number of transactions in the block INN. The SNA W$ can for example be convenient for measuring the number of transactions waiting in one single block, e.g. prior to a WAITIF block, or being 'served' in a particular ADVANCE block. The use of such a W$ in an IF-block instead of a Q$ can decrease the number of blocks used, if obtaining the Q$-value would otherwise require the inclusion of an ARRIVE–DEPART pair.

The last new SNA to be presented here is C1, the value of the relative clock. This SNA is written *without* $ or a name, since there is only one relative clock. (The difference between the absolute and the relative clock, non-existent in the programs until now, will be explained in Section 18.8.)

An interesting use of the SNA C1 is in a function that relates the average arrival rate to the time of day. In this way the arrival rate can vary depending on the time of day. For example, a store has a rush hour in the late afternoon, while there is more of a lull earlier in the day. Let us assume that there is an average IAT of 40 minutes between 8 a.m. and 3 p.m. and of 10 minutes between 3 and 6 p.m. The store opens at 8 a.m. and closes at 6 p.m., i.e. 10 hours or 600 minutes later. The following function defines this arrival pattern:

```
AVIAT  FUNCTION C1,D2
420,40/600,10
```

This discrete function implies that between time 0 and 420, i.e. 8 a.m. and 3 p.m., the average IAT is 40 minutes, and between time 420 and 600, i.e. 3 and 6 p.m., the average IAT is 10 minutes. The block GENERATE FN$AVIAT*FN$XPDIS will then sample IATs following a negative exponential distribution with an average value of 40 minutes for the first seven hours of simulated time, i.e. between 8 a.m. and 3 p.m., and with an average value of 10 minutes for the last three hours.

This function can be used in a program that deals with the following issue: in a store with the customer arrival pattern following the function AVIAT defined as above, i.e. with the rush hour between 3 p.m. and 6 p.m., there is at present only one salesperson working. Management is contemplating the hiring of another salesperson to work part-time. What are the most suitable working hours for this person? The most immediate answer would perhaps be to hire the part-timer for the three busiest hours between 3 p.m. and 6 p.m. To study the effect of such a decision Program 14.1 can be used.

The 'part-timer at home' segment requires further comment, although it is similar to the lunch segment in Program 11.2. The problem dealt with here, which arose earlier in Exercise 11.1, is how to model a store employing one full-timer and one part-timer. In the STORAGE statement the capacity of the store is defined as 2, i.e. the maximum number of people working at any single time. The idea behind the 'part-timer at home' segment, is that in order to make the part-timer *unavailable* for serving customers from 8 a.m. to 3 p.m., he is made busy by a 'home event'. This 'home event' commences at time 0. (The A and B operands of the GENERATE block in the 'at home' segment are both 0 by default.) Only *one* 'home event' will be generated during the simulation (D operand is 1).

The 'home event' has priority over ordinary customers (E operand is 1) in order to ensure that the 'home event' makes the part-timer busy (through the ENTER block), before a customer does so. The 'home event' then holds the part-timer in the ADVANCE block for 420 minutes, between 8 a.m. and 3 p.m. When the 'home event' releases the part-timer at 3 p.m., he or she is made available to serve customers in the store for the remainder of the day.

Let us now experiment with the working time of the part-timer. For example, how much longer will customers have to wait, if he or she starts half an hour later, e.g. at 450 instead of at 420? To investigate this, we change the time in the ADVANCE block of the 'home event' segment from

**Program 14.1**

```
        simulate
stor    storage      2
aviat   function     c1,d2
420,40/600,10
* Customer segment
        generate    fn$aviat*fn$xpdis
        arrive      lin
        enter       stor
        depart      lin
        advance     25+5*fn$snorm
        leave       stor
        terminate
* Part-timer at home segment
        generate    ,,,1,1
        enter       stor
        advance     420
        leave       stor
        terminate
* Stop segment
        generate    600
        terminate   1
        start       1
        end
```

420 to 450 (= Program 14.1b). Since waiting lines do not pile up immediately when the rush hour starts, and waiting times hence increase only slightly by delaying the start of the part-timer, it might be suitable to have the part-timer start at 3.30 instead of 3 p.m. and save half an hour's salary. The adjustment of the work force to this type of fluctuation in arrival patterns is one type of practical problem for which GPSS is very suitable.

In a similar way the probability of going to a certain address could be allowed to vary over time. Let us look at Program 8.2 again. We can allow the probability of error to increase over time by defining the following function:

```
ERPRO FUNCTION C1,C2
0,0.1/4800,0.2
```

The block GOTO FIX,0.15 is then replaced by IF RN2 < FN$ERPRO,FIX.

## 14.2 Built-in mathematical and logical functions

Micro-GPSS also has other built-in functions, apart from the statistical functions presented in Chapter 13. There are 15 functions altogether, divided into two groups, A (mathematical functions) and B (logical functions).

The functions, presented below, are used as FN$name followed by a *parenthesized expression*, which constitutes the value of the independent variable, i.e. the *x*-value, of the function, corresponding to the A operand of the FUNCTION definition (see Chapter 12). The important difference is that within the parentheses we can use not only an SNA, but also a full *expression*. Note furthermore that a constant within parentheses refers to a value, in contrast to the statistical functions, where it referred to the number of a random number generator.

[A] *Mathematical functions*. Except for FN$DEC, these have the same names as in BASIC and should hence be familiar to many readers.

1. ABS gives the absolute value of the argument A, i.e. if $A < 0$, FN$ABS(A) = $-A$; else FN$ABS(A) = A.

2. INT truncates A, if non-integer, to the nearest lowest integer, e.g. FN$INT(2.23) = 2.

3. DEC calculates the decimal fraction part of a number, e.g. FN$DEC(2.23) = 0.23.

4. EXP calculates the exponential value of A, e.g. FN$EXP(1) = 2.718.

5. LOG computes the natural logarithm of A, i.e. LOG is the inverse of EXP. Thus FN$LOG(FN$EXP(A)) = A. Combining EXP and LOG we can calculate 'raised to the power of'. Thus A raised to the power of B can be calculated as FN$EXP(B $\star$ FN$LOG(A)).

6. SGN calculates the sign of A; i.e. if $A < 0$, FN$SGN(A) = $-1$; if $A = 0$, FN$SGN(A) = 0 and if $A > 0$, FN$SGN = 1.

7. SIN calculates the sine of the argument given in *degrees*, e.g. FN$SIN(0) = FN$SIN(360) = 0. In GPSS this trigonometric function is mainly used to depict cyclical fluctuations, e.g. of demand. An example of such use is given later in this section.

8. SQR calculates the square-*root*. Thus FN$SQR(9) = 3. (The square can be calculated by multiplying the number by itself.) It should be noted at this point that, e.g., FN$SQR(RN5) will sample from a standardized triangular distribution with the mode $m = 1$ (see Section 13.8). RN5 is here the random fraction number sampled, e.g. 0.64 leading to FN$SQR(RN5) = 0.8.

**[B]** *Logical functions*, i.e. functions that are used for assigning logical values of 0 or 1 depending on the value of the argument.

1. EQ0 is a logical function testing for *equality* with 0. Thus FN$EQ0(A) = 1, if A = 0 and FN$EQ0(A) = 0, if A <> 0. Note that the third character of EQ0 (as well as that of GT0, GE0, LT0, LE0 and NE0 below) is a zero.

2. NOT is a logical function performing the same task as EQ0 but is mainly meant to be used for reversing the truth value, thus FN$NOT(1) = 0 and FN$NOT(0) = 1.

3. GT0 tests whether or not A > 0. Thus FN$GT0(A) = 1, if A > 0 and = 0, if A ≤ 0.

4. GE0 tests whether or not A ≥ 0. Thus FN$GE0(A) = 1, if A ≥ 0 and = 0, if A < 0.

5. LT0 tests whether or not A < 0. Thus FN$LT0(A) = 1, if A < 0 and = 0, if A ≥ 0.

6. LE0 tests whether or not A ≤ 0. Thus FN$LE0(A) = 1, if A ≤ 0 and = 0, if A > 0.

7. NE0 tests whether or not A <> 0. Thus FN$NE0(A) = 1, if A <> 0 and = 0, if A = 0.

These logical functions can be used, among other things, for testing whether several conditions hold simultaneously in an IF statement. Thus in Program 13.3, for example, the two statements IF S$STOR > 10,NOBUY and IF ORDER=U,NOBUY could be replaced with *one* statement: IF FN$GT0(S$STOR−10)+F$ORDER > 0,NOBUY (where F$ORDER is the current contents of the facility ORDER). This single block is, however, more difficult to understand than the two separate blocks.

Finally let us study an example that uses the mathematical function SIN. Let us take as a starting point Program 13.3 which concerns a book store. We now assume that demand for the book fluctuates cyclically over the year, although the *average* demand remains as one per day. At the start of the simulation year (e.g. late September) the average demand is one book per day, and increases to two books per day one quarter later (just before Christmas). Demand returns to the level of one book per day three months later, decreasing to almost zero another quarter later (in the middle of the summer), only to return to one per day at the end of the simulation year. Figure 14.1 illustrates these fluctuations.

Since the number of degrees (= 360) is a good approximation of the number of days of the year, this curve can be approximated by a function $1 + \sin(day)$, where *day* is the number of days from the simulation start. Since in Program 13.3 there are only 5 days (= working days) a week and C1

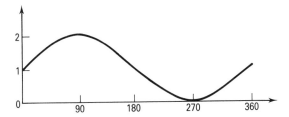

**Figure 14.1** $1 + \text{FN\$SIN(day)}$

has a maximum value of 250 during a year instead of 360, it is therefore necessary to multiply C1 by $360/250 = 1.44$ to obtain the true day. Average daily demand can thus be defined as $1 + \sin(1.44 \star \text{C1})$.

Since we wish to generate average time in days between each potential sale, average IAT is determined as 1/(sales per day). For example, if sales per day were 2, IAT would be 0.5, i.e. there would be half a day between two sales. Thus, in this case average $\text{IAT} = 1/(1 + \sin(1.44 \star \text{C1}))$. However, since $\sin(270) = -1$ and division by zero is forbidden, this is approximated with $1/(1.05 + \sin(1.44 \star \text{C1}))$.

Thus in this program there is an average IAT of $1/(1.05 + \text{FN\$SIN}(1.44 \star \text{C1}))$ and customers, who arrive according to an exponential distribution with this average IAT, are generated by the block GENERATE FN\$XPDIS/(1.05+FN\$SIN(1.44*C1)). If this statement replaces GENERATE FN\$XPDIS of Program 13.3, a new program, Program 14.2, is obtained. Only the first few lines of this are listed, the rest being identical to Program 13.3.

If this program is run, almost the same number of customers, orders, sales and lost sales are obtained as in Program 13.3, but the average waiting time increases dramatically, reflecting the inability of the proposed inventory policy to handle peak demand.

**Program 14.2** First part

```
        simulate
  stor  storage
  *    Customer segment
        generate    fn$xpdis/(1.05+fn$sin(1.44*c1))
        if          stor=e,nodir
        leave       stor
        terminate
  nodir goto         nosel,.6
```

## 14.3 Functions with addresses

Micro-GPSS has two more types of function, both using function definition statements. One of these functions must use so-called savevalues in the A operand of this statement. Since I have not yet dealt with savevalues, it is necessary to wait until Chapter 20 to study this type of function.

The other type of function are functions that provide the address of a block as the dependent variable. The independent variable can be any type of SNA, but RN$j$ is most frequently used. The function is defined by the user and is always of the *discrete* type, i.e. the B operand of the function definition statement is D$j$, where $j$ is the number of pairs. Thus the function header statement is similar to that of other statements. The function *data* statements are different. While the first member in each pair, the independent $x$-value, is still a number, the second member in each pair, the dependent $y$-value, is a symbolic address, i.e. a name starting with three letters.

An example is function FN$CHOIC below, leading in 60 percent of all cases to the address MEAT, in 20 percent to the address FISH and in 20 percent to the address CHEES, depending on what RN4 value is sampled.

```
CHOIC FUNCTION RN4,D3
.6,MEAT/.8,FISH/1,CHEES
```

In micro-GPSS a function address, such as e.g. FN$CHOIC, can be used instead of any ordinary address. Such an address is probably most useful in an unconditional GOTO statement, replacing several stochastic GOTO statements. Program 14.3 demonstrates the power of this function address construction. Let us consider the situation in Exercise 8.1. In addition to a meat counter with two servers and a fish counter with one server, there is a cheese counter with one server with a service time ranging from 2 to 18 minutes. Let us now assume that customers go to just *one* of these counters and that 60 percent go to the meat counter, 20 percent to the fish counter and 20 percent to the cheese counter.

The transfer done by GOTO FN$CHOIC could have been carried out using two stochastic GOTO statements, but such a construction would invite logical errors. First there would be GOTO MEAT,.6, whereby 60 percent go to MEAT and the remaining 40 percent to the next block. If this block were GOTO FISH,.2, 20 percent of the 40 percent, i.e. only 8 percent of the total, would go to FISH. Instead we want 20 percent of the total, i.e. 50 percent of the remaining 40 percent to go to FISH. It is thus necessary to write GOTO FISH,.5. When there are more addresses and numbers are more complicated than above, the advantage of the address function over several stochastic GOTOs becomes even greater.

**Program 14.3**

```
        simulate
meat    storage     2
        qtable      meat,0,10,10
choic function      rn4,d3
.6,meat/.8,fish/1,chees
        generate    6,3
        goto        fn$choic
* Meat counter
meat    enter       meat,q
        advance     16,8
        leave       meat
        terminate
* Fish counter
fish    seize       fish,q
        advance     20,3
        release     fish
        terminate
* Cheese counter
chees   seize       chees,q
        advance     10,8
        release     chees
        terminate
        generate    480
        terminate   1
        start       1
        end
```

**Exercise 14.1** (Based on case study 4A in Schriber, 1974)

In a one-line, one-server queuing system, arrivals occur in a Poisson pattern (i.e. according to the exponential distribution) with a mean rate of 12 arrivals per hour. Service is also performed exponentially, but the mean service time depends on the content of the waiting line ahead of the server. The dependence is shown in the table below:

| Contents of the waiting line | Mean service time (minutes) |
|---|---|
| 0 | 5.5 |
| 1 or 2 | 5.0 |
| 3, 4 or 5 | 4.5 |
| 6 or more | 4.0 |

Build a GPSS model of the system, then use the model to estimate the effective mean service time. If the arrival rate increases to the extent of one additional arrival per hour, will the server still be able to handle the flow of customers, or will the waiting line tend to become longer and longer? Run the model for 500 customers!

---

### Exercise 14.2  (Based on Exercise 3.47 in Banks and Carson, 1984)

People arrive at a newspaper stand with an InterArrival Time that is exponentially distributed with a mean of 0.5 minutes. Fifty-five percent of the people buy just the morning paper, while 25 percent buy the morning paper and a *Wall Street Journal*. The remainder buy only the *Wall Street Journal*. One clerk handles the *Wall Street Journal* sales, while another clerk handles morning paper sales. The time it takes to serve a customer is normally distributed with a mean of 40 seconds and a standard deviation of 4 seconds for all transactions. Collect statistics on queues for each type of clerk. Simulate for four hours.

---

### Exercise 14.3

Cars arrive at a bridge at a rate of 15 per minute, but with IATs following the exponential distribution. The average speed is dependent on the number of cars on the bridge. If there are no other cars, a car can drive at 60 mph; if there are 30 cars at 50 mph; if 100 cars at 40 mph; if 200 cars at 30 mph and if 500 cars at 20 mph. Ninety-five percent of all cars drive at between 80 and 120 percent of this average speed. The length of the bridge is four miles. Simulate for 1000 cars to estimate the average time in minutes to cross the bridge.

---

### Exercise 14.4

Modify Program 12.4 to take into account a varying intensity of customer arrivals during the day and the possibility of hiring a part-timer as the second salesperson. Assume that the store is open between 9 a.m. and 6 p.m. Average IAT is 25 minutes 9 a.m.–11 a.m.; 15 minutes 11 a.m.–1 p.m.; 30 minutes 1 p.m.–4 p.m. and 10 minutes 4 p.m.–6 p.m. The specific arrival times are exponentially distributed. The part-timer is willing to work any four hours in a row. Should the part-timer be hired to work between 11 a.m. and 3 p.m. or between 2 p.m. and 6 p.m., if the objective is to sell as much as possible? Assume that all factors other than those mentioned here are as in Program 12.4.

## Exercise 14.5

Modify Program 13.3 by incorporating the possibility of influencing sales by changing the price. Assume that annual potential sales of the book, i.e. the number of students per year during 250 working days who ask for the book, is a function of price as follows: $q = ap^{-b}$, where $q$ represents potential sales, $p$ the price, $a$ a scale factor and $b$ the price elasticity constant. Let $a = 30\,000$ and $b = 1.5$ (implying that sales go up by 1.5 percent if price goes down by 1 percent). Simulate for both a price of 25 and a price of 30. All other factors are the same as in Program 13.3.

## Exercise 14.6

Orders arrive at a factory at the rate of 20 every hour, following an exponential distribution. There are orders for three types of good: 40 percent are of type A, 35 of type B and 25 of type C. They each require processing in a special machine. Processing in the A machine takes $6 \pm 4$ minutes, in the B machine $9 \pm 3$ minutes and in the C machine $12 \pm 5$ minutes. Simulate for a working week of 50 hours to study to what extent orders are held up at the various machines.

# 15 Print-out and savevalues

## 15.1 Introduction

Until this point in the book only standard output has been received. This has been given automatically at the end of the simulations by the GPSS processor, without allowing the programmer to select what is printed. This chapter deals with blocks and control statements in micro-GPSS that allow increased flexibility as regards the output.

I shall first discuss the savevalue concept. This allows us to obtain any kind of value printed in the standard output obtained at the end of the simulation. Savevalues can also be used for other important purposes, e.g. storing different values permanently. In micro-GPSS, savevalues mainly obtain their values through various forms of LET statements, studied in Section 15.2. Savevalues can also be assigned values through a special IF block, as discussed in Section 15.3.

After this, in Section 15.4, we shall study the PRINT block, which allows us to obtain print-out also *during* the simulation, i.e. prior to the standard output at the end of the simulation.

Finally, Section 15.5 covers the use of the block TABULATE and the control statement TABLE for producing tables for any kind of SNA, similar to those that QTABLE creates for queues.

## 15.2 LET statements and savevalues

In this section we shall examine the savevalue concept. This concept has two functions. First, it allocates memory in which to save any temporary value. It is thus similar to a (single-precision real) variable in a GPL like FORTRAN. Secondly, every such value is printed in the final standard output.

# The LET block

The most common way of creating savevalues in micro-GPSS is by the use of the LET block. Since each savevalue with a particular name is completely unique, the value given to a savevalue will remain until the end of the simulation, unless it is changed by some transaction going through this or another block referring to this savevalue. The LET concept can also be used in connection with parameters, the subject of the next chapter. This chapter, however, deals only with savevalues.

> The LET concept of micro-GPSS covers three concepts in GPSS V. LET used for savevalues, as in this chapter, corresponds to the SAVEVALUE block and the INITIAL statement in GPSS V and LET used for parameters, as in the next chapter, corresponds to the GPSS V ASSIGN block. (A different LET concept exists in GPSS/H.) For the sake of increased compatibility ASSIGN, INITIAL and SAVEVALUE are also allowed in micro-GPSS (see Appendix B).

The SNA of the savevalue is denoted by X followed by $ and then the symbolic name of the savevalue. Because of X being the 'class letter' of the savevalue it is sometimes, e.g. in error codes, called the X-value for short.

Since the LET block is a combination of GPSS V blocks, we are free to choose a suitable block symbol. The simple symbol shown in Figure 15.1 has the advantage of allowing space for fairly long B operands in the form of expressions. (In some IBM manuals this symbol is also suggested as an alternative symbol for both ASSIGN and SAVEVALUE blocks, i.e. the blocks replaced by LET.) The A operand, which is compulsory, consists of X$ followed by the name of the savevalue, i.e. the variable name.

**Figure 15.1** Block symbol of LET

The B operand is the value to be given to the variable of the A operand. The B operand can be a constant, an SNA or an expression, and is compulsory.

The simple LET block works in a pure *assign* mode, where the value of the B operand is given to the savevalue in the A operand. Thus LET X$COST = 27 implies that the savevalue X$COST acquires the value 27. Note that the comma between the A and B operands of this LET block is replaced by an =. (The statement LET X$COST=27 is more comprehensible than LET X$COST,27.) Likewise LET X$FVAL=FN$VAL implies that X$FVAL obtains the current value of the function VAL and LET X$REVNU=X$PRICE⋆X$QUANT implies that X$REVNU obtains the value of the product of X$PRICE and X$QUANT.

A common use of savevalues is to provide for the print-out of values of other SNAs. All savevalues are automatically printed in the standard output obtained at the end of the simulation. If an SNA value is placed into a savevalue at a particular time, the print-out of this particular SNA value is then secured. For example, the print-out of the current contents of the storage STOR at time 80 can be secured by the following segment:

```
generate  80,,,1
let       x$sto80=s$stor
terminate
```

At time 80 one special transaction is generated that places the value of S$STOR into X$STO80. A part of the final standard output is a print-out of the value of STO80, which will contain the contents of storage STOR at time 80, provided X$STO80 has not been changed since then.

## The LET control statement

LET can be used not only as a block, but also as a *control* statement. As mentioned above, all savevalues are (like most other SNAs) set to 0 at the start. There might, however, be reasons to give a savevalue a positive value prior to the start of the simulation. This can be done by a LET control statement. Most commonly, the B operand of the LET *control* statement is a positive *constant* that is given to the savevalue at the start of the simulation. Thus LET X$COST=25, placed somewhere at the beginning of the program prior to the first GENERATE block, will assign the value 25 to the savevalue X$COST at the start of the simulation.

For B operand of the LET *control* statement, it is also possible to use another X$-value that has been assigned a value through a LET control statement *earlier* in the program. Thus LET X$COST=25 could be followed by the control statement LET X$PRICE=X$COST. However, in the *control* statement the B operand cannot be an expression or an SNA other than a savevalue used earlier. This is the main difference in syntax between the LET control statement and the LET block.

One important use of the LET control statement is when there is a need to run a program several times with different values of some parameter that occurs several times in the program. Instead of a constant having to be changed in several places in the program, it is then only necessary to change *one* savevalue.

For example, the effect on total profits from changes in a decision variable can be tested by repeated simulations. This decision variable could then appear in the calculation of, for example, both sales and costs. Instead of writing the decision variable as a constant in several places, all of which have to be changed for each run of the program, it is easier to use a savevalue. At the beginning of the program, after SIMULATE, a LET statement gives a value to this decision variable for a particular run of the program. Another benefit is that the output clearly shows the value given to the decision variable.

For example, in Program 12.5, it might be appropriate to use a control statement LET X$INCAS=80000 and in the morning segment to then write ENTER CASH,X$INCAS instead of ENTER CASH,80000.

Furthermore, in Program 8.1 X$WORKR could have been used as the D operand of the GENERATE block and the number of workers set by an initial LET X$WORKR=4. As seen in Appendix A, micro-GPSS allows a savevalue that has been given its value through a LET control statement to be used instead of a numerical constant, e.g. as the D operand of a GENERATE block.

Another example of the use of LET control statements is the definition of storage capacity. In Chapter 7 the A operand of the STORAGE statement was defined as an integer constant. Micro-GPSS (but not GPSS V) thus also allows a savevalue as the A operand of STORAGE, provided that it has obtained a value through a LET control statement earlier in the program.

I shall now give an example of a program (Program 15.1) that uses both LET blocks and LET control statements for savevalues to produce a print-out of the total profits obtained during a day. Let us modify an earlier example, Program 12.4, where we calculated total sales during a day, dependent on the number of salespeople. By the use of savevalues, the print-out can also include the profits associated with the particular hiring policy.

Let us assume that gross profits are 30 percent of sales and that each salesperson costs \$80 per day. Profits can thus be defined as $0.3 * S\$REVNU - 80 * X\$CAPAC$. This program starts with LET X$CAPAC=1 and next uses X$CAPAC as the A operand of the STORAGE statement.

A print-out of the total profit made over the day is obtained since the stop transaction calculates the savevalue X$PROF. The effect of this stop segment is that, at stop time 480, the final profit is calculated, based on the current value of S$REVNU, the total sales of the day. Since the profit is assigned to the savevalue X$PROF, it is included in the final output.

Besides the ordinary block, queue and storage statistics, we also obtain in this case a print-out of savevalues, looking as follows:

| Contents of savevalues (non-zero) | |
|---|---|
| Savevalue name | Value |
| CAPAC | 1.00 |
| PROF | 518.20 |

With the A operand of STORAGE set instead to 2 (= Program 15.1b), the following output is obtained:

| Contents of savevalues (non-zero) | |
|---|---|
| Savevalue name | Value |
| CAPAC | 2.00 |
| PROF | 848.90 |

If several runs yield similar results, the hiring of an additional salesperson would be recommended.

**Program 15.1**

```
          simulate
          let        x$capac=1
 sal      storage    x$capac
 revnu storage
 serv     function   rn2,c2
0,20/1,30
 limit  function    rn3,d6
.1,1/.3,2/.55,3/.75,4/.9,5/1,6
 sales  function    rn4,c5
0,0/.25,10/.5,40/.75,100/1,500
          generate   18,6
          if         q$sal>=fn$limit,bye
          enter      sal,q
          advance    fn$serv
          enter      revnu,fn$sales
          leave      sal
 bye      terminate
          generate   480
          let        x$prof=0.3*s$revnu-80*x$capac
          terminate  1
          start      1
          end
```

## The LET+ and LET− blocks

In certain programs there might be blocks where a savevalue is increased, e.g. in cases when the savevalue is used as a counter. Instead of writing, e.g. LET X$COUNT=X$COUNT + 1, we can, however, use a simpler construction with the operation code LET+, i.e. LET in an *increase* mode. We can then write LET+ X$COUNT,1. We can read this as 'LET's increase X$COUNT by 1'. Here the + follows immediately after the T of LET without any intervening blank space as part of the operation word.

In addition the A and B operands are separated with a comma in this case, to make clear the distinction from the pure assign mode. The block symbol is as in Figure 15.1 except that there is a + immediately after LET and the equal-sign is omitted.

The LET− block, i.e. the LET block in the *decrease* mode, is very similar. Instead of LET X$CASH=X$CASH−X$PAY, it is possible to write LET− X$CASH,X$PAY. This can be read as 'LET's decrease X$CASH by X$PAY' or 'let's decrease cash by the payment'. All the other statements about LET+ above hold in a similar way for LET−. It should be noted that since control statements cannot involve calculations, LET+ and LET− only exist as blocks. Their use will be demonstrated in Program 15.5.

## 15.3 The IF block in assignment mode

Chapter 9 dealt with an IF block where the A and B operands formed part of a test condition and the C operand was the address of the block to which the transaction went if this test condition was true. Micro-GPSS also has another IF block, where the A and B operands are *SNAs* or *constants* as in the IF blocks in SNA mode, but where the C and D operands are like the A and B operands of the LET block in pure assignment mode. The C operand is thus a savevalue (or parameter, see Chapter 16), while the D operand is a constant, an SNA or an expression. If the test condition involving the A and B operand is true, the value of the D operand is assigned to the savevalue (or parameter) of the C operand. To emphasize that the assignment of a value is involved and to make the block easy to understand, the C and D operands are separated by = instead of a comma. (There are special restrictions governing the formation of complex operands which depend on the implementation.)

The block symbol in Figure 15.2 is a combination of the ordinary IF symbol and the LET symbol. Thus the block IF X$GNORM<0,X$GNORM=0 implies a test of whether X$GNORM < 0 and if this is true, X$GNORM is set to 0; otherwise X$GNORM retains its original value. This is very similar to the BASIC statement IF GNORM < 0 THEN GNORM = 0. This block will be used in Program 15.2, where the ADVANCE block uses the normal distribution 10 ⋆ FN$SNORM + 25. Since there is almost a 1 percent risk of this ADVANCE time becoming negative, causing a halt in program execution, this value, called X$GNORM, is instead set to 0.

If in this program the IF block is deleted (= Program 15.2b), the program might stop.

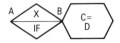

**Figure 15.2** Block symbol of the IF block in assignment mode

**Program 15.2**

```
        simulate
stor    storage     2
        generate    18*fn$xpdis
        enter       stor,q
        let         x$gnorm=fn$snorm*10+25
        if          x$gnorm<0,x$gnorm=0
        advance     x$gnorm
        leave       stor
        terminate
        generate    4800
        terminate   1
        start       1
        end
```

## 15.4 The PRINT block

Until this point, even when using savevalues, I have only discussed GPSS concepts that yield print-out at the *end* of the simulation, i.e. when the termination counter is set to 0. A standardized report is then obtained, always including the block statistics and, depending on whether there are any facilities, storages, queues (AD sets), tables and/or savevalues, a full print-out of statistics on these items is also produced.

It might, however, be desirable also to obtain a print-out of the current values of some SNAs *during* the simulation. In some cases it might not be sufficient to obtain, e.g., queue or storage values only at the end of the simulation, but there might also be a need to know these values at certain intervals during the simulation. This print-out of values prior to the simulation stop can be accomplished by the use of the PRINT block. It should be stressed that this is a block, i.e. is included in the block diagram, and has to be activated by a transaction.

The block symbol is similar to the printed output symbol of conventional flow charts. The A operand is one of the following four types:

1. An SNA, allowing for the print-out of *one* specific value.

2. A single letter, allowing for the print-out of a whole *group* of statistics.

3. An expression.

4. Text within quotes.

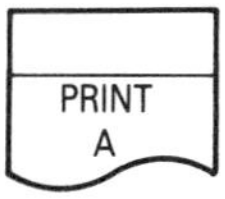

**Figure 15.3** Block symbol of PRINT

## 1. SNA print-out

I shall first deal with the case of A being an SNA. Micro-GPSS (but not GPSS V) allows for the print-out of specific SNAs. The A operand is a specific SNA like Q$LIN, S$STOR, C1 etc. The print-out will contain both the name of the SNA, as given in the A operand, and the actual value of the SNA.

In order to obtain a print-out at a certain time, it is usually most convenient to have a special segment which deals with the print-out. For example, the following segment causes the length of the waiting line, Q$SAL, to be printed out every 100 minutes of simulation time:

```
generate  100
print     q$sal
terminate
```

A program stopping at time 480 with this segment included would provide a print-out of the length of the waiting line of SAL at times 100, 200, 300 and 400. If a print-out is only required at time 100, there must be D operand = 1 in the GENERATE block, i.e. GENERATE 100,,,1.

As an example let us study Program 15.3, based on Program 6.1 but with the waiting line printed every 100 minutes. In order to see clearly what time the print-out refers to, the block PRINT C1 is included prior to PRINT Q$SAL.

This provides a chance to study how the waiting line builds up during the day. The output obtained prior to the standard report is in Table 15.1. The output of such a PRINT SNA construction can also be used for debugging a program (see Appendix D).

## 2. Group print-out

I shall now discuss the case when the A operand is a single letter. This letter determines which group of statistics is to be printed:

**Program 15.3**

```
simulate
generate    18,6
seize       sal,q
advance     25,5
release     sal
terminate
generate    100
print       c1
print       q$sal
terminate
generate    480
terminate   1
start       1
end
```

**Table 15.1** Non-standard output of Program 15.3

| C1 | 100.00 |
|---|---|
| Q$SAL | 2.00 |
| C1 | 200.00 |
| Q$SAL | 4.00 |
| C1 | 300.00 |
| Q$SAL | 5.00 |
| C1 | 400.00 |
| Q$SAL | 6.00 |

A refers to **All** of the standard report, otherwise obtained at the end of the simulation.

B refers to **Block** statistics.

C refers to the relative and absolute **Clock**.

F refers to **Facility** (and storage) statistics.

Q refers to **Queue** (AD set) statistics.

S refers to **Storage** (and facility) statistics.

T refers to **Tables**.

X refers to savevalues (**X**-values).

In micro-GPSS, where the aim is always to use the simplest constructions possible, this symbol is the A operand. Hence, in micro-GPSS,

PRINT A prints *all* statistics of any type, PRINT B prints *all* the block statistics, ..., and PRINT X prints *all* the savevalues.

GPSS V also allows for this type of print-out (except for the A = print all), but the letter is placed as the C operand; e.g. PRINT S of micro-GPSS must be written in GPSS V as PRINT ,,S. In order to increase compatibility with GPSS V, micro-GPSS also allows this form.

To exemplify the use of group print-out, let us change PRINT C1 and PRINT Q$SAL in Program 15.3 to PRINT C and PRINT Q to obtain Program 15.4.

**Program 15.4**

```
simulate
generate    18,6
seize       sal,q
advance     25,5
release     sal
terminate
generate    100
print       c
print       q
terminate
generate    480
terminate   1
start       1
end
```

The first part of the output of Program 15.4 is in Table 15.2.

## 3. Print-out of the value of an expression

In micro-GPSS a PRINT block can also print the value of an expression, as in PRINT 0.3*S$REVNU−X$CAPAC*80. In this case the value will not be preceded by any name.

## 4. Text print-out

Finally, micro-GPSS also allows a PRINT block to print text of a maximum length of 50 characters placed within quotation marks. If single quotation marks, i.e. ' ', are used the text within the quotation marks will be printed on

**Table 15.2** Start of output of Program 15.4

```
relative clock    100.00 absolute clock    100.00
```

| Queue (AD set) | Maximum contents | Average contents | Total entries | Zero entries | Percent zeros |
|---|---|---|---|---|---|
| TIM | 2 | 0.86 | 6 | 1 | 16.67 |

| Queue (AD set) | Average time/trans | $Average time/trans | Current contents |
|---|---|---|---|
| TIM | 14.38 | 17.25 | 2 |

$Average time/trans=average time/trans excluding zero entries

```
relative clock    200.00 absolute clock    200.00
```

| Queue (AD set) | Maximum contents | Average contents | Total entries | Zero entries | Percent zeros |
|---|---|---|---|---|---|
| TIM | 4 | 1.77 | 12 | 1 | 8.33 |

| Queue (AD set) | Average time/trans | $Average time/trans | Current contents |
|---|---|---|---|
| TIM | 29.43 | 32.11 | 4 |

$Average time/trans=average time/trans excluding zero entries

one line followed by a line feed. Thus we can print out headings, comments or blanks (by PRINT ' ').

If double quotation marks, i.e. " ", are used there will be *no* line feed, i.e. the next value to be printed by a PRINT SNA or PRINT expression block will come on the same line as the text within the double quotation marks. (Double quotation mark print-out cannot be used just before a group print-out block.) If this PRINT "text" block is followed by a PRINT SNA block then the SNA name will not be printed. The SNA will then be preceded by the text on the same line. In this way more appropriate names can be given to the SNA values.

The difference between the two types of quotation mark can be demonstrated by the following print-out taking place when the (relative) simulation clock is 100:

PRINT 'Time is' and PRINT C1 will lead to

```
Time is
C1        100.00
```

PRINT "Time is" and PRINT C1 will lead to

```
Time is  100.00
```

## Suppression of standard output

Since there is the possibility of obtaining more selective statistics by using the PRINT block, the standard output might not be required when the termination counter is set to 0 and the simulation stops. This standard print-out can be suppressed by including NP (for No Printing) as the B operand of the START control statement, e.g. as in START 1,NP.

Inserting a B operand NP into Program 15.4 (making it 15.4a) will hence cause output to detail only queues at times 100, 200, 300 and 400. No final output is obtained.

## A simple cash flow example

In order to summarize what has been learnt thus far about LET and PRINT blocks, I shall discuss a simple example involving profit and cash flow calculations. Program 15.5 deals with a corporation that buys and sells certain machines. It pays the producer cash directly for each unit, but provides its customers with credit. In this simple program we disregard the interest on this credit; a more complicated version will be presented in Program 19.5.

Let us first assign values to some variables: price, cost per unit and initial cash. FN$SALES is the annual sales in number of units, defined by five pairs of data as a continuous function of price. Thus if price is, e.g., 30, 60 units will be sold. Note that no price below 10 or above 50 can be used.

In the customer segment, the GENERATE block samples IATs that follow an exponential distribution with an average number of days between two orders of 360/FN$SALES. If, for example, 36 units are sold per year, there is an average of 360/36 = 10 days between two orders.

Each order implies first of all that X$SAL, which is the total sales in dollars for this quarter, is increased by the price of the product X$PRICE. Likewise X$TCOST, i.e. total costs, is increased by X$COST, the unit cost of the sold product. Since this amount X$COST has to be paid right away, X$CASH is decreased by this amount.

The ADVANCE block represents the actual credit time. This follows an Erlang distribution with the parameter $n = 3$. The average credit time is 45 days which would very approximately correspond to a modal value of around 30 days (see Figure 13.9). This distribution implies that the majority of customers pay within a little more than a month, but a few customers use a credit time which is two or three times longer. After this time the customers pay, which increases CASH by the price of the product.

The report segment produces a report each quarter. First the total profits of the quarter are calculated as sales − total costs. Next the time of the report is printed and then all the savevalues. Finally, X$SAL and

**Program 15.5**

```
            simulate
            let          x$price=25
            let          x$cost=15
            let          x$cash=100
   sales function        x$price,c5
   10,310/20,110/30,60/40,40/50,30
 * Customer segment
            generate     fn$xpdis*360/fn$sales
            let+         x$sal,x$price
            let+         x$tcost,x$cost
            let-         x$cash,x$cost
            advance      45*fn$rlng3
            let+         x$cash,x$price
            terminate
 * Report segment
            generate     90
            let          x$prof=x$sal-x$tcost
            print        c
            print        x
            let          x$sal=0
            let          x$tcost=0
            terminate    1
 *
            start        4,np
            end
```

X$TCOST are set to 0 so that the next report will concern only the values for that quarter.

The report segment also functions as a stop segment. With the A operand of START set to 4, the simulation is stopped after four report transactions have gone through TERMINATE 1, each decreasing the termination counter by 1.

In the initial LET control statements it is possible to work with different values of X$PRICE, X$COST and X$CASH for the purpose of experiments and sensitivity analysis. Setting these values to 25, 15 and 100 the output shown in Table 15.3 is obtained for the first quarter.

A clearer output can be obtained by using PRINT followed by text. For instance it is possible to write the report segment of Program 15.6 below. Except for the report segments, Programs 15.5 and 15.6 are identical.

**Table 15.3** Reports for the first quarter for Program 15.5

```
relative clock        90.00 absolute clock        90.00

Contents of savevalues (non-zero)
Savevalue name          Value
      PRICE             25.00
      COST              15.00
      CASH              10.00
      SAL              525.00
      TCOST            315.00
      PROF             210.00
```

**Program 15.6** Report segment

```
* Report segment
        generate    90
        let         x$prof=x$sal-x$tcost
        print       ' '
        print       ' '
        print       "Day number"
        print       c1
        print       ' '
        print       "Sales             "
        print       x$sal
        print       "Total costs       "
        print       x$tcost
        print       '------------------------------'
        print       "Total profits     "
        print       x$prof
        print       '=============================='
        print       "Cash              "
        print       x$cash
        let         x$sal=0
        let         x$tcost=0
        terminate   1
```

Program 15.6 produces the report in Table 15.4 for the first two quarters.

# 15.5 TABULATE and TABLE

In Chapter 6 I introduced the QTABLE statement that allows us to obtain a print-out of tables with statistics over the time spent in queues and AD sets.

**Table 15.4** Reports for the first two quarters of Program 15.6

```
Day number             90.00

Sales                      525.00
Total costs                315.00
------------------------------
Total profits              210.00
==============================
Cash                        10.00


Day number            180.00

Sales                      475.00
Total costs                285.00
------------------------------
Total profits              190.00
==============================
Cash                       225.00
```

In many cases it is helpful to obtain similar tables for any kind of SNA. This can be done by a combination of the block TABULATE and the control statement TABLE.

I shall begin by discussing the TABLE statement. There are five similarities with the QTABLE statement, as presented in Chapter 6:

1. There are four operands.

2. The B operand is the upper limit of the lowest class, often set to 0.

3. The C operand is the class width.

4. The D operand is the number of classes.

5. The statement should come after SIMULATE but before the first GENERATE block.

There is a further similarity which was not dealt with in Chapter 6. In that chapter only one table was used and it was not given a name. If several QTABLE tables are used in a program it is advisable (although not compulsory) to give them a name in order to distinguish them. This is done by writing a table name in front of the word QTABLE, i.e. in the address field. As regards TABLE, the name of the table is likewise written in the address field, i.e. before the word TABLE. For TABLE the name is, however, *compulsory*.

The major difference between QTABLE and TABLE, however, concerns the A operand, which for TABLE is the name of the SNA for which statistics are required in the table, e.g. S$STOR, Q$LIN, X$CASH, W$INN, etc.

An example of a TABLE statement is CATAB TABLE X$CASH,0,100,20.

This statement yields a table of 20 classes of the savevalue X$CASH, measured in units of 100, i.e. with the instances or observations of negative or zero cash in the first class, the instances of 0.01–100 dollars in cash in the second class, etc.

In order to gather statistics, i.e. to make observations, for TABLE a special block, TABULATE, is required. (For QTABLE this is done implicitly by the DEPART blocks.)

The symbol of the TABULATE block is illustrated in Figure 15.4. The TABULATE block has a compulsory A operand, which is the name of the TABLE in which the data gathered by the block will be presented.

**Figure 15.4** Block symbol of TABULATE

In Program 15.7 there is a block TABULATE CATAB, CATAB being defined as in the above example.

**Program 15.7**

```
        simulate
catab table       x$cash,0,100,20
      let         x$price=25
      let         x$cost=15
      let         x$cash=100
 sales function   x$price,c5
10,310/20,110/30,60/40,40/50,30
*
      generate    fn$xpdis*360/fn$sales
      let+        x$sal,x$price
      let+        x$tcost,x$cost
      let-        x$cash,x$cost
      advance     45*fn$rlng3
      let+        x$cash,x$price
      terminate
*
      generate    10
      tabulate    catab
      terminate   1
*
      start       90
      end
```

Since the A operand of CATAB is X$CASH, it can be determined that the
TABULATE block will gather statistics on the value of X$CASH at each
moment when a transaction enters this TABULATE CATAB block.

Program 15.7 is a modification of Program 15.5. Instead of printing
quarterly reports, it produces a table (see Table 15.5) on the amount of cash,
measured every 10 days during one quarter.

From Table 15.5 it can be seen that cash has been zero or negative
several times during the first quarter. This could not be seen from the report
at the end of the quarter in Table 15.4.

**Table 15.5** Part of table produced by Program 15.7

```
Table  CATAB
Entries in table Mean argument Standard deviation Sum of arguments
        90            928.22           632.16           83540.00

   Range           Observed    Per cent   Cumulative Cumulative
                   frequency   of total   percentage remainder

          -   0        5        5.56         5.56       94.44
   0.01 -  100         6        6.67        12.22       87.78
 100.01 -  200         3        3.33        15.56       84.44
 200.01 -  300         5        5.56        21.11       78.89
 300.01 -  400         3        3.33        24.44       75.56
   ...
1600.01 - 1700         5        5.56        84.44       15.56
1700.01 - 1800         6        6.67        91.11        8.89
   Overflow            8        8.89       100.00        0.00
   Average value of overflow            1845.63
```

## Exercise 15.1

Modify Program 6.1 so that Average time/trans, printed in the queue statistics, is also
obtained as a savevalue. Total waiting time is first calculated by adding C1, i.e. the
value of the relative clock, to this time at each exit from the queue and subtracting C1
from this time at each entry into the queue. At stop time, the *product* of C1 and the
number of customers remaining in the queue (in the block prior to SEIZE) is also
added to the total time. This total waiting time is then finally divided by the number of
entries into the queue. (In Section 18.6 a much simpler, but less instructive, method
for doing this will be presented.)

**Exercise 15.2** (Based on case study 4A in Schriber, 1974)

Run the model of Exercise 14.1 again for 500 customers, but now to obtain a print-out after every 100th customer. (Hint: the decimal fraction of N/100 is = 0 for every such customer. Use FN$DEC, see Section 14.2.)

**Exercise 15.3** (Based on case study 5A in Schriber, 1974)

Modify Program 8.1 to incorporate the following features:

1. Arrange to have the average daily profit realized for each alternative included in the model output. Base the profit calculation on the following cost information.

   | | |
   |---|---|
   | Worker's salary | $3.75 per hour |
   | Oven cost | $80 per 10-hour work day |
   | | (independent of utilization) |
   | Raw material | $2 per pot |
   | Value of *finished* pot | $7 per pot |

2. Let the number of workers be a variable, using a savevalue, and simulate for four, five and six workers.

3. Make it easy to change the number of days to be simulated by specifying it as a savevalue.

**Exercise 15.4** (Based on case study 5B in Schriber, 1974)

In a retail store, the daily demand for a given item is normally distributed with a mean and standard deviation of 10 and 2 units, respectively. Whenever the retailer's stock-on-hand drops to or beneath a predetermined point, called the re-order point, he places a stock-replenishment order with his supplier regarding a specific replenishment amount, called the re-order quantity, provided there is no unfilled order. The replenishment order arrives at the retail store 6 to 10 days after it was placed. The time between placing the replenishment order, and its arrival at the retail store, is termed lead-time. The lead-time distribution is as follows:

| Lead-time (days) | Relative frequency |
|---|---|
| 6 | 0.05 |
| 7 | 0.25 |
| 8 | 0.30 |
| 9 | 0.22 |
| 10 | 0.18 |

Demand that arises when the retailer is out of stock is lost; that is, customers whose demand cannot be satisfied immediately go elsewhere to carry out their business.

The retailer wants to know how his experience of stocking the item will vary, depending on where he sets the re-order point.

Build a GPSS model for the retailer's situation. Design the model to obtain a table on 'lost daily sales' and 'number of units carried in inventory'. Run the model to estimate these two distributions when the re-order quantity is 100, and the re-order point is 80. Shut off the model after a simulation of 1000 days. Ignore any 'weekend problems', by assuming that the retailer does business seven days a week and that a replenishment order in transit continues to proceed toward its destination on Saturdays and Sundays.

---

### Exercise 15.5  (Based on Example 5 in Birtwistle, 1979)

Motorists wishing to cross the strait between the mainland and a small island have to use a ferry. The ferry is moored on the mainland overnight and starts work promptly each day at 7 a.m. It shuttles to and fro between the mainland and the island until approximately 10 p.m. when the service closes down for the night. The ferry has a capacity limit of six cars. When the ferry arrives at a quay, the cars on the ferry are driven off, and then any waiting cars (up to a maximum of six) are driven on. When the ferry is fully loaded, or the quay queue is empty, the ferry leaves that side of the strait and starts another crossing. When the ferry has completed a round trip and deposited any passengers on the mainland, the captain checks the time. If it is 9.45 p.m. (i.e. 21.45 hours) or later, he closes down the service for the night.

Both on the mainland and the island, cars arrive on average at a rate of nine per hour, following an exponential distribution. Crossing times follow the normal distribution with a mean of 8 minutes and a standard deviation of 0.5. It takes 0.5 minutes to drive on or drive off the ferry.

Run the model for one working day under the following initial conditions: at time 7 a.m., there are three cars waiting on the mainland and one on the island. Produce a table of the number of cars on the ferry at each crossing.

# 16 Parameters

## 16.1 The parameter concept

This chapter covers one of the most powerful ideas in GPSS, the parameter. Since it is also the part of GPSS that is most difficult to learn and use, this first section will spend a considerable time explaining the main ideas behind this concept. In Section 16.2 we shall study examples of the use of LET blocks as applied to parameters. Finally Section 16.3 deals with another block, SELECT, which when combined with parameters allows for very powerful programming.

The parameter is an SNA (Standard Numerical Attribute), which is linked to a *transaction*. Each transaction carries with it a certain number of parameters. A parameter is in this respect very similar to the priority level that we studied in Chapter 11. Just as each transaction has its own specific priority level, each transaction can have its own value of a specific parameter, as will be explained in detail below.

In micro-GPSS each transaction can have 12 parameters. (In GPSS V more can be created by special actions.) The parameters are distinguished only by a number. With the parameter being denoted as P, the parameters of a transaction are thus called P1, P2, P3 etc. Since the program examples in this book will only need three parameters at the most, there will not be any reason to use any other parameters apart from P1, P2 and P3 in this book, since the memory required is dependent on the highest parameter number.

Because of the fundamental difference between parameters and other SNAs, to be explained in more detail later, the naming of parameters is completely different from that of other SNAs. Symbolic names are not allowed, nor is there any P$-value. Because of this special characteristic of parameters and because there can be no more than 12 parameters, micro-GPSS follows GPSS V (but not GPSS/H) in only allowing parameters to be called P$j$, where $j = 1 \ldots 12$.

The value of a parameter can be *regarded* as the value in a memory cell in a matrix. (The actual implementation is, however, quite different.) Since

**Table 16.1** Hypothetical parameter matrix

| | | Number of parameter | | | |
|---|---|---|---|---|---|
| | | 1 | 2 | 3 | 4 . . . |
| | 1 | | | | |
| | 2 | | | | |
| ITN | 3 | | P(3,2) | | |
| | 4 | | | | |

every transaction can be thought of as having an internal number (unknown to the user) and since every parameter has a number, P2 for the third (generated) transaction in the simulation can be thought of, for instance, as the cell P(3,2) in a matrix. This is illustrated by the hypothetical parameter matrix P in Table 16.1. The rows are the values of the Internal Transaction Number (ITN) and the columns the numbers of the parameters, 1 . . . 12.

At this point it should be stressed that the memory cell referred to when a parameter is called upon depends on which transaction goes into the block that calls on the parameter. When a transaction which has ITN 3 enters a block using parameter P2, this can be thought of as a reference to the cell P(3,2) in this imaginary parameter matrix. When the next transaction, e.g. with ITN 4, reaches this block, parameter P2 refers to the cell P(4,2) in this matrix.

The value in a memory cell can be accessed only as long as the transaction with the ITN of the cell is active in the simulation. Once the transaction goes into a TERMINATE block, the value in this cell can no longer be accessed, i.e. it is lost for the simulation.

The LET block can be used to store the value of a parameter in such a memory cell. The effect of several transactions coming to such a block can be illustrated with the aid of the following simple segment:

```
generate    10
let         p1=c1
advance     25
terminate
```

Table 16.2 shows the development of the parameter values produced by this segment. The * denotes the time of generation and the † refers to the time of termination of the transaction.

At time 30, when the transactions with the internal numbers ITN = 1–3 have been generated, P(1,1) = 10, P(2,1) = 20 and P(3,1) = 30. At time 35, transaction 1 is terminated and the value of P(1,1) is lost. The transaction generated at time 40 can now take the ITN of 1, since the old transaction

**Table 16.2** Example of parameter values

| * | † | ITN | P1 |
|---|---|-----|----|
| 10 | 35 | 1 | 10 |
| 20 | 45 | 2 | 20 |
| 30 | 55 | 3 | 30 |
| 40 | 65 | 1 | 40 |
| 50 | 75 | 2 | 50 |

with number 1 is 'dead'. Then P(1,1) can be set to 40. Likewise, at time 50, with the old number 2 dead, the new transaction takes the ITN of 2 and sets P(2,1) = 50.

Before going into more detail about parameters, I shall first examine some differences between savevalues and parameters. Both represent memory locations, but, while a savevalue only needs *one* memory cell, representing one number, a parameter, e.g. P1, usually refers to several cells in memory, as has been seen in Table 16.1. Furthermore, while the savevalue remains for the whole simulation once it has been created, a parameter value is, as mentioned, linked to a transaction and is available only while this transaction is active in the simulation. It is lost when the transaction goes into the TERMINATE block.

A parameter, not a savevalue, must be used when one needs to keep track of a characteristic or attribute that can be connected to more than one transaction at the same time. For example, in Program 16.1, the number of items in each shopping cart must be represented by a parameter, since there can be several shopping carts at the same time in the store, each with a different number of items.

Another example is when a particular period of credit has been determined for each payment and this is used in the calculation of interest on each payment after the credit period has elapsed. The period of credit must then be placed into a parameter and *not* a savevalue, since this value would most likely be changed by another transaction before it is time to calculate the interest on the first payment (see Program 19.5).

Since parameter values are lost when a transaction is terminated, but a savevalue is permanent, one use of a savevalue is to save some feature of a parameter, e.g. to establish the highest value that a certain parameter obtains during a simulation.

# 16.2 The LET block applied to parameters

The LET block can be used in micro-GPSS to give a value to a parameter. The LET block as applied to parameters works, just as it does for savevalues, in three different modes.

## 1. The pure assign mode

In this case LET is the operation, the A operand is P$j$ (with $j = 1 \ldots 12$) and the B operand is the value assigned to the parameter in the A operand. For example, LET P1=7 implies that parameter 1 is assigned the value 7. This is equivalent to a statement in a GPL (such as FORTRAN) such as P(ITN,1) = 7.

## 2. The increase mode

In the increase mode, the operation is LET+, the A operand is P$j$ and the value of the B operand is added to the current value of the parameter in the A operand. Thus LET+ P2,FN$NUMB is equivalent to LET P2=P2+FN$NUMB and implies that the value of parameter 2 is increased by the value of the function NUMB, corresponding in a GPL to P(ITN,2) = P(ITN,2) + FNNUMB($x$).

## 3. The decrease mode

In the decrease mode, the operation is LET−, the A operand is P$j$ and the value of the B operand is subtracted from the current value of the parameter of the A operand. Thus, LET− P1,7 is equivalent to LET P1=P1−7 and implies that the value of the parameter 1 is decreased by 7, corresponding in a GPL to P(ITN,1) = P(ITN,1) − 7.

I shall illustrate the use of the LET block for parameters with two examples.

## Example 1 – Program 16.1

The first example deals with a store where customers go through two aisles and pick up goods. The time spent in an aisle will depend on the number of items picked up in this aisle. The customer then comes to a checkout counter, where the time spent depends on the total number of items purchased in the store. The block diagram of the customer segment is in Figure 16.1.

Let us assume that customers arrive on average every 11 seconds, following an exponential distribution. They next join the AD set TOTIM, which measures the total time spent in the store, since DEPART TOTIM is just before TERMINATE.

The first LET block represents aisle 1. This is a LET block functioning in pure assign mode. It assigns the value of the random function AYL to parameter 1 of each transaction. Parameter 1 will then contain the number of items to be chosen in this aisle. It can be seen from function AYL that a number between 0 and 9 will be sampled. In micro-GPSS the function value FN\$AYL will generally not be an integer number. Therefore the value is truncated using the function FN\$INT so that between 0 and 8 items are assigned to P1, since, e.g., FN\$INT(8.99) = 8.

The block LET P2=P1 assigns this number of items to parameter 2, which represents the number of items put into the shopping cart. Thus the number of items in the shopping cart is now set equal to the number of items picked in the present aisle, in this case the first aisle.

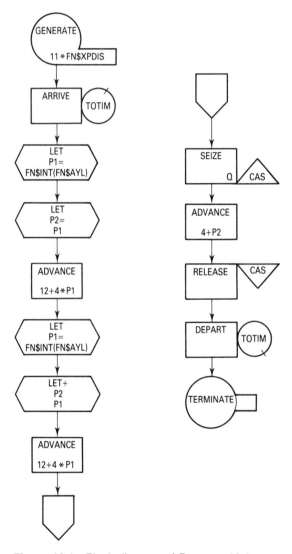

**Figure 16.1** Block diagram of Program 16.1

**Program 16.1**

```
        simulate
  ayl   function   rn2,c2
0,0/1,9
* Customer segment
        generate   11*fn$xpdis
        arrive     totim
* first aisle
        let        p1=fn$int(fn$ayl)
        let        p2=p1
        advance    12+4*p1
* second aisle
        let        p1=fn$int(fn$ayl)
        let+       p2,p1
        advance    12+4*p1
* cashier
        seize      cas,q
        advance    4+p2
        release    cas
        depart     totim
        terminate
* Stop segment
        generate   3600
        terminate  1
        start      1
        end
```

Next the transaction spends time in this first aisle via the block
ADVANCE $12 + 4 * P1$. The service time depends on the number of items
picked up in this aisle, i.e. on the transaction's parameter 1 value. There is a
basic choosing time of 12 seconds and each item requires 4 seconds.

The customer then goes into the second aisle. Again the function AYL
determines at random how many items are chosen in this aisle. This number
is again given to parameter 1. Parameter 1 hence holds the number to be
chosen in the present aisle, which is now aisle 2. An ADVANCE block uses
this value of P1 to determine how long the customer spends in the second
aisle.

The customer puts these items into the shopping trolley. The block
LET+ P2,P1 adds the P1 value, i.e. the number of items picked in aisle 2, to
P2, which before this addition contained the number of items picked in aisle
1. Now P2 will contain the *total* number of items selected so far, i.e. both in
aisle 1 and aisle 2.

The customer next comes to the checkout counter. There is also a need for statistics on actual waiting times in front of the checkout counter, so Q is used in the B operand of the SEIZE block. There is a single cashier, the facility CAS. The service time spent with the cashier is dependent on P2, i.e. the total number of items selected, with a fixed time (independent of number of items purchased) of 4 seconds, plus a time of 1 second per item. The simulation is run for one hour, i.e. 3600 seconds.

## Example 2 – Program 16.2

In the next example the parameter will be used in a more complicated and more powerful way. In order to understand this better, first note that until

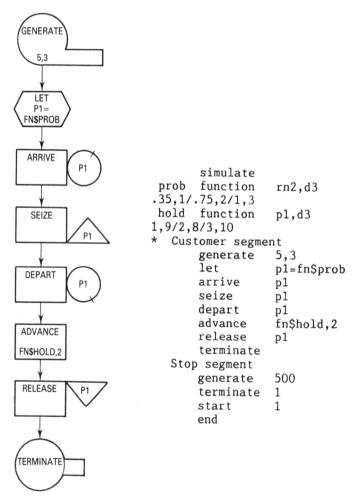

```
        simulate
prob  function    rn2,d3
.35,1/.75,2/1,3
hold  function    p1,d3
1,9/2,8/3,10
*   Customer segment
        generate    5,3
        let         p1=fn$prob
        arrive      p1
        seize       p1
        depart      p1
        advance     fn$hold,2
        release     p1
        terminate
Stop segment
        generate    500
        terminate   1
        start       1
        end
```

**Figure 16.2** Block diagram and listing of Program 16.2

now only symbolic names have been used for facilities, storages, queues (or AD sets), etc. At the start of execution of the program, the processor translates these symbolic names into numbers. It has already been mentioned that it is possible in GPSS V, but *not* micro-GPSS, to use numbers instead of symbolic names, but it must be stressed that this can lead to very dangerous confusion. For example, SAL and 1 used in the same program might inadvertently refer to the same storage (see, e.g., Schriber, 1974, p. 236).

Micro-GPSS uses the numerical designation of servers and queues only in connection with parameters and there is *never* any danger of this confusion. (There is no danger of confusion in GPSS V either, *provided* there are no symbolic names for servers and queues in the program.) In Programs 16.2–16.6, I shall first deal with the case when there are no symbolic names and where micro-GPSS and GPSS V hence function in the same way.

If parameters are allowed in the place of symbolic names for servers, it is possible to have a block SEIZE P1, for instance, which will imply SEIZE 1, SEIZE 2 or SEIZE 3, depending on what value, 1, 2 or 3, has been assigned to the parameter P1. Likewise, ARRIVE P2 can imply ARRIVE 1, ARRIVE 2, ..., ARRIVE 5, depending on whether P2 is 1, 2, ... or 5. This is a very important feature in GPSS, allowing for very compact programs as will be shown in Program 16.2.

This program deals with a store with three different salespeople, each running his or her own part of the store and each with a separate waiting line. (Alternatively it could be a barber shop with three barbers, where every customer has a preferred barber.) Thirty-five percent of the customers go to server 1, 40 percent go to server 2 and 25 percent to server 3. The three servers have different service times: server 1 needs 9 minutes, server 2 needs 8 minutes and server 3 needs 10 minutes on average. Actual service times can vary from average time *minus* 2 minutes to average time *plus* 2 minutes.

The block diagram and program listing of Program 16.2 are shown in Figure 16.2. There is only *one* customer segment, with all customers generated by the same GENERATE block. Immediately after GENERATE, a LET block determines which of the three servers and queues each customer should go to. The block LET P1=FN$PROB will assign to the arriving customer the number 1 with the probability 0.35, the number 2 with the probability 0.4 and the number 3 with the probability 0.25. This can be thought of as giving each customer a ticket with a number that tells him which queue and server he has to go to. This number is then put into P1.

The customer then comes to the block ARRIVE P1. If number 1 is located in parameter P1, he or she will go into queue 1; if the customer has number 2, into queue 2, etc. At this point it should be stressed that Q cannot be used in the B operand of a SEIZE block, *if* the A operand is a parameter. It is therefore necessary to use an ARRIVE–DEPART set for measuring queuing time here.

Likewise, SEIZE P1 implies that if the transaction has obtained number

1, it will try to obtain service from server 1; if number 2, from server 2, etc. If the customer is denied access to a server, e.g. server 1, because the server is busy, then the customer is, in the processor sense, put on a special waiting list, representing those waiting in front of server 1. In this case the customer *cannot* go to another server, even if this facility is idle. (Selection of a free server has to be modeled differently, as shown in Program 16.3.)

Next the customer comes to the block DEPART P1, which acts like the 'mirror image' of ARRIVE P1, implying that the customer leaves the queue joined earlier.

The customer then comes to the block ADVANCE FN$HOLD,2. The FN$-value is the A operand and the constant 2 is the B operand. Hence the service time is a rectangular distribution, implying that service times vary between FN$HOLD − 2 and FN$HOLD + 2. The value of FN$HOLD is dependent on the number of the customer's parameter 1 so that FN$HOLD is 9 if the number in P1 is 1, and 8 if the number is 2, etc.

The block RELEASE P1 encountered next allows the customer to free the chosen server and the TERMINATE block finally removes the customer from the system.

It can be seen that the customer segment is compact, although it deals with three separate servers. Without using the parameter concept it would have been necessary to divide the customer segment into three separate parts, each with a similar sequence of blocks. The use of the parameter concept greatly enhances both the compactness and the simplicity of the program.

In the facility and queue statistics in Tables 16.3 and 16.4 it can be seen that there are three facilities and three queues.

**Table 16.3** Facility statistics of Program 16.2

| Facility | Average utilization | Number entries | Average time/tran |
|---|---|---|---|
| 1 | 0.63 | 35 | 8.95 |
| 2 | 0.59 | 36 | 8.14 |
| 3 | 0.53 | 27 | 9.83 |

**Table 16.4** Part of queue statistics of Program 16.2

| Queue (AD set) | Maximum contents | Average contents | Total entries | Zero entries | Percent zeros |
|---|---|---|---|---|---|
| 1 | 1 | 0.12 | 35 | 17 | 48.57 |
| 2 | 2 | 0.15 | 36 | 19 | 52.78 |
| 3 | 1 | 0.10 | 27 | 15 | 55.56 |

## 16.3 The SELECT block

In the preceding section the LET block was used for giving each transaction the desired parameter number. As noted, the LET block in Program 16.2 made a customer choose a specific server irrespective of whether it was free or whether there was a long waiting line in front of it. In contrast, this section deals with situations where customers go to the checkout counter with the shortest waiting line, as in a supermarket. In order to deal with such *parallel* servers, each with its own waiting line, it is necessary to use another block, SELECT, which can also give a value to a parameter of a transaction.

In micro-GPSS the SELECT block has either a MIN or MAX mode. I shall here focus on the MIN mode, which is the most commonly used mode. (A more advanced example using the SELECT MAX mode is given in Section 20.5.) The purpose of the SELECT MIN block is to search for the lowest value of some SNA, e.g. queue lengths or storage contents.

The block symbol is shown in Figure 16.3. The mode indicator MIN or MAX is in a circle to the left, and there is also a rectangle with the word SELECT and below that the operands; to the right a triangle is added. The operation code is SELECT MIN, with *one* blank space between SELECT and MIN.

**Figure 16.3** Block symbol of SELECT MIN

SELECT MIN uses four operands, all compulsory. Micro-GPSS uses the A, B, C and D operands.

> In GPSS V the E operand *must* be used instead of the D operand, requiring an additional comma. For the sake of compatibility, this usage is also possible in micro-GPSS (see Appendix B).

I shall begin with the D operand. This contains the SNA for which the lowest value will be sought. For example, if D is Q, the queue lengths will be searched; if D is S, the storage contents will be sifted, etc.

The B and C operands contain the lower limit and the upper limit of the reference numbers of the SNA that will be searched. To make this more comprehensible, let us remember that each queue, facility or storage at execution time will be represented by a reference number. If, for example, B = 2, C = 10 and D = Q, the processor will search through queue 2, 3, . . . , 10 to determine which one of these queues has the lowest value, i.e. the lowest current contents. We are interested in the reference number of this queue. Hence, if, for example, queues 2–5 have four members, queue 6 has two members and queues 7–10 have three members, then queue 6 would be the shortest queue. It is this reference number (in this case 6) that is looked for.

If two queues are equally long, the queue with the lower reference number will be selected, i.e. if in the example above queue 4 also had two members, 4 would be the selected number, since $4 < 6$.

The selected reference number will now be placed in the parameter, whose number is that of the A operand. The A operand is hence the number of the parameter into which one puts the reference number of that entity which has the lowest value out of the set of values of the SNA mentioned in the D operand.

I hope that an example of a SELECT block will make this clearer.

SELECT MIN 1,1,6,Q will search through queues 1 to 6 for the shortest waiting line, i.e. lowest contents, at the time when the transaction comes into the SELECT block, and will place this number into parameter 1. Note that the A operand is 1, *not* P1. Since the A operand of SELECT always refers to a parameter, P is unnecessary, and hence *not* allowed in micro-GPSS.

It is difficult to fully comprehend how this works without looking at a complete program. Let us therefore study Program 16.3 which simulates the six checkout counters of a supermarket. Earlier in the book Program 9.2 modeled a similar situation but with only two checkout counters. It might be appropriate to review the essentials of this program first.

The customers behave as follows: a customer first of all goes to a checkout counter if the cashier there is idle. If no cashier is idle, the customer goes to the checkout counter that has the shortest waiting line. If all checkout counters are equal in the respect of being idle or of having the same waiting line length, then the customer will go to the checkout counter with the lowest number.

As in Program 9.2 we can, by putting an ARRIVE block in front of the SEIZE block and a DEPART block after the RELEASE block (see Figure 9.3), obtain a value Q, such that $Q = 0$ if the cashier is idle; $Q = 1$, if the cashier is busy but there is no waiting line; and $Q > 1$, if there is a waiting line (since Q is the length of the waiting line + 1). By allowing each customer to select the checkout counter with the lowest of these Q values, we ensure that the policy described above is adhered to.

Figure 16.4 contains the block diagram with the program listing. This program provides a good example of the power of the parameter concept when combined with the SELECT block. This program, dealing with six checkout counters, contains far fewer blocks than Program 9.2, which allowed for only two checkout counters.

As regards the functioning of the program, the key is the block SELECT MIN 1,1,6,Q. As we have seen, this block allows each transaction to

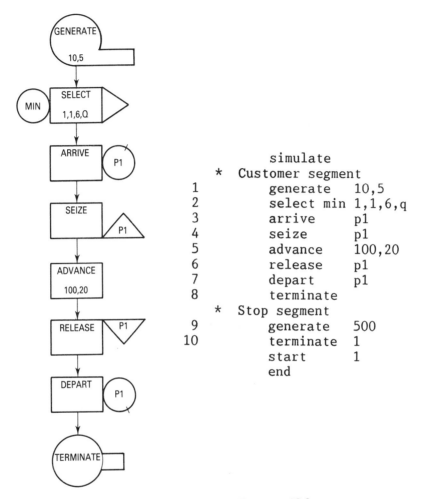

```
              simulate
    *    Customer segment
    1          generate    10,5
    2          select min  1,1,6,q
    3          arrive      p1
    4          seize       p1
    5          advance     100,20
    6          release     p1
    7          depart      p1
    8          terminate
    *    Stop segment
    9          generate    500
    10         terminate   1
               start       1
               end
```

**Figure 16.4** Block diagram and listing of Program 16.3

scan through on arrival all Qs with numbers 1 to 6, to see which Q is the smallest and then place the number of this Q into parameter 1. The transaction will join the AD set with this number and then try to seize the facility with the same number. After going through the ADVANCE block, allowing for the same expected service time by each server, the customer will release the same facility he or she seized earlier. The customer will then, before leaving the store, leave the AD set, consisting of all customers being served or waiting in front of that checkout counter.

In order to understand more precisely how the program functions, let us study the arrivals of the first two customers. When the first customer arrives, the values of Q1 ... Q6 are all 0, since all Q-values of micro-GPSS are set to

0 at the start of the simulation. Hence AD set 1 will be regarded as the one with the smallest value. As mentioned, the SNA with the lower number is chosen when two SNA values are equal. The customer thus goes into AD set 1 and seizes facility 1. If the second customer arrives while facility 1 is busy with the first customer, then since $Q1 = 1$ and $Q2 \ldots Q6 = 0$, Q2 is regarded as having the lowest Q-value and the second customer goes to AD set 2 and seizes facility 2.

It is important to note that in GPSS it is not necessary to define the AD sets or facilities that are going to be used in advance. The values Q1, Q2, etc. are available, but already set to 0 when the first customer arrives. The transactions can use facilities 1, 2, ... etc., needing only the block SEIZE P1. In fact, the GPSS processor has a fairly large number of pre-defined facilities, AD sets (or queues) and storages, which can be brought into use as they are required.

Let us now examine the output, looking first at the block statistics shown in Table 16.5. In these block statistics it is not possible to distinguish between the different checkout counters. Only the total number of customers who are waiting at all the checkout counters is given (21) in the current count of block 3. As far as the processor is concerned, however, the customers will be waiting on *separate* waiting lists, internal to the computer, which ensures that there really are six separate waiting lines.

**Table 16.5** Block statistics of Program 16.3

| Number | Adr. | Oper. | Current | Total |
|--------|------|-------|---------|-------|
| 1 | | GENER | 0 | 51 |
| 2 | | SELEC | 0 | 51 |
| 3 | | ARRIV | 21 | 51 |
| 4 | | SEIZE | 0 | 30 |
| 5 | | ADVAN | 6 | 30 |
| 6 | | RELEA | 0 | 24 |
| 7 | | DEPAR | 0 | 24 |
| 8 | | TERMI | 0 | 24 |
| 9 | | GENER | 0 | 1 |
| 10 | | TERMI | 0 | 1 |

Let us now consider the facility statistics shown in Table 16.6. Average utilization usually follows the general pattern that the lower the facility number, the higher the utilization. This is due to the fact that when the Q-value is the same for two checkout counters, customers go to the one with the lower number.

Let us finally turn to the queue statistics in Table 16.7. The total number of customers waiting at each checkout counter can be obtained by deducting 1, i.e. the person being served, from the current contents. It can be

**Table 16.6** Facility statistics of Program 16.3

| Facility | Average utilization | Number entries | Average time/tran |
|---|---|---|---|
| 1 | 0.99 | 5 | 98.92 |
| 2 | 0.97 | 5 | 97.17 |
| 3 | 0.95 | 5 | 95.36 |
| 4 | 0.94 | 5 | 94.21 |
| 5 | 0.92 | 5 | 92.37 |
| 6 | 0.90 | 5 | 89.83 |

seen that the sum of these numbers $(27 - 6 = 21)$ is the same number as the current count of block 3 in Table 16.5.

While program 16.3 contained a SELECT MIN block with Q in the D operand, selections can also be done with other SNA types in the D operand. Let us learn one more SNA in this context – F. F fulfils the same function for facilities as S does for storages, i.e. the *current* contents of the facility. F is either 0 or 1, since the contents cannot exceed 1 for a facility. Alternatively, F may be regarded as a busy indicator. F is 1 when the facility is busy; 0 when it is idle.

Whatever the interpretation, the block SELECT MIN 1,1,6,F, will search through facilities 1 ... 6 to see if any facility is idle. If F is 0 for any

**Table 16.7** Queue statistics of Program 16.3

| Queue (AD set) | Maximum contents | Average contents | Total entries | Zero entries | Percent zeros |
|---|---|---|---|---|---|
| 1 | 5 | 2.88 | 9 | 0 | 0.00 |
| 2 | 5 | 2.55 | 9 | 0 | 0.00 |
| 3 | 5 | 2.45 | 9 | 0 | 0.00 |
| 4 | 4 | 2.34 | 8 | 0 | 0.00 |
| 5 | 4 | 2.20 | 8 | 0 | 0.00 |
| 6 | 4 | 1.97 | 8 | 0 | 0.00 |

| Queue (AD set) | Average time/trans | $Average time/trans | Current contents |
|---|---|---|---|
| 1 | 160.16 | 160.16 | 5 |
| 2 | 141.57 | 141.57 | 5 |
| 3 | 136.16 | 136.16 | 5 |
| 4 | 146.28 | 146.28 | 4 |
| 5 | 137.26 | 137.26 | 4 |
| 6 | 123.28 | 123.28 | 4 |

$Average time/trans=average time/trans excluding zero entries

**Program 16.4**

```
        simulate
*   Customer segment
        generate    10,5
        select min 1,1,6,f
        if          p1=u,bye
        arrive      p1
        seize       p1
        advance     100,20
        release     p1
        depart      p1
    bye terminate
*   Stop segment
        generate    500
        terminate   1
        start       1
        end
```

facilities, then the entity number of the lowest numbered idle facility will be put into P1. If no facility is idle, i.e. all six checkout counters are busy, the entity number 1 of the first facility is put into P1.

In order to have a reasonably realistic example of SELECT MIN with F in the D operand, let us 'convert' our supermarket to a bank with separate waiting lines for the tellers and where all the customers are very impatient. Customers choose the lowest numbered free server, but if no one is free they leave the bank. This is modeled by Program 16.4.

Program 16.4 demonstrates that micro-GPSS also allows a parameter in the A operand of an IF block in the server mode. Thus customers can leave if the facility represented by the number in P1 is in use.

Let us now model this same bank somewhat more realistically by assuming that customers go away, if the shortest of all waiting lines already has a certain number of customers, e.g. 2. Since the AD set as used here measures the total number of customers at a teller, the waiting line is one person less. Thus, if we test whether a waiting line is 2, we must test whether the corresponding AD set is 3 (2 waiting + 1 being served).

In order to modify the program in this way, there is a need to access an SNA-value, corresponding to a Q$NAME. For parameters, which do not have symbolic names, a Q$-construction cannot be used. Instead Q* is used, followed by the number of the parameter. In this case, when we refer to the length of the AD set whose number is held in parameter 1, we use Q*1. This use of SNAs with *, called indirect addressing, is discussed in more detail in Chapter 20.

The block SELECT MIN 1,1,6,Q will now search through AD sets 1 to 6

**Program 16.5**

```
        simulate
*   Customer segment
        generate    10,5
        select min 1,1,6,q
        if          q*1=3,bye
        arrive      p1
        seize       p1
        advance     100,20
        release     p1
        depart      p1
  bye   terminate
*   Stop segment
        generate    500
        terminate   1
        start       1
        end
```

**Program 16.6**

```
        simulate
        let         x$max=5
* Customer segment
        generate    10,5
        select min 1,1,x$max,q
        arrive      p1
        seize       p1
        advance     100,20
        release     p1
        depart      p1
        terminate
* Part time worker
        generate    360
        let         x$max=6
        terminate
* Stop segment
        generate    500
        terminate   1
        start       1
        end
```

to find the one with the minimum length. The number of this AD set is hence put into parameter 1. The length of this AD set can be accessed by Q*1. Since a customer leaves if the shortest AD set has reached 3, we write IF Q*1=3,BYE. Program 16.5 is then obtained.

To further illustrate the power of the SELECT block we shall change Program 16.3 into Program 16.6 to allow for a part-timer. As the C operand of the SELECT block X$MAX is used. The control statement LET X$MAX=5 has the supermarket start with five checkout counters open. At time 360 the block LET X$MAX=6 increases the number of open checkout counters to six. All customers arriving after time 360 will then choose the shortest of *six* waiting lines.

None of the program examples studied so far in this chapter has used symbolic names for servers, AD sets or queues, but only parameters have been used to refer to these types of entities. We finally turn to the case where some facilities are referred to by symbolic names and some are referred to by parameters.

In GPSS V problems could arise from this since a symbolic name and a parameter could then refer to the same number, e.g. if LOCK was the facility 1 and there was a block SEIZE P1, where P1 could take the value 1. This has

**Program 16.7**

```
            simulate
    stor    storage
    *   Customer segment
            generate    10,5
            waitif      lock=u
            select min  1,1,6,q
            if          q*1=3,bye
            enter       stor
            arrive      p1
            seize       p1
            advance     100,20
            release     p1
            depart      p1
            leave       stor
    bye     terminate
    *   Stop segment
            generate    500
            seize       lock
            waitif      stor=ne
            terminate   1
            start       1
            end
```

been a major cause of faulty programming in GPSS V, causing some very treacherous logical errors. In a GPSS program with many symbolic names, it is cumbersome to keep track of what values the parameters can take. Furthermore, it becomes difficult to introduce a new facility name into an old program.

In order to allow for safer programming, micro-GPSS is constructed so that a parameter *never* takes the same internal number as that given to a symbolic name of a server. In micro-GPSS you *never* have to worry about what internal number will be given to a symbolic name. Thus micro-GPSS avoids one of the greatest disadvantages of GPSS V.

This mixture of symbolic names and parameters for servers is illustrated by Program 16.7, where Program 16.5 has been changed to allow for closing the store properly, in line with the method discussed in connection with Program 10.1.

It should be stressed that if this program is rewritten in GPSS V after the necessary general modifications and also including a RELEASE SAL before TERMINATE 1, completely misleading results would be obtained from a syntactically correct program. It would be necessary to have 2 and 7, instead of 1 and 6, in the C and D operands of SELECT to obtain a correctly functioning program.

## Exercise 16.1 (Case study 4B in Schriber, 1974)

A small grocery store consists of three aisles and a single checkout counter. Shoppers arrive at the store in a Poisson pattern, i.e. according to an exponential distribution, with a mean InterArrival Time of 75 seconds. On arrival each customer takes a basket and may then go down one or more of the three aisles, selecting items for purchase. The time required to shop an aisle, and the number of items selected for purchase in the process, are uniformly distributed random variables. The parameters of these distributions as well as the probability of going down any particular aisle, are shown below.

| Aisle | Probability of going down the aisle | Time required to travel down the aisle (seconds) | Number of items selected during travel |
|-------|-------------------------------------|--------------------------------------------------|----------------------------------------|
| 1 | 0.75 | $120 \pm 60$ | $3 \pm 1$ |
| 2 | 0.55 | $150 \pm 30$ | $4 \pm 1$ |
| 3 | 0.82 | $120 \pm 45$ | $5 \pm 1$ |

When shopping is complete, the customers queue up first-come, first-served at the checkout counter. In this area, each customer chooses an additional $2 \pm 1$ 'impulse items' for purchase. A customer's checkout time depends on the number of items chosen. Checkout time is 3 seconds per item. After checking out, a customer leaves the basket at the front of the store and departs.

Build a GPSS model for the grocery store, then use the model to simulate an eight-hour day. Measure the utilization of the checkout person, and the maximum length of the waiting line at the checkout counter. Assuming there is no limit to the number of shopping baskets, also determine the maximum number of baskets in use at any one time.

---

**Exercise 16.2**  (Case study 4D in Schriber, 1974)

Customers arrive at a bank in an exponential pattern at a mean rate of 200 per hour. Eight teller windows are open at the bank at all times. A separate waiting line forms ahead of each teller. If a teller is free when a customer enters the bank, the customer immediately goes to that teller. Otherwise, he or she joins whichever waiting line is the shortest. Customers then remain in that line on a first-come, first-served basis until they have transacted their business, after which they leave the bank.

The various types of business which customers transact fall into five categories. The relative frequencies of these categories and the corresponding mean service time requirements are as follows:

| Category of business | Relative frequency | Mean service time (seconds) |
|---|---|---|
| 1 | 0.10 | 45 |
| 2 | 0.19 | 75 |
| 3 | 0.32 | 100 |
| 4 | 0.24 | 150 |
| 5 | 0.15 | 300 |

In each category service time is exponentially distributed. No customer transacts business in two or more categories in a single visit to the bank.

Another bank in the vicinity has introduced a 'Quickline' queuing system. In this system, customers entering the bank form a single line. Whenever a teller becomes available, the customer at the head of the line goes to that teller.

Build a GPSS model which gathers waiting line information for the bank's operation, both as it currently exists, and for a change to a Quickline system. Run the model for a five-hour day in each case.

---

**Exercise 16.3**  (Exercise 3.51 in Banks and Carson, 1984)

The InterArrival Time for parts needing processing is defined as follows:

| InterArrival Time (seconds) | Proportion |
|---|---|
| 10–20 | 0.20 |
| 20–30 | 0.30 |
| 30–40 | 0.50 |

There are three standard types of part: A, B and C. The proportion of each part, and the mean and standard deviation of the normally distributed processing times, are as follows:

| Part type | Proportion | Mean (seconds) | Standard deviation (seconds) |
|---|---|---|---|
| A | 0.5 | 30 | 3 |
| B | 0.3 | 40 | 4 |
| C | 0.2 | 50 | 7 |

Each machine processes any type of part, one part at a time. Use simulation to compare one, two or three machines working in parallel.

## Exercise 16.4 (Based on example in Bobillier *et al.*, 1976, p. 117)

A real-time computer serves three terminals which can send four types of message. When they arrive, the messages enter a queue and wait for processing. The queue is handled in arrival order (FIFO). The InterArrival Times and processing time (both in milliseconds) of each message depend on its source as follows:

| Source number | InterArrival Times | Processing time |
|---|---|---|
| 1 | 4500 ± 2000 | 350 |
| 2 | 3000 ± 800 | 320 |
| 3 | 2000 ± 700 | 240 |

The distribution of the various types of message, which is the same for all terminals, and the additional processing time required for each type is as follows:

| Message type | Frequency | Processing time |
|---|---|---|
| 1 | 0.30 | $500 \pm 100$ |
| 2 | 0.50 | $400 \pm 100$ |
| 3 | 0.10 | $250 \pm 50$ |
| 4 | 0.10 | $900 \pm 200$ |

Simulate the system for 10 minutes (600,000 milliseconds) to determine waiting times for messages from each source.

## Exercise 16.5

Modify Program 8.1 in such a way that each worker finishes work for the day and goes home as soon as he or she has produced 14 pots.

## Exercise 16.6

Modify Program 15.1 in the following ways: customers arrive following an exponential distribution, with an average InterArrival Time of 2 minutes at 9 a.m., of 1.5 minutes at 3 p.m. and of 1 minute at closing time 6 p.m., i.e. more and more customers arrive as the day goes on. Normally seven people work full-time (eight hours a day) in the store. The store is closed in a 'proper manner' as in Program 10.1. The simulation is to be used for deciding whether to hire part-timers to work at the end of the afternoon. The part-timers are paid $10 an hour. There is a separate waiting line in front of each salesperson. All other factors are as in Program 15.1. Carry out a couple of simulations with one or two part-timers, starting at what you would consider to be a suitable time. Make a comparison based on the profits from the operations. Investigate both for the case of each salesperson having a separate waiting line and the case of a joint waiting line for all salespeople.

## Exercise 16.7  (Program SIMPLQ in Jennergren, 1984)

This program simulates a single-server queuing situation. Customers arrive every 60 seconds. The service times of successive customers are uniform random variables between 10 and 90 seconds. The program simulates 50 cycles, where one cycle begins and ends with an idle period for the server. For each cycle, the program calculates (1) the sum of individual waiting times for all customers served during the cycle and (2) the number of customers served during the cycle.

# 17 Help statements

## 17.1 HELP as a block

The HELP block differs from other GPSS blocks in that it does not carry out any specific task. Rather it allows the GPSS programmer to do virtually anything by using a FORTRAN subroutine (or possibly another General Programming Language like C or Pascal). The name HELP indicates that it was originally seen as a kind of life-saver, when the programmer was *not* able to program a specific requirement in ordinary GPSS. The syntax of the HELP block is different for different GPSS versions; only the HELP block of micro-GPSS is presented here.

This first section of the chapter will be slightly more technical than other sections and will be somewhat easier to understand for readers who have an elementary knowledge of FORTRAN or a similar General Programming Language.

In micro-GPSS the HELP block has eight operands and is represented by the symbol shown in Figure 17.1. The A operand, written to the right of the symbol, is the name of the FORTRAN subroutine that is called. In accordance with the general GPSS rules, the name has a maximum of five characters.

**Figure 17.1** Block symbol of HELP

The B, C, D, E, F, G and H operands are SNAs or constants. The B–H operands are optional, but if one of them is defaulted on (e.g. D) then the remaining ones *must* also be defaulted on (e.g. E–H). The B–H operands contain the values that are transferred to the FORTRAN subroutine. At the moment of transfer these values are transformed into real (i.e. floating-point) numbers. If there is a B operand, the FORTRAN subroutine must have as its argument the variable VALUE defined by a statement REAL VALUE(7), i.e. as a vector with 7 values. The value of the B operand will be placed in VALUE(1), the value of the C operand in VALUE(2), etc. and finally the value of the H operand in VALUE(7).

The FORTRAN subroutine can do whatever processing is required. The RETURN statement of the subroutine will bring execution back to the GPSS program. On returning, values are transferred *back* to each operand of the HELP block in the GPSS program, *provided* the operand contains a savevalue, i.e. an X$-value.

If the operand contains a constant or an SNA other than a savevalue, the value of the operand is *not* changed. Hence, if the program has, e.g., HELP FPRIN,C1,X$VAL, then at return from the subroutine FPRIN, the value of the B operand, C1, does *not* change, but the C operand X$VAL takes the value which VALUE(2) had in the subroutine FPRIN before RETURN to the GPSS program.

Thus, there is free transfer of the 7 different operand values (B–H) *to* the subroutine, but the transfer *back* to the GPSS program is restricted to savevalues. The reason for this restriction in micro-GPSS is one of safety. Assume as above that C1, the time of the simulation clock, is the B operand in a HELP block calling on FPRIN. Suppose furthermore that VALUE(1) is inadvertently changed in the subroutine FPRIN. Then, if C1 was allowed to change, the simulation clock would by mistake be given a completely new value, most probably leading to strange simulation results.

Limiting the data imported from the subroutine to savevalues hence increases programming safety. No major loss in programming power occurs, since there are other means for transferring values back to the GPSS program. For example, a subroutine can transfer a value to a parameter indirectly by first giving it to a savevalue and then having a LET block give the value of the savevalue to the parameter.

As mentioned in Chapter 1, micro-GPSS has in some respects a more powerful FORTRAN interface than other GPSS versions. Not only can GPSS call subroutines in FORTRAN, but a FORTRAN program can in turn call the whole micro-GPSS system, which then in turn can call on FORTRAN subroutines. In this way, some well-structured large programs can be written. It is, however, outside the scope of this book to deal with this case, as well as other cases when the GPSS user writes his own FORTRAN program. Such an interface between a user-written FORTRAN program and the micro-GPSS system requires access to the micro-GPSS object code, distributed separately together with documentation on how to use it.

There are, however, also FORTRAN subroutines which are already part of the micro-GPSS system. The idea is that by incorporating these subroutines, which can be called by HELP, the micro-GPSS system can adjust in a flexible manner to new demands without changing its simple basic syntax.

Several of these subroutines are specific to specific operating systems. For example, there is a subroutine GODOS, specifically for DOS on PCs. HELP GODOS will allow for a temporary exit from the GPSS system to DOS, and a return to GPSS by typing EXIT. There are furthermore special subroutines for interfacing with other systems, e.g. memory resident graphic packages, like Graph-in-the-Box Analytic. These subroutines allow instant graphics for both block and table statistics and for 'tailor-made' statistics (see Section 17.2).

There are also subroutines that are common to *all* versions of micro-GPSS. Future additions to this set of common subroutines are likely, but this book deals with the subroutines that are included in all micro-GPSS versions as of 1990.

Most of these are presented in this chapter. In this section it will only be mentioned that HELP PAUSE allows execution to halt until any key is pressed. We shall study subroutines for graphics in Section 17.2; for interactive input of data *during* simulation in Section 17.3 and at the *start* of simulation in Section 17.4; for creation of 'new SNAs' in Section 17.5 and for matrix operations in Section 17.6. Finally in the next chapter it will be seen how it is possible to use HELP blocks in order to carry out repeated runs of a GPSS program coupled with statistical analysis and optimization.

A complete list of the subroutines that are incorporated into the specific micro-GPSS system is given in the file HELP.DOC included in the same software package as the micro-GPSS interpreter.

## 17.2 HELP FPRIN for graphics

FPRIN is a subroutine that is mainly useful for creating graphics. A simple example, Program 17.1 (based on Program 15.5), will illustrate the use of the subroutine FPRIN. Let us suppose that there is a need to follow cash development very carefully, registering every change in cash. The block HELP FPRIN,C1,X$CASH is then placed after each of the savevalue blocks implying a change in cash in Program 15.5. Only two quarters are simulated.

The subroutine FPRIN does two things: first, it prints, during execution of the program, the value of the B and C operands together with some text each time the subroutine is called. For Program 17.1, the print-out shown in Table 17.1 will be obtained prior to the ordinary output.

Besides this print-out on the screen (or on paper), the program will write all this data, but without the text, in a file called PROG171.PRN. More generally, the name of this result file is the name of the program without any . in the name, *plus* the extension .PRN. When running GPSS on, e.g., a PC, this result file can be used together with an external graphics package, e.g. that of LOTUS 1–2–3, for producing a graph. For example, the graph shown in Figure 17.2 could be obtained.

**Program 17.1**

```
         simulate
         let           x$price=25
         let           x$cost=15
         let           x$cash=100
  sales function       x$price,c5
  10,310/20,110/30,60/40,40/50,30
*
         generate      fn$xpdis*360/fn$sales
         let+          x$sal,x$price
         let+          x$tcost,x$cost
         let-          x$cash,x$cost
         help          fprin,c1,x$cash
         advance       45*fn$rlng3
         let+          x$cash,x$price
         help          fprin,c1,x$cash
         terminate
*
         generate      90
         terminate     1
         start         2,np
         end
```

**Table 17.1** Start of print-out of Program 17.1

| Value at | 0.48 is | 85.00 |
|----------|---------|-------|
| Value at | 3.62 is | 70.00 |
| Value at | 4.40 is | 55.00 |
| Value at | 5.50 is | 40.00 |
| Value at | 14.13 is | 25.00 |

...

From this graph it is clear that cash will be negative even in the first quarter. A similar graph can be obtained instantly by using a corresponding subroutine GPRIN in micro-GPSS versions that are combined with a memory resident graphics package, such as Graph-in-the-Box Analytic.

As an alternative to a PRINT statement, a HELP block calling on FPRIN can also be used for tracing the development of some key value step by step during program execution. This is often a useful device when searching for a logical error in a program.

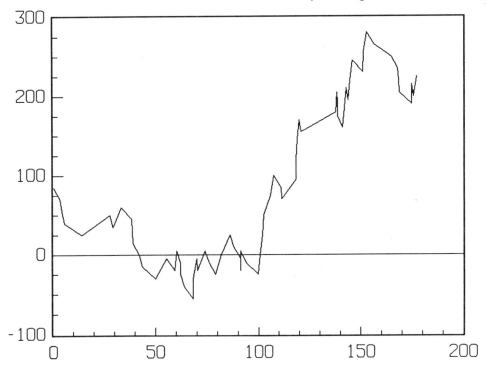

**Figure 17.2** Graphical output from Program 17.1

## 17.3 Interactive input using HELP LETSA

This section contains another example of a powerful use of HELP and a subroutine, namely for obtaining interactive input to the program during the run of the simulation. With the aid of the subroutine LETSA, it is possible to provide different inputs depending on what output is obtained in the course of the simulation.

LETSA is a subroutine that reads a value from the keyboard and gives it to the savevalue mentioned in the B operand of the block HELP LETSA,B. When a transaction reaches, for example, the block HELP LETSA,X$VAL, the computer writes the prompt 'Give value of X$VAL', the user types a value, and this is then assigned to X$VAL. Thus, HELP LETSA,X$VAL works to some extent like a block LET X$VAL=inval, where inval is the value keyed in. 'LETSA' can be viewed as an abbreviation of 'LET SAvevalue ='. Program 17.2, an extension of Program 17.1, exemplifies LETSA.

**Program 17.2**

```
            simulate
            let        x$price=25
            let        x$cost=15
            let        x$cash=100
   sales function      x$price,c5
   10,310/20,110/30,60/40,40/50,30
   *  Decision segment
            generate   ,,,1
   begin help          letsa,x$time
            advance    x$time
            help       fprin,c1,x$cash
            help       letsa,x$price
            goto       begin
   *   Order segment
            generate   fn$xpdis*360/fn$sales
            let+       x$sal,x$price
            let+       x$tcost,x$cost
            let-       x$cash,x$cost
            if         x$cash>0,nxt
            help       fprin,c1,x$cash
            help       letsa,x$price
   nxt      advance    45*fn$rlng3
            let+       x$cash,x$price
            terminate
   *  Stop segment
            generate   90
            terminate  1
            start      2,np
            end
```

There is first of all a *decision segment*, where *one* transaction is generated at the very beginning of the simulation, as in the traffic light segment of Program 10.2. Next there is a block HELP LETSA,X$TIME, where X$TIME is the time in days until the next decision is to be taken. This is a value keyed in by the user. The transaction of the decision segment will then wait in the ADVANCE block during this time before it comes back and prints the values of time and cash and asks for a decision.

If the user sets X$TIME to 10 the first time, i.e. when the simulation clock is 0, the first decision on price will be made at time 10. The computer will then in HELP FPRIN,C1,X$CASH provide information about the present state of cash and in HELP LETSA,X$PRICE ask for a new value of price. The computer then goes back to BEGIN to ask again how many days are to elapse before a new decision is to be taken and the process repeats itself.

In the *order segment* there are the following four new or revised blocks:

```
        if       x$cash>0,nxt
        help     fprin,c1,x$cash
        help     letsa,x$price
   nxt  advance  45*fn$rlng3
```

In this part of the segment the program allows a new decision concerning price whenever cash becomes negative. If cash is positive, the two HELP blocks are by-passed and execution proceeds to the address NXT. If cash is negative (or zero), the computer first prints the present values of time and cash. Next the user is asked to input a new value on X$PRICE.

Table 17.2 contains the first part of the output.

## 17.4 HELP as a control statement

In the previous section HELP was used as a block, implying that the call to the FORTRAN subroutine was carried out in connection with a transaction entering a HELP block. This is the only way that all *other* GPSS systems use HELP. However, micro-GPSS also allows HELP as a control statement, inserted prior to the first GENERATE block in the program. The call to the FORTRAN subroutine will then take place at the very start of execution. The HELP control statement is hence executed only *once* and does *not* require any

**Table 17.2** Start of output from Program 17.2

```
 Give value of X$TIME
10
 Value at      10.00 is    40.00
 Give value of X$PRICE
25
 Give value of X$TIME
20
 Value at      30.00 is    35.00
 Give value of X$PRICE
20
 Give value of X$TIME
30
 Value at      41.36 is    -5.00
 Give value of X$PRICE
30
   . .
```

transaction for its initiation. Otherwise the syntax rules are the same as for the HELP block. Some HELP subroutines work in the same way whether called by a block or a control statement. One example is LETSA.

The control statement HELP LETSA,X$VAL can be regarded as equivalent to, for example, the following three blocks:

```
generate  ,,,1,2
help      letsa,x$val
terminate
```

One transaction is generated at the very start, before *any* other transactions (due to the priority value of 2 in the E operand, which is assumed to be the highest priority), with the sole purpose of calling LETSA.

Program 17.3 illustrates the use of the HELP LETSA control statement. This somewhat larger, but important, program is based on Program 13.3 and the reader is advised to re-read Section 13.6. Like Program 13.3, Program 17.3 has four segments.

The customer segments of the two programs are identical (except for two extra addresses), as are the entering inventory segments. In the re-ordering segments there are some differences as can be seen by comparing Figure 17.3 with Figure 13.8.

Immediately after GENERATE 5, in Program 17.3 there is a block LET+ X$INVEN,S$STOR. This implies that each week the current storage level S$STOR, i.e. the 'storage level of the week', is added to X$INVEN. X$INVEN thus becomes the total number of 'storage unit-weeks', which multiplied by the storage cost per week for one unit will give total annual storage costs, used when calculating profits.

Furthermore, in the third block of the segment, the general re-ordering level is expressed as a variable, X$RPLEV, instead of the fixed constant 10, as used in Program 13.3. Likewise, in the eighth block, the ordered quantity is expressed generally as X$ORDQ, instead of just 5.

In order to study the stop segment let us look at the whole program listing below. In this listing comments have been added to all blocks that differ from Program 13.3. The stop segment contains an additional LET block to calculate the profits using V$PROF. There is also a block PRINT X to print savevalues, since NP has been added to the START to suppress standard print-out.

The use of V$PROF requires a definition of the variable PROF for calculating the profit associated with various values of the decision variable, i.e. the quantity to be ordered. This VARIABLE definition requires further explanation.

Let us first calculate the revenue. Assume that $10.00 is made on every book sold directly and $7.00 on each book sold to a waiting student. (Mailing and packing costs come to $3.00.) The total number of books sold directly is the number of transactions having entered the first LEAVE block. In order to

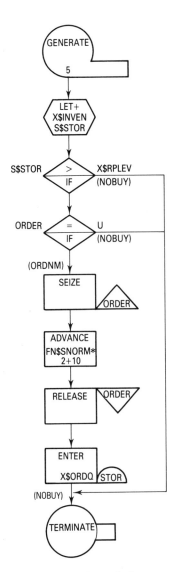

**Figure 17.3** Re-ordering segment of Program 17.3

calculate this number of entries, the address DIR is given to this block. Hence N$DIR is the total number of books sold directly. Likewise the address LATER is put in front of the second LEAVE block, making N$LATER the total number of books sold later.

From this revenue, are deducted the total costs of holding inventories. The cost per week of holding one unit in the inventory is X$STOCO. As I have already described, the total number of storage unit-weeks, X$INVEN is

**Program 17.3**

```
        simulate
stor    storage
        help        letsa,x$ordq
        let         x$rplev=10
        let         x$stoco=1
        let         x$orco=4
prof    variable    n$dir*10+n$later*7-x$inven*x$stoco-n$ordnm*x$orco
* Customer segment
        generate    fn$xpdis
        if          stor=e,nodir
dir     leave       stor        ! The address DIR added
        terminate
nodir goto          nosel,.6
        arrive      tim
        waitif      stor=e
        depart      tim
later leave         stor        ! The address LATER added
        terminate
nosel terminate
* Re-ordering segment
        generate    5
        let+        x$inven,s$stor ! Number of orderweeks added up
        if          s$stor>x$rplev,nobuy ! Don't buy if enough stocks
        if          order=u,nobuy
ordnm seize         order       ! Address ORDNM added
        advance     fn$snorm*2+10
        release     order
        enter       stor,x$ordq ! Enter ORDQ units into stocks
nobuy terminate
* Entering inventory segment
        generate    ,,,1
        enter       stor,30
        terminate
* Stop segment
        generate    250
        let         x$profi=v$prof ! Profits are calculated
        print       x           ! Profits are printed
        terminate   1
*
        start       1,np        ! No standard output
        end
```

calculated in the inventory segment. X$INVEN ⋆ X$STOCO is hence the total inventory cost.

Finally the total purchasing cost is deducted. The cost per order is X$ORCO. With ORDNM as the address of the ordering segment, N$ORDNM is the total number of orders and hence N$ORDNM ⋆ X$ORCO is the total purchasing cost. Total profit, PROF, hence becomes N$DIR ⋆ 10 + N$LATER ⋆ 7 − X$INVEN ⋆ X$STOCO − N$ORDNM ⋆ X$ORCO.

Finally, the values of the re-ordering level and the quantity to be ordered are set in the control statements. The re-ordering level, X$RPLEV, which is not going to be changed very frequently here, is given its value, e.g. 10, by the statement LET X$RPLEV = 10.

Let us now experiment with different ordering quantities. X$ORDQ is, as noted, used as the B operand of ENTER in the re-ordering segment, implying that each order brings X$ORDQ books into the storage STOR. In the original example, five books were purchased each time, but now a method for changing this quantity easily is required. One way would be to use a statement LET X$ORDQ = B, where B stands for an integer value that would be changed with an editor between the runs.

A more convenient method, used here, is to allow for an interactive input of this quantity using the control statement HELP LETSA,X$ORDQ.

When running the program, the question 'Give value of X$ORDQ' will appear in the listing of the program directly after the HELP statement, as shown in Table 17.3. The user will then type the value of X$ORDQ, e.g. 5 (followed by a return), after which the program listing continues. This would correspond to a statement LET X$ORDQ = 5.

**Table 17.3** Partial listing at run time of Program 17.3

```
          simulate
     stor  storage
          help        letsa,x$ordq
  Give value of X$ORDQ
5
```

## Suppression of program listing

When the program is to be run several times, with only one value changed each run, it is usually preferable not to have large amounts of output each time. We have already studied how to avoid the print-out of a standard report by having NP in the B operand of the START statement. The program listing can also be very easily suppressed in micro-GPSS: the very *first* line of the program, i.e. *prior* to SIMULATE, then consists only of $ in column 1.

Thus Program 17.3 can be revised by inserting a line containing only $

at the top of the program. The start of this revised program, Program 17.3b, then looks as follows in its original form.

---

**Program 17.3b** The first lines of original code

```
$
simulate
stor storage
help letsa,x$ordq
```

---

The program is then not listed and when running this program repeatedly, only the output of Table 17.4 is obtained.

**Table 17.4** Output from Program 17.3b

```
What is the name of the GPSS program file
   at most 25 characters allowed
prog17.3b
 Give value of X$ORDQ
5

   Contents of savevalues (non-zero)
   Savevalue name          Value
        ORDQ                5.00
        RPLEV              10.00
        STOCO               1.00
        ORCO                4.00
        INVEN              86.00
        PROFI             862.00
 Do you want to stop?   Y, N or new name
n
 Shall same program be repeated? Y, N or new name
y
 Shall seeds be reset? Y or N
y
 Give value of X$ORDQ
10

   Contents of savevalues (non-zero)
   Savevalue name          Value
        ORDQ               10.00
        RPLEV              10.00
        ...
        PROFI            1698.00
```

In order both to suppress the program listing and to have all output written into a file (see Section 3.11), %$ must be written, i.e. with % first and $ in column 2. Then only output will be written into the file. If the first line of Program 17.3b had been %$, the savevalue statistics, but *not* the dialogue, in Table 17.4 would have been written into the file PROG173B.PRN.

If users who are unfamiliar with GPSS are going to run a program like Program 17.3b as a decision aid, it is less desirable to ask the user to input X$ORDQ and give back savevalue statistics as above. Therefore in order to make it possible to obtain more user-friendly interactive dialogues, the micro-GPSS system also includes another subroutine for interactive input, INPUT. The only difference from LETSA is that INPUT does *not* provide any prompting text. This has to be supplied in some other way.

In the case of HELP INPUT used as a *block*, this can be done by a preceding PRINT block with text within single quotes. In the case of HELP INPUT used as a *control* statement, i.e. as discussed in this section, it can be handled by a special type of comment available only in micro-GPSS. As mentioned in Chapter 3, comment lines start in GPSS with a ⋆ in column 1. Micro-GPSS also allows for comment lines that start with ! in column 1. These comment lines function in the same way as the lines with ⋆, except that they overrule the non-listing command of $, i.e. they will be printed or listed even when the rest of the program is not listed.

Program 17.3b can now be modified into Program 17.4 which is more user-friendly. It uses HELP INPUT preceded by comment lines with !. To provide more user-friendly results, the stop segment uses PRINT X$PROFI preceded by PRINT blocks with text within double quotation marks. The program listing below only includes the parts that are different from Program 17.3, i.e. the first few control statements and the stop segment.

**Program 17.4** First control statements and stop segment

```
$
          simulate
   stor   storage
 ! We want to determine the optimal order quantity
 ! Give number of units to be ordered each time
          help        input,x$ordq
          let         x$rplev=10
 ...
 * Stop segment
          generate    250
          let         x$profi=v$prof ! Profits are calculated
          print       "Order quantity"
          print       x$ordq
          print       "Profits       "
          print       x$profi
          terminate   1
```

The program produces the dialogue in Table 17.5.

**Table 17.5** Output from Program 17.4

```
What is the name of the GPSS program file
   at most 25 characters allowed
prog17.4
         ! We want to determine the optimal order quantity
         ! Give number of units to be ordered each time
  5
   Order quantity              5.00
   Profits                   862.00
```

# 17.5 HELP SNAQS for accessing values of attributes in print-outs

By a HELP block calling the subroutine SNAQS it is possible to access the value of any attribute for which a value will later be printed in the facility, storage or queue (AD set) statistics, and transfer this to a savevalue. This savevalue can then be used in other blocks, e.g. IF blocks. A SNAQS block can be used at *any* time during the simulation and hence produce *current* values, as contrasted with those of the final standard output. In this way a kind of 'new SNAs' can be created in micro-GPSS with user-determined names. (GPSS V has over 50 different SNAs all with different abbreviations.)

The B operand of HELP SNAQS is the related 'typical' SNA, i.e. in the case of facility statistics F$name, in the case of storage statistics S$name and in the case of queue or AD set statistics Q$name, where name is the name of the facility, storage or AD set for which the particular piece of information is desired. The first letter thus corresponds to the symbol used in group print-outs (see Section 15.4).

The C operand is a number denoting which item in the print-out will be accessed. It corresponds to one of the numbers used in Tables 4.3, 6.1 or 7.5. For example, if the B operand is Q$SAL, a C operand of 2 would refer to Average contents and of 6 to Average time per transaction.

Finally the D operand is the savevalue into which the value thus accessed is placed.

The block HELP SNAQS,F$SAL,1,X$AVUSE thus assigns the value of Average Utilization of SAL to the savevalue X$AVUSE and the block HELP SNAQS,S$STOR,7,X$MAXST places the Maximum Contents of the storage STOR into the savevalue X$MAXST.

The use of the subroutine SNAQS can be illustrated by Program 17.5 which is a modification of Program 6.1.

**Program 17.5**

```
simulate
generate    18,6
seize       sal,q
advance     25,5
release     sal
terminate
generate    480
help        snaqs,f$sal,1,x$avuse
help        snaqs,q$sal,6,x$avtim
terminate   1
start       1
end
```

Table 17.6 contains the savevalue output of this program, with the same values as the corresponding data in Table 4.3 and Table 6.1.

**Table 17.6** Savevalue output from Program 17.5

```
Contents of savevalues (non-zero)
Savevalue name          Value
    AVUSE               0.97
    AVTIM              67.25
```

# 17.6 HELP MATIN for the creation of a data spreadsheet

Program 17.1 exemplified how HELP FPRIN could be used to create two sequences of values, one of the time and one of some other SNA value, e.g. X$CASH. In the simulation of a business, one is, however, often more interested in creating a whole matrix or spreadsheet, e.g. with values on sales, costs, profits, cash, etc. for several periods.

In micro-GPSS, this can be done using the subroutine MATIN called by the block HELP MATIN,B,C,D. The B operand is the row number of the matrix, the C operand is the column number and the D operand is the value to be placed into the cell of row B, column C. At the end of the program run the whole matrix will be written into the file *name*.MAT, where *name* is the name of the program with any . deleted.

I shall illustrate this by expanding Program 15.5 into Program 17.6.

**Program 17.6**

```
        simulate
        let          x$price=25
        let          x$cost=15
        let          x$cash=100
 sales function      x$price,c5
10,310/20,110/30,60/40,40/50,30
* Customer segment
        generate     fn$xpdis*360/fn$sales
        let+         x$sal,x$price
        let+         x$tcost,x$cost
        let-         x$cash,x$cost
        advance      45*fn$rlng3
        let+         x$cash,x$price
        terminate
* Report segment
        generate     90
        let+         x$num,1
        let          x$prof=x$sal-x$tcost
        help         matin,1,x$num,x$sal
        help         matin,2,x$num,x$tcost
        help         matin,3,x$num,x$prof
        help         matin,4,x$num,x$cash
        let          x$sal=0
        let          x$tcost=0
        terminate    1
        start        6,np
        end
```

All the changes concern the report segment (besides an increase in the A operand of START to 6). This segment starts with LET+ X$NUM,1. Since X$NUM is initially set to 0, X$NUM becomes 1 at time 90, 2 at time 180, etc., i.e. X$NUM is the number of the quarter. The next block calculates the profits X$PROF. The value of X$SAL is then placed into row 1 in the column X$NUM of the present quarter. Likewise the values of X$TCOST, X$PROF and X$CASH are placed into rows 2, 3 and 4 respectively, in the column X$NUM of the present quarter. After this X$SAL and X$TCOST are set to 0, since these values only refer to the value of the present quarter.

There is no immediately visible output, since the micro-GPSS system writes the whole matrix into the file PROG176.MAT. If this file is displayed (e.g. on a PC by TYPE PROG176.MAT), the matrix in Table 17.7 is obtained. This is not very easy to read, but a more readable matrix can be obtained in micro-GPSS by supplying a pre-arranged text frame, called *name*.FRM, where *name* is the name of the program with any . deleted. Let us assume that there is already a file PROG176.FRM, e.g. as in Table 17.8. The purpose of the frame is that the lines either contain text or they start with an 'underlining character', i.e. −, = or _ . The text will be placed in front of a data line in *name*.MAT, while an 'underlining character' in column 1 of a line will produce a line with this character in *every* column. The resulting matrix is written into the file *name*.TXT (where *name* is defined as above). Thus on the basis of PROG176.FRM Program 17.6 will also produce PROG176.TXT shown in Table 17.9. If there is no frame with the program name, only *name*.MAT is obtained as well as a warning that *name*.FRM is missing.

**Table 17.7** Contents of PROG176.MAT

| | | | | | |
|---|---|---|---|---|---|
| 525.00 | 475.00 | 350.00 | 650.00 | 775.00 | 475.00 |
| 315.00 | 285.00 | 210.00 | 390.00 | 465.00 | 285.00 |
| 210.00 | 190.00 | 140.00 | 260.00 | 310.00 | 190.00 |
| 10.00 | 225.00 | 515.00 | 675.00 | 910.00 | 1200.00 |

**Table 17.8** Contents of PROG176.FRM

```
Sales
Costs
-----
Profits
=====
Cash
```

**Table 17.9** Contents of PROG176.TXT

| | | | | | | |
|---|---|---|---|---|---|---|
| Sales | 525.00 | 475.00 | 350.00 | 650.00 | 775.00 | 475.00 |
| Costs | 315.00 | 285.00 | 210.00 | 390.00 | 465.00 | 285.00 |
| ------ | ------ | ------ | ------ | ------ | ------ | ------ |
| Profits | 210.00 | 190.00 | 140.00 | 260.00 | 310.00 | 190.00 |
| ====== | ====== | ====== | ====== | ====== | ====== | ====== |
| Cash | 10.00 | 225.00 | 515.00 | 675.00 | 910.00 | 1200.00 |

Finally note that micro-GPSS also contains subroutines for *reading* data from a matrix.

HELP MATRE,B,C in a program will read a matrix with B rows and C columns from the file *name*.MAT. Since reading a file is usually only carried out once during the simulation, HELP MATRE is used as a control statement.

The block HELP MATUT,B,C,D will assign the value of the cell at row B and column C of this matrix to the savevalue in D.

These two subroutines can be illustrated by Program 17.7 which produces a quarter by quarter report on the basis of PROG177.MAT which is a copy of PROG176.MAT of Table 17.7. The output for the first quarter is in Table 17.10.

---

**Program 17.7**

```
simulate
help        matre,4,6
generate    90
let+        x$num,1
help        matut,1,x$num,x$sal
help        matut,2,x$num,x$tcost
help        matut,3,x$num,x$prof
help        matut,4,x$num,x$cash
print       "Quarter"
print       x$num
print       ' '
print       "Sales   "
print       x$sal
print       "Costs   "
print       x$tcost
Print       '--------------------'
print       "Profits"
print       x$prof
print       '===================='
print       "Cash    "
print       x$cash
print       ' '
print       ' '
terminate   1
start       6,np
end
```

---

The size of the matrix to be used in the MATIN, MATRE and MATUT subroutines is implementation dependent. For information about this and other details concerning the functioning of these subroutines, see the file HELP.DOC of the specific micro-GPSS system.

**Table 17.10** Report of first quarter of Program 17.7

```
Quarter                1.00

Sales                525.00
Costs                315.00
----------------------------
Profits              210.00
============================
Cash                  10.00
```

## Exercise 17.1

Rewrite Program 12.5 so that the progress of cash can be followed transaction by transaction. If you have a graphics package produce a graph for the development of cash over the day. Simulate for three days.

## Exercise 17.2 (Based on case study 2E in Schriber, 1974)

Rewrite Exercise 8.4 so that you can (a) calculate the total costs of lost production, repairers and reserve machines, assuming a repairer costs $3.75 per hour, a back-up machine $30 per day and the hourly cost penalty for having fewer than 50 machines in production is $20 per machine, and (b) interactively change the value of both the number of repairers and the number of reserve machines. Run the program for various combinations of values on these two variables from 1 to 3 to study variations in costs.

## Exercise 17.3 (Based on case study 4C in Schriber, 1974)

In a foundry, finishing work on castings is done by a machine. Only one worker is needed to operate such a machine. The work itself consists of a sequence of two processes, Process 1 and Process 2. The steps to do the finishing work are:

1. Perform Process 1.

2. Re-position the casting on the machine.

3. Perform Process 2.

4. (a) Unload the finished casting from the machine.

(b) Store the finished casting.
(c) Fetch the next rough casting from the storage area.
(d) Load this rough casting onto the machine.
(e) Return to Step 1 above.

An overhead crane is needed at each step involving movement of the casting, i.e. Steps 2 and 4 above. Whenever a crane is not being used for one of these steps, it is in an idle state.

The finishing machine goes repeatedly through a single closed cycle consisting of the four steps listed above. The crane, on the other hand, can go through each of two distinct cycles, depending on whether it is being used for Step 2 or Step 4. The times (in minutes) required to perform Steps 1 and 3 in the finishing process are as follows:

| Time for Process 1 | Cumulative frequency | Time for Process 2 | Cumulative frequency |
|---|---|---|---|
| < 60 | 0.00 | < 80 | 0.00 |
| 70 | 0.12 | 90 | 0.24 |
| 80 | 0.48 | 100 | 0.73 |
| 90 | 0.83 | 110 | 1.00 |
| 100 | 1.00 | | |

The handling of the casting in Step 2 requires $15 \pm 5$ minutes. The sequence described by Step 4 takes $30 \pm 5$ minutes.

Management wants a GPSS simulation of the finishing department. It wants to determine what utilizations would result if the number of machines served by a single crane were three, four, five or six. Secondly, it wants to know what the effect would be if two cranes were used to serve a group of 10 machines; or if three cranes were used to serve a group of 15 machines. For each condition, which is input interactively, simulate for five 40-hour work weeks. In case of conflict Step 2 is to be given priority over Step 4.

## Exercise 17.4

Modify Program 7.1 so that the cost of waiting for the customers is calculated and printed, assuming that they value their time at an average of $6.00 an hour.

## Exercise 17.5

Modify Program 17.3 so that it produces in *one* table a report for each quarter (i.e. every 62.5 working days) on direct sales, delayed sales, inventory costs, ordering costs and profits, all in dollars.

## Exercise 17.6

Two firms produce identical products sold only by them. If one firm has a higher price than the other, it will not meet any primary demand, i.e. it can only sell if the other firm has not enough stocks. If it has a lower price, it faces a demand intensity corresponding to potential annual sales $q = ap^{-b}$, where $a = 30\,000$ and $b = 1.5$ (see Exercise 14.5). Actual demand in the form of order arrivals follows an exponential distribution with the average time between two orders inversely proportional to $q$. If both firms have identical prices they split the demand. If a customer demanding a product from one firm cannot get it from this firm because of empty stocks, he will try to purchase the product from the other firm, regardless of the price charged by this firm. If this firm cannot supply it either, the customer goes back to the first firm and signs up to buy from them when their inventories are no longer empty.

At the start of each month, each firm orders new products which arrive after 10 days. Each firm also announces a new price for the month, which goes into effect immediately. All customers, even those who signed up for a product earlier, pay the current price. Firm 1 has a cost of $7.00 per unit, while firm 2 has a cost of only $6.00 per unit. The price and purchasing decision of each month are made interactively after print-out of the last month's sales and profits and the inventory level at the end of the month of each firm. Write a program that simulates this situation so that it can be used by two students sitting at a PC or terminal, playing the roles of the two firms, e.g. in a lab session in economics.

## Exercise 17.7

Modify Program 11.2 so that correct statistics for facility utilization are also obtained.

# 18 Experimentation with GPSS models

## 18.1 Introduction

The basis for this chapter is the principle, stressed earlier, that a program should never be run just once, since the result of a single run depends on the use of *one* specific set of random numbers. If the program is run with another set of random numbers, there would most probably be different results. In order to find out to what extent results depend on the use of a particular set of random numbers, a simulation program should be run several times, each time with a different set of random numbers. Section 18.2 covers five possible methods of running the same program with different sets of random numbers and Section 18.3 contains a comparison between two of these methods.

Section 18.4 deals with another issue, namely how to change one or a few particular items in a program from one run to another in a systematic manner in order to make experiments with the simulation model. It focuses on probably the most powerful aspect of simulation, namely the systematic determination of the effect of changes in specific decision variables.

Section 18.5 deals briefly with the important topic of statistical analysis of data from different simulation runs and in Section 18.6 it will be seen how HELP statements can facilitate such analysis. Finally, Section 18.7 touches on how antithetic random numbers can reduce variance and Section 18.8 on how so-called starting-up effects can be avoided.

## 18.2 Running a program with different random numbers

First of all, the following should be stressed: if any of the programs are run several times, without any changes and starting the GPSS processor anew each time, *exactly* the same results would be obtained each time. The reason for this is quite simple. If exactly the same program is run several times, exactly the same sequence of random numbers will be used every time. As already mentioned in Chapter 2, each sequence of random numbers generated by the same generator starts with the same starting number – seed – and, as a given transformation formula is used, in each run the same sequence of numbers is repeated.

Since the results obtained might very well depend on the specific set of random numbers, it is necessary to run a program with *different* sets of random numbers. The question is how this can be done. In this section I shall discuss five possible ways of doing this in micro-GPSS, of which the first two have already been mentioned briefly above. The first two as well as the last one are unique to micro-GPSS.

## 1. Re-run program without resetting seed

In Chapter 3 it was noted that in micro-GPSS a program can be re-run without leaving the micro-GPSS system. When, after a program run, the GPSS processor asks whether we wish to stop the program, we answer N(o) and when it then asks whether we wish to re-run the same program we answer Y(es). Asked whether the seeds are to be reset, we answer N(o). The program will now be re-run, but with a different set of random numbers. For each random number generator, it will start with the number derived from the last random number of the preceding run. In this way we can re-run the program, time and again, with different results. (This dialogue method samples random numbers and hence produces the same results as if a number of CLEAR statements had been used; see method 4 below.)

## 2. SIMULATE with an A operand

If at the outset it has already been decided how many times to re-run the program, in micro-GPSS the desired number of runs can be obtained by using the A operand of the SIMULATE block. Thus SIMULATE 5 will cause the program to run five times.

There are two major differences between this method and the 'dialogue' method above under 1.

1. SIMULATE with an A operand will print all output in a stream, i.e. the computer will not wait for the typing of the return key between each specific item of output. The reason is that the output in the case of an A operand is probably so large that the user is not interested in seeing the output on the screen, but only requires it printed on paper.

2. The set of random numbers is different. The principles for the choice of random numbers in the SIMULATE A case will be explained in Section 18.3.

Finally it should be noted that this A operand in micro-GPSS can be a savevalue, namely X$SIM. In this case the micro-GPSS processor will ask for the value of X$SIM, which the user types in. In this way the number of runs can be easily determined at run time. (This construction thus works as if SIMULATE X$SIM had been preceded by HELP LETSA,X$SIM, which is illegal since SIMULATE has to be the first statement.)

## 3. RMULT

The RMULT control statement can be used for obtaining different random number sequences produced by a specific random number generator. RMULT is the operation and there can be up to eight operands, A, B, C, D, E, F, G and H. The A operand refers to the first, the B operand to the second and the H operand to the eighth random number generator. Hence the A operand affects RN1 and the B operand RN2, etc.

The operand has to be a positive integer constant with a maximum of five digits, which gives an initial value that determines the seed of the random number generator. (In GPSS V it should also be odd.) If different values are assigned to an operand, then different random numbers can be generated.

If an operand has its default value, the standard initial value will be assigned to the corresponding random number generator. In micro-GPSS this initial value is $j$ for the $j$th random number generator, i.e. 1 for the A operand, 2 for the B operand, etc. The seed is then in turn set to an odd number that is determined by an implementation-dependent function of this value $j$. This implies that all random number generators have by default *different* seeds in micro-GPSS. (In GPSS V the default seed is the same for all random number generators.) If there is no RMULT statement at all, these standard initial values are assigned to all eight random number generators, i.e. programs would be executed as above.

Thus, if a different result is required when running a program by using RMULT, it is necessary to assign a non-standard initial value to at least one of the random number generators used. If a number other than $j$ is used as the $j$th operand (i.e. something other than 1 for the A operand, 2 for the B operand, etc.), it is certain that different random numbers will be sampled than in the standard case and hence different results obtained.

If a program is to be re-run by using RN1 and RN2 with different random streams, the control statement RMULT 3,5 could be included, for instance. If RN3 and RN5 need to be changed RMULT ,,7,,9 can be included. In the last case note that we default on the A, B, D (and the F–H operands), since we only wish to change the C and E operands.

The RMULT method is used most simply as follows: when re-running a program, just insert the appropriate RMULT statement, after SIMULATE, but before the first GENERATE block. Let us illustrate the use of RMULT by inserting RMULT 5 into Program 4.1, obtaining Program 18.1 as follows:

**Program 18.1**

```
simulate
rmult      5
generate   18,6
seize      sal
advance    25,5
release    sal
terminate
generate   480
terminate  1
start      1
end
```

As seen from the facility statistics in Table 18.1, slightly different results are obtained from those obtained from Program 4.1. Note, for example, that the average utilization of SAL is now 0.95 to be compared to 0.97 in Table 4.3.

**Table 18.1** Facility statistics of Program 18.1

| Facility | Average utilization | Number entries | Average time/tran |
|----------|---------------------|----------------|-------------------|
| SAL      | 0.95                | 19             | 24.05             |

Re-running a program using RMULT is of particular interest when you wish to re-run a program, one run at a time, after having studied the output of earlier runs. It is thus a kind of substitute for method 1, i.e. the dialogue. One difference is that RMULT provides more control over which random number seed is used.

## 4. CLEAR

The control statement CLEAR is used in micro-GPSS as a substitute for SIMULATE with an A operand. In GPSS V (but not GPSS/H) it is the only possible method if you wish to re-run a program a specified number of times (e.g. five times) and this is known from the outset. The use of the control statement CLEAR is a more efficient method than using RMULT, but less efficient than SIMULATE with an A operand.

The idea behind CLEAR is very different from that of RMULT. The CLEAR statement has no operands in micro-GPSS and is placed *after* the first START statement, to be followed by another START statement.

I shall demonstrate the use of CLEAR with the following version of Program 4.1 which allows it to be run twice, each time with a different set of random numbers.

**Program 18.2**

```
simulate
generate     18,6
seize        sal
advance      25,5
release      sal
terminate
generate     480
terminate    1
start        1
clear
start        1
end
```

This program would produce the facility statistics shown in Table 18.2. In order to explain how the CLEAR statement works in this case, it must first be stressed that the GPSS interpreter follows the control statements in sequential order, until it reaches a START statement. In this case it goes from SIMULATE to the statement START 1, which sets the termination counter to 1 and then starts the execution of all blocks *above* this START statement. Once the termination counter becomes 0 again (by TERMINATE 1 in the stop segment), execution control is, after print-out of the results, passed back to the statement *after* the first START 1.

In all earlier programs there has been an END statement immediately after START 1 and in micro-GPSS execution is then returned to the top

**Table 18.2** Facility statistics of Program 18.2

| Facility | Average utilization | Number entries | Average time/tran |
|---|---|---|---|
| SAL | 0.97 | 19 | 24.61 |

| Facility | Average utilization | Number entries | Average time/tran |
|---|---|---|---|
| SAL | 0.96 | 19 | 24.13 |

level of GPSS, allowing the user to run another program or to stop the simulation. In this case, however, CLEAR comes after START 1 and simulation will now continue with CLEAR instead.

The idea behind CLEAR is that the model is 'cleared' in the sense that *all* statistics are re-initialized and all internal waiting lists and the list of future events are cleared of transactions. All GPSS entities and attributes are set back to their original status with only *one* important *exception*, the *random* number streams, implying that a generator will *not* start with the seed, but will continue in the stream from where it had stopped. CLEAR also initiates the scheduling of the first transaction for each segment.

When the GPSS processor comes to the second START 1 statement, it will again set the termination counter to 1 and then execute all the blocks above. It will thus re-run the whole program from the beginning again, but now with the difference that it will use other random numbers.

In Program 18.2 above, the first run of the program used the first 47 RN1 random numbers. (This can be calculated on the basis of the block statistics of the first run.) When the program is re-run after CLEAR, it starts with the 48th RN1 number and the second run of the program will utilize RN1 numbers 48–93. These numbers are different from the first 47 numbers and hence a different outcome will be obtained, as seen in the facility statistics in Table 18.2.

The average utilization of SAL in the second run, 0.96, is different from the 0.95 obtained with RMULT 5 in Table 18.1 and also from the 0.97 in the first run. In each of these three cases different sets of random numbers have been used.

It should be stressed that none of these three values of the average utilization is more correct than the others. Each of these values can be viewed as sampled from the set of all possible values that can be obtained by running the program with any possible sequence of random numbers.

## 5.  Use of different random number generators

It should finally be mentioned that in micro-GPSS (but not GPSS V) there will be a different set of random numbers if one switches from one random number generator to another. The reason for this is that in micro-GPSS, as noted above, RMULT has $j$ as a default value for the $j$th operand, i.e. an RMULT statement RMULT 1,2,3,4,5,6,7,8 has been implicitly assumed. For example, a switch from RN2 to RN3 in the function definition statement in Program 12.2 would lead to a change in the results.

Such a switch is generally not recommended as a means of obtaining different random numbers, since methods 1 and 2 are much easier to use. Micro-GPSS, in contrast to GPSS V, uses different seeds for the different random numbers for another reason.

Let us imagine a situation where every other random number is used for sampling IATs and every other is used for sampling service time, and RN2 is used for the IATs and RN3 for the service times. In the case of GPSS V, where the same seed is used for every random number generator, two *parallel* sequences of identical random numbers will be used for the two processes. This would imply that when there is a long IAT there is also a long service time and likewise that when there is a short IAT there is also a short service time. Thus the required independence between IATs and service times would be violated.

In micro-GPSS, independence between IATs and service times is retained in this case, since the ADVANCE block uses a random number sequence that is completely different from the one used by the GENERATE block. To achieve the same independence in GPSS V would require an RMULT statement.

If for some reason the *same* seed was required for several random number generators, in micro-GPSS it would then be necessary to use an RMULT statement, e.g. RMULT 1,1,1. It appears, however, that the need for independence between the random numbers is far more important and that such an RMULT statement would seldom be used for that purpose in micro-GPSS.

## 18.3 Comparison between CLEAR and SIMULATE A

Since it is fairly tedious to write a large number of repeated CLEAR and START statements, micro-GPSS has a great advantage over GPSS V by allowing for the production of repeated runs by using SIMULATE A. There is also another advantage, besides the convenience, of using SIMULATE with an A operand as opposed to a set of repeated CLEAR and START statements. The SIMULATE A construction is such that it facilitates proper experimental design.

In order to be able to design experiments properly (which is discussed in Section 18.4), it is important to be able to assume that, e.g., the third run of the program will always use the same random numbers, regardless of the value of the decision variable. Thus the result of the third run should not be affected by how many random numbers are used by the first and second runs.

Hence, SIMULATE with an A operand corresponds to a program in GPSS V followed by (A − 1) sets of the following three control statements:

1. A CLEAR statement

2. An RMULT statement and

3. A START statement.

The CLEAR statement is, as before, without operands. The RMULT statement will set the A operand (i.e. the initial value for random number generator 1) for the second run to 9, the B operand to 10, etc.; for the third run it will set the A operand to 17, the B operand to 18, etc. Generally for the $i$th run the initial value for the $j$th random number generator is set to $(i - 1) \star 8 + j$. The hypothetical START statement will take the same A and B operands as in the real START statement.

Hence the two programs, 18.3a and b, are equivalent.

**Programs 18.3a and 18.3b**

```
simulate    4                    simulate
generate    18,6                 generate    18,6
seize       sal                  seize       sal
advance     25,5                 advance     25,5
release     sal                  release     sal
terminate                        terminate
generate    480                  generate    480
print       f                    print       f
terminate   1                    terminate   1
start       1,np                 start       1,np
end                              clear
                                 rmult       9
                                 start       1,np
                                 clear
                                 rmult       17
                                 start       1,np
                                 clear
                                 rmult       25
                                 start       1,np
                                 end
```

# 18.4 Experimenting with the model

The most important use of simulation is experiments on a model representing a real system, in order to study the effect of a proposed change in this real system. For example, it is possible to study how many more customers would stay and hence how profits would change, if the number of salespeople increases from one to two. Thus, before hiring the second salesperson it is possible to know in advance something of the effect of this hiring. It is therefore a very natural focus within GPSS to carry out experiments by running the same program with two or more values of a decision variable (such as number of salespeople) to see the effect of this change.

The focus of this chapter is thus on the choice between a number of values of a specific decision variable, e.g. the number of salespeople to hire. In principle there could be several values to compare, but for the sake of simplicity, the analysis will be limited here to the choice between two values. A choice between more than two values can always be made by a succession of choices between two values. For example, when choosing between one, two and three salespeople, you can first compare one and two salespeople and then compare the 'best' of one or two salespeople with three salespeople.

When the term 'best' is used here, it does not necessarily have to refer to one single attribute or objective, such as profits, but it could equally refer to some combined evaluation of several attributes, such as profits and liquidity. How this combined evaluation would be made is outside the scope of this text. In the examples studied only one criterion will be used, but it should be stressed that this is purely for the sake of simplicity. It would be quite straightforward to expand the analysis to several objectives. The possibility of including multiple objectives in a simple way is in fact, as mentioned briefly in Chapter 1, one of the advantages of simulation over optimization.

We shall hence proceed to compare the results for two different values of a decision variable. To make the analysis more concrete, let us illustrate it with the case dealt with in Program 15.1, i.e. the choice between one and two salespeople in a store, where the criterion for the choice is the profits per day.

There are two main alternatives as regards the methodology for carrying out the comparative analysis for such a choice:

1. First we make a number of runs, e.g. 10, for the case of one salesperson, each time with different seeds in the random number generators and hence different sets of random numbers, and then we estimate within what limits the 'true' average profit would lie with a certain confidence. (The concept 'true' average is discussed in Section 18.5.) Next we make a number of such runs for the case of two salespeople and estimate within what limits this average profit would then lie. Each set of runs is hence made completely independent of the other. In fact there is no need for the number of runs to be equal.

2. The comparisons are made in *pairs* of runs. In each pair of runs, one run deals with the case of one salesperson and the other run with the case of two salespeople. In each pair, the *only* difference between the runs is the value of the decision variable, i.e. the number of salespeople. What is important is that in each pair the InterArrival Times of the customers, as well as the service times of the first salesperson, are the same. For each pair a difference in profits is then calculated. This is due only to the difference in the number of salespeople. Since the different pairs of

runs use different seeds and hence different sets of random numbers, the different pairs will lead to varying differences in profits. Each pair of runs hence samples one difference in profits out of all possible differences. The final step is then to determine the 'true' average of these differences in profits and base a decision on this.

As will be demonstrated in Section 18.5, the second method of pair-wise comparisons is usually more efficient in the sense that a conclusion as to which is the better alternative can be drawn on the basis of fewer runs. The main part of our discussion will hence be devoted to this method.

In this section two aspects of the use of this method in GPSS will be discussed: (a) how to ensure that the two runs in any *one* such pair of runs are comparable in the sense that the only difference refers to the decision variable and (b) how to make a *number* of such runs in a simple manner.

## 1. Control of conditions in a single pair of runs

In order to make the runs with one and two salespeople comparable, there should first of all be the same customer arrival pattern in the two cases. The difference in outcome should not be due to more people arriving in one case than the other, for example.

Firstly it is necessary to ensure that each of the two runs uses the *same* initial value – seed – of random number generator *j*. A general way to do this is as follows: each condition is run as a separate program. For example, one program can first be written with the base condition, e.g. one salesperson. This base program is then copied, and the copy is given a slightly different name. Next, the decision variable in the copy is changed, e.g. to two salespeople. Each of the two programs is then run with the same initial value of a certain random number stream.

However, even if the programs use the same random number seeds for both values of the decision variable, it is still not possible to rule out that the differences in results between two values can be due to random factors. For example, the customer arrival and service time patterns might be different. This risk is run in programs which have random numbers in more than one block, e.g. when there is both a GENERATE and an ADVANCE block with random variations.

Let us consider the example of the store with one or two salespeople. Firstly, let us compare Programs 6.1 and 7.6, where Program 6.1 is equivalent to Program 7.6 with STOR STORAGE 1. In order for the simulation runs of these two situations to be comparable, exactly the same customer arrival pattern is required in the two simulations. However, since both the GENERATE and the ADVANCE block use constants in the A and B operands and hence the same random number stream RN1, there would probably *not* be the same customer arrival pattern.

The reason for this is as follows: the first few customer arrivals will be the same, because initially the same random numbers are used for the arrival of the first and second customers in both programs. However, after a short while, there will be a customer who will have to wait in the case of one salesperson, while the same customer will go into service in the case of two salespeople. Let us assume that this customer is generated using the fifth RN1 random number. Then the sixth random number is used for sampling service time in the two-salespeople case, while it is used for sampling the next IAT in the one-salesperson case. From this moment on, a different set of random numbers is used for the generation of the customers in the two cases.

It sometimes happens that there are more customers in the case of one salesperson than in the case of two salespeople. This might happen, for instance, if both programs have the seed set by the use of 4 as the initial value for the first random number generator (e.g. by using RMULT 4). In such a case it is not possible to distinguish clearly how much of the difference in waiting time is due to one more salesperson and how much is due to a different set of random numbers producing more customer arrivals.

In order to avoid this problem, different, i.e. dedicated, random number generators must be used for the GENERATE block and the ADVANCE block. For example, the first random number generator RN1 can be reserved for the GENERATE block and RN2 for the ADVANCE block as in Program 12.2. This program is repeated here, called Program 18.4.

**Program 18.4**

```
          simulate
   stor   storage     2
   serv   function    rn2,c2
0,20/1,30
          generate    18,6
          enter       stor,q
          advance     fn$serv
          leave       stor
          terminate
          generate    480
          terminate   1
          start       1
          end
```

The GENERATE block is the same as in Program 7.6, since RN1 is retained here. If RN2 is used for the rectangular distribution, as noted earlier, the simple ADVANCE block with constants in the A and B operands cannot be used, since this way of using the rectangular distribution uses RN1 only. Instead a continuous function must be used, as discussed in Chapter 12.

If this program is run with different values of the number of salespeople, the same number of customer arrivals is always obtained, irrespective of the seeds set for the random number generators. The reason for obtaining exactly the same number of arrivals, regardless of the number of salespeople, is that the same random numbers from RN1 are used for generating the customers in both programs. Likewise, as RN2 is only used for the ADVANCE block, the same random numbers are used for the service times in the one-salesperson case as are used for the corresponding number of customers served first in the two-salespeople case. Hence the first, e.g. 19, service times will be identical in the two cases and the remaining, e.g. 8, service times are used only in the two-salespeople case. Therefore, the service times are also comparable. The difference between the two cases will be entirely due to the number of salespeople.

## 2. Control of conditions in repeated pairs of runs

To be able to draw any conclusion on the basis of a comparison between the two conditions (one or two salespeople), several runs of each condition would be required. We wish to know how this difference varies for different sets of random numbers. In order to have different pairs of runs produce different sets of random numbers, different seeds need to be used for the different pairs of runs. Different seeds can be obtained by using different initial values in the operands of the RMULT statement.

In micro-GPSS this can be done very simply by the use of SIMULATE with an A operand since, as noted in Section 18.3, this assigns the $i$th run (index $= i$) the initial value $(i - 1) \star 8 + j$ for random number generator $j$.

Comparisons can be made as follows:

A. The one-salesperson case with index $i = 1$, compared to the two-salespeople case also with index $i = 1$.

B. The one-salesperson case with the index 2, compared to the two-salespeople case also with the index 2.

C. The one-salesperson case with the index 3, compared to the two-salespeople case also with the index 3, etc.

For example, in the comparison pair A the only difference between the two runs concerns the number of salespeople: both simulation runs use the same index 1 and the same initial value $j$ for random number generator $j$. Thus they use the same set of random numbers and consequently the same customer arrivals and the same service times.

To illustrate this, I shall use a slightly modified version of Program 15.1, called Program 18.5a.

---

**Program 18.5a**

```
        simulate    10
        let         x$capac=1
sal     storage     x$capac
revnu   storage
serv    function    rn2,c2
0,20/1,30
limit   function    rn3,d6
.1,1/.3,2/.55,3/.75,4/.9,5/1,6
sales   function    rn4,c5
0,0/.25,10/.5,40/.75,100/1,500
* Customer segment
        generate    18,6
        if          q$sal>=fn$limit,bye
        enter       sal,q
        advance     fn$serv
        enter       revnu,fn$sales
        leave       sal
bye     terminate
* Stop  segment
        generate    480
        let         x$prof=0.3*s$revnu-80*x$capac
        print       x$prof
        terminate   1
        start       1,np
        end
```

---

Note that RN1 is used for the IATs, RN2 for the service times and RN3 and RN4 for the functions LIMIT and SALES. In order to obtain only the interesting profits, we use PRINT X$PROF and START 1,NP in the stop segment.

Program 18.5a produces 10 different runs with one salesperson, each run with a different set of random numbers, successively giving, e.g., RN1 seeds based on the initial values 1, 9, 17, . . . . Program 18.5b (not shown here but differing only with 2 instead of 1 in the B operand of the initial LET statement) yields 10 new runs, dealing with the two-salespeople case. Again RN1 is successively allocated seeds based on the initial values 1, 9, 17, . . . , implying that runs 1 of both programs constitute one pair, 1a + 1b (with the index 1), runs 2 another pair, 2a + 2b (with the index 2), etc.

Thus the difference in profits between runs 1a and 1b, between runs 2a and 2b, between runs 3a and 3b, etc. can be established and then it can be seen how much these differences vary among the pairs of runs. This variation of the difference in profits over the runs would be entirely due to random factors. By running 10 such pairs it is possible, using statistical methods to be discussed in Section 18.5, to establish the limits within which the 'true' average, as regards the difference in profits, is likely to lie.

## 18.5 Statistical analysis of output

As discussed earlier, the output of a simulation is dependent on what random numbers are used. If the program is run several times with different random numbers each time, different results, e.g. different profits, would most probably be obtained. Running a program e.g. 10 times and noting 10 different values of the profits can be viewed as drawing at random 10 samples from a set containing all possible profit values that could be obtained by running the program with all possible sets of random numbers.

An important question must then be asked: what is the average value of all these *possible* profits, i.e. what is the 'true' average value of profits? We shall call the hypothetical set of all possible results (e.g. profits) the *population* and we are hence interested in estimating the average of this population, calling it $\mu$. Assume we have sampled $n$ values (e.g. 10 values). We can then estimate the population average on the basis of the average of the simulation results $\bar{x}$ and the standard deviation of the simulation results $s$, defined as

$$\sqrt{\frac{1}{n-1}\sum_1^n (x_j - \bar{x})^2}$$

For estimating the limits within which we are likely to find the population average, we shall use Student's $t$-distribution, discussed in detail in many textbooks on statistics. This distribution provides a value $t(n-1, \alpha/2)$, such that we can estimate that the population average will, with the probability of $1-\alpha$, be such that

$$\bar{x} - (s/\sqrt{n}) \star t(n-1, \alpha/2) \le \mu \le \bar{x} + (s/\sqrt{n}) \star t(n-1, \alpha/2)$$

$\alpha$ is hence the probability that the value of $\mu$ will be outside these two limits, i.e. there is a probability $\alpha/2$ that $\mu$ is smaller than the lower limit $\bar{x} - (s/\sqrt{n}) \star t(n-1, \alpha/2)$ and of $\alpha/2$ that it is larger than the upper limit $\bar{x} + (s/\sqrt{n}) \star t(n-1, \alpha/2)$.

For $n = 10$: $\bar{x} - (s/3.16) \star t(9, \alpha/2) \le \mu \le \bar{x} + (s/3.16) \star t(9, \alpha/2)$ and for $n = 5$: $\bar{x} - (s/2.24) \star t(4, \alpha/2) \le \mu \le \bar{x} + (s/2.24) \star t(4, \alpha/2)$.

It is often desirable to estimate the limits within which the population average will lie with 95 percent confidence. This implies that $\mu$ is allowed to lie outside the limits with a probability $\alpha$ of 0.05, i.e. with a probability of 0.025 of the population average being lower than the lower limit and with the same probability of it being higher than the upper limit. A table of Student's $t$-distribution, to be found in most statistical textbooks, shows that $t(9,.025) = 2.26$ and $t(4,.025) = 2.78$.

Since $(s/3.16) \star 2.26 = 0.72s$, it can be seen that for the case of 10 runs, i.e. with n = 10, $\mu$ is such that $\bar{x} - 0.72s \leq \mu \leq \bar{x} + 0.72s$. For the case of 5 runs $\mu$ is such that $\bar{x} - 1.24s \leq \mu \leq \bar{x} + 1.24s$.

Hence, 10 runs provide a much better estimate than 5 runs. As the number of runs increases, the increase in precision of the estimates slows down. For the case of 15 runs, $t(14,.025) = 2.15$ and the limits are $\bar{x} \pm 2.15/3.87s = \bar{x} \pm 0.55s$. For the case of 25 runs, $t(24,.025) = 2.06$ and the limits are $\bar{x} \pm 0.41s$. There is a rapidly decreasing pay-off in terms of increased precision from increasing the number of runs. Since each simulation run is not without cost, it might in many cases be appropriate to stop at 10 runs.

At this point it should be mentioned that when $n = 7$ it can be concluded with 95 percent confidence that $\bar{x} - s \leq \mu \leq \bar{x} + s$, since $\sqrt{7}$ is roughly the same as $t(6,0.025)$.

I shall illustrate this with the case of 10 runs. Suppose a program is run with SIMULATE 10, and assume that the following 10 numbers are obtained, representing, for example, the profits of a certain strategy: 2030, 1965, 2536, 1985, 2344, 1900, 2412, 2055, 2145 and 1960. The average is 2133 and the standard deviation $s = 221$. Hence the lower limit of $\mu$ is $2133 - 0.72 \star 221 = 1974$ and the upper limit is $2133 + 0.72 \star 221 = 2292$.

It can then be estimated that, if this program was run a very large number of times, e.g. several thousand times, the average profits would lie between 1974 and 2292 in 95 percent of all runs.

The example above was limited to a *single* program being run. The same methodology can, however, also be used, when two experimental conditions are run in pairs. Program 18.5 for comparing one salesperson *vs.* two salespeople, uses in each pair of runs the same specific sets of random numbers, but uses different sets of random numbers for different pairs of runs. For each pair of runs, i.e. each set of random numbers, a pair of profits is obtained referring to one and two salespeople, respectively.

The difference in profits can be calculated for each pair, thus yielding one difference value for each set of random numbers. If this difference value is regarded as sampled from the total set of such difference values which would be obtained when running such paired comparisons for all possible different sets of random numbers, the methodology presented above can be used.

**Table 18.3** Comparison of results of Programs 18.5a and 18.5b

| Profits | | |
|---|---|---|
| 1 salesperson case | 2 salespeople case | Difference in profits |
| | | case 2–case 1 |
| 518.20 | 848.90 | 330.70 |
| 417.70 | 475.40 | 57.70 |
| 480.70 | 626.90 | 146.20 |
| 207.70 | 235.40 | 27.70 |
| 457.90 | 519.80 | 61.90 |
| 375.70 | 639.50 | 263.80 |
| 386.80 | 491.60 | 104.80 |
| 607.90 | 897.20 | 289.30 |
| 293.50 | 341.30 | 47.80 |
| 323.80 | 324.50 | 0.70 |

To demonstrate this I shall use the output of Programs 18.5a and 18.5b. There are 10 pairs of profits leading to the differences shown in Table 18.3. The average difference is 133.06 and the standard deviation of the differences is 119.34. Using the methodology presented above, it can be estimated with 95 percent confidence that the average difference due to one more salesperson of all possible simulation runs of the program will lie between 47.70 and 218.42.

It can furthermore be estimated that the hiring of an additional salesperson will lead to better results with a probability of more than 97.5 percent. In 2.5 percent of all cases the population average $\mu$ would be $\leq 47.70$ and thus in 97.5 percent of the cases $\mu \geq 47.70$. Hence $\mu > 0$ in certainly more than 97.5 percent of all cases.

In this context the following should be noted: using the same method it can be estimated with 95 percent confidence that the profits in the one-salesperson case will lie between 323.78 and 490.20 and in the two-salespeople case between 384.41 and 695.69. Since the upper limit in the one-salesperson case is higher than the lower limit in the two-salespeople case, no firm conclusions can be drawn solely on the basis of these estimates of the *separate* profits, in contrast to the difference method. This is an example of the greater power of the paired comparisons approach.

In this section we have studied only one method of analysis. It has the advantage of being fairly simple and fairly widely applicable. It is, however, based on the assumption that the distribution of observations does not deviate strongly from the normal distribution. This is often true if $n$ is not very small. It should be stressed that there are many other, often more sophisticated, methods of analysis, but it is outside the scope of this book to cover these methods.

# 18.6 Using HELP to carry out the statistical analysis

The statistical analysis above can be made automatically if in Program 18.5a LET X\$CAPAC=1 is replaced with HELP VALIN,X\$CAPAC and PRINT X\$PROF with HELP VALUT,X\$PROF and the A operand of SIMULATE is deleted, resulting in Program 18.6.

**Program 18.6**

```
        simulate
        help        valin,x$capac
 sal    storage     x$capac
 revnu storage
 serv   function    rn2,c2
0,20/1,30
 limit function     rn3,d6
.1,1/.3,2/.55,3/.75,4/.9,5/1,6
 sales function     rn4,c5
0,0/.25,10/.5,40/.75,100/1,500
* Customer segment
        generate    18,6
        if          q$sal>=fn$limit,bye
        enter       sal,q
        advance     fn$serv
        enter       revnu,fn$sales
        leave       sal
 bye    terminate
* Stop segment
        generate    480
        let         x$prof=0.3*s$revnu-80*x$capac
        help        valut,x$prof
        terminate   1
        start       1,np
        end
```

Running this program produces a dialogue and output like the one shown in Table 18.4. After typing GPSS, you give \$ as the answer to the first demand for the name of the program file. (In this case you must always start by invoking GPSS.) By giving \$, a call to micro-GPSS is made in a special way allowing for repeated runs of the program combined with statistical analysis. When micro-GPSS again asks for the name of the program file, you answer PROG18.6.

**Table 18.4** Output from Program 18.6 with two alternatives

```
gpss
.....
  What is the name of the GPSS program file
    at most 10 characters allowed
$
 What is the name of the GPSS program file
prog18.6
 Optimization or statistical analysis?
 For optimization give more than two alternatives
 Number of alternatives?
2
 Lowest value ?
1
 Highest value ?
2
 Number of runs?
10

 Result = Result(  1) - Result(  2)

 Result in run  1  -330.70

 Result in run  2   -57.70
 After  2 runs:
 Average:   -194.20   Standard deviation:    193.04
 With 95 percent probability:
 Average lies  between  -1928.57 and   1540.17

 Result in run  3  -146.20
 After  3 runs:
 Average:   -178.20   Standard deviation:    139.28
 With 95 percent probability:
 Average lies  between   -524.23 and    167.83
...
 Result in run  6  -263.80
 After  6 runs:
 Average:   -148.00   Standard deviation:    123.96
 With 95 percent probability:
 Average lies  between   -278.11 and    -17.89

 With 97.5 percent probability:
   2 has a higher value than    1
...
 Result in run 10    -0.70
 After 10 runs:
 Average:   -133.06   Standard deviation:    119.34
 With 95 percent probability:
 Average lies  between   -218.42 and    -47.70

 With 97.5 percent probability:
   2 has a higher value than    1
```

Next micro-GPSS asks for the number of alternatives. If a statistical analysis is required you answer 1 or 2. (3 or more will give you optimization.) Since a comparison between two alternatives is required here you answer 2. (Later in this section the program will also be run for one alternative.)

Micro-GPSS next asks for the lowest value. This value refers to the SNA in the B operand of the HELP VALIN,B statement. Since this is X$CAPAC, answering first 1, and next 2 to the question about the highest value, is equivalent to running a paired comparison between the results of X$CAPAC = 1 on the one hand and X$CAPAC = 2 on the other hand.

The number of runs (10) is next specified. This will hence be equivalent to running 18.5a and 18.5b, both with SIMULATE 10, with the difference that the output is now X$PROF of X$CAPAC = 1 *minus* X$PROF of X$CAPAC = 2. The fact that the difference is calculated with regard to X$PROF is determined by X$PROF being the B operand of the block HELP VALUT,B.

Thus HELP VALIN,B and HELP VALUT,B form a kind of pair, where the B operand of HELP VALIN specifies the input variable and the B operand of HELP VALUT specifies the output variable. In the case of *two* alternatives the output will then refer to the *difference* between the result for the lower value of the input and the result for the higher value of the input. (The usage of the savevalue B of VALIN as a *constant* is restricted in some implementations, see HELP.DOC.)

In this case for each run the difference in results for the two values of X$CAPAC is obtained, based on runs with the same initial values for the random number generators. The results are the same as those on the right in Table 18.3. (Table 18.4, however, lists the result for X$CAPAC = 1 minus the result for X$CAPAC = 2, and not vice versa as in Table 18.3. Hence the many minus signs in Table 18.4.)

In each run, except the first one, there will also be an estimate of the limits within which the population average μ will lie with 95 percent confidence, based on the formulae in the preceding section. It can be seen that the interval decreases as additional runs are made. In this case, it is also found for run 6 and onwards that with at least 97.5 percent confidence the results of X$CAPAC = 2 are higher than those of X$CAPAC = 1, i.e. that higher profits are obtained with two salespeople than with one.

If you wish to estimate the limits within which the profits from two salespeople actually lie, Program 18.6 is re-run, this time limiting the analysis to only one alternative, as shown in Table 18.5. You ask for only one alternative and set the value of this alternative as the lowest value. The result refers only to this particular alternative. Apart from this, the principles behind the output are similar to those of the two alternatives case in Table 18.4.

Finally I shall demonstrate how HELP VALIN and HELP VALUT can be used for optimization. In order to obtain a suitable example let us modify

**Table 18.5** Output from Program 18.6 with one alternative

```
 Number of alternatives?
1
 Lowest value ?
2
 Number of runs?
10

 Result in run  1    848.90

 Result in run  2    475.40
 After  2 runs:
 Average:    662.15    Standard deviation:    264.10
 With 95 percent probability:
 Average lies  between   -1710.70 and   3035.00
 ....
 Result in run 10    324.50
 After 10 runs:
 Average:    540.05    Standard deviation:    217.59
 With 95 percent probability:
 Average lies  between    384.41 and    695.69
```

Program 17.3, which deals with the determination of the order quantity in the book store. Only two changes are made: HELP LETSA,X$ORDQ is replaced with HELP VALIN,X$ORDQ and PRINT X with HELP VALUT,X$PROFI. X$ORDQ is thus the decision variable to be changed and X$PROFI is the result. Since the resulting new Program 18.7 is so similar to Program 17.3, it is not listed. It is sufficient to show an example of the output in Table 18.6. In this case six alternatives are asked for with 5 as the lowest value and 30 as the highest. The program then asks for the number of the optimization run. The number given here determines what seeds are given to the random number generators. A different number here will lead to a different set of seeds and hence a different set of random numbers. In fact the number $i$ used here will lead to the same seeds as used for each value when run the $i$th time with SIMULATE A. Number 1 will thus yield the same result for X$ORDQ = 5 as was obtained in Program 17.3 when run only once (see Table 17.4). Various samples of optimization runs can thus be drawn by running the program many times.

Note that the optimum seems to lie somewhere in the vicinity of 15–20. Besides proceeding to other optimization runs with other random numbers, the program could be run next with only two alternatives, 15 and 20, but with many runs, as in Table 18.4.

**Table 18.6** Output from Program 18.7

```
What is the name of the GPSS program file
    at most 25 characters allowed
$
What is the name of the GPSS program file
prog18.7
Optimization or statistical analysis?
For optimization give more than two alternatives
Number of alternatives?
6
Lowest value ?
5
Highest value ?
30
Give number of the optimization run
1
Result of      5.0 =      862.00
Result of     10.0 =     1698.00
Result of     15.0 =     1761.00
Result of     20.0 =     1791.00
Result of     25.0 =     1637.00
Result of     30.0 =     1512.00
```

## 18.7 Variance reduction with antithetic random numbers

As noted above, the interval within which it could be estimated that the actual average result $\mu$ would lie with 95 percent confidence, was highly dependent on the standard deviation. The lower the standard deviation, or rather the square of it, i.e. the variance, the smaller the interval. Thus reduction of this variance is an alternative to simply making more runs when attempting to obtain a more precise estimate of $\mu$.

One of the simplest and most intuitively appealing ways of variance reduction is the use of antithetic random numbers. For a sequence of uniform random fraction numbers $u_1, u_2, u_3 \ldots u_n$, the corresponding sequence of antithetic random numbers is $1 - u_1, 1 - u_2, 1 - u_3 \ldots 1 - u_n$. Thus, if the 'ordinary' random number is low, the antithetic one is high and *vice versa*. In Table 18.7 there are two random number sequences, of which the one on the right consists of the antithetic values of the numbers on the left. This table might make it easier to understand the advantage of using the antithetic random numbers as a *complement* to the ordinary random number stream. While a simulation based on the random numbers on the left would imply values which are too high (the average is 0.7), a simulation based on the

**Table 18.7** Random numbers and their antithetic values

| a | b |
|------|------|
| 0.44 | 0.56 |
| 0.35 | 0.65 |
| 0.17 | 0.83 |
| 0.90 | 0.10 |
| 0.71 | 0.29 |
| 0.94 | 0.06 |
| 0.96 | 0.04 |
| 0.94 | 0.06 |
| 0.68 | 0.32 |
| 0.97 | 0.03 |
| *a* | *b* |

numbers on the right would imply values which are too low. The two simulations would thus counter-balance each other.

When a short sequence of random numbers is used there is a risk of an average substantially different from 0.5. Thus for simulations that use only a small number of random numbers the availability of antithetic random numbers is important. Since it is thus of interest to be able to generate antithetic random numbers, micro-GPSS provides a very simple method for producing such numbers, namely by the B operand of the SIMULATE statement. If this B operand has the value **A** for **A**ntithetic, a program with this SIMULATE statement will produce random numbers that are antithetic in regard to the numbers produced by a program that is identical apart from the omission of the B operand in the SIMULATE statement.

I shall illustrate this by two simple programs, 18.8a and 18.8b, which produce the two streams *a* and *b* in Table 18.7.

**Program 18.8**

```
simulate                          simulate     ,a
generate    1                     generate     1
print       rn5                   print        rn5
terminate   1                     terminate    1
start       10                    start        10
end                               end
       a                                 b
```

Note that in Program 18.8b there is ,A in the operand field of SIMULATE, since the A operand is defaulted on.

# 18.8 Eliminating starting conditions with RESET

In this final section I shall discuss another important phenomenon which might influence the relevance of the comparison of different simulation runs. This has to do with the fact that in a simulation there will often be *starting* conditions at the beginning of the run which have no correspondence in reality. This is particularly true when the process being modeled has no true beginning in reality, but where the simulation has to start at what is often an arbitrary time.

Let us take as an example the inventory policy of a company such as the one modeled in Program 13.3, which investigated the effect of an inventory policy during 250 days. We do not only want to study the case when the company first started with this product at the beginning of the simulation run. It is more likely that it has been selling this product for years, but the investigation has to be started at some point in time. If the simulation is started with 30 units in the inventory and with no students waiting for delivery of the book, as in Program 13.3, the conditions during the first simulated days will be different from the conditions during the rest of the run. For example, in the case of five books being re-ordered each time the stocks would soon be depleted and a number of students would be waiting.

Thus the initial conditions, with substantial stocks and no waiting line, are different from the later conditions, with small stocks and several students waiting. Since these later conditions will prevail for the rest of the simulation, they will be called 'steady state' conditions. As the initial conditions in this example are only caused by the start-up of the simulation and have no counterpart in reality, it is preferable to eliminate the effects of these initial conditions on the statistics, by focusing the statistics exclusively on the real steady state conditions.

The way to eliminate these initial conditions in GPSS is through the use of the RESET statement. This is a control statement used in a similar fashion to CLEAR. The first START is followed by RESET, then followed by a new START. This implies that the simulation temporarily halts to carry out RESET when the termination counter is reset to 0. After this the simulation starts with the new START statement.

The RESET statement will reset statistics, but in contrast to CLEAR it will not remove any transactions from the future events list or the waiting lists, nor will it carry out the initial scheduling of the first transactions. The principle of RESET is that the simulation will proceed as usual after the processor has reached the START after RESET, but that the gathered statistics will refer only to the part of the simulation that comes after the RESET statement has been invoked.

More specifically, the RESET statement consists of only the operation code RESET. The RESET statement will set all statistical items (Standard

Numerical Attributes) back to their initial value (usually 0) with the following important exceptions:

1. As for the CLEAR statement, the random number streams are *not* reset to the seeds. When the simulation starts again (due to the START after RESET), the program proceeds with that random number in each stream, which comes after the one most recently used in the execution prior to RESET.

2. The ABSOLUTE CLOCK is *not* set back to 0, but the RELATIVE CLOCK is. For the first time it is now clear why there are two different clocks. The ABSOLUTE CLOCK measures the time from the simulation start, while the RELATIVE CLOCK measures the time from the last RESET activity.

3. The *current* count of each block is *not* reset to 0, since the current count represents the number of transactions, which at the time of RESET are waiting in different blocks. The *total* count will, however, be reset to 0, so that the total count will now represent all transactions that enter a block after the RESET time.

4. The savevalues are *not* reset to 0 but retain their values.

I shall illustrate the use of RESET by Program 18.9 which is a slight extension of the inventory example of Program 13.3, but which simulates initial conditions during 50 days and produces statistics for the steady state conditions during 250 days. The only difference when compared to Program 13.3 is the end of the program. Program 18.9 has a stop segment, followed by control statements as follows:

**Program 18.9** Final part

```
generate    50
terminate   1
start       1,np
reset
start       5
end
```

The stop segment will decrease the termination counter by 1 every 50 days. The first use of START 1,NP implies that the program first runs for 50 days, but without any print-out for the first 50 days. After this, execution passes to the first statement after START 1, i.e. to RESET, which will reset the statistics so that they will henceforth refer only to the time after RESET, i.e. to time after the ABSOLUTE CLOCK is 50. Execution next proceeds to

START 5. The termination counter is then set to 5. The execution of the program then continues.

When AC (ABSOLUTE CLOCK) is 100, and RC (RELATIVE CLOCK) is 50, TERMINATE 1 decreases the termination counter by 1 to 4. At RC = 100 and AC = 150, the termination counter is decreased from 4 to 3 etc. and finally at RC = 250 (AC = 300) the termination counter is decreased from 1 to 0 and the simulation stops. Statistics referring to the most recent 250 days are then obtained, but the total simulation has been run for 300 days.

Finally I will discuss how it can be determined what is a suitable length of run for the initial conditions, i.e. how to decide when initial conditions still prevail and when steady state conditions have been reached. One way is as follows: the time is divided into fairly small units, e.g. in this case 10 days. Next it is necessary to establish which SNA is the best indicator of whether a steady state has been obtained or not, and have only this SNA printed out. Let us assume it is Q$TIM. On this basis, the final part of the program is changed, resulting in Program 18.10.

**Program 18.10** Final part

```
generate    10
let+        x$acloc,c1
print       x$acloc
print       q$tim
terminate   1
start       1,np
reset
start       1,np
reset
.....
end
```

The stop segment of Program 18.10 first computes the *absolute* clock (remember that C1 is the *relative* clock). It next prints the absolute clock and then the value Q$TIM to be studied.

There are hence a great many RESET and START 1,NP pairs and there will be a print-out of the absolute clock as well as of Q$TIM every 10 days. As long as the value of Q$TIM varies greatly from 10-day period to 10-day period, initial conditions still prevail. When the values of the 10-day periods begin to be fairly similar, the steady state condition has probably been reached.

## Exercise 18.1

Customers arrive at a store every 25 seconds on average, following an exponential distribution. Service time is likewise 25 seconds on average, following an exponential distribution. The store owner contemplates whether one or two salespeople should be used. The average waiting line measured two hours after opening needs to be studied. Five simulation runs for the case of one salesperson are initially to be made. Write programs in the *five different* ways described in Section 18.2 and run them to compare the output in the five cases.

## Exercise 18.2 (Case study 3C in Schriber, 1974)

Modify the program of Exercise 11.2 so that in a single batch run, 10 different days of operation will be simulated for the tool-crib problem. In addition to controlling experimental conditions, arrange the model so that both the 'no priority' and 'priority' queue disciplines are investigated with the same program. (Note that as priority value a savevalue determined in an initial LET or HELP statement can be used.) The resulting output will provide two samples, each consisting of 10 different 'average queue content' estimates for the corresponding disciplines. Compute the mean and standard deviation for each of these two samples. How much better is the priority distinction discipline based on samples?

## Exercise 18.3 (Case study 5D in Schriber, 1974)

The InterArrival Times of cars approaching a gas station with the intention of possibly stopping for service are distributed as follows:

| InterArrival Time (seconds) | Cumulative frequency |
|---|---|
| <0 | 0.00 |
| 100 | 0.25 |
| 200 | 0.48 |
| 300 | 0.69 |
| 400 | 0.81 |
| 500 | 0.90 |
| 600 | 1.00 |

Service times for cars are distributed as follows:

| Service time (seconds) | Cumulative frequency |
|---|---|
| <100 | 0.00 |
| 200 | 0.06 |
| 300 | 0.21 |
| 400 | 0.48 |
| 500 | 0.77 |
| 600 | 0.93 |
| 700 | 1.00 |

A car stops for service only if the number of cars already waiting for service is less than or equal to the number of cars currently being served. (That is, a car stops only if the driver perceives that not more than one car per attendant is already waiting to be served.) Cars which do not stop go to another gas station, and therefore represent lost business.

The gas station is open from 7 a.m. until 7 p.m. Cars arriving later than 7 p.m. are not accepted for service. Any cars already waiting in line at 7 p.m. are served, however, before the attendants leave for the night.

It is estimated that the profit per car served averages $1, excluding attendants' salaries and other fixed costs. Attendants earn $2.50 per hour and are only paid for working a 12-hour day, even if they stay beyond 7 p.m. to finish serving waiting cars. The other fixed costs amount to $75 per day.

The station's owner wants to determine how many attendants he should hire to maximize his daily profit. Build a GPSS model simulating the operation of the station, then use the model to provide the answer. Simulate with each attendants-hired configuration for five different days. Design the model to control experimental conditions, so that the various alternatives are investigated under identical sets of circumstances.

## Exercise 18.4

Alter the program of Exercise 8.4 so that it produces statistics referring to the steady state conditions. First write one version of the program to determine when steady state conditions begin, by allowing a study of the changes in the utilization of machinery week by week. Next write another version to produce statistics for the steady state, simulating a period roughly twice the length of the initial conditions. Compare the results, as well as simulation time, with those of Exercise 8.4.

# 19 SPLIT and ASSEMBLE blocks

## 19.1 Introduction

In this chapter I shall deal with the two remaining blocks in micro-GPSS, namely SPLIT and ASSEMBLE. The SPLIT block is used for making copies of a transaction; its syntax is presented in Sections 19.2 and 19.4 and an example of its use for reneging in Section 19.3. The ASSEMBLE block, used for deleting copies of transactions created in a SPLIT block, is presented in Section 19.5. Finally, in Section 19.6 we shall study a program which is larger than any earlier presented program and which deals with the simulation of the financial effects of sales and inventory policy.

## 19.2 The SPLIT block

Until now the only way for transactions to enter the simulation was by a GENERATE block. The SPLIT block is another block in which transactions are created. The SPLIT block, however, will only allow for the creation of *copies* of transactions that are already in the simulation. The original transactions must hence enter the simulation through a GENERATE block. When an original transaction reaches the SPLIT block, one or several copies of this transaction will then be created. These copied transactions will acquire exactly the same characteristics (parameters, priority, etc.) as the original transactions had when reaching this block.

In micro-GPSS the SPLIT block can have A, B and C operands. The A operand, a positive integer value (a constant or a savevalue), is the number of copies to be created in the SPLIT block. Normally, this is a small number. The examples below are limited to the case when the A operand is 1, implying that only one copy is created from each transaction entering the SPLIT block.

The B operand is the address of the block to which these copies of the transaction are sent. There cannot be any default values of these A and B operands, since the processor must know both how many copies are to be created and where these copies are to be sent. The C operand is the so-called serialization parameter. This operand, which is more complicated, though optional, will be described in Section 19.4.

The block symbol of the SPLIT block is shown in Figure 19.1. There is a rectangle with the operation SPLIT at the top of the rectangle and with the A and C operands further down in the rectangle. One arrow points down to the next block, where the original transaction goes. The second arrow points to the right and has the B operand (within parentheses), showing where the copy or copies will go.

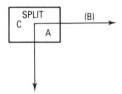

**Figure 19.1** Block symbol of SPLIT

One of the uses of the SPLIT block is to allow for some *concurrent* activity initiated by the transaction, as in Program 19.1. This deals with a simple version of a company's simulation of a product possibly leading to repeated sales. As seen in the block diagram in Figure 19.2, the original 'customer' transaction is the sale of one unit. This sale of one unit will later lead to two concurrent paths of activities: one financial path, involving credits of varying lengths of time, and one other path, representing the possibility of a repeated purchase later in time. Since the timing of a possible repeated purchase is completely independent of the time elapsed before the customer pays his bill, there must be two separate paths. This in turn requires that two identical transactions emerge from the SPLIT block.

More specifically, sales orders are generated, following an exponential distribution, with an average InterArrival Time of 360/FN$SALES. FN$SALES represents annual potential sales in number of units and 360/FN$SALES is hence the average time between each order of one unit.

Each sales order then comes to the SPLIT block, where it is copied: along one path there is the original transaction going downwards, dealing with financial aspects, and along the other path is the copy going right to RETUR, dealing with repeated sales.

Let us first look at the financial path (similar to Program 15.5). The first LET+ block adds the sales revenue of one unit (= the price) to the total sales revenue SAL. The next LET+ block adds the cost of this unit to total costs. The following LET− block deducts the cost of the sold unit from cash. In this

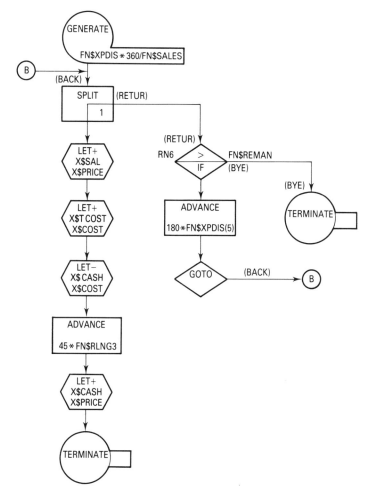

**Figure 19.2** Block diagram of customer segment of Program 19.1

simple model it is assumed that the payment corresponding to the cost of a sold unit occurs at the same time as the sales of the product. Program 19.5 will use more complicated, yet more realistic, assumptions.

The sales transaction next comes to an ADVANCE block, where it is delayed a time 45 ⋆ FN$RLNG3, representing the time between the sales of the goods and the time when the payment from the customer is received. It is thus assumed that the average payment time is 45 days, and that the actual credit time follows an Erlang distribution with the parameter $n = 3$, dependent on RN4 by default, as described in Section 13.7.

After the ADVANCE block there is another LET+ block, representing payment by the customer. This block increases cash with the sales amount, i.e. the price.

**Program 19.1**

```
        simulate
*
        let         x$price=27
        let         x$cost=21
        let         x$cash=200
*
 sales function     x$price,c5
10,60/20,40/30,25/40,20/50,15
 reman function     x$cost,c5
8,0/12,.4/15,.6/20,.7/40,.8
*
* Sales segment
        generate    fn$xpdis*360/fn$sales
 back   split       1,retur
        let+        x$sal,x$price
        let+        x$tcost,x$cost
        let-        x$cash,x$cost
        advance     45*fn$rlng3
        let+        x$cash,x$price
        terminate
*
 retur  if          rn6>fn$reman,bye
        advance     180*fn$xpdis(5)
        goto        back
 bye    terminate
*
        generate    360
        let         x$prof=x$sal-x$tcost
        terminate   1
        start       1
        end
```

I shall now discuss the right-hand part representing the repeated sales. First there is an IF block which checks whether a random number is larger than the value of the function REMAN. If this is true, the transaction goes to BYE without repeated sales. Otherwise it goes to the next block and repeated sales occur. This IF block is similar to a statistical GOTO block, but instead of writing, e.g., GOTO BYE,.2, there is a probability FN$REMAN that can take different values, e.g. 0.2, 0.3 etc., depending on the product quality (see below).

If the sampled random number is such that the customer will make a repeated purchase, he goes to the next block, the ADVANCE block. Here he is delayed half a year, or 180 days, on average, with the delay following an exponential distribution (using RN5), implying that some customers wait much longer than the average before they repeat their purchases. After this, the customer transaction goes to BACK to repeat the whole purchasing process all over again.

Note that FN$XPDIS uses RN2, FN$RLNG3 RN4 and FN$XPDIS(5) RN5. In this way each GENERATE and ADVANCE block has its own random number generator.

I shall now discuss the details that are not covered by the block diagram.

First, initial values are given to the savevalues PRICE, COST and CASH. The idea is that these are the variables that one would like to experiment with, by changing them between different runs. Next, SALES, i.e. annual sales, is defined as a continuous, decreasing function of price. This demand function for the original purchase implies, e.g., that if price increases from 20 to 30 (thousands), then sales volume is reduced from 40 to 25 units. Prices are assumed to lie between 10 and 50 (thousands).

The probability of a repeated purchase is then defined as a function of production cost, implying a function of quality. The higher the unit production cost, the higher the quality and the higher also the probability that the customer will buy another unit. When the cost is 8 (thousand), the product is so inferior that no one wishes to repeat the purchase. No costs over 40 (thousand) are contemplated.

The sales segment has already been explained. The stop segment stops the simulation after one year (= 360 days) and calculates profits as sales revenue minus total costs.

## 19.3 An example of reneging

SPLIT blocks are also useful for modeling reneging, e.g. a customer leaves a waiting line, if he has not been served within a certain number of minutes.

A SPLIT block is needed for the following reason. Once a customer starts waiting in front of a server, he remains in a passive waiting state until all customers waiting in front of him have obtained service. In micro-GPSS, there is no direct way of taking a customer out of a waiting line before it is his time to be served. Hence we divide each customer into two fictitious 'half-persons'; the left half goes as a normal customer into the waiting line; the right half stays outside of this line, waiting to renege after a certain time.

When it is time for the left half to leave the waiting line and go into service, it checks if the right half has already reneged, in which case it leaves the system. If instead it is served before reneging time, it sends a signal to the right half that it has left the waiting line. It also updates the waiting line statistics and then goes into service.

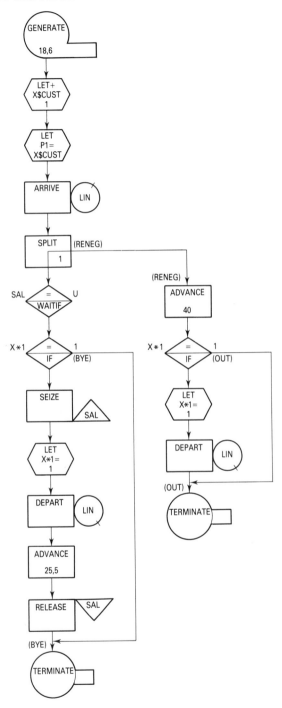

**Figure 19.3** Customer segment of Program 19.2

**Program 19.2**

```
        simulate
* Customer segment
        generate    18,6
        let+        x$cust,1
        let         pl=x$cust
        arrive      lin
        split       1,reneg
        waitif      sal=u
        if          x*1=1,bye
        seize       sal
        let         x*1=1
        depart      lin
        advance     25,5
        release     sal
 bye    terminate
*   reneging section
 reneg advance      40
        if          x*1=1,out
        let         x*1=1
        depart      lin
 out    terminate
* Stop segment
        generate    480
        print       q
        terminate   1
        start       1,np
        end
```

When it is time for the right half to renege, it checks whether the left half has already gone into service. If this is the case, it simply leaves the system. Otherwise it signals to the left half that it has reneged, updates the waiting line statistics and leaves.

An example of a program using this procedure is Program 19.2, which is similar to Program 6.1 but allows reneging.

Before turning to the details of this block diagram, it remains to be discussed how the two halves can signal to each other. An important problem here is that several signals, all for different customers, might exist at the same time in the system. Hence, each customer transaction must have its own signal. In order to allow this, a block LET+ X$CUST,1 first keeps track of the number of each customer. X$CUST becomes 1 after the first customer arrival, 2 after the second one etc. Next LET P1=X$CUST assigns this number to parameter 1 of each customer transaction. Thus P1 = 1 for the first customer, P1 = 2 for the second etc.

It is helpful to remember how Q⋆1 was used in Program 16.5 to denote the length of the queue (or AD set) with the number held in parameter 1. Likewise, savevalues can be created using this method of indirect addressing. X⋆1 is thus a whole sequence of values (like X(1), X(2), etc. in a GPL) with *one* particular value for *each* customer transaction. Hence X⋆1 can be used to denote whether a customer has stopped waiting, i.e. has either reneged or gone into service. In that case X⋆1 = 1. Otherwise, i.e. if the customer is still waiting, X⋆1 keeps its initial value 0.

I shall now discuss the details of the block diagram of the customer segment shown in Figure 19.3.

First the values 1, 2, 3, etc. are assigned to P1. Next the customer goes into the ARRIVE block to measure total waiting time. He or she then proceeds to the SPLIT block which makes one copy of the customer transaction corresponding to the right part of the person, and sends it to the address RENEG. Since the SPLIT block also gives the values of the parameters of the original to the copy, both 'halves' of the customer have the same value of P1, but they share *one* joint X⋆1-value. Thus both the left and the right half of customer 1 can access one X⋆1 (like X(1) in a GPL), while the two halves of customer 2 access another X⋆1 (like X(2)), etc.

The original transaction, i.e. the left half, next goes into the block WAITIF SAL=U, where the customers are kept waiting as long as SAL is busy. When SAL becomes idle, an IF block checks whether the right half of the customer has already reneged, i.e. if X⋆1 = 1. If that is the case the left half just leaves through BYE TERMINATE. If X⋆1 = 0, i.e. the initial value, the left half of the customer makes SAL busy. In the block LET X⋆1=1 it sends the signal to the right half that it has stopped waiting. It then updates the waiting line statistics through DEPART LIN and remains in service $25 \pm 5$ minutes before leaving service and the system.

The right half in the reneging section will first wait a certain time in the ADVANCE block, in this case 40 minutes. It is then time to renege. If the left part has already gone into service, i.e. if X⋆1 = 1, the right half leaves through OUT TERMINATE. Otherwise, i.e. if the left half is still waiting in front of SAL, the right half reneges. It sends a signal to the left half by LET X⋆1=1 and then goes through the DEPART block, in order to determine correct waiting times, before leaving the system.

Since only output of the queue statistics is required, PRINT Q is placed in the stop segment and NP as B operand in the START statement.

## 19.4 The C operand of the SPLIT block

The C operand is the number of the so-called *serialization parameter*. It is a positive constant (in the range from 1 to 12) that gives the number of the parameter to be used. When the transaction enters the SPLIT block, the value of this parameter is increased by 1 for the parent, i.e. the original transaction, by 2 for the first copy, by 3 for the second copy, etc., i.e. generally by $j + 1$ for the $j$th copy. If, for example, the transaction has *not* changed any parameter before coming to the SPLIT block, then SPLIT 4,NEXT,1 will place 1 into P1 of the parent, 2 into P1 of the first copy, 3 into P1 of the second copy, etc. The value of the serialization parameter makes it easy to determine later in the program whether a transaction is a parent or a copy. Defaulting on the C operand causes no value to be assigned to any parameter.

One use of the serialization parameter is to send different copies in a simple way to one of several addresses, which are given as values in a function of the parameter. This can be illustrated by Program 19.3, which sends a transaction and its copies in parallel to one of five different machines. In this simple example there is only a print-out of the name of each machine to show that it has been properly reached.

**Program 19.3** with part of output

```
            simulate
    adr     function    p1,d5
    1,mac1/2,mac2/3,mac3/4,mac4/5,mac5
            generate    10,5
            split       4,next,1
    next    goto        fn$adr
    mac1    print       'Machine 1'
            terminate
    mac2    print       'Machine 2'
            terminate
    mac3    print       'Machine 3'
            terminate
    mac4    print       'Machine 4'
            terminate
    mac5    print       'Machine 5'
            terminate
            generate    40
            terminate   1
            start       1,np
            end
Machine 1
Machine 2
Machine 3
Machine 4
Machine 5
..
```

Here the original and four copies are sent from the SPLIT block to the next block with the address NEXT. From this block, in turn, the five transactions are sent to five different addresses.

## 19.5 The ASSEMBLE block

While the SPLIT block divides a transaction into several transactions, the ASSEMBLE block merges several such transactions, coming from the *same* original, back into *one* transaction again.

The ASSEMBLE block has only one operand, the A operand, which is the number of transactions that are merged into one transaction. Hence, if a SPLIT block has created one copy of a transaction and there is a need to merge the original and the copy, the A operand is set to 2. The A operand is thus the number of transactions to be removed *plus one*.

The block symbol of the ASSEMBLE block is a rectangle resembling an envelope with a flap on which the value of the A operand is written, as shown in Figure 19.4.

**Figure 19.4** Block symbol of ASSEMBLE

The merger of transactions cannot take place before the number of transactions specified in the A operand have entered the ASSEMBLE block. These transactions must all belong to the same assembly set in the sense that they are either the original transaction itself or copies of the same original transaction or copies of such copies, etc.

If the members of an assembly set differ in some way, e.g. with regard to value of the serialization parameter discussed earlier, it might be important to know that in micro-GPSS the merger process is such that the *last* transaction to reach the ASSEMBLE block is kept and all the remaining ones eliminated. It might therefore very well happen that the original is eliminated and some copy kept. In general this is, however, without any particular consequence.

Let us now study another type of problem for which GPSS is appropriate, namely problems dealing with project time planning. One important aspect of project time planning is that a project, such as the construction of a building or a ship, is composed of various activities and that work on certain activities cannot start before work on other activities has been completed. The time needed for each activity is often not fixed but rather of a stochastic nature. These kinds of project time problem are often dealt with using computer methods like CPM (Critical Path Method) and PERT (Program Evaluation and Review Technique).

Some of these methods assume a given time requirement for each activity. Other versions of these methods allow for stochastic variations of a particular type, often requiring a so-called Beta distribution. One is generally interested in determining the time that the whole project will take, i.e. in cases with stochastic activity times, the probability of different total times. In general the methods mentioned above also have the weakness that they do not always produce a correct estimate of the distribution of total project times. In some cases an estimate of the time variation is only obtained for *one* specific sequence of so-called critical activities. Furthermore, resource limitations are generally not considered explicitly.

An alternative method, allowing for any kind of distribution of activity times, is to run a great number of simulations, using, e.g., GPSS. For each simulation, total time can be computed and the potential variations in total time can be estimated. Resource limitations are taken into account.

Let us consider a very simple GPSS example involving a project, e.g. the construction of a house, with only four activities: first there is an activity A, e.g. the construction of the frame of a building. Next are two activities B and C, which can start only when A is completed, but can be carried out independently, i.e. at the same time. These could be the plumbing and electrical wiring. Finally there is an activity D, e.g. interior painting, which can start only when B and C have *both* been completed.

In this simple program let us assume that for each of these activities there is only one person (with a special machine) available. When a person has completed his or her part on one house, he or she can, if it is possible, start to do the same kind of work on the next house. We shall assume different distributions for the service completion times: for A an exponential distribution, for B and C rectangular distributions and for D a normal distribution.

A total of 100 houses are to be built. The whole project can be represented by Figure 19.5. The simple Figure 19.5 can next be transformed into the GPSS block diagram of Figure 19.6. On the basis of this, Program 19.4 can be written.

The production of each of 100 houses starts as soon as activity A can start for each house. The block ARRIVE TOTTI (and the corresponding DEPART block just before TERMINATE) measures the total production time for a house, starting from the moment that activity A starts, i.e. the house has been able to seize MACH1.

After going through activity A, work is sent by the SPLIT block simultaneously to activity B and activity C. Both of these activities lead into MAC4 ASSEMBLE 2, which allows production to continue with activity D only when both of these two activities B and C are completed.

From the output of the table (not shown here), it is possible to see that,

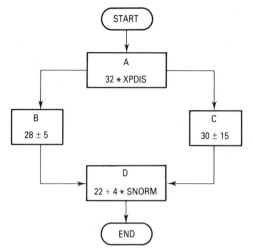

**Figure 19.5** Production flow of Program 19.4

**Program 19.4**

```
        simulate
        qtable        totti,100,100,20
*
        generate      ,,,100
*   Activity A
        seize         mach1
        arrive        totti
        advance       32*fn$xpdis
        release       mach1
        split         1,mac3
*   Activity B
        seize         mach2
        advance       28,5
        release       mach2
        goto          mac4
*   Activity C
mac3    seize         mach3
        advance       30,15
        release       mach3
*   Activity D
mac4    assemble      2
        seize         mach4
        advance       22+4*fn$snorm
        release       mach4
        depart        totti
        terminate     1
*
        start         100
        end
```

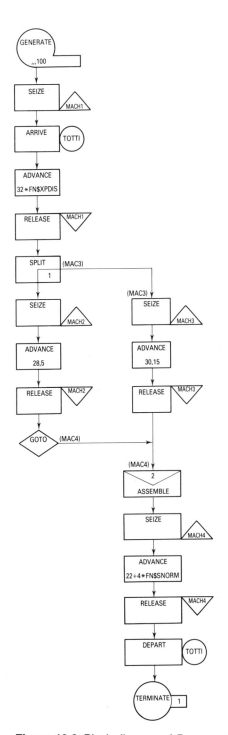

**Figure 19.6** Block diagram of Program 19.4

although the sum of the average times of the critical path A–C–D is $32 + 30 + 22 = 84$ hours, fewer than 20 of the 100 houses would take less than 100 hours. Some houses would in fact take more than 400 hours!

## 19.6 An integrated financial simulation model

In this section I shall discuss a model that is larger than the models presented earlier. It deals with a type of simulation that is of importance for a great many corporations, namely the simulation of the financial effects of sales and inventory policy. This model will be built largely on Programs 13.3, 17.3 and 19.1.

The simulation concerns a company which buys a product from a manufacturer and then resells it on the market. Demand for the product is dependent on both price and product quality. Demand is also a function of earlier sales: some customers will, after varying periods of time, return to buy an additional unit of the product. Because of this, demand will increase over time.

Sales first lead to an increase in accounts receivable. The time after which customers pay varies stochastically. The inventory policy involves determining both the re-ordering level and the re-ordering quantity, i.e. when to re-order and how much to re-order each time. By running the simulation with various random number sequences, it is possible to estimate the probability that the corporation will run out of cash at a specific combination of price, product quality and inventory policies.

This Program 19.5 consists of four segments: a sales segment, an entering inventory segment, a re-ordering segment and a report segment.

The *sales segment* is very similar to the sales segment of Program 19.1, as can be seen by comparing Figure 19.2 with Figure 19.7. The part of the segment that deals with the customers who return for repeat purchases is the same. The other part of the segment to the left in Figure 19.7, dealing with financial consequences, contains, however, several blocks not found in Figure 19.2.

The GENERATE block, creating purchasing orders, is followed by an IF block, IF STOR=E,LOST, implying that if there are no units left in the inventory, the customer goes to a competitor and the order is lost. The number of lost orders is added up in the savevalue LOST.

After the SPLIT block the original transaction, dealing with the financial consequences, comes to the block LEAVE STOR, implying that it decreases the contents in storage by one unit. The blocks LET+ X$SAL,X$PRICE and LET+ X$TCOST,X$COST are the same as in Program 19.1, adding up sales and costs of goods. In Program 19.5 these costs are, however, not connected with immediate payments. The payments (= cash outflow) for purchased

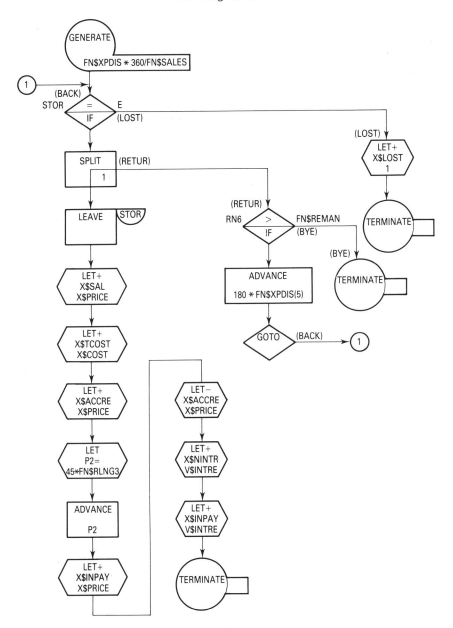

**Figure 19.7** Sales segment of Program 19.5

goods are handled in the re-ordering segment (see below) in Figure 19.8, while in Program 19.1 the company immediately re-purchased one unit of the product when one was sold.

Program 19.5 also keeps track of accounts receivable. The sale of one unit here leads to the immediate increase in accounts receivable, handled by the block LET+ X\$ACCRE,X\$PRICE.

Next there is, as in Program 19.1, a delay in payments of 45 days on average, following an Erlang distribution. In Program 19.5, this time, 45 ⋆ FN\$RLNG3, is placed in parameter 2, i.e. there is a time delay of $P2 = 45 \star FN\$RLNG3$.

It should be explained why a parameter is needed here instead of a savevalue. A particular value of FN\$RLNG3 and hence of P2 is sampled for *each* payment and used for the calculation of interest on each payment *after* the elapse of this time P2. Therefore 45 ⋆ FN\$RLNG3 cannot be put into a savevalue, since this savevalue would most probably be changed by another transaction before the interest on the first payment has been calculated.

The payments made after this delay are registered as an increase in cumulative cash inflow by the block LET+ X\$INPAY,X\$PRICE and as a corresponding decrease in accounts receivable by the block LET− X\$ACCRE,X\$PRICE.

The company also obtains an interest payment V\$INTRE, which is defined in the variable INTRE (at the top of the program) as price ⋆ interest-bearing credit time (in days) ⋆ interest per day. The total credit time has already been placed in parameter 2. From this an interest-free credit time of 30 days is deducted. (In the few cases when this leads to a negative interest-bearing credit time, the negative interest payments can be regarded as cash discounts for simplicity.) The daily interest rate is 24/36 000, corresponding to an annual rate of 24 percent. This interest payment is next added to NINTR, the cumulative net interest as well as to INPAY, cumulative cash inflow.

The *entering inventory segment* is similar to the corresponding segment in Program 17.3. This brings a certain number of units (in this case 2) into storage, which is the opening balance of inventory at the start of the simulation.

I shall now turn to the *re-ordering segment* of Figure 19.8, which is based on the re-ordering segment of Program 17.3, shown in Figure 17.3. The first part of the left-hand side of the inventory segment in Figure 19.8 is almost identical to that part of Figure 17.3. The only difference is that Program 19.5 does *not* measure the weekly inventory, since all inventory costs in this case refer to interest costs and are thus incorporated in other ways into the model. (Furthermore, there are no fixed costs for each purchase.)

The first addition to the segment (as compared to Figure 17.3) is the block LET P1=X\$ORDQ⋆X\$COST. For each replenishment purchase, this

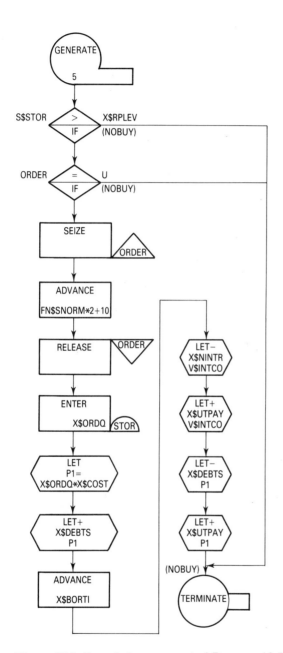

**Figure 19.8** Re-ordering segment of Program 19.5

block calculates the total purchase expenditure as the ordered quantity multiplied by the purchasing cost per unit. This value is then saved in the parameter P1 as the borrowed amount. The block LET+ X$DEBTS,P1 then increases debts by this amount.

The company's payments to the supplier are delayed in the ADVANCE block for the total borrowing time X$BORTI, which is a decision variable. At the end of this time, the company first has to pay V$INTCO in interest on the borrowed amount of P1 dollars. At the top of the program, V$INTCO is defined as $P1 * (X\$BORTI - 20) *$ the daily interest rate $(20/36\,000 = 20$ percent annually). Thus 20 days are interest free. These interest costs V$INTCO of a particular purchase are deducted from the net interest results NINTR by the block LET − X$NINTR,V$INTCO. At the same time the total cumulative cash outflow X$UTPAY increases by these interest costs. Finally as the borrowed amount P1 is paid back, the debts decrease and the cumulative cash outflow increases by this amount P1.

The explanation of the *report segment* does not require any block diagram, but can best be studied directly from the program listing. This segment generates a report every 90th day, i.e. at the end of each of six quarters (see START 6,NP).

In this report segment the number of the quarter X$NUM first increases by 1. Next the net cash-flow X$CASFL is calculated as X$INPAY − X$UTPAY and added to total cash X$CASH. The value of inventories X$INVEN is S$STOR ∗ X$COST = the number of units in storage multiplied by purchasing cost per unit. The quarter's closing balance of assets is cash + accounts receivable + inventories, and profits are sales − total costs + net interests.

Next there are 13 different HELP statements which will place the results into a result matrix. The columns are determined by X$NUM, the number of the quarter and the rows, 1–13, represent, in order: sales revenues, total (purchasing) costs, net interest, profits, cash inflow, cash outflow, net cash-flow, cash balance, accounts receivable, inventories, total assets, debts, and equity = assets − debts. These HELP statements call on the subroutine MATIN (see Section 17.6), which at the end of each quarter puts each value into an internal result matrix and finally at the end of the run (when a program stop is requested) writes the whole matrix into a file with the name PROG195.MAT.

Finally in the report segment, sales, cash inflow, cash outflow, total costs and net interests are all set to 0, since these are to be quarterly values.

As already mentioned, the result matrix in its raw form containing only numbers is written into a file called PROG195.MAT. If a file PROG195.FRM is supplied with text, Program 19.5 will also produce a more readable table, PROG195.TXT, as shown in Table 19.1. If Table 19.1 is examined more closely, it can be seen that the closing balance of cash is positive at the end of each quarter. It is tempting to draw the conclusion that the company will *not*

**Program 19.5** First half of program

```
          simulate
  stor    storage
*
          let           x$borti=50
          let           x$ordq=10
          let           x$price=27
          let           x$cost=21
          let           x$rplev=6
          let           x$cash=200
*
  intco variable        p1*(x$borti-20)*20/36000
  intre variable        x$price*(p2-30)*24/36000
*
  sales function        x$price,c5
 10,60/20,40/30,25/40,20/50,15
  reman function        x$cost,c5
 8,0/12,.4/15,.6/20,.7/40,.8
* Sales segment
          generate      fn$xpdis*360/fn$sales
  back    if            stor=e,lost
          split         1,retur
          leave         stor
          let+          x$sal,x$price
          let+          x$tcost,x$cost
          let+          x$accre,x$price
          let           p2=45*fn$rlng3
          advance       p2
          let+          x$inpay,x$price
          let-          x$accre,x$price
          let+          x$nintr,v$intre
          let+          x$inpay,v$intre
          terminate
  retur   if            rn6>fn$reman,bye
          advance       180*fn$xpdis(5)
          goto          back
  bye     terminate
*
  lost    let+          x$lost,1
          terminate
* Entering inventory segment
          generate      ,,,1
          enter         stor,2
          terminate
```

**Program 19.5** Second half of program

```
* Re-ordering segment
        generate    5
        if          s$stor>x$rplev,nobuy
        if          order=u,nobuy
        seize       order
        advance     fn$snorm*2+10
        release     order
        enter       stor,x$ordq
        let         p1=x$ordq*x$cost
        let+        x$debts,p1
        advance     x$borti
        let-        x$nintr,v$intco
        let+        x$utpay,v$intco
        let-        x$debts,p1
        let+        x$utpay,p1
 nobuy  terminate
* Report segment
        generate    90,,,,1
        let+        x$num,1
        let         x$casfl=x$inpay-x$utpay
        let+        x$cash,x$casfl
        let         x$inven=s$stor*x$cost
        let         x$asset=x$cash+x$accre+x$inven
        let         x$prof=x$sal-x$tcost+x$nintr
        help        matin,1,x$num,x$sal
        help        matin,2,x$num,x$tcost
        help        matin,3,x$num,x$nintr
        help        matin,4,x$num,x$prof
        help        matin,5,x$num,x$inpay
        help        matin,6,x$num,x$utpay
        help        matin,7,x$num,x$casfl
        help        matin,8,x$num,x$cash
        help        matin,9,x$num,x$accre
        help        matin,10,x$num,x$inven
        help        matin,11,x$num,x$asset
        help        matin,12,x$num,x$debts
        help        matin,13,x$num,x$asset-x$debts
        let         x$sal=0
        let         x$inpay=0
        let         x$utpay=0
        let         x$tcost=0
        let         x$nintr=0
        terminate   1
*
        start       6,np
        end
```

**Table 19.1** Final result matrix of Program 19.5

| Sales | 108.00 | 270.00 | 297.00 | 270.00 | 459.00 | 459.00 |
|---|---|---|---|---|---|---|
| Dir. costs | 84.00 | 210.00 | 231.00 | 210.00 | 357.00 | 357.00 |
| Net interest | -2.86 | -1.51 | 0.07 | -1.51 | -0.33 | -3.41 |
| Profits | 21.14 | 58.49 | 66.07 | 58.49 | 101.67 | 98.59 |
| Cash in | 54.64 | 190.99 | 300.57 | 244.99 | 462.17 | 489.59 |
| Cash out | 213.50 | 213.50 | 213.50 | 213.50 | 213.50 | 427.00 |
| Cash flow | -158.86 | -22.51 | 87.07 | 31.49 | 248.67 | 62.59 |
| Cash | 41.14 | 18.63 | 105.70 | 137.18 | 385.85 | 448.44 |
| Acc. rec. | 54.00 | 135.00 | 135.00 | 162.00 | 162.00 | 135.00 |
| Inventories | 168.00 | 168.00 | 147.00 | 147.00 | 210.00 | 273.00 |
| Assets | 263.14 | 321.63 | 387.70 | 446.18 | 757.85 | 856.44 |
| Liabilities | 0.00 | 0.00 | 0.00 | 0.00 | 210.00 | 210.00 |
| Equity | 263.14 | 321.63 | 387.70 | 446.18 | 547.85 | 646.44 |

get into any liquidity problems under the examined conditions.

However, the closing balance of the second quarter, 18.63, appears to be somewhat low. Since the closing balance of the first quarter is 41.14 and the cash outflow during the second quarter is 213.50, the possibility that the company will fall into financial difficulties sometime during the second quarter cannot be ruled out. It could very well happen that cash outflows come prior to cash inflows.

In order to investigate this, GPSS' dynamic capability of providing information about any critical event is utilized. For this purpose a procedure similar to that used in Program 17.1 is adopted. The development of the savevalue X$CASH is traced at *every* instance of time when there are cash inflows or outflows. In order to do so Program 19.5 is altered as follows:

1. After LET+ X$INPAY,V$INTRE (before TERMINATE) in the sales segment, the three blocks LET+ X$CASH,X$PRICE, LET+ X$CASH,V$INTRE and HELP FPRIN,C1,X$CASH are inserted. Since LET+ X$INPAY,X$PRICE takes place at exactly the same time as LET+ X$INPAY,V$INTRE, cash only needs to be measured in connection with the last of these two blocks.

2. After LET+ X$UTPAY,P1 in the inventory segment, the three

blocks LET– X$CASH,V$INTCO, LET– X$CASH,P1 and HELP FPRIN,C1,X$CASH are inserted.

3. In the entering inventory segment a block HELP FPRIN,C1,X$CASH is included to obtain entering cash in the graph.

4. In the report segment the block LET+ X$CASH,X$CASFL is deleted, since X$CASH is determined in the other segments.

This revised program (Program 19.6, which does not require a separate listing) produces data, both on the screen and in the file PROG196.PRN, on all the changes in X$CASH. On the basis of this data it is possible, as for Program 17.1, to generate a graph looking, e.g., as in Figure 19.9. In this diagram it can be seen somewhat surprisingly, that in this simulation the company will run out of cash in the *first* quarter; on day 65 to be exact, as can be seen from the data in PROG196.PRN. However, contrary to expectations there is *no* instance of negative cash in the *second* quarter.

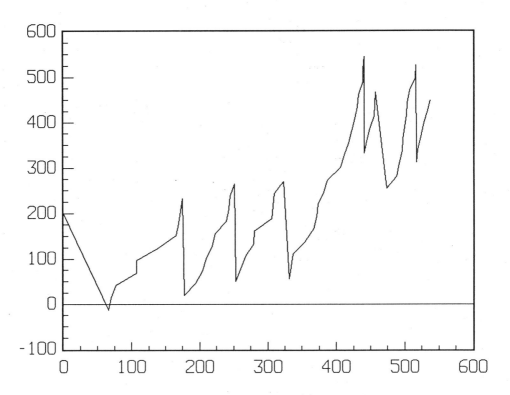

**Figure 19.9** Graphical output from Program 19.6

The above discussion illustrates the deficiency of models that only produce data at a limited number of pre-defined times. The financial crisis on day 65 cannot be seen from the *periodic*, in this case quarterly, reports. In all cases where the closing balance of one period is smaller than cash outflow during the next period, the risk of the company having a negative cash balance some day during the period cannot be ruled out. In such a case it might be worthwhile to investigate with dynamic simulation whether or not there will be a negative cash balance at *any* time during the period.

In all cases where cash inflows and outflows occur in large quantities, which happens, e.g., for companies selling a small number of highly priced items, this kind of discrete-event simulation, allowing for day-to-day cash control, is a very important complement to any method of cash forecasting that allows for only end-of-the-period estimates. The simulation program should of course be run many times with different seeds to give an estimate of the probability of a financial crisis.

---

### *Exercise 19.1* (Case study 6C in Schriber, 1974)

A certain machine uses a type of part which is subject to periodic failure. Whenever the part fails, the machine must be turned off. The failed part is then removed, a good spare part is installed if available, or as soon as one becomes available, and the machine is turned on again. Failed parts can be repaired and re-used. The lifetime of a part is normally distributed, with a mean of 350 hours and a standard deviation of 70 hours. It takes 4 hours to remove a failed part from the machine. The time required to install a replacement part is 6 hours. Repair time for a failed part is normally distributed, with mean and standard deviation of 8 and 0.5 hours, respectively.

The machine operator is responsible for removing a failed part from the machine, and installing a replacement part in its place. There is a repairer who is responsible for repairing failed parts. The repairer's duties also include repair of items routed from another source. These other items arrive according to a negative exponential distribution with a mean arrival time of 9 hours. Their service-time requirement is 8 ± 4 hours. These other items have a higher repair priority than the failed parts used in this particular machine.

Build a GPSS model for this machine-and-parts system, then use the model to estimate the fractional utilization of the machine as a function of the number of spare parts provided in the system. Study the system under the alternative assumptions that zero, one and two good spare parts are provided initially. Run each simulation for the equivalent of five years, assuming 40-hour work weeks.

## Exercise 19.2 (Case study 7D in Schriber, 1974)

The network in Figure 19.10 represents a series of subprojects which must be carried out to complete an overall project. A pair of circles (nodes) connected by a directed line segment is used to depict each particular subproject. For example, node 1 is connected to node 2, depicting what is called subproject 1-to-2. Each directed line segment is labeled to show how many people and how many time units are required to perform the corresponding subproject. Subproject 1-to-2 thus requires four people, and takes 14 ± 6 time units to complete.

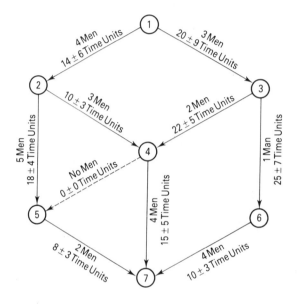

**Figure 19.10** Precedence network for Exercise 19.2

The network in Figure 19.10 also displays the precedence constraints on the various subprojects, indicating which subprojects must be completed before other subprojects can be started. For example, subprojects 2-to-4 and 3-to-4 must be completed before subproject 4-to-7 can be started. Similarly, subproject 5-to-7 cannot be initiated until subproject 2-to-5 is finished, and until the subprojects leading into node 4 have been completed. (Note that the dashed line leading from node 4 to node 5 represents a dummy subproject, requiring no people and no time. The dummy simply expresses a timing constraint with respect to initiation of subproject 5-to-7.)

There is a need to know how much time is required to complete the overall project, or more precisely to estimate the distribution of the 'project completion time' random variable. This distribution depends on the subproject completion-time distributions, and on the precedence relations involved. Project completion time also depends on the available labor.

Build a GPSS model to simulate the undertaking of the overall project shown in Figure 19.10. Use the model to investigate behavior of the completion-time variable, as a function of the number of people (varying e.g. between 5 and 12) assigned to work on the project. Also estimate the distribution of the random variable 'number of people-in-use' at each level.

---

### *Exercise 19.3* (Program BARBER in Jennergren, 1984)

Up to four barbers work in a barber shop. Intervals between successive customers are exponential, with an average of one every 10 minutes during time 0–120 and 225–390 (minutes after opening) and one every 5 minutes during time 120–225. No customers are generated after 390 but customers already in the system are served. Lunch hour is as follows: barber 1: 60–90; barbers 2 and 4: 90–120; barber 3: 240–270. A barber goes for lunch as soon as his lunch hour begins, if he is idle; otherwise as soon as he finishes the customer being served.

There are three waiting chairs. If an entering customer cannot be served at once he will leave immediately with the following probabilities: 0.1 if all three waiting chairs are empty; 0.3 if at least two waiting chairs are empty; 0.5 if one waiting chair is empty and 1 if no such chair is empty. After having waited 15 minutes, a customer leaves unserved with a probability of 0.5. Service time is normal with a mean of 20 minutes and a standard deviation of 5 minutes. Simulate to determine the number of customers served per day for different numbers of barber (1 . . . 4).

---

### *Exercise 19.4* (Exercise 13–5 in Gordon, 1975)

A party of 100 people is taken to a football game in four buses, each of capacity 25. When the game is over, each person returns independently to the bus that brought him to the game. The time taken to reach a bus is normally distributed with mean values of 10, 12, 15 and 18 minutes for the four buses. In each case the standard deviation is 2 minutes. When a bus is full, it leaves, and arrives home after a drive that is normally distributed with a mean of 80 and a standard deviation of 5 minutes. Begin a simulation from the time the game finishes and find the time at which the last bus arrives home.

# 20 Remaining micro-GPSS features

## 20.1 Introduction

In this chapter I shall present all features of micro-GPSS which have not yet been dealt with: the B operands of PREEMPT and TABULATE (in Sections 20.2 and 20.3 respectively), parameters used for storages (in Section 20.4), indirect addressing using parameters (in Section 20.5), functions of a savevalue defined by an expression in the B operand (in Section 20.6), the logical SEIZE block (in Section 20.7) and the C operand of WAITIF for the simultaneous testing of several conditions (in Section 20.8). Finally, I shall discuss two topics that do not involve any new micro-GPSS concepts, but which require some comments, namely the waiting until a certain relationship between two SNAs holds (in Section 20.9) and the construction of subroutines (in Section 20.10). From the outset it should be stressed that this chapter contains some of the more difficult aspects of micro-GPSS.

## 20.2 The B operand of PREEMPT

In Chapter 11 we studied PREEMPT with only an A operand. Micro-GPSS also allows for an optional B operand with the code PR. If there is no B operand, as in Programs 11.5 and 11.7, preemption occurs only if the current user of the facility is not itself a preempter. If there is a B operand PR, preemption occurs only if the preempter, i.e. the transaction that has reached this PREEMPT block with PR, has a higher priority level than the current user of the facility. The B operand is mainly used when there is a need to be able to interrupt a transaction that earlier interrupted another transaction. The B operand can also be used in order to interrupt a 'seizer', i.e. a transaction making a facility busy via a SEIZE block, but *only* if the would-be preempter has a higher priority.

As regards the block symbol, the B operand can be written in the lower left-hand corner of the rectangle as shown in Figure 20.1.

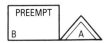

**Figure 20.1** Block symbol of PREEMPT with B operand

The use of PREEMPT with a B operand is illustrated by Program 20.1, which is a simplification of Case 7B in Schriber (1974, p. 433). Schriber states the problem behind this program as follows:

> A certain city owns and operates a garage in which maintenance and repair work is performed on city-owned vehicles. Included among these vehicles are motor-pool cars, heavy-duty trucks and so on. The city is not large; as a result, the garage is equipped with only one service bay, and employs only one mechanic. This means that service can be performed on only one vehicle at a time.
>
> All of the city-owned vehicles are regularly scheduled to come in to the garage for maintenance work. The number of vehicles coming in on a scheduled basis is uniformly distributed from 2 to 4. The time required to service one of these vehicles varies uniformly from 1.5 to 2.5 hours. Vehicles scheduled to come in on a given day are all left in the garage at the end of the preceding day. They are therefore already waiting at the garage when each work day begins. A work day itself consists of 8 hours.
>
> Under certain conditions, regularly scheduled maintenance work which is in progress can be interrupted, so that the service bay can be used for a more important purpose. In particular, the city attempts to keep a full fleet of police cars operating at all times. The police cars are in use 24 hours per day, under demanding conditions. Whenever there is a problem with one of these cars, the car is brought immediately to the garage for unscheduled service. If another vehicle is undergoing scheduled maintenance at the time, the just-arrived police car is permitted to preempt the service bay, so that its repair can begin without delay. However, a police car in need of unscheduled repair is not permitted to preempt another police car on which unscheduled repair is in progress.
>
> Police cars arrive for unscheduled service in a Poisson stream (i.e. following an exponential distribution) with a mean interarrival time of 48 hours. Of course, if the garage is not open when they arrive, they must wait until 8 a.m. before servicing can begin. Their service time is exponentially distributed, averaging 2.5 hours.

The system is simulated for 25 days assuming that the garage is open 7 days a week. Of particular interest is how long the police cars have to spend at the garage.

First the *ordinary vehicles* are modeled. The first problem to handle is the arrival of 2–4 such vehicles a day. This is most conveniently handled by having a 'master vehicle' arrive at 8 a.m. each day. The first such vehicle is generated at time 0 = simulation start = 8 a.m. the first day and then another master vehicle every 24 hours. Next 1–3 *copies* are made of this master vehicle. As seen in Figure 20.2, these copies are made in a SPLIT block with the A operand = the number of copies as a savevalue X$JOB. X$JOB has obtained a value, 1, 2 or 3, in the preceding statement LET X$JOB=FN$INT(FN$JOBS), where FN$JOBS produces real values from 1 to 3.999 . . . and FN$INT consequently truncates these values to 1, 2 or 3.

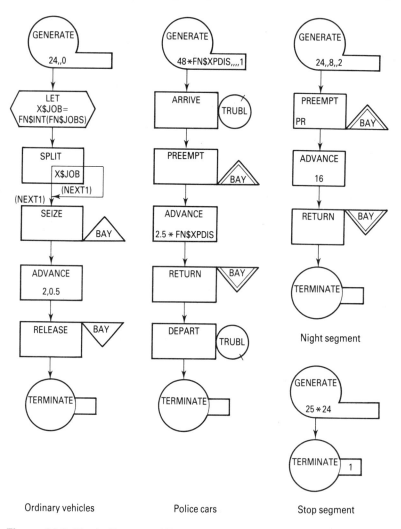

Ordinary vehicles          Police cars          Stop segment

**Figure 20.2** Block diagram of Program 20.1

**Program 20.1**

```
        simulate
 jobs   function    rn1,c2
0,1/1,4
* Ordinary vehicles
        generate    24,,0
        let         x$job=fn$int(fn$jobs)
        split       x$job,next1
 next1 seize        bay
        advance     2,0.5
        release     bay
        terminate
* Police cars
        generate    48*fn$xpdis,,,,1
        arrive      trubl
        preempt     bay
        advance     2.5*fn$xpdis
        return      bay
        depart      trubl
        terminate
* Night segment
        generate    24,,8,,2
        preempt     bay,pr
        advance     16
        return      bay
        terminate
* Stop segment
        generate    25*24
        terminate   1
*
        start       1
        end
```

All copies as well as the 'master vehicle' go to the next block, the SEIZE block, and then proceed to use the bay, before releasing the bay and finally leaving the system.

Let us now turn to the segment for *police cars*. They arrive with an InterArrival Time of 48 * FN$XPDIS and since they have a higher priority than the ordinary vehicles, the E operand of the GENERATE block is 1. Since there is a need to measure the time that the police cars have to spend at the garage, the next block is ARRIVE TRUBL. The police cars go into the block PREEMPT BAY, since they are allowed to interrupt service for ordinary vehicles. The police cars spend 2.5 * FN$XPDIS hours being repaired. After this they 'return' the bay to the ordinary vehicle that was interrupted. Finally, DEPART TRUBL measures the time when the police cars leave the garage.

Let us now study what can be called the *night segment*. The purpose of this segment is to close down the bay for the night at 4 p.m. each day. Then all work in progress will be interrupted. Hence a night transaction is generated every 24 hours, but arriving the first time 8 hours after the start of the simulation (the C operand = 8). Thus this night transaction will arrive at 4 p.m. each day.

Since the night transaction is to interrupt all work in progress at the bay, it must go into a PREEMPT BAY block. Since police cars might already be preempting ordinary vehicles, the night transaction must also be able to preempt the police cars. In order to achieve this, the night transaction is generated with a higher priority than the police cars (e.g. 2) and the PREEMPT block uses a B operand PR. Thus the work in progress on the police cars will also be interrupted. The night transaction then holds the bay for 16 hours and at 8 a.m. the next day it will return the bay to the work that was interrupted.

Finally a stop segment closes down the simulation after 25 days of 24 hours.

## 20.3 The B operand of TABULATE

In Chapter 15 the TABULATE block was introduced, but there it only had an A operand which contained the name of the table into which the data to be tabulated would go (see Section 15.5). The TABULATE block also has an optional B operand. In micro-GPSS this B operand is an integer constant or savevalue that determines the *number* of times that the value of the SNA in the A operand of the corresponding TABLE is to be entered into this table *each* time a transaction enters the TABULATE block. Since in Chapter 15 the value was only entered once, the default value of the B operand is obviously 1.

As regards the block symbol, the B operand is written in the lower right-hand corner of the rectangle as shown in Figure 20.3.

**Figure 20.3** Block symbol of TABULATE with B operand

In order to demonstrate the B operand of TABULATE, let us return to the situation in Program 20.1. It might be of interest to know for what percentage of total time there are no police cars in the garage and what percentage of total time there are one, two, three, etc., held up by maintenance and hence unavailable for duty.

In order to establish this, the time during which there are different numbers of police cars in the garage needs to be tabulated. Thus, each time the contents of the AD set TRUBL are about to change it is necessary to record the current contents and how long it has had this contents, i.e. the time since the contents of TRUBL were last changed. That many time units thus need to be entered into the class representing the current contents.

An example should make this clear. Let us assume that the first police car comes to the garage at time 63.2. Since the B operand is an integer, 63 hours need to be entered into the class representing the contents 0. To accomplish this, the following three additional blocks are placed in the police car segment before the block ARRIVE TRUBL:

```
LET        X$TIM=FN$INT(C1)-X$LAST
TABULATE   LENTH,X$TIM
LET        X$LAST=FN$INT(C1)
```

LET X$TIM=FN$INT(C1)−X$LAST implies that X$TIM is defined as the present hour (= 63) minus X$LAST, the hour when the contents of TRUBL last changed. At this first arrival, X$LAST has the initial value of 0. TABULATE LENTH,X$TIM then implies that X$TIM (= 63) hours are put into the class 0 of the table LENTH, since Q$TRUBL (A operand of table LENTH) is still 0. LET X$LAST=FN$INT(C1) means that X$LAST is updated to the present hour of 63.

The next change in Q$TRUBL takes place, e.g., at hour 72 when this first police car is to leave the garage. To record this accurately, the three statements above are also inserted before the DEPART block. LET X$TIM=FN$INT(C1)−X$LAST sets X$TIM to 72 − 63 = 9. TABULATE LENTH,X$TIM puts 9 hours into the class representing a current contents of 1. LET X$LAST=FN$INT(C1) updates X$LAST to 72.

The only thing remaining is to have correct records at simulation stop. Hence the first two of these blocks are also included in the stop segment, so that LENTH is updated, e.g. that Q$TRUBL was 2 for the last 10 hours (600 − 590). There is obviously no need to update X$LAST here.

By adding these blocks and a table definition with a class width of 1 to Program 20.1, Program 20.2 is obtained.

Program 20.2 will produce Table 20.1. In this table there is a total of 600 entries into the table corresponding to the 600 hours simulated. During 459 hours, i.e. 76.5 percent of the time, no police cars were off duty for maintenance; during 124 hours, i.e. 21 percent of total time one police car was off duty and during 17 hours, i.e. 3 percent of total time, two or three cars were off duty due to maintenance.

**Program 20.2**

```
         simulate
 lenth table          q$trubl,0,1,10
 jobs  function       rn1,c2
0,1/1,4
* Ordinary vehicles
         generate     24,,0
         let          x$job=fn$int(fn$jobs)
         split        x$job,next1
 next1 seize          bay
         advance      2,0.5
         release      bay
         terminate
* Police cars
         generate     48*fn$xpdis,,,,1
         let          x$tim=fn$int(c1)-x$last
         tabulate     lenth,x$tim
         let          x$last=fn$int(c1)
         arrive       trubl
         preempt      bay
         advance      2.5*fn$xpdis
         return       bay
         let          x$tim=fn$int(c1)-x$last
         tabulate     lenth,x$tim
         let          x$last=fn$int(c1)
         depart       trubl
         terminate
* Night segment
         generate     24,,8,,2
         preempt      bay,pr
         advance      16
         return       bay
         terminate
* Stop segment
         generate     25*24
         let          x$tim=c1-x$last
         tabulate     lenth,x$tim
         terminate    1
         start        1
         end
```

**Table 20.1** Table produced by Program 20.2

Table  LENTH

| Entries in table | Mean argument | Standard deviation | Sum of arguments |
|---|---|---|---|
| 600 | 0.28 | 0.58 | 169.00 |

| Range | | Observed frequency | Per cent of total | Cumulative percentage | Cumulative remainder |
|---|---|---|---|---|---|
| – | 0 | 459 | 76.50 | 76.50 | 23.50 |
| 0.01 – | 1 | 124 | 20.67 | 97.17 | 2.83 |
| 1.01 – | 2 | 6 | 1.00 | 98.17 | 1.83 |
| 2.01 – | 3 | 11 | 1.83 | 100.00 | 0.00 |

Remaining frequencies are all zero

# 20.4 Parameters for storages

Chapter 16 introduced parameters. This is quite a difficult topic and the treatment in Chapter 16 was far from comprehensive.

In Chapter 16 parameters only referred to facilities and queues (AD sets). It should be added that parameters can also refer to *storages*. Thus it is possible to have ENTER P1 as well as LEAVE P1. (In contrast to GPSS V, micro-GPSS does not, however, allow parameters as A operands of PREEMPT and RETURN blocks.) However, the capacities of such parameter storages, i.e. storages referred to by parameters, must be defined in a special way. Since micro-GPSS does not allow the mixing of symbolic names and numbers referred to by a parameter, we cannot define the capacities of parameter storages using names. Instead STORAGE statements referring to parameter storages must have numbers in the A operand, numbered consecutively and starting with 1. All such STORAGE statements must come prior to STORAGE statements concerning storages with symbolic names.

QTABLEs can also be used for producing tables of queues referred to by a parameter. In such a case a *number* in the A operand refers to the queue.

Using parameters the problem of Program 14.3, dealing with a store with meat, fish and cheese counters, can be solved in a more compact fashion, namely by Program 20.3.

Compared with Program 14.3, Program 20.3 has fewer blocks, since all transactions go through the same sequence of blocks. With regard to the blocks, Program 20.3 is similar to Program 16.2. The only major difference is using ENTER and LEAVE instead of SEIZE and RELEASE.

Program 20.3 can be explained in a similar manner to Program 16.2. Initially, each customer is assigned a number P1 = 1, 2 or 3, indicating which

**Program 20.3**

```
        simulate
1       storage      2
2       storage      1
3       storage      1
choic function      rn4,d3
.6,1/.8,2/1,3
ave     function     p1,d3
1,16/2,20/3,10
half    function     p1,d3
1,8/2,3/3,8
meatq qtable        1,0,10,10
        generate     6,3
        let          p1=fn$choic
        arrive       p1
        enter        p1
        depart       p1
        advance      fn$ave,fn$half
        leave        p1
        terminate
        generate     480
        terminate    1
        start        1
        end
```

counter he is to go to. ARRIVE measures the time for his arrival at this counter, ENTER allows him to attempt to move into service and DEPART measures the time of his leaving the waiting line at this counter. Next ADVANCE determines the average and half-width of the service time for this counter and keeps him in service for a time sampled from a rectangular distribution based on these two values. Finally LEAVE allows him to move out of service at this counter.

Compared to Program 14.3, more control statements are, however, needed. First there are three STORAGE statements, since the two facilities (the fish and cheese counters) must be defined as storages with a capacity of 1 so that the blocks ENTER P1 and LEAVE P1 can refer to them. Note the numbers 1–3 in the address field, instead of meat, fish and cheese. Furthermore, there are two additional functions: one for the average time, being 16, 20 or 10, depending on whether P1 is storage 1, 2 or 3; another for the half-width of the rectangular distribution, being 8, 3 or 8.

Furthermore, the CHOIC function is different from Program 14.3, where the dependent variable was an address label. Here it is instead a parameter number that is sampled. Finally, there is a QTABLE definition with 1 in the A operand, giving us the desired statistics for waiting at the *meat* counter.

## 20.5 Indirect addressing

SNAs followed by ⋆ were studied in connection with Program 16.5. Q⋆1 was used to refer to the length of the AD set (or queue) with the number given by the current value of parameter 1. Likewise Program 19.2 used X⋆1 to refer to the savevalue which has the same number as the current value placed in P1. Q⋆1 and X⋆1 can be thought of as Q(P1) and X(P1), respectively.

The use of SNA⋆*j*, where *j* is a parameter number 1 . . . 12, is called *indirect addressing*. In micro-GPSS the number of the particular SNA within this group of SNAs is *not* given directly as, e.g., Q4, but only indirectly as Q⋆1 when e.g. P1 = 4.

In micro-GPSS this indirect mode of addressing an SNA can be used for the following eight SNAs: F, N, P, R, Q, S, W and X. In GPSS V the usage of indirect addressing is more general. Since the use of indirect addressing very often leads to hard-to-find logical errors, micro-GPSS restricts the use of indirect addressing to the cases where the advantages of indirect addressing, according to the author's experience, appear to outweigh the increased risks of logical errors.

The usage of Q⋆*j* and X⋆*j* has been demonstrated earlier. The use of F⋆*j*, referring to the busy status of a facility, is fairly similar to the use of Q⋆*j*. I shall illustrate this by changing Program 16.4 slightly, replacing the block IF P1=U,BYE with IF F⋆1=1,BYE. This results in identical output, since F⋆1, i.e. the number of customers held in the facility whose number is in P1, is 1 only if P1=U.

The use of S⋆*j* and R⋆*j*, referring to the contents of and the remaining unused capacity of a storage, can be exemplified by altering Program 20.3 slightly (resulting in Program 20.3b). Below ENTER P1, PRINT S⋆1 and PRINT R⋆1 are written. The output obtained is shown in Table 20.2. Note that micro-GPSS prints two names: the original name of indirect addressing and the 'actual' name, i.e. with the current number held in the parameter. Also note that micro-GPSS will treat a storage with capacity 1 just like a facility in the output. Thus, the symbol F will replace the symbol S in such cases.

As regards W⋆*j* and N⋆*j*, referring to the current and total block counts, the number held in the parameter will be that of the block number, which can be seen in the extended listing. The usage of W⋆*j* and N⋆*j* is, however, rare.

Finally I shall discuss the most complicated type of indirect addressing, namely using P⋆*j*. P⋆*j* refers to the value of the parameter whose number is

**Table 20.2** First part of output from Program 20.3b

```
F*1= F3        1.00
R*1= R3        0.00
F*1= F2        1.00
R*1= R2        0.00
S*1= S1        1.00
R*1= R1        1.00
S*1= S1        2.00
R*1= R1        0.00
..
```

to be found in parameter *j*. Thus if P2 holds the value 5, and P4 holds the value 2, P*4 is 5.

Program 20.4 illustrates the use of P*j: a supermarket has three checkout counters at its northern exit and two checkout counters at its southern exit. Forty-five percent of the customers go to the southern exit. At each exit the customers go to the checkout counter which is free and, if all are busy, to the one with the shortest waiting line. The store's manager is interested in finding out how the longest of all the waiting lines at the five counters varies over the day. He wants a report on this printed out every 10 minutes during the eight-hour day.

In the customer segment there is at each exit a segment part similar to that of Program 16.3. At the northern exit, P1 will be assigned the number 1, 2 or 3 of the checkout counter that has the fewest customers; at the southern exit, P2 will be given the number 4 or 5 of the counter that has the fewest customers.

In the report segment, starting every 10 minutes, the first SELECT block determines which of the checkout counters 1–3 at the northern exit has the most customers and puts this number into P1. Next the actual number of customers at this counter, Q*1, is put into P1. P1 then contains the number of customers at the busiest checkout counter of the northern exit.

Likewise, SELECT MAX 2,4,5,Q and LET P2=Q*2 determine P2 as the number of customers at the busiest checkout counter of the southern exit.

Finally, SELECT MAX 3,1,2,P determines P3 as 1 or 2 depending on whether the counter with the most customers is at the northern or southern exit. Finally P*3, i.e. the number of customers at the busiest counter, is printed. The output is shown in Table 20.3.

**Program 20.4**

```
            simulate
* Customer segment
            generate    0.7*fn$xpdis
            goto        south,0.45
*    northern exit
            select min 1,1,3,q
            arrive      p1
            seize       p1
            advance     3,0.4
            release     p1
            depart      p1
            terminate
*    southern exit
  south select min 2,4,5,q
            arrive      p2
            seize       p2
            advance     3,0.4
            release     p2
            depart      p2
            terminate
* Report segment
            generate    10
            select max 1,1,3,q
            let         p1=q*1
            select max 2,4,5,q
            let         p2=q*2
            select max 3,1,2,p
            print       p*3
            terminate   1
            start       48
            end
```

**Table 20.3** Start of output of Program 20.4

| | | |
|---|---|---|
| P*3= | P1 | 1.00 |
| P*3= | P1 | 2.00 |
| P*3= | P1 | 2.00 |
| P*3= | P2 | 1.00 |
| P*3= | P1 | 2.00 |
| P*3= | P1 | 3.00 |
| P*3= | P1 | 4.00 |
| P*3= | P2 | 4.00 |
| P*3= | P2 | 3.00 |
| P*3= | P2 | 3.00 |

. . . .

## 20.6 Functions defined by an expression

Micro-GPSS allows for one more type of function, namely a function defined by an *expression* in the B operand. (This is not available in GPSS V.)

The independent variable of the A operand must be a named savevalue, i.e. X$name. This savevalue should not be used anywhere else in the program. This function definition statement is similar to the VARIABLE statement, but more flexible. It is also in line with the DEF FN statement in BASIC.

An example of such a function definition statement is

```
FUN FUNCTION X$VAL,X$VAL * FN$EXP(- X$RATE * X$VAL)
```

This is similar to DEF FNFUN(XVAL) = XVAL * EXP(- RATE * XVAL) in BASIC. (Students of OR might recognize the function as the present value of a cost, originally 0, that increases each year by 1, discounted at the rate of 100 RATE percent.)

The A operand, which can be regarded as the formal argument of the function, is used in the expression of the B operand. The function is called by FN$name with a constant, an SNA or an expression as the calling argument given within parentheses. This calling argument provides the actual value to be used by the savevalue of the A operand which is the formal argument. Thus, when the value of the expression in the B operand is calculated, the savevalue (given in the A operand) is assigned the value of the argument within parentheses of the calling FN$name.

Using the function FUN as defined above, FN$FUN(10) would imply that X$VAL is set to 10 and that FN$FUN would be calculated as 10 * FN$EXP (- X$RATE * 10). Likewise, if C1 = 5, FN$FUN(C1 + 5) is also 10 * FN$EXP (- X$RATE * 10).

Program 20.5, using the function FUN as defined above, exemplifies the use of expression-defined functions.

The program calculates the derivative of the function FN$FUN by defining the derivative of a function as

$$\frac{\text{FN\$FUN}(x + delta) - \text{FN\$FUN}(x)}{delta}$$

Instead of allowing delta to go towards 0, it is given a fairly small value, dependent among other things on the precision of the computer system (see textbooks in numerical analysis). The important thing to note here is that this expression can be written in *one* block. Using a VARIABLE expression, two more blocks would be needed. I shall leave it as an extra exercise for the reader to rewrite Program 20.5 using a VARIABLE definition instead of this new kind of function definition. This exercise would probably make the

**Program 20.5**

```
        simulate
fun     function    x$val,x$val*fn$exp(-x$rate*x$val)
        generate    ,,,1
        let         x$delta=0.001
        let         x$rate=.05
back    help        letsa,x$kvan
        if          x$kvan=0,bye
        print       x$kvan
        print       (fn$fun(x$kvan+x$delta)-fn$fun(x$kvan))/x$delta
        goto        back
bye     terminate   1
        start       1,np
        end
```

convenience of expression-defined functions clear.

Finally, note that in some micro-GPSS versions the B operand of FUNCTION can be a name, allowing for graphic input of the function (see GPSSDOC).

## 20.7 The logical SEIZE block

In this section I shall discuss another micro-GPSS feature not found in GPSS V, namely the *logical* SEIZE block. The logical SEIZE block is distinguished by having an L as the B operand. The block symbol is the same as that of Figure 6.1 if L replaces Q. The L as B operand has the effect that a block SEIZE A,L will turn the facility A into a *logical facility*. This implies that when a transaction tries to obtain service from the logical facility A and facility A is busy, the transaction will *not* wait in front of the SEIZE block, but simply enter the SEIZE block and go straight through it. Since the facility is already busy, the busy indicator is not changed. If the logical facility A is idle, the SEIZE A block functions just like an ordinary SEIZE block and the busy indicator is switched on.

When a transaction comes to a block RELEASE A, and facility A has become busy by means of a block SEIZE A,L, the only thing that happens is that facility A becomes idle. If the logical facility is not busy when the transaction reaches the RELEASE block, the transaction just goes straight through without anything happening.

The reason for this logical SEIZE block in micro-GPSS is that in some cases a facility is not used to give service, but rather to send a message to a

WAITIF block or an IF block in server mode. It is then necessary to avoid putting the transactions into a waiting line when the facility is busy, in the sense that it already has an 'on' status.

I shall illustrate this with Program 20.6, dealing with a road which pedestrians want to cross. Let us take Program 10.2 as a starting point and assume that the road has the same characteristics, as regards traffic, as street 2 in that program. The red light segment will, however, be different, since the lights are controlled by pedestrians, who arrive in a random fashion according to a negative exponential distribution on average every 10 seconds. The pedestrians can turn on the red light for the cars by pressing a button. The red light for the cars (and the green light for the pedestrians) will then stay on for 20 seconds, although most pedestrians can cross the street in a shorter time.

The reason for using a logical SEIZE block with an L as B operand instead of just an ordinary SEIZE block (as in Program 10.2) is that it might very well happen that a new pedestrian arrives while an earlier one is crossing the street. If there was no L as B operand, the new pedestrian would stop and wait until the red light for the cars (and green light for the pedestrians) is turned off and then immediately press the button to get a red light for the cars again. In fact, if Program 20.6 is run without the L in the B operand of the SEIZE block (Program 20.6b), enormous waiting lines of pedestrians would build up.

The natural assumption is rather that a pedestrian will start crossing the street without pressing the button if he has a green light (and the cars a red one) when he arrives. This assumption is precisely what is covered by the logical SEIZE block. If the facility is busy on the transaction's arrival at the block, the transaction goes straight through it.

Earlier a SEIZE block was used for sending similar messages to other blocks, e.g. in Programs 10.2 and 13.3, without using L as B operand of the SEIZE block. Using L was not necessary in these cases, since there was no risk of getting a waiting line in front of the SEIZE block. In Program 10.2 there was only *one* light transaction and hence there could never be a second transaction waiting. In Program 13.3, where facility ORDER was used as a logical indicator that an order was under way, the block SEIZE ORDER was preceded by the block IF ORDER=U,BYE. Hence SEIZE ORDER could only be reached in those cases when the facility ORDER was idle.

## 20.8 Simultaneous testing of several conditions

In Chapter 10 I discussed the WAITIF block, which allows for a testing of *one* specific condition concerning either a facility or a storage. A more complicated situation occurs when we want to test several conditions for

**Program 20.6**

```
        simulate
* Light segment
        generate    10*fn$xpdis
        seize       red,1
        advance     20
        release     red
        terminate
* Street segment
        generate    12,4
        queue       dir
        if          red=u,wait
        advance     10,3
        goto        join
 wait   waitif      red=u
        advance     30,15
 join   depart      dir
        terminate
* Stop segment
        generate    14400
        terminate   1
        start       1
        end
```

waiting concerning servers simultaneously. In micro-GPSS this testing is done using a sequence of several WAITIF blocks.

If there are two WAITIF blocks one after another, there is, however, the problem that a transaction might go through the first block at one time, but the second block at another later time. It is then not certain that when the transaction goes through the second block, it would still be allowed to go through the first one, i.e. that the two conditions for stop waiting are fulfilled *simultaneously*. It is therefore necessary to perform something like an additional test that would send the transaction back to the first WAITIF block to check if the waiting conditions of this block still held when the transaction had gone through the second WAITIF block.

I shall illustrate this with a situation to be dealt with in Program 20.7 presented below. It is necessary to test whether two facilities, STORM and TUG, are simultaneously idle; otherwise the transaction, a ship, has to wait. Using WAITIF blocks as defined in Chapter 10 we would write

```
waitif  storm=u
waitif  tug=u
```

The ship first waits until STORM is idle; then the ship proceeds to wait until

TUG is idle. When TUG is idle, it is necessary to check that STORM is idle at the *same* time. If STORM is now in use, the ship should go back to wait in front of the first block while STORM is in use.

In order to allow for this kind of check, micro-GPSS allows the WAITIF block to have a C operand. This is an integer constant that specifies how many blocks the transaction should go back for such a check. More precisely, the C operand of a WAITIF block specifies the number of immediately preceding WAITIF blocks that must also *simultaneously* allow the transaction to go through, if the transaction is to go through this block with the C operand. (In a block diagram the C operand can be written below WAITIF in the bottom corner of the diamond.)

In this case it is necessary to go back only one block to WAITIF STORM=U to check that the ship is allowed through this block at the *same* time as it is allowed to go through the block WAITIF TUG=U. Thus WAITIF TUG=U,1 is written. Thus the following two blocks will have transactions wait correctly if there is a storm and/or the tug is busy, i.e. until there is no storm and a free tug at the same time:

```
waitif   storm=u
waitif   tug=u,1
```

Let us complicate this test by requiring that the ship *also* has to wait if the storage BERTH is full. In this case there are three blocks that have to be fulfilled simultaneously. Hence when the ship has gone through the last of these blocks, it is necessary to go back *two* blocks to check that this block still allows the ship to go through. The C operand 2 is added to the last block in this WAITIF block sequence. The simultaneous testing is thus done by the following three blocks:

```
waitif   storm=u
waitif   tug=u
waitif   berth=f,2
```

It is now possible to study the problem behind Program 20.7, which is a simplified version of Case study 6a in Schriber (1974). Tankers arrive at a port every $11 \pm 7$ hours. There is one tug at the port. Tankers require the services of this tug for two hours to move into a berth and later to move out of the berth. Loading takes $18 \pm 4$ hours. The area experiences frequent storms and no berthing or deberthing of a tanker can take place when a storm is in progress. Storms last between 2 and 6 hours. The time between the end of one storm and the start of the next one follows a negative exponential distribution with a mean of 48 hours.

In the segment generating the storm there is a single transaction involved as in the light segment of Program 10.2. There is hence no risk of any new storm starting before the old storm is over and no need for a *logical* SEIZE block.

**Program 20.7**

```
            simulate
berth  storage      3
*   Storm segment
            generate    ,,,1
next   advance      48*fn$xpdis
            seize       storm,1
            advance     4,2
            release     storm
            goto        next
*   Port segment
            generate    11,7
            arrive      area
            waitif      storm=u
            waitif      tug=u
            waitif      berth=f,2 ! 2 preceding WAITIF blocks involved
            seize       tug
            enter       berth
            advance     2
            release     tug
            advance     18,4
            waitif      storm=u
            waitif      tug=u,1    ! 1 preceding WAITIF block involved
            seize       tug
            advance     2
            release     tug
            leave       berth
            depart      area
            terminate
*   Stop segment
            generate    24*365
            terminate   1
            start       1
            end
```

In the port segment we measure the total time that the ships spend at the port by the ARRIVE and DEPART blocks. After the ARRIVE block, there are the three blocks described above that simultaneously test whether there is no storm, a free tug *and* a free berth before the tug can proceed to berth the ship. After loading, there are the two blocks that simultaneously test whether there is no storm and a free tug, both necessary for deberthing. Note that a ship occupies a berth as soon as it starts berthing and frees it only when deberthing is finished.

Finally, the stop segment allows for the simulation of a year.

This concludes the presentation of new micro-GPSS details. For a summary of the syntax refer to Appendix A.

## 20.9 Waiting for relations between SNAs to hold

In Chapter 10 the WAITIF block was studied. This can, as A operand, only use a server name and, as B operand, only employ a symbol (U, NU, E, NE, F or NF). In contrast to the IF block, it is *not* possible to use SNAs or constants as A and B operands. The reason for this is that the micro-GPSS processor has to continually check whether a change has occurred that could affect a WAITIF block. Since a WAITIF block refers only to a specific server the required amount of such checking is small. If instead the WAITIF block could refer to any SNA, such checking would have to occur with *every* event. This could lead to extremely long run times.

The lack of a specific block allowing for waiting with regard to any SNAs implies that a logical SEIZE block construct can be used to allow for waiting. I shall illustrate this with Program 20.8, which is a modification of Program 13.3. Instead of every customer buying just one item, a customer buys one, two or three items. This number of items is sampled from the function NUMBR and then stored in P1. If this number of items P1 is not in stock at customer arrival, the buyer will not buy *any* items directly but will go into a waiting line at the address NODIR. He indicates that there is a shortage by putting the logical facility SHORT into use. The customer will now wait if and as long as this facility SHORT is in use. This shortage can be overcome by the arrival of goods in the re-ordering segment. A customer can then leave the WAITIF block and take P1 units out of the replenished stock.

Since there might be many customers waiting in the WAITIF block, it might very well happen that stocks are depleted again before all waiting customers have been able to obtain their P1 units. Hence, when each customer leaves the WAITIF block, a check is made as to whether there are at least P1 units in stock.

If this is not the case, there is a new shortage and the customer is sent back to the address LACK, where the logical facility SHORT is put into use. The customer then goes back into the waiting line. In order to ensure the *first* place in the waiting line, the customer is assigned the highest possible priority through the block PRIORITY C1 before going back to LACK to wait for another delivery of goods.

The only change in the re-ordering segment compared to Program 13.3 is that the facility SHORT is released upon arrival of new products as a signal to the WAITIF block in the customer segment.

**Program 20.8**

```
        simulate
 numbr function    rn4,d3
.4,1/.75,2/1,3
 stor   storage
* Customer segment
        generate    fn$xpdis
        let         p1=fn$numbr
        if          s$stor<p1,nodir
        leave       stor,p1
        terminate
*
 nodir arrive       tim
 lack  seize        short,1
        waitif      short=u
        priority    c1
        if          s$stor<p1,lack
        depart      tim
 later leave        stor,p1
        terminate
* Reordering segment
        generate    5
        if          s$stor>20,nobuy
        if          order=u,nobuy
        seize       order
        advance     fn$snorm*2+10
        release     order
        release     short
        enter       stor,20
 nobuy terminate
* Entering inventory
        generate    ,,,1
        enter       stor,30
        terminate
* Stop segment
        generate    250
        terminate   1
*
        start       1
        end
```

# 20.10 Subroutines in micro-GPSS

In certain programs, some segments have identical parts. Instead of repeating the same sequence of blocks, it is possible to write shorter programs using a subroutine to which transactions from several segments can go. It is important when writing such a subroutine to ensure that a transaction will return to the same segment that it originally left. This can be accomplished by the use of a parameter and an address function dependent on this parameter. This is illustrated by Program 20.9.

Two types of transaction come to a bar, singles and couples. There is a joint subroutine section concerning the use of a bartender, whose serving time is independent of whether the transaction is single or a couple. This

**Program 20.9**

```
          simulate
  stor    storage     8
  retur   function    p1,d2
1,ret1/2,ret2
* Singles
          generate    10*fn$xpdis
          enter       stor
          let         p1=1
          goto        sub
  ret1    leave       stor
          terminate
* Pairs
          generate    20*fn$xpdis
          enter       stor,2
          let         p1=2
          goto        sub
  ret2    leave       stor,2
          terminate
* Joint subroutine section
  sub     seize       fac
          advance     10,10
          release     fac
          goto        fn$retur
* Stop segment
          generate    540
          terminate   1
          start       1
          end
```

subroutine starts with the address SUB. In each segment the block GOTO SUB is preceded by a block assigning a numerical characteristic (1 for singles, 2 for couples) to parameter 1. Hence, when a transaction leaves the subroutine by GOTO FN$RETUR, parameter 1, being 1 or 2, will determine whether the next block has the address RET1 or RET2.

## Exercise 20.1 (Based on exercise 3.42 in Banks and Carson, 1984)

A computer center substation has two terminals. On arrival users choose the terminal with the shortest waiting line. Students arrive at a rate of one every $8 \pm 2$ minutes. They can be interrupted by professors, who arrive at a rate of one every $12 \pm 2$ minutes. There is one systems analyst who can interrupt anyone, but students are interrupted before professors. The systems analyst spends $6 \pm 4$ minutes on the terminal and arrives every $20 \pm 5$ minutes. Professors and students spend $4 \pm 2$ minutes on the terminal. If a person is interrupted, that person joins the head of the queue and resumes service as soon as possible. Simulate for 50 professor or analyst jobs. Estimate the mean length of the waiting line of students.

## Exercise 20.2 (Example 7 in Birtwistle, 1979)

Tankers arrive periodically at a harbor and discharge their cargo into shore tanks. When a shore tank is full, or nearly so (has less than 20 K (= thousand) tons capacity free), its contents are automatically transferred to the refinery. While this transfer is taking place, a shore tank may not be filled by a tanker. Tankers arrive eight per hour on average, exponentially distributed. The time needed to set up a pump is 0.5 hours. The pumping rate is 1 K tons per hour and the discharge rate is 4 K tons per hour. Tanker loads are either 15, 20 or 25 K tons, all equally likely. All shore tanks have a capacity of 70 K tons.

Run the simulation for 1000 continuous hours with the five shore tanks. Initially, two shore tanks are empty and free; one is currently discharging and will be free after 8 hours, and the other two are currently being loaded and will be freed after 12 (with 45 K tons still free) and 3.5 hours (with 25 K tons free) respectively. The first tanker arrives at time 0.

## Exercise 20.3

A small elevator has space for only one person and goes between two levels. People wanting to go up arrive at the rate of one every 10 minutes, following an exponential distribution, while people wanting to go down arrive only every 20 minutes (also following an exponential distribution), since many prefer to walk down the stairs. The elevator takes 2 minutes in each direction. On the ground-level there is only a button for going up and on the top-level only a button for going down. If the elevator is on the top-level and someone on the ground-level is pressing the button for going up (and there is no one waiting to go down), the elevator goes down empty. In a corresponding manner the elevator goes up empty, if someone on the top-level is pressing the going down button and the elevator is on the ground-level and no one wants to go up. Simulate a day of 20 hours to determine the utilization of the elevator. In the morning the elevator is on the ground-level.

---

### Exercise 20.4 (Example DEPOT by L. P. Jennergren)

A wholesaler has a depot, where goods are delivered by truck. The goods are brought to the customers by van. The depot opens at time 0 and closes at time 360 (time in minutes). After time 360 no additional vehicles (trucks or vans) are allowed into the depot, but the trucks and vans already in the depot finish their tasks.

Arrival distributions: the time between two trucks or two vans arriving follows an exponential distribution with the average times of 30 minutes for trucks and 5 minutes for vans.

The serving of the trucks and vans takes place on the second floor in the depot. An elevator is used to get there. This elevator has space for one truck *or* one van. The time to transport a vehicle up or down varies between 1.5 and 2.5 minutes, equally distributed. This time includes driving the vehicle in and out of the elevator. If the elevator travels empty it takes exactly 1 minute up or down.

The servicing of the trucks or vans takes place at special loading bays. There are at present two bays for trucks and three for vans. (Each kind of vehicle must use its own type of bay.) The servicing is carried out manually by a team of workers. A team can service either a truck or a van. The time per truck follows the normal distribution with an expected value of 30 and a standard deviation of 5 minutes. The time for a van is also normally distributed with an expected value of 10 and a standard deviation of 3 minutes. The teams work all day. (Lunch break is disregarded.)

The following rules are used to control the traffic: the trucks have priority over vans, both when waiting at the elevator and at the bays. The vehicles wait in two lines at the elevator, one for trucks, one for vans, until there is a bay free for the particular type of vehicle. They are then brought upstairs to the bay. (This time is included in the 1.5–2.5 minutes for the elevator.) The vehicle might then have to wait until a team is free to give service. The elevator goes up or down empty if there is some vehicle waiting on the other floor.

Management has observed considerable waiting times, in particular for the vans. In order to reduce these times, management contemplates

1.  an increase in the number of teams from 3 to 4;

2.  an increase in the number of bays for *vans* from 3 to 4.

Simulate the effect of these proposals! (Hint: Do Exercise 20.3 first.)

# 21 How to proceed in simulation

We have now reached the last chapter of this book. Hopefully, the book has given the reader an understanding of the potential of discrete-event stochastic simulation for giving insights and thus decision-support for a wide variety of practical problems. The reader might therefore want to learn more about simulation and its uses and carry out more work in this area. This last chapter thus contains a discussion of how to proceed in simulation.

One of the best ways to learn more about simulation is to work with concrete examples. If the reader wants examples from books and has already done the exercises in this book, a good source for some additional problems is Schriber (1974). Many of Schriber's case studies have been solved in this book, but several remain. Suggested micro-GPSS solutions for all the Schriber case studies (except 7C involving PREEMPT P1) are available on a special diskette. Schriber's book also contains many exercises without a commented solution.

The best examples are, however, most probably problems encountered in real life.

When working on a practical problem using the ordinary low-cost student version of micro-GPSS, the user might 'hit the ceiling', e.g. with regard to the number of blocks and statements, the number of transactions that can be in the system at the same time, number of servers, queues, savevalues, etc. (The exact numerical restrictions in the student version might vary somewhat between different implementations and dates of release, but are described in GPSSDOC of the specific micro-GPSS system. The student version is, however, always sufficient for running the programs and solutions to the exercises in this book.) By switching to a professional version of micro-GPSS, available from the author, any such restrictions can be lifted and the only restriction will be the size of the computer's memory. It might also be of interest to have the possibility of animation.

One might also 'hit the ceiling' when a program takes too long to run in micro-GPSS, especially if it is run many times. It might then be advisable to use GPSS/H for the simulation runs. The program can be developed in micro-GPSS and then using a special translator, available from the author, the micro-GPSS code can be translated into GPSS/H code. The GPSS/H compiler will compile this code into machine language and the program will then in most cases run much faster.

Finally one might 'hit the ceiling' in the sense that it is very difficult to represent the problem with a program in ordinary micro-GPSS. There are then several possibilities.

You can try to stay within the micro-GPSS system using HELP blocks calling on subroutines written in FORTRAN or some other General Programming Language. This alternative is probably most helpful if you wish to produce some special output, e.g. in the form of graphics. There is then no need to know the details of the inner workings of the micro-GPSS interpreter, which would probably be necessary if you wanted to influence the actual simulation by these subroutines.

Another alternative is to proceed to full GPSS. As mentioned previously, GPSS V has 48 different block types and GPSS/H over 60, while micro-GPSS has only 22. The question is then whether a problem that is difficult to represent in micro-GPSS could be suitable for representation in full GPSS. It is difficult to give a general answer to this question.

There are certainly a few problems that are difficult to solve in micro-GPSS, but that can easily be solved in full GPSS. On the other hand, micro-GPSS was constructed with the aim that the 22 block types should cover almost all of what the 48 blocks of GPSS V cover (see Chapter 1). It is therefore the author's opinion that the sphere of real problems for which full GPSS is suitable is not much larger than that of the problems for which micro-GPSS is the most suitable alternative.

In order to decide whether a certain problem, unsuitable for micro-GPSS, might be suitable for full GPSS, it is probably necessary to consult a GPSS textbook. Again, I recommend Schriber (1974) as the first source, because of its great pedagogical merit. It should, however, be stressed that Schriber (1974) does not cover all 48 block types of GPSS V, but only 31. Among books that cover all the GPSS V block types are Gordon (1975) and Bobillier *et al.* (1976). These books are difficult for the beginner, but can be understood after reading Schriber (1974) first.

For those specifically interested in GPSS/H, two new books have recently appeared, namely Banks *et al.* (1989) and Schriber (1990). Both books are elementary and present in detail only about one-third of all the GPSS/H block types. These books hence cover much less ground in terms of applications than either Schriber (1974) or this book. However, they devote a substantial part of the text to the GPSS/H interactive debugging system, which none of the earlier books covers at all.

As mentioned above, it is quite possible that if the problem is not suitable for micro-GPSS, it is not suitable for full GPSS either. In such a case the best strategy is probably to proceed to one of the other simulation languages, like Simscript or Simula. Simula, for example, which has the

General Programming Language Algol 60 as a core, is in principle able to handle *any* kind of problem.

For a person with a GPSS background, having perhaps already done some preliminary programming of the problem in micro-GPSS, a good stepping stone towards general Simula is a package similar to GPSS written in Simula. The most well-known package is DEMOS, described in Birtwistle (1979). It should be stressed that to be able to use DEMOS correctly for more complex problems, it is first necessary to know Simula fairly well, which in turn requires a knowledge of Algol.

There are obviously several other alternatives for a more general programming approach to simulation, e.g. simulation languages based on Pascal, Modula 2 and ADA or perhaps even Prolog or Smalltalk. For a more general survey of different software systems for simulation, see Kreutzer (1986), Pidd (1989) and Watson and Blackstone (1989).

Finally, it should be mentioned that proceeding in simulation might also imply learning more about the various statistical and experimental techniques used in simulation. There are a great many excellent books on these subjects, for example Banks and Carson (1984) and Solomon (1983), both of which also contain many useful references.

# Appendix A
# Summary of micro-GPSS syntax

## Notations and definitions

| | |
|---|---|
| b | blank, i.e., default value of non-compulsory operand |
| e | expression = string of 4–59 characters containing at least one of (, ), +, −, ⋆, /, or . |
| i | integer value (non-negative): constant or x$n |
| j | integer constant: 1 ... 12 if Pj; 1 ... 8 if RNj; else 1 ... |
| k | real value (non-negative): constant or x$n |
| n | symbolic name of 3 letters + 0–2 letters or digits |
| digit | 0 ... 9 |
| letter | A ... Z or a ... z |
| SNA | See list below |
| SNA1 | FN$n, Pj, P⋆j, X$n, X⋆j, V$n |
| SNA2 | SNA excluding FN$n and V$n |
| G | Group print symbol: A, B, C, F, Q, S, T, X |
| tx | text string of at most 50 characters within " " or ' ' |
| x$n | X$n value with value given in *preceding* LET or HELP control statement |
| ( ) | Character within the parentheses optional |
| <=> | =, <, >, <=, >= or <> (used instead of , as separator) |

## SNA: Standard Numerical Attributes

| | |
|---|---|
| C1 | Time of relative clock |
| F$n | Contents of facility n |
| FN$n | Value of function n |
| N$n | Number of transactions having entered the block with address n |
| Pj | Value of parameter j |
| PR | Priority value |

Q$n    Number of members of AD set n or length of queue n
R$n    Remaining unused capacity of storage n
RNj    Random number generated by random number generator j
S$n    Contents of storage n
V$n    Value of variable expression n
W$n    Number of transactions currently in block with address n
X$n    Savevalue n

$n can be replaced by ⋆j except after FN and V

## Blocks

|  | A |  | B | C | D | E |
|---|---|---|---|---|---|---|
| ADVANCE | k,e,SNA1,b |  | k,e,SNA1,b |  |  |  |
| ARRIVE | n,Pj |  |  |  |  |  |
| ASSEMBLE | i,X$n |  |  |  |  |  |
| DEPART | n,Pj |  |  |  |  |  |
| ENTER | n,Pj |  | i,e,SNA,Q,b | Q,b |  |  |
| GENERATE | k,e,SNA1,b |  | k,e,SNA1,b | k,b | i,b | k,b |
| GOTO | n,FN$n |  | (0).j,b |  |  |  |
| HELP | n |  | k,e,SNA,b | C − H same as B |  |  |
| IF | k,e,SNA | <=> | (−)k,e,SNA | n,FN$n |  |  |
|  | n,Pj | = | U,NU,F,NF, E,NE | n,FN$n |  |  |
|  | k,e,SNA | <=> | (−)k,e,SNA | Pj,P⋆j, X$n,X⋆j | = | (−)k,e,SNA |
| LEAVE | n,Pj |  | i,e,SNA,b |  |  |  |
| LET(±) | Pj,P⋆j, X$n,X⋆j | = | (−)k,e,SNA |  |  |  |
| PREEMPT | n |  | PR,b |  |  |  |
| PRINT | SNA,tx,e,G |  |  |  |  |  |
| PRIORITY | k,e,SNA |  |  |  |  |  |
| RELEASE | n,Pj |  |  |  |  |  |
| RETURN | n |  |  |  |  |  |
| SEIZE | n,Pj |  | L,Q,b |  |  |  |
| SELECT MIN | j |  | i,X$n | i,X$n | F,N,P,Q, |  |
| MAX |  |  |  |  | R,S,W,X |  |
| SPLIT | i,X$n |  | n,FN$n | i,b |  |  |
| TABULATE | n |  | i,X$n,b |  |  |  |
| TERMINATE | i,b |  |  |  |  |  |
| WAITIF | n,Pj | = | U,NU,F,NF, E,NE | j,b |  |  |

# Control statements

| Address | | A | B | C–D | E–H |
|---|---|---|---|---|---|
| | CLEAR | | | | |
| | END | | | | |
| n | FUNCTION | SNA2 | Cj,Dj,e,n | | |
| | HELP | n | k,X$n,b | k,X$n,b | k,X$n,b |
| | LET | X$n    = | k | | |
| n,b | QTABLE | n,j | i | i | |
| | RESET | | | | |
| | RMULT | i,b | i,b | i,b | i,b |
| | SIMULATE | j,X$SIM,b | A,b | | |
| | START | i | NP,b | | |
| n,j | STORAGE | i,b | | | |
| n | TABLE | SNA | i | i | |
| n | VARIABLE | e | | | |

# Short description of micro-GPSS blocks

(The letters **A** . . . **H** refer to operands **A** . . . **H**, if not indicated otherwise.)

ADVANCE delays the transaction during a time sampled from the rectangular distribution **A ± B**, where **A** and **B** in turn can be values sampled from other distributions. The default values of **A** and **B** are 0.

ARRIVE implies that the transaction becomes a member of the AD set ('statistical queue') with the name **A** and that the time of entry into this block is noted.

ASSEMBLE destroys copies made in an earlier SPLIT block. One remaining copy (or the original) is allowed to leave the ASSEMBLE block only when **A** transactions, which are either an original transaction or copies of this transaction made in a SPLIT block, have arrived at the block.

DEPART implies that the transaction leaves the AD set with the name **A** and that the time of entering into this block is noted. The time between entry into the corresponding ARRIVE block and entry into this block is then calculated and saved for use in the AD set statistics.

ENTER means that the transaction attempts to bring **B** units into storage **A**, where **B** is, or is truncated to, an integer value. The transaction will enter storage **A** only if **A** has a free capacity of at least **B** units. The default value of **B** is 1. If **B** contains just the letter Q, the effect with regard to entry is the same as if **B** had a value of 1. If **B** (or **C** if **B** holds a numerical value) contains Q, queue statistics are gathered for storage **A** exactly as if *every* block ENTER **A** was preceded by a block ARRIVE **A** and succeeded by a block DEPART **A**, where **A** is the name of the storage **A** of this ENTER block with Q.

GENERATE creates transactions with InterArrival Times (IATs) sampled from the rectangular distribution **A** ± **B** where **A** and **B** in turn can be values sampled from other distributions. Default values of **A** and **B** are 0. **C** is the time of the creation of the first transaction from the block, with the default value being the first sampled IAT. **D** is the maximum number of transactions that can be created before simulation stop. The default value is 32 000. **E** is the priority number of the transactions (≥ 0 but < 100 000) with the implication that in waiting lines transactions with a higher priority number will go ahead of transactions with a lower priority number and that for events scheduled to occur at the same time, events with a higher priority are executed prior to those with a lower priority number. The default value of **E** is 0.

GOTO exists in two versions:

1. Unconditional GOTO. The transaction is sent to the block with the address **A**.

2. Statistical GOTO. The transaction is sent to the block with the address **A** with the probability **B** and to the next block with the probability 1 − **B**.

HELP calls on the FORTRAN subroutine with the name **A** and transfers the values of **B**−**H** to this subroutine and, if the operand contains X$n, sends a value back to this operand.

IF works in two modes:

1. IF in SNA-mode compares the value of **A** with the value of **B** according to the relationship (>, >=, =, <>, <, <=) given between the **A** and **B** operands.

2. IF in server-mode tests for the server with the name **A** if the condition given in **B** (U, NU, E, F, NE, NF) is true.

If this test condition, e.g. **A** > **B** or **A** = U, is true, the transaction is sent to the block with the address of **C**. If the test condition is false, the transaction continues to the next block.

In the SNA mode, the IF block can also work in an assignment mode using a D operand: if the test condition is true, the C operand obtains the value of the D operand.

LEAVE brings **B** units out of the storage **A**. The default value of **B** is 1.

LET assigns the value of **B** to the parameter or savevalue given in **A**.
    In the case of LET+, the value of **B** is added to the value of **A**, and in the case of LET−, the value of **B** is subtracted from the value of **A**.

PREEMPT implies that a transaction trying to get service from a busy facility will, in the case of *no* **B**, interrupt the service given to a transaction that has made the facility busy at a SEIZE block, and in the case of **B** being PR, interrupt the service given to a transaction with a lower priority. At interruption, the interrupted transaction's remaining time in the ADVANCE block is saved.

PRINT causes the print-out either of a single SNA value, of the value of an expression, of text within quotes or of a total set of statistics corresponding to the symbol in **A**: A = all standard statistics, B = block statistics, C = clock time, F = facility and storage statistics, Q = queue (AD set) statistics, S = storage and facility statistics, T = tables and X = savevalues.

PRIORITY gives the transaction the value of **A** as a new priority number with the same implications as **E** of the GENERATE block.

RELEASE frees the facility **A**.

RETURN implies that a transaction which has made facility **A** busy at a PREEMPT block will free this facility. If the transaction at PREEMPT had interrupted service for some other transaction, this other transaction can now get back into service (in the ADVANCE block) for the remaining service time.

SEIZE implies that the transaction attempts to obtain service from facility **A**. If the facility is not busy, the transaction can enter the SEIZE block and make the facility busy. If the facility is busy, the transaction will wait in front of the facility when **B** is *not* L. If **B** is L, the SEIZE block will make the facility work as a logic switch, implying that the transaction will also enter the SEIZE block if the facility is busy. If **B** is Q, statistics will be collected regarding the facility in the same way as if *every* SEIZE block with this facility name **A** was preceded by a block ARRIVE **A** and succeeded by a block DEPART **A**.

SELECT searches through all SNAs of the type given in **D** from number **B** to number **C** and puts the number of that entity, which for MIN has the lowest value and for MAX the highest value, into the parameter with the number **A**.

SPLIT makes **A** copies of the transaction and moves them to the block of the address in **B**. **C** is the optional number of the serialization parameter j and the value of Pj of the original transaction is increased by 1, of the first copy by 2, of the second copy by 3, etc.

TABULATE implies that the value of the SNA which is given in **A** of the TABLE statement whose address has the same name as **A** of the TABULATE block, is placed into the table statistics. **B** is an optional weighting implying that the above-mentioned value is put **B** times into the table. The default value of **B** is 1.

TERMINATE removes the transaction from the system and decreases the termination counter by **A**. If the termination counter thereby becomes 0 (or negative), the simulation is stopped. The default value of **A** is 0.

WAITIF implies that, if the relationship = **B** (where **B** is U, NU, E, F, NE, NF) is true for server **A**, the transaction will wait in front of the WAITIF block as long as this condition is true. Otherwise it will try to enter the next block. **C**, which is optional, indicates the number of immediately preceding WAITIF blocks that the transaction must be able to pass through at the same time as the block with this **C**.

# Short description of micro-GPSS control statements

CLEAR first resets all statistics. Both clocks are reset to 0, but random numbers are *not* reset. It further clears all internal waiting lists and the list of future events, and frees all servers. Finally it initiates the re-scheduling of the first transaction for every GENERATE block.

END is the last statement of every GPSS program.

FUNCTION defines a function with the name given in the address field. **A** is an SNA defining the independent variable of the function. **B** is either Cj, Dj, an expression or a name. The letter C implies a continuous function and the letter D a discrete function; j is the number of data-pairs used for defining the function. The expression defines the function mathematically in terms of a savevalue given in A. (In some implementations **B** can be a filename containing data-pairs given by graphic input.)

HELP as a control statement works like the HELP block with the exception that **B–H** must be constants or savevalues.

LET as a control statement works like the LET block with the exception that **A** can only be a savevalue and **B** a constant or a savevalue that has obtained a value in a preceding LET or HELP statement.

QTABLE defines a table to be printed automatically in the standard output, regarding an AD set or a queue. **A** is the name of either an AD set (= **A** of an ARRIVE and a DEPART block) or of a queue (**A** of a SEIZE or an ENTER block with **Q** in **B** or **C**). **B** is the upper limit of the lowest class, **C** the class width (of the intermediate classes) and **D** the number of classes.

RESET sets all SNAs back to their initial value with the following exceptions: the random numbers, the *absolute* clock, the *current* count of each block and all savevalues.

RMULT sets the seeds of the random number generators as follows: **A** determines the seed of random number generator 1, **B** of generator 2, ... and **H** of generator 8. The default value is j for generator j, i.e., 1 for generator 1 (set in **A**), 2 for generator 2 (= **B**) etc.

SIMULATE signals that simulation, and not only syntax checking, is to take place. **A** is the number of times the program shall be run with different seeds each time. If **B** is the letter A, the simulation is run with antithetic random numbers.

START initiates the simulation run. **A** is the initial value of the termination counter. If **B** is NP, no standard output is produced when the termination counter reaches 0 or turns negative.

STORAGE defines the storage with the name given in the address field to have the capacity **A**. The default value of **A** is 2 billions.

TABLE causes a table regarding the SNA in **A** to be printed automatically in the standard output. **B**, **C** and **D** have the same meaning as for QTABLE.

VARIABLE defines, as the value of the expression in **A**, a value V$name, where name is given in the address field.

# Appendix B
# Alternative forms for increased compatibility with GPSS V

|                        | A            | B          | C       | D | E              |
|------------------------|--------------|------------|---------|---|----------------|
| *Blocks*               |              |            |         |   |                |
| ASSIGN                 | j(±)         | (−)k,SNA   |         |   |                |
| GATE U,NU,SE,SF, SNE,SNF | n,Pj       | n,b        |         |   |                |
| PRINT                  |              |            | G       |   |                |
| QUEUE                  | n,Pj         |            |         |   |                |
| SAVEVALUE              | n(±),Pj(±)   | (−)k,SNA   |         |   |                |
| SELECT MIN  MAX        | j            | `  i,X$n   | i,X$n   |   | F,N,P,Q, R,S,W,X |
| TEST G,GE,E, NE,L,LE   | k,SNA        | (−)k,SNA   | n,FN$n  |   |                |
| TRANSFER               | .j           |            | n,FN$n  |   |                |
|                        |              | n,FN$n     |         |   |                |
|                        |              |            |         |   |                |
| *Control statements*   |              |            |         |   |                |
| FVARIABLE              | e            |            |         |   |                |
| INITIAL                | X$n          | k          |         |   |                |

# Appendix C
# The GPSSMENU program

The program GPSSMENU is obtainable on a separate diskette (or tape). This program allows for a dialogue by which the user can produce a micro-GPSS program very simply, mainly by choosing various alternatives in different menus. The input is mainly done by choosing a single letter or number or just pressing the enter-key. This program will also guide the user to the correct micro-GPSS syntax.

The GPSSMENU program is mainly used for writing a new program from scratch or a major part of a new program. The editing of a program already written is more easily done using an editor, preferably one that is memory resident (see GPSSDOC). Rewriting a single line with a syntax error can generally be done within the ordinary micro-GPSS system.

The GPSSMENU program can be started in two different ways, either with the command GPSSMENU or the simple command GP. The difference is that GPSSMENU will run only this specific menu-program, while GP will first run this menu-program and then start the actual micro-GPSS program. GP can be seen as a combination of the commands GPSSMENU and GPSS.

After the start, the GPSSMENU program will first ask if you want to start the program with SIMULATE (without any operand). In that case simply press the enter-key. Otherwise, by answering N, you have a chance either to add operands to SIMULATE or to start the program (part) with something else.

After having dealt with SIMULATE, e.g. by just pressing the enter-key for SIMULATE without operands, the whole control statement menu is displayed. This menu contains all the control statements (except SIMULATE) plus at the bottom a choice for a switch to the block menu. The choice is made either by a number (1 ... 14) or, generally more conveniently, a single letter. This is the letter marked in upper case. For all choices except two, the first letter is used. The two exceptions are rMult and stOrage (R means Reset and S Start). The choice of letter or number must be followed by the enter-key.

B (or 14) brings us to the block menu. This menu consists of the 22 micro-GPSS blocks and a choice C (or 23) to get us back to the control statement menu. In the block menu, the choice is made by one or two letters (or by a number 1 . . . 23). The first of these two letters to be typed is always the first letter of the block. If two letters are needed, the second letter is often the second letter of the block (ARrive, ASsemble, GOto, SPlit and TAbulate), but in other cases the second letter is the most 'typical' one (LeaVe, PreeMpt, Prioritem, ReTurn and SeLect).

When a certain block or control statement has been chosen, the choice of the operands for this block or control statement is made. The possible alternatives for the operands are presented. Default values are chosen by just pressing the enter-key.

In this connection it should be stressed that GPSSMENU is particularly helpful for writing the function data statements. On the basis of the number of pairs it will ask for data, pair after pair, first for the *x*-value, then for the *y*-value.

After all the choices have been made, the program displays the whole line with the operation and operands and asks if this line should be changed. If you wish to change the whole line answer Y. Then the operation and operands are discarded and you return to the menu you started from and a new attempt for this line can be made. If you just want to add an address, answer A and you can then write the address to be put in front of the operation. Otherwise, i.e. if the line is correct, simply press the enter-key to return to the block menu or control statement menu, but this time the line which has just been input will be saved. You will also see the line incorporated in the listing of the program to the right of the menu. This listing contains the 23 most recently input lines.

In this way you can input line after line of the program. To end the program, you have to be in the control statement menu and choose E (or 2). When you press return a final time to show that you really want to end the program, you are asked for the name under which this GPSS program will be saved. If you just press return as an answer to this question, the file will be saved under the name of GPFILE.

This ends the run of the GPSSMENU program. If it has been started by the GP command, the micro-GPSS program then starts right away. When the GPSS program asks you for the name of the GPSS program file, you answer with the name under which the newly created program has been saved, e.g. GPFILE, if you used the default file name by just pressing return at the last question in the GPSSMENU.

Finally I shall illustrate the use of GPSSMENU by examining how Program 3.1 can be created using this program.

Start by the command GP. Since you only want to run the program once, press return on the question of SIMULATE and get to the control statement menu. Next you need to have the GENERATE block, so type B (and enter) to get to the block menu and then G to obtain GENERATE. For the A operand write 18 and for the B operand 6. As you do not want any more operands just press return. After the display of GENERATE 18,6 again press return, since this was correct. You then return to the block menu.

Now type T for TERMINATE and then write 1 as the A operand. After the display of TERMINATE 1, which is correct, press enter and return to the block menu. You now need START, so first write C to get to the control statement menu. In this menu write S for Start and next write 50 as the A operand. At the display of START 50 press return. Since this is the whole program you type E for End. Since you really want to finish, press return once again and as an answer to the name of the file just press return to have the file saved as GPFILE. Next GPSS is started and you then answer GPFILE to run the program just created.

# Appendix D
## Debugging of programs in micro-GPSS

If simulation is going to be used for decision support, it is of paramount importance that the programs work correctly as intended. Therefore, a major consideration behind the development of micro-GPSS has been that it should be easy to write correctly functioning simulation programs. Program safety has been given high priority.

This appendix will deal briefly with how to find, correct and avoid errors in a micro-GPSS program.

Errors can generally be divided into three types:

1. Syntax errors, implying that the micro-GPSS syntax of a particular block or control statement has been violated. Such errors are usually found in the initial phase of the program run, in connection with the listing of the program, before actual execution, i.e., when the simulation clock is still 0.

2. Execution errors are errors found during the actual simulation phase, i.e. usually when the simulation clock is $> 0$. Although each specific block of the program is correct, some actual value produced is illegal and the simulation is halted.

3. Logical errors are errors obtained when the simulation has been carried out for the desired time or desired number of transactions, but the results are not correct. In some cases the existence of a logical error is obvious in that the results are completely out of line with expectations; in other more dangerous cases only careful analysis of the results can establish that they are incorrect.

Syntax errors are the least troublesome, since they can generally be located to a specific block or control statement, and logical errors are of course the most problematic ones. With this in mind, micro-GPSS has been constructed, as already discussed in Chapter 1, with the aim that logical errors should be avoided as far as possible. Hence many of the most common dangerous logical errors in GPSS V (see e.g. Bobillier *et al.*, 1976, pp. 391–7) cannot be made in micro-GPSS (e.g. 1 and SAL referring to the same facility, GENERATE acting strangely when followed by a SEIZE block, FN$ as B operand implying multiplication, ASSIGN with P1 as B operand, etc.).

An important factor which increases the safety when programming in micro-GPSS is indeed the limitation of the number of block types. Some of the most complicated GPSS V blocks have been omitted, since they are difficult to understand and invite faulty programming. Programming safety is also increased by micro-GPSS being more restrictive as regards the operands that can be used, limiting them, e.g. as regards ADVANCE, to SNAs that could be meaningful in order to avoid strange errors.

Micro-GPSS furthermore tries to stop errors at an early stage, by allowing an error to be found while it is still a syntax error, rather than allowing it to develop into a logical error. One example is the requirement that all storages be defined. (GPSS V gives 'forgotten' storages a very large default capacity.)

Because of these factors, logical errors that are difficult to find are much less likely to occur in micro-GPSS than in GPSS V and supersets of this, such as GPSS/H. Consequently, there is much less need for a debugging system in micro-GPSS than in, e.g., GPSS/H, which comes with a very extensive debugging system, requiring substantial efforts to learn. To the extent that debugging is required in micro-GPSS, a spectrum of methods available within the ordinary micro-GPSS system, and hence presented earlier in this book, can be used for such debugging as will be discussed in this appendix. I shall carry out this discussion regarding the search for and treatment of errors with reference to each of the three types of error discussed above, i.e. syntax, execution and logical errors.

# Syntax errors

In micro-GPSS, syntax errors are discovered as the program is listed in its extensive form. When the processor finds a syntax error, it produces an error message and displays the line at which the error is found. The user now has the chance to re-type this line correctly. After the line has been re-typed (and the enter key has been pressed), the program is listed again from the beginning with the corrected line saved as part of the program instead of the incorrect one. If there are several syntax errors in the program, the procedure is repeated for each error until all syntax errors have been removed.

This facility for line correction cannot be used if the syntax error found on one line really depends on an error on an earlier line. One example is ENTER STO, when there is no preceding definition of the storage STO. This leads to an error located at this line, although the error might lie in the programmer having forgotten to define STO. It is then meaningless to change

the block ENTER STO, since a definition of STO needs to be inserted earlier
in the program. Instead of typing a corrected line, simply press the enter-key
and this gives you the choice of either leaving the micro-GPSS system
completely or, in some systems, leaving it temporarily to use a memory
resident editor (see GPSSDOC). In either case, you next need to use an editor
for the insertion of the STORAGE statement, after which the program can be
re-run. In some other cases the line to be re-typed might be so long that it is
more convenient to do character editing in an editor rather than re-type the
whole line. (For very long programs this line editing is suppressed.)

It should also be mentioned that the processor might assign an error
to a line that is completely correct, but where a preceding line causes
the error. An example is GENERATE FN$FUN immediately preceded
by FUN FUNCTION RN2,D4. An error is assigned to the line with
GENERATE FN$FUN, saying that the data are incorrect. The reason is that
D4 in the function definition statement implies that the next line is a data
statement. If this data statement is forgotten, the processor reads the
GENERATE line as the data statement.

Some error messages reflect the fact that since micro-GPSS has a
completely free format and *no* reserved words, the processor cannot rule out
that a certain operation word, e.g. SEIZE, is used as an address or as a
facility. SEIZE SEIZE SEIZE is syntactically correct (the first SEIZE is an
address, the third a facility name), but SEIZE SEIZE 3 is not. The error could
either be that the numerical facility 3 is illegal (the first SEIZE is an address)
or that 3 is an illegal comment (there is no address; comments must be
preceded by !). In cases when a word can be either an operation or an address,
the error message could look somewhat strange to the user who would not
think of using an operation word as an address.

Some other syntax error messages reflect the way the micro-GPSS
processor works, e.g. that expressions are translated into internal variables
(V$-values).

It has been the author's aim that the error messages should be as clear
as possible to make correction easy. However, all possible ways of making
errors cannot be predicted and no doubt some error messages might still be
misleading. Thus an on-going task in the improvement of micro-GPSS is to
produce better error messages. Everyone who has received a strange or
misleading error message is kindly asked to send a program listing to the
author (address on p. ii). If you include your name and address, your efforts
will not be unrewarded.

It should finally, in this context of syntax errors, be mentioned that
there are a few syntax errors that occur after the listing of the program, but
with simulation time still 0. These errors often refer to undefined entities. An
example is that there is no block with the address BYE, although there is a
block GOTO BYE. These errors do not pinpoint any specific line as incorrect,
since the processor obviously cannot determine which block lacks the address.
Thus the correction must be done using an editor.

# Execution errors

Execution errors are found after the listing of the entire program, when the actual execution has started and simulation time generally is $> 0$. In this case an error causes a halt in the simulation. Generally there is a message regarding the block in which the error has occurred, followed (unless START has NP) by a print-out of all the standard statistics, now referring to the time when the error occurred and simulation halted.

An example of a simulation error is Program 12.5b where $50,000 in initial cash is insufficient and there is an error due to negative contents of a server, i.e. of the storage CASH.

Some execution errors will be dependent on which micro-GPSS version is used. As mentioned in Chapter 20 the student version is limited in several ways, e.g. with regard to the number of transactions that can be in the system at the same time. An error due to too many transactions in the system would occur in the student version in Program 4.1 if the time was changed from 480 to 48 000. There would then be too many customers in the waiting line. However, if this program is run using the professional version, there would not be any such error, since this version allows many more transactions to be active in the system.

A similar problem might occur if a LEAVE, RELEASE or RETURN block is forgotten. Then the server will remain busy with the first customer for the rest of the simulation, even if this customer has terminated. All other customers have to wait in the system.

A special kind of execution error is the eternal loop, where no block TERMINATE A will be reached. This could happen, for instance, if the only TERMINATE block is preceded by a block IF X$VAL > X$EPS,BACK, and X$VAL remains larger than X$EPS. In this case there is no way out other than by interrupting the run by a break command or possibly by re-booting the system.

A very long run, perhaps appearing as an eternal loop, is caused by a GENERATE with $A = B = 0$ and no D operand. This will then cause 32 000 transactions to be generated, which can take quite a while. Another error, often similar to an eternal loop, is a lock-in effect, e.g. where some transactions cannot release facility A before they have seized facility B, but other transactions cannot release facility B before they have seized facility A.

Another example of a lock-in effect is as follows: a janitor opens a door and lets waiting customers in and then immediately closes the door again. The customers waiting for the door to be opened cannot get moving until the janitor transaction is stopped. However, a transaction continues as many blocks as possible until it is stopped by an ADVANCE or TERMINATE block or has to wait for a server or at a WAITIF block. Hence before he is brought to a halt, the janitor transaction both opens and closes the door and the customers are 'locked in'. If a dummy ADVANCE block, i.e. an ADVANCE block with a default A operand (= 0), is inserted after the opening of the door but before the closing of it, these transactions can get moving, thereby breaking the lock-in.

# Logical errors

As mentioned above, logical errors can either be manifest immediately because of unexpected and unreasonable results, or not be apparent until later in the form of misleading results. The latter case is of course the most troublesome one. It is far better for the programmer to find the logical error than the ultimate user, i.e. the decision maker. It is hence important that the simulation programmer investigates the program results to look for potential logical errors.

In some cases the programmer could use other methods, e.g. analytical ones from queuing theory, to check that the program produces the expected results, at least for steady state conditions, obtainable for long simulation times. Other checks involve the scrutiny of the standard output and the use of special print-out.

The standard output should first be checked for absence of spelling mistakes, since an important source of errors in computer programming is due to the misspelling of variable names. SIMULA as well as many General Programming Languages like Pascal require that all variables be declared before use, which implies that misspelt variable names are stopped as syntax errors. Traditionally GPSS has, however, *no* declarations, which leads to compact programs, but risks logical errors, due to misspelt names. Micro-GPSS, however, requires *storage* names to be declared. Furthermore, by adhering to the GPSS V restriction of names having only five characters instead of allowing longer names, the risk of spelling errors is contained somewhat. Yet spelling mistakes cannot be ruled out. Hence it is important to glance through the list of names of servers, queues (AD sets) and savevalues to check that there are not two similar names like, e.g., GAT0R and GATOR (where 0 (zero) instead of O (upper case o) is a spelling mistake).

The study of the standard output should furthermore include the block statistics. All blocks with a *total* count of 0 should be investigated. Why have no transactions passed through this block? One cause could be a missing GENERATE block. Very high *current* counts for certain blocks should also be considered. Do they represent justified waiting?

A scrutiny of facility and storage statistics, in particular with regard to utilization, might also reveal logical errors. Is 0 or 100 percent utilization reasonable? Queue (AD set) statistics can also yield some information, in particular the relationship between maximum and current contents of a queue. If they are the same it probably indicates that there is a steadily increasing waiting line. Is this reasonable?

Both in the search for possible logical errors and in the pin-pointing of the source of a manifest error, special non-standard print-outs can be helpful. In micro-GPSS this refers especially to the block PRINT SNA, e.g. PRINT X$value. If you also want to follow development through time, HELP FPRIN,C1,X$value can be useful, in particular since a graph can be made from this.

In case such 'tracing' produces too much output, print-out can be limited to a specific time or some other factor. For example, printing can be started at time X$TIME if the PRINT block is preceded by a block IF C1<X$TIME,NEXT, where NEXT is the address of the block after PRINT. Likewise printing can start when a storage STOR is full if WAITIF STOR=NF precedes the PRINT block.

Other special print-outs include the print-out of block statistics at certain time intervals, or as an alternative to this, the print-out of N$address and W$address for the most interesting blocks. It might also be useful to test the functioning of a user-defined function by print-out of a table, produced by a special TABULATE block, over the distribution of values produced by this function. Finally, animation can in some cases be suitable for debugging when using the professional version. Further hints on debugging of GPSS programs can be found in Bobillier *et al.*, 1976, pp. 245–58.

At the end of this appendix, it should be stressed that certain features in micro-GPSS are probably more prone to cause logical errors than others. This refers mainly to indirect addressing, especially the use of P*j, and the use of PREEMPT and RETURN blocks. It might hence be wise to be extra careful when using these constructs. Finally, if there are errors which appear to be inexplicable even after very careful analysis, you are welcome to contact the author (address given on p. ii).

# References

Banks, J. and J.S. Carson II (1984) *Discrete-Event System Simulation*, Prentice Hall: Englewood Cliffs, NJ.

Banks, J., J.S. Carson II and J.N. Sy (1989) *Getting Started with GPSS/H*, Wolverine Software Corp.: Annandale, VA.

Birtwistle, G.M. (1979) *DEMOS: A system for discrete event simulation on Simula*, Macmillan: London.

Birtwistle, G.M., O.-J. Dahl, B. Myhrhaug and K. Nygaard (1973) *SIMULA BEGIN*, Auerbach: Philadelphia.

Bobillier, P.A., B.C. Kahan and A.R. Probst (1976) *Simulation with GPSS and GPSS V*, Prentice Hall: Englewood Cliffs, NJ.

Caroll, J.M. (1987) *Simulation Using Personal Computers*, Prentice Hall: Englewood Cliffs, NJ.

Davies, R.M. and R.M. O'Keefe (1989) *Simulation Modelling with Pascal*, Prentice Hall: Hemel Hempstead.

Gordon, G. (1975) *The Application of GPSS V to Discrete System Simulation*, Prentice Hall: Englewood Cliffs, NJ.

Gordon, G. (1979) 'The design of the GPSS language', in Adams, R.N. and Dagramici, A. (eds), *Current Issues in Simulation*, Wiley: NY.

*GPSS/PC User Manual* (1985) Version 1.1, Minuteman Software: Stow, Mass.

Greenwood, A.G. (1988) *Queuing and Simulation Models for Business: The $(SP^2)$ simulation pedagogic support package*, Northeastern University: Boston.

Henriksen, J.O. (1983) *State-of-the-Art GPSS*. Paper presented at the 1983 Summer Computer Simulation Conference, 1983, Vancouver B.C., Canada.

Henriksen, J.O. (1985) *The Development of GPSS/85*. Paper presented at the 18th Annual Simulation Symposium, Tampa, Florida.

Henriksen, J.O. and R.C. Crain (1983) *GPSS/H User's Manual*, 2nd ed., Wolverine Software: Annandale, VA.

Jennergren, L.P. (1984) *Discrete-Events Simulations Models in Pascal/MT+ on a Microcomputer*, Studentlitteratur: Lund.

Kreutzer, W. (1986) *System Simulation: Programming styles and languages*, Addison-Wesley: Sydney.

McMillan, C. and R.F. Gonzales (1973) *Systems Analysis: A computer approach to decision making*, Richard D. Irwin: Homewood, Illinois.

Pidd, M. (1984) *Computer Simulation in Management Science*, Wiley: Chichester.

Pidd, M. (ed.) (1989) *Computer Modelling for Discrete Simulation*, Wiley: Chichester.

Schmidt, B. (1980) *GPSS-FORTRAN*, Wiley: Chichester/NY.

Schriber, T.J. (1974) *Simulation Using GPSS*, Wiley: NY.

Schriber, T.J. (1990) *An Introduction to Simulation Using GPSS/H*, Wiley: NY.

*Simon 75 Reference Manual* (1976), Robin Hills: Camberley.

Solomon, S.L. (1983) *Simulation of Waiting-Line Systems*, Prentice Hall: Englewood Cliffs, NJ.

Watson, H.J. and J.H. Blackstone Jr (1989) *Computer Simulation*, 2nd ed., Wiley: NY.

# Index